Bernard Tomson
&
Norman Coplan

ARCHITECTURAL
&
ENGINEERING
LAW

**SECOND
EDITION**

REINHOLD PUBLISHING CORPORATION
A subsidiary of Chapman-Reinhold, Inc.

NEW YORK   AMSTERDAM   LONDON

To Rose and Joan

Foreword

EDWARD DURELL STONE

After World War II, when I returned from the service, it was impossible to find office space in New York. I established temporary headquarters in Great Neck, and there I encountered Bernard Tomson—first as a client for a new home, and next as a legal adviser in helping me reestablish my architectural practice. We soon became fast friends. Shortly thereafter I met Norman Coplan, Bernard Tomson's partner, and together their advice and guidance in legal and professional matters became indispensable. After Bernard Tomson went on the bench, Norman Coplan continued to represent me, as well as many other leading architectural and engineering firms in the United States.

One of the dividends from this association may indeed be this book, since through our association both Judge Tomson and Norman Coplan became aware of and interested in the architect's problems and their implications—moral, ethical and legal. This led to their monthly column entitled "It's the Law" published by *Progressive Architecture,* to their membership on the faculty of the School of Architecture of Pratt Institute, and to their collaboration on several books and articles in the construction field.

The architectural profession is profoundly indebted to Judge Tomson and Norman Coplan for their intelligent guidance in a field in which the architect, owing to pressures of his own profession, is neither properly aware nor advised—and in which a traditional architectural education does not provide the proper background.

Their interest in these matters has transcended architectural law and dry legalities. I believe that their broad social interest includes the provision of a beautiful environment for our country. By aiding the architect, the builder and the owner, they are, in a large measure, contributing toward the enrichment of man's environment.

Most building projects today involve the expenditure of millions of dollars, and it behooves all of us entrusted with the responsibility of great sums of other people's money to be acquainted with all details of this trust. Therefore, this book will perform a great social service, mandatory

v

for government officials, business enterprises, professionals in the arts of building, and individuals who embark on the complexities of building projects.

It is an honor for me to salute Judge Tomson and Norman Coplan as friends, creative professionals, and as men who accept a social responsibility of contemporary life.

Preface

Legal problems are inherent in every stage of an architect's or engineer's dealings with his clients, with his partners, with contractors, in the day to day execution of a project—in fact in every step taken or contemplated. However, no matter how conscientious a professional or business man may be about referring legal matters to his attorney, expense and time provide natural limitations to this procedure. Moreover it is not feasible or desirable that the minutiae of every day's business be submitted to an attorney's scrutiny. Everyone associated with the building industry must of necessity be armed with some basic acquaintance with the legal problems involved in each situation as it develops. Sometimes this fund of knowledge is adequate to dispose of the problem as it arises. Sometimes reference to other material (such as this book) is sufficient. Sometimes this fund of knowledge is required only for the purpose of indicating that a serious problem is presented which should be submitted to a lawyer. When legal questions of immediate or potential importance are presented, a lawyer should be consulted. In the long run, not to do so is folly. The resulting difficulties are not necessarily demonstrated by anything as dramatic as a law suit. They exert a more subtle influence in the form of unnecessary trouble, anxiety and expense.

The first edition of this book was published in 1951. Since that date, the law has changed. Many legal principles applicable to problems of the building industry that were deemed settled in 1951 either have been modified or are open to question today. For example, the potential liability of an architect or engineer for injuries, caused by defective plans or inadequate supervision, to third persons with whom he has no contractual relationship has been greatly extended in recent years. This field of law as well as many other aspects of particular significance to the building industry continue to evolve. It is important, therefore, that in dealing with the legal concerns of the industry, knowledge of the law be current.

The format of the chapters and their subdivisions in this book were designed to avoid repetitious discussion and yet serve equally the needs of the building industry, the student and the lawyer. In general, each chapter contains a brief statement of general principles and a further discussion of the chapter heading followed by citations, arranged according to states. I trust that in this way the architect, engineer, contractor, student or lawyer will readily be able to find in each chapter or subdivision a discussion (with references) of the problems with which he is concerned.

The authors wish to express their deep gratitude and appreciation to Louis Tomson for his invaluable assistance in editing the manuscript and to Daniel Subotnik for his dedicated research.

BERNARD TOMSON

NORMAN COPLAN

July, 1967

Contents

PART ONE

LICENSE LAWS FOR THE ARCHITECT, ENGINEER, SURVEYOR, AND GENERAL CONTRACTOR

CHAPTER ONE

State regulation of professional practice and building construction

Statutes regulating the practice of architecture, professional engineering, land surveying, and building construction are upheld as a valid exercise of the state police power because they are in the interest of public health, safety and welfare.

All but a negligible number of states have enacted legislation controlling those who engage in occupations dealing with the planning and construction of buildings and other structures. Regulatory legislation has been enacted in recognition of the need to protect the public against persons who are not qualified by training and experience to render successfully and efficiently the services they offer to perform for compensation.

Broadly speaking, the statutes require that those intending to engage in the named pursuits secure from the proper authority a license or certificate to practice. These enactments create a board, commission, or other regulatory authority given the task of certifying candidates who meet the qualifications established by the legislature. The boards in many instances have broad powers to prescribe their own rules and regulations within these standards. They are likewise authorized to revoke existing licenses on any of the grounds specified in the statutes. To insure enforcement, state laws generally make violations of the act misdemeanors and prescribe attending penalties.

While the courts almost universally justify these laws on the grounds of public welfare, they are also necessary to protect the qualified professional individual from unethical competition by unskilled and incompetent practitioners. It is important that professional societies recognize the unfortunate consequences of such competition and it is largely owing to their efforts that such protective legislation has been enacted.

3

A reliable body of practitioners qualified to cope with present-day construction needs can exist only when good licensing statutes with adequate governmental enforcement is coordinated with the activities of professional groups alert to the importance of the problem.

Judicial concern with the statutes has addressed itself mainly to the questions of interpretation. The problem of defining the limits of each profession is made difficult by reason of the close interrelation of pursuits in the building field. Nevertheless, the legislators and the courts have treated the professions individually as separate and distinct occupations.

A NUMBER OF DEFINITIONS have been adopted by legislatures and courts in allocating to each profession its particular functions. Although the duties incidental to one profession may overlap those in another, the fundamental distinction between them is carefully maintained, and any unwarranted excursion into a related, controlled occupation is prohibited.

A broad definition of architectural services within the meaning of the registration statute is:

> "(The) rendering or offering to render service to clients by consultations, investigation, evaluations, preliminary studies, plans, specifications, contract documents and a coordination of structural factors concerning the esthetic or structural design and supervision of construction of buildings or any other service in connection with the designing or supervision of construction of buildings located within the boundary of the Commonwealth, . . ." *Pa. Stat. Ann. Tit.* 63 §28 (1959).

For other statutory definitions, see references to individual state license laws on pages 15–16.

Cal.   *Payne v. DeVaughn,* 77 Cal. App. 399, 246 Pac. 1069 (1926).

Colo.   *Heron v. Denver,* 131 Colo. 501, 283 p. 2d 647 (1955).

La.   *Rabinowitz v. Hurwitz-Mintz Furniture Co.,* 19 La. App. 811, 133 So. 498 (1931).

   C. G. Kershaw Contracting Co. v. Crowley, 149 So. 181 (1933).

Ill.   *Gastaldi v. Reuterman,* 345 Ill. App. 510, 104 NE 2d 115 (1952).

Ky.   *Board of Education v. Elliot,* 276 Ky. 790, 125 S.W. 2d 733 (1943).

N.Y.   *Hecht v. Commuter's Cafe, Inc.,* 193 Misc. 170, 80 N.Y.S. 2d 861 (1948). "A 'design' becomes an architectural design only when it is drawn for the purpose of construction according to architectural detail, in scale, and in accordance with the principles of mathematics, aesthetics, and the physical sciences."

U.S.   *Leavy v. Rosenthal,* 104 F. Supp. 496 (D.C. Mich. 1952). The practice of engineering is typically defined as "The practice of a profession which engages in the application of mathematics and the physical sciences ... for the development, production, functioning of engineering processes, apparatus, machines, equipment, facilities, structures, work or utilities.... Such practice includes consultation, investigation, research, surveys, planning, designing, direction and supervision and such other services or acts as are a necessary part of such practice." *Pa. Stat. Ann. Tit.* 63 §149 (1959).

IN THE FOLLOWING CASES THE COURT'S DECISION turned on whether the services offered constituted the practice of engineering within the meaning of the relevant practice statute.

Minn. *Dick Weatherton's Associated Mechanical Services Inc. v. Minn. Mutual Life Ins. Co.*, 257 Minn. 184, 100 N.W. 2d 819.

Miss. *State Board of Registration for Professional Engineers v. Rogers*, 239 Miss. 35, 120 So. 2d 772, rehearing 121 So. 2d 720 (1960).

N.Y. *Engel v. Ansco Photoproducts, Inc.*, 229 App. Div. 241, 240 N.Y.S. 737 (1930), *aff'd*, 256 N.Y. 615, 177 N.E. 163 (1931). Consulting engineer for camera company, employed to furnish company with new inventions, was not practicing professional engineering within meaning of license statute.

Usdin v. Kvatinetz, 69 N.Y.S. 2d 634 (1947). "Professional engineering" is practiced whenever services named therein are performed in connection with a machine, but only when they are involved with safeguarding of life, health, or property.

Ohio *Ohio Soc'y of Professional Engineers v. Hulsander*, 86 Ohio App. 497, 89 N.E. 2d 119 (1949). In contempt proceedings for allegedly violating injunction restraining defendant from practicing professional engineering, evidence that his business activities related solely to the design or fabrication of manufactured products under exemptive provisions of statute was insufficient to warrant conviction.

Va. *Clark v. Moore*, 196 Va. 878, 86 S.E. 2d 37 (1955).

U.S. *Keller v. Baumgartner*, 153 F. 2d 474 (1946). Unlicensed engineer employed as a sales agent, in giving incidental advice to purchasers as to type and manner of use of machinery he sold, was not practicing engineering within the meaning of the license law of Wisconsin.

Although the scopes of architectural and engineering practice significantly overlap, a distinction along industrial–non-industrial lines has occasionally been given effect in the cases. Alternatively, the court in *State of Maine v. Beck*, 156 Me. 403, 165 A. 2d 463 (1960) suggested that architects were trained to understand the esthetic, psychological and cultural aspects of construction, while the engineering approach was seen as largely utilitarian.

Where these distinctions are not consciously recognized, state case law must be closely scrutinized in view of the fact that the courts are unwilling to accept the whole area of activity of the one as completely within the province of the other.

La.   *Rabinowitz v. Hurwitz-Mintz Furniture Co.,* 19 La. App. 811, 133 So. 498 (1931). "An architect is defined as one who, skilled in the art of architecture, designs buildings, determining the disposition of both their interior and exterior space together with structural embellishments of each and generally supervises their construction, while a 'civil engineer' is one whose field is that of structures, particularly foundations, and who designs and supervises construction of bridges, great buildings, etc."

N.J.   *Gionti v. Crown Motor Freight Co.,* 128 N.J.L. 407, 26 A. 2d 282 (1942). A registered engineer, not licensed as an architect, may not recover for the value of architectural services rendered since the state statutes distinguish the two professions, and a license to practice in one does not carry the right to practice in both.

N.Y.   *Goldschlag v. Deegan,* 135 Misc. 535, 238 N.Y.S. 3 (1929), *aff'd,* 254 N.Y. 545, 173 N.E. 859, *cert. den.* 282 U.S. 876 (1930). In the absence of rules, declared by the proper authorities, for the determination of what shall constitute fitness to be an architect, an engineer may not hold himself out as an architect.

Utah   *Smith v. American Packing & Provision Co.,* 102 Utah 351, 130 P. 2d 951 (1942). ". . . the field of professional engineering involves the making of plans, designs, and the supervision of construction; but we believe such plans, designs and supervision must all relate to engineering problems, projects, or undertakings."

The practice of land surveying is typically defined to include the "measuring of area's land surfaces, streams, bodies of water and swamps for their correct determination and description, for the establishment, reestablishment, ascertainment or description of land boundaries, corners, divisions, distances and directions, the plotting and monumenting of lands and subdivisions thereof, and mapping and topographical work." *Pa. Stat. Ann.* 37:682 (1964).

For statutory definitions, see reference to individual state license laws on pages 18–20.

Ala.   *Evans v. State,* 125 Ala. App. 335, 146 So. 287 (1933). Surveyor held not a "civil engineer" within statute requiring license for practicing profession of civil engineering.

Cal. *Severance v. Ball*, 93 Cal. App. 56, 268 Pac. 1068 (1928).

Hill v. Kirkwood, 161 Cal. App. 2d 346, 326 P. 2d 599 (1958).

Iowa *Op. Atty. Gen.* §58 (1932). A registered engineer may not practice land surveying without qualifying as a land surveyor and without a specific grant of such privilege in his certificate as a registered engineer.

Ore. *Opp. Atty. Gen.* (1924–1926). A "municipal engineer" may not practice as a land surveyor in laying out a new street without qualifying as a land surveyor.

Landscape architecture has been defined as a distinct and separate profession. Under the New York statute, for example, it is described as follows:

"A person practices landscape architecture within the meaning and intent of this article who performs professional services such as consultation, investigation, reconnaissance, research, planning, design, or responsible supervision in connection with the development of land areas where, and to the extent that the dominant purpose of such services is the preservation, enhancement or determination of proper land uses, natural land features, ground cover and planting, naturalistic and aesthetic values, the settings and approaches to structures or other improvements, natural drainage and the consideration and determination of inherent problems of the land relating to erosion, wear and tear, blight or other hazards." *N.Y. Education Law*, §7320.

The constitutionality of the statute requiring the licensing of landscape architects has been upheld on the ground that it is an appropriate exercise of the "police power" of the state in that the practice of landscape architecture involves the public health, safety and welfare (*Paterson v. University of State of New York*, 14 N.Y. 2d 432).

State statutes typically exempt the following persons from the requirements of professional licensing laws.

1. Recent arrivals in the state who are licensed in the state of previous residence or place of business (rarely applied to architects).
2. Persons working under the supervision of a licensed architect, engineer, or surveyor.
3. Architects rendering engineering services incidental to their architectural practice. Engineers rendering architectural or surveying services incidental to their engineering practice.
4. Persons designing alterations of existing structures which alterations are valued at or below a certain dollar amount (often $10,000).
5. Persons designing or supervising construction of buildings for their own use.

6. Persons involved in the designing or supervision of construction of farm buildings.
7. Persons in the professional employ of the Government of the United States.

State statutes are by no means uniform in this area and should be individually scrutinized by anyone hoping to fall within any of the above exemptions.

There is no contractor practice statute which can be called typical. The California statute is to a degree representative.

"The term contractor . . . is synonymous with the term builder and . . . a contractor is any person who undertakes to, or offers to undertake to, or purports to have the capacity to undertake to or submits a bid to, or does himself or by or through others, construct, alter, repair, add to, subtract from, improve, move, wreck or demolish any building, highway, road, parking facility, railroad, excavation or other structure, project, development or improvement, or to do any part thereof. . . ." *California Business and Professions Code §7026 (1964).*

For statutory definitions, see reference to individual state license laws on page 21.

Ark.   *Arkansas State Licensing Bd. for Gen'l Contractors v. Lane,* 214 Ark. 312, 215 S.W. 2d 707 (1948). An employee who devoted all of his time to the work of his employer at a weekly wage, and who, in superintending the construction of a theatre building for the owners, hired and fired no one and was no more than a general overseer, held not to be a contractor within the meaning of the license law.

Cal.   *MacIntyre v. Angel,* 240 P. 2d 1947.
       Machinery Engineering Co. v. Nickel, 226 P. 2d 78.

D.C.   *Wilson v. District of Columbia,* 26 App. D.C. 110 (1905). Bricklayer, making contracts with builders or general contractors to lay part of all of bricks required in work is not a "building contractor" within meaning of law requiring building contractors to procure licenses.

La.   In a number of early cases, determination of the scope of contractors' licensing statutes has involved Article 206 of the Louisiana Constitution exempting from the payment of a license tax persons pursuing mechanical trades.
       New Orleans v. Bayley, 35 La. Ann. 545 (1883). A mechanic who works at his trade with his own hands and employs others to assist him in his work is exempt from the license tax in pursuance of Article 206 of the Constitution. To same effect see *New Orleans v. Lagman,* 43 La. Ann. 1180, 10 So. 244 (1891).

Theobalds v. Connor, 42 La. Ann. 787, 7 So. 689 (1890). A mechanic who employs others in the erection of buildings and superintends the work is a general contractor within the license law although he performs mechanical work occasionally. To same effect see *New Orleans v. O'Neil*, 43 La. Ann. 1182, 10 So. 245 (1891); *New Orleans v. Pohlmann*, 45 La. Ann. 219, 12 So. 116 (1893); *New Orleans v. Leibe*, 45 La. Ann. 346, 12 So. 625 (1893). See also *State v. McNally*, 45 La. Ann. 44, 12 So. 117 (1893).

Nev.   *Peck v. Woomack*, 65 Nev. 184, 192 P. 2d 874 (1948). To qualify for a license under the statute relating to general contractors, it is not necessary for the applicant to qualify as to competency, skill, or experience in a particular trade or classification within the general scope of the building or construction trades.

N.M.   *Kaiser v. Thomson*, 55 N.M. 270, 232 P. 2d 142.
       Fischer v. Rangokes, 59 N.M. 463, 286 P. 2d 312.

Okla.   *Ex parte Unger*, 22 Okla. 755, 98 Pac. 999 (1908). House and sign painter who is engaged in contract work held not required by statute to procure a contractor's license.

Tenn.   *Ross-Frankel, Inc. v. State*, 179 Tenn. 320, 165 S.W. 2d 590 (1942). Statutory provision defining contractors and the scope of their activities does not apply to the furnishing and installation of unattachable and removable store fixtures.

THE PROHIBITION AGAINST ENGAGING in a particular activity for which an individual is not legally qualified has been held to include a prohibition against his use of titles and designations relating to these specific occupations.

Iowa   *Op. Atty. Gen.* 312 (1928). A company manufacturing barn equipment having an architectural department cannot use the term "architect" or "architectural" in connection with such department if it receives compensation directly or indirectly for its designs.

Mich.   *Op. Atty. Gen.* No. 595 (Oct. 3, 1947). A registered professional engineer is not entitled to advertise himself as an "architectural engineer."

Minn.   *Op. Atty. Gen.* 10–A (June 23, 1947). An "architectural designer," who is not a registered architect, cannot prepare plans for the alteration of a public building where total cost comes within section of statute requiring registration.

N.Y.   *Varall v. Morton*, 68 N.Y.S. 2d 710, *aff'd*, 272 App. Div. 801, 71 N.Y.S. 2d 893 (1947). Civil Service Commission of New York

City properly refused to change petitioner's name from assistant architect to architect, since to do so would have violated former Sec. 1476 of Education Law which forbids a person to hold himself out as an architect if unlicensed, and petitioner in this case had no license to practice architecture.

Op. Atty. Gen. 1933, 48 St. Dep't. 151. A person not duly licensed as an engineer or surveyor is unauthorized to use such terms or titles.

Ohio   *Op. Atty. Gen.* No. 478 (1949). In his advertisements an individual, not registered or exempted as a professional engineer, may not use the word "engineer" or "engineering" in connection with the words, "tax consultant," "business manager," or "accountant."

Pa.   *Registration of Consulting Interior Architects*, 12 Pa. D. & C. 780 (1919). A person using the title "consulting interior architect" holds himself out as an architect and therefore must register as an architect.

Tenn.   *State Bd. of Examiners v. Standard Engineering Co.*, 157 Tenn. 157, 7 S.W. 2d 47 (1928). Persons using name and letterhead implying that they are engineers held subject to engineering statute, even though they are licensed plumbers doing only such work as plumbers ordinarily undertake.

Wash. *Meyer v. Simpson*, 209 P. 2d 294.

Wis.   *33 Op. Atty. Gen.* 55 (1944). Use of classification "professional engineering employer" for collective bargaining purposes is permitted although it includes persons not qualified under the licensing statute. The term, for collective bargaining purposes, does not deceive anyone and has a restricted and harmless effect.

25 Op. Atty. Gen. 346 (1936). Use of the title "designer," "house designer," or "building designer" has been permitted to a person performing architectural service for private residences or farm buildings since by statute, services relative to this type of construction are exempted from license requirements.

26 Op. Atty. Gen. 384 (1937). The term "architrator" when used with intent to practice architecture constitutes a violation of the licensing statute unless the user is registered or exempt from its provisions.

THE POWER TO REGULATE THESE PROFESSIONS is sometimes delegated by the state to a municipality.

Cal.   *Horwith v. Fresno*, 74 Cal. App. 2d 443, 168 P. 2d 767 (1946). When statute licensing an occupation has been enacted by the state, a municipality cannot impose additional local requirements. If the field is fully occupied by a state statute, the city ordinance is void.

Colo. *Heron v. Denver*, 131 Colo. 501, 283 P. 2d 647 (1955). Even where the power to regulate is not expressly given, regulations in the interest of the public health, safety, and welfare will be upheld.

Fla. *State v. St. Petersburg*, 133 Fla. 766, 183 So. 304, 309 (1938). "It is elementary that that character of legislation which the State legislature has the power to enact, regulating a trade or business, it may delegate to the legislative authority of a municipality to enact for the regulation of trades and businesses within the jurisdiction of such municipality."

Mo. *Siemens v. Shreeve*, 317 Mo. 736, 296 S.W. 415 (1927). Unless the municipality is specifically authorized by statute or charter provision to regulate a professional or business, the power cannot be exercised.

Neb. *Grey v. Omaha*, 80 Neb. 526, 114 N.W. 600 (1908). Where there is no express power granted to a city to license or regulate the business of constructing sidewalks, an ordinance to license and regulate such business is unreasonable and void.

Okla. *Ex parte Unger*, 22 Okla. 755, 98 Pac. 999 (1908). State power granted to municipality to levy occupational tax on contractors. Held, that section of ordinance covering persons doing contract work illegal and void as not within the municipality's grant of power.

It should be noted that the right to practice architecture or other professions may be subject to "privilege" or "occupational" taxes, requiring state or municipal licenses.

Ala. *Brown Plumbing & Heating Co. v. McDowell*, 240 Ala. 485, 200 So. 104 (1941); *Pate v. State*, 243 Ala. 44, 8 So. 2d 516 (1942).

Ariz. *Arizona Tax Comm'n. v. Frank Harmonson Co.*, 63 Ariz. 452, 163 P. 2d 667 (1945).

Ga. *La Grange v. Whitley*, 180 Ga. 805, 180 S.E. 823 (1935).

Ill. *People ex rel Laist v. Lamee*, 251 Ill. 527, 96 N.E. 346.

Miss. *Stone v. Greene*, 199 Miss. 6, 23 So. 2d 542 (1945); *Cook v. Stone*, 192 Miss. 219, 5 So. 2d 223 (1941).

Mo. *St. Louis v. Hertzel*, 88 Mo. 128 (1885).

Ohio *Wolpa v. Hambly*, 20 Ohio App. 236, 153 N.E. 135.

Okla. *Ex parte Marler*, 140 Okla. 194, 282 Pac. 353 (1929).

S.C. *Wilson & Edwards v. Greenville*, 65 S.C. 426, 43 S.E. 966 (1903); *Simons-Maybrant Co. v. Query*, 146 S.C. 185, 143 S.E. 808 (1928).

Tenn.   *Cook v. Memphis,* 94 Tenn. 692, 30 S.W. 742 (1895); *Beck v. Cobb,* 174 Tenn. (10 Beeler) 104, 124 S.W. 2d 228 (1939); *McGill & Daugherty v. Kefauver,* 175 Tenn. 667, 137 S.W. 2d 279 (1940).
Va.   *Deirick v. Commonwealth,* 122 Va. 906, 95 S.E. 392 (1918).

WHILE TAX AND LICENSE LAWS ARE GENERALLY UPHELD as a valid exercise of the police power, courts have declared statutes and ordinances unconstitutional which set up discriminatory and arbitrary classifications.

Ala.   *McLendon v. State,* 179 Ala. 54, 60 So. 392 (1912). Statute excluding Confederate soldiers from the payment of certain professional occupational taxes was held to be invalid.
Ill.   *Doe v. Jones,* 327 Ill. 387, 158 N.E. 703 (1927). Statute licensing land surveyors, but exempting those in governmental employment, held invalid.
Ky.   *Young v. Lexington,* 235 Ky. 822, 32 S.W. 2d 410 (1930). Licensing ordinance classifying painting contractors on the basis of the "volume of business" carried on was upheld.
Pa.   *Commonwealth v. Humphrey,* 288 Pa. 280, 136 Atl. 213 (1927). Act registering engineers held unconstitutional as creating unjustifiable classification since it wholly exempted from registration "officers and employees of a corporation engaged in interstate commerce."
Tenn.   See *Chalker v. Birmingham & N.W. Ry.,* 249 U.S. 522 (1919) *infra.*
Wis.   *Milwaukee v. Rissling,* 184 Wis. 517, 199 N.W. 61 (1924), *aff'd,* 271 U.S. 644 (1926). Licensing ordinance providing separate classification of journeymen and electrical contractors held valid.
Wyo.   *State v. Sheridan,* 25 Wyo. 347, 170 Pac. 1 (1918). Ordinance taxing "cement" sidewalk contractors and excluding other kinds of sidewalk contractors was invalid.
U.S.   *Chalker v. Birmingham & N.W. Ry.,* 249 U.S. 522 (1919), reversing *Wright v. Jackson Constr. Co.,* 138 Tenn. 145, 196 S.W. 488 (1917). Statute taxing construction companies according to location of their chief offices held invalid.
   Williams v. McCartan, 212 Fed. 345 (1914). Licensing ordinance discriminatory against non-resident of city held invalid.

THE LEGALITY OF A PARTNERSHIP OR A CONTRACT for a joint venture entered into between architects or engineers and unlicensed persons has sometimes been upheld.

Cal.   *Joseph v. Drew,* 225 P. 2d 504 (1950). Licensed architects could form a partnership with a licensed building contractor who was not licensed as an architect under statute permitting such partnership provided the name of the architects appears on all instruments of service while unlicensed members are not designated as architects.

Colo. *Mitchell v. Jones,* 104 Colo. 62, 88 P. 2d 557 (1939). A contract, entered into by plaintiff and defendant whereby the plaintiff was to secure architectural contracts for the defendant, assist governing boards in preparing and submitting P.W.A. applications, and supply supervision of work in return for part of the architect's fees, is not invalid on the ground that it is in contravention of public policy.

School Dist. v. Central Savings Banks & Trust Co., 113 Colo. 487, 159 P. 2d 361 (1945). Written contract whereby architect agreed that ⅔ of fees for services rendered in employment procured by consultant "will be remitted" to consultant authorized the consultant to collect at least ⅔ of the fees due for architectural services, and consultant acquired a lien on funds due as compensation for services rendered by architect in employment procured by consultant when fund representing such compensation came into existence.

Ill. *Haynes v. East St. Louis Council,* 258 Ill. App. 38. A partnership consisting of architects, one of whom was not licensed, could recover for services rendered.

CHAPTER TWO

Registration and licensing laws

The registration laws pertaining to the architectural profession fall into two categories: (a) those which restrict use of the title "architect," and (b) those which restrict the practice of architecture.

Corporations in almost every state are either barred from the practice of architecture, professional engineering, or land surveying, or are permitted to practice provided (a) the principal officers are licensed, or (b) the persons in responsible charge of the work are licensed.

No restrictions are placed upon the formation of partnerships by persons engaged in these occupations, but in some states partnerships *as such* are not entitled to be licensed or to engage in practice.

Among the jurisdictions providing licensing requirements for architects, four may be designated as "title" states, in that they do not restrict the practice of architecture, but merely ban the use of the name "architect" or any modification thereof by those who have not complied with the registration requirements.

A typical interpretation given "title" statutes is found in a Wisconsin case stating: "The evident purpose (of the statute) is the protection of the public from misinterpretation and deceit, and its prohibition is no broader than is called for by this purpose." *Fischer v. Landisch*, 203 Wis. 254, 234 N.W. 498, 499 (1931).

Forty-six jurisdictions now have "practice" statutes, some of which, however, to some extent, do not effectively bar those not licensed from practicing.

There is no uniform rule with regard to the practice of architecture, engineering, or surveying by corporations. Statutes differ as to the permissibility of practice by corporations, and where there is no explicit statutory provision, one must look to judicial decisions.

In a number of states, similar qualifications for practice are required

14

of corporations and partnerships. Partnerships as such may not be entitled to a license for practice, but no restriction is placed on the formation of partnerships for engaging in these activities so long as the individual members are licensed.

A TYPICAL "TITLE" STATUTE reads as follows:

"No person shall assume the title architect or 'registered architect,' or shall use any other word, letters or figures indicating or implying that the person using them is an architect or registered architect...." *The W. Va. Code of 1961 §§2956–2965.*

In the following states "title" statutes are in force:
Iowa   *Iowa Code Ann.* §§118.1–118.14 (1949).
Md.   *The Ann. Code of the Public Gen'l Laws of Md. art.* 43, §§513–528 (1957).
Washington   Rev. Code of Wash. Ann. cit 18 §§18.08.100–18.08.270.
W.Va.   *The W.Va. Code of 1961* §§2956–2965.
Wyo.   *Wyoming Stat. 1957* §§33–24–33–39.

AN EFFECTIVE PRACTICE STATUTE reads:

"In order to safeguard life, health, and property, no person shall practice architecture in this state, or use the title architect or any title, sign, card, or device to indicate that such person is practicing architecture or is an architect, unless such person shall have secured from the regents a license...." *N.Y. Educ. Law* §7302.

In the following states, "practice" statutes are in force. Each statute should be carefully examined for exceptions which may emasculate the licensing requirements. See for example, the South Carolina statute post which, though in form is a "practice" statute, actually offers no more protection than a "title" statute because it excepts everyone not holding himself out as an architect from its provisions. The citations are to the entire statutory section relating to architecture.
Ala.   *Ala. Code* tit. 46, §§8–20 (1958) (Supp. 1963).
Alaska   *Alaska Stat. 1962* c. 48, §§08.48.010–08.48.430.
Ariz.   *Ariz. Rev. Stat. Ann.* tit. 32, §§101–145 (1956).
Ark.   *Ark. Stat. 1947,* 1957 Replacement, §§71–301–71–313 (Supp. 1963).
Cal.   *Cal. Bus. and Prof. Code* §§5500–5604 (1962) (1964 Supp.).
Colo.   *Colo. Rev. Stat. 1963* 10–1–1–10–1–22.
Conn.   *Conn. Gen. Stat. Ann.* §§20–288–20–298 (1960).
Del.   *Del. Code Ann.* tit. 24, §§301–319 (1953) (Supp. 1964).

D.C.   *Dist. Col. Code* §§2–1001–1031 (1961).

Fla.   *Fla. Stat. Ann.* §§467.01–467.17 (1951) (Supp. 1964).

Ga.   *Ga. Code Ann.* §§84–301–84–322 (1955) (Supp. 1963).

Hawaii   *Rev. Laws of Hawaii 1955* c. 166, §§1–14 (Supp. 1963).

Idaho   *Idaho Code* §§54–301–54–310 (1957).

Ill.   *Ill. Ann. Stat.* c. 10½, §§1–20 (1963).

Ind.   *Ind. Ann. Stat.,* 1961 Replacement, §§63–101–63–129.

Kan.   *Kan. Stat. Ann.* art. 6–101–6–123 (1964).

Ky.   *Ky. Rev. Stat. Ann.* §§323.010–323.990 (1963).

La.   *La. Stat. Ann.* tit. 37, §§141–161 (1964).

Mass.   *Mass. Ann. Laws* c. 112, §§60A–600 (1957).

Mich.   *Mich. Stat. Ann.* c. 156, §§18.84(1)–18.84(27) (1957) (Supp. 1963).

Minn.   *Minn. Stat. Ann.* §§326.02–326.16 (1945).

Miss.   *Miss. Code 1942 Ann.,* recompiled 1956, §§8632–01–8632–23 (Supp. 1962).

Mo.   *Stat. Mo. Ann.* §§327.010–327.290 (1949) (Supp. 1964).

Mont.   *Mont. Rev. Code 1947 Ann.,* 1962 Replacement, §§66–101–66–115 (Supp. 1965).

Neb.   *Neb. Rev. Stat. 1943,* Reissue of 1958 as amended by 1963 Cum. Supp., §§81–839–81–856.

Nev.   *Nev. Rev. Stat.* 623.010–623.390 (1963).

N.H.   *N.H. Rev. Stat. Ann. 1955* c.310:1–310:30.

N.J.   *N.J. Stat. Ann.* §§45:1–1–45:3–16 (1963).

N.M.   *N.M. Stat. 1953* §§67–12–1–67–12–19 (Supp. 1963).

N.Y.   *N.Y. Educ. Law* §§7301–7312 (1961) (Supp. 1964).

N.C.   *N.C. Gen. Stat.,* 1965 Replacement, §§83–1–83–15.

N.D.   *N.D. Century Code* §§43–03–01–43–03–21 (1960).

Ohio   *Ohio Rev. Code Ann. 1964* §§4703.01–4703.99.

Okla.   *Okla. Stat. Ann.* tit. 59, §§45.1–45.24 (1963).

Ore.   *Ore. Rev. Stat.* §§671.010–671.090 (1963).

Pa.   *Pa. Stat. Ann.* tit. 63, §§21–33 (1959) (Supp. 1964).

Puerto Rico   *Laws of P.R. Ann.* tit. 20, §§681–710 (1961) (Supp. 1964).

R.I.   *R.I. Gen. Laws 1956* §§5–1–1–5–1–29 (Supp. 1964).

S.C.   *S.C. Code of Laws 1962* §§56–51–56–63. (Supp. 1964).

S.D.   *S.D. Code 1939* §§18.0101–18.0116, as amended by 1960 Supp. to S.D. Code of 1939 §§18.0101–18.0119.

Tenn.   *Tenn. Code Ann.* §§62–201–62–222 (1955) (Supp. 1964).

Tex.   *Vernon's Ann. Rev. Civil Stat. of The State of Texas* art. 249a, §§1–14 (1959).

Utah   *Utah Code Ann. 1953*, Replacement 1963, §§58–1–1–58–1–43 and
    58–3–1–58–3–7.

Vt.   *Vt. Stat. Ann.* tit. 26, §§121–210 (1959) (Supp. 1964).

Va.   *Va. Code 1950* §§54–17–54–41 (1950) (Supp. 1964).

Wis.   *Wis. Stat. Ann.* §§101.31(1)–101.31(14) (1957) (Supp. 1965).

REGISTRATION STATUTES are diverse in scope and effectiveness. Many of
them contain ambiguous provisions which require interpretation by the
courts.

Ohio   *Ohio Rev. Code Ann. 1964* §§4703.01–4703.99. The statute pro-
    vides that no one shall practice architecture without a license, but
    it is further provided: "(This act) shall not prevent persons other
    than architects from filing application for building permits or ob-
    taining such permits, providing the drawings for such buildings
    are signed by the authors with their true appellation as engineer,
    contractor, carpenter, or other appellation, but without the use of
    any form of the title architect, nor shall it prevent such persons
    from designing any building or supervising the construction thereof
    for their own use."
    In *McGill v. Carlos*, 39 Comm. Pl. 502, 81 N.E. 2d 726, 728, 729
    (1947) the Court in interpreting the statute said:

    "The court feels that these two exceptions were intended pri-
    marily to enable an owner to design plans and specifications for
    the construction of a building for his own use and when required,
    to file and obtain a building permit therefor." The court decided
    that "a builder who is not a registered architect may not prepare
    complete plans and specifications for the construction of a build-
    ing for another, when expert knowledge and skill are required
    in such preparation, and that such laws apply to persons engaging
    in single, isolated transactions as well as persons attempting to
    practice architecture as a business or profession."

S.C.   *Code of Laws of S.C. 1962* §§56–51–56–63. After requiring a
    license of those who practice architecture in the state, the South
    Carolina statutes provide the following exception: "Nothing in this
    chapter shall be construed to apply to contractors, builders, me-
    chanics or *private individuals making plans and erecting buildings*,
    so long as they do not hold themselves out to the public as archi-
    tects." this provision, though contrary to the tenor of the practice
    statute, seems explicit. Nevertheless, the court found that the
    defendant violated the statute when he prepared "detailed speci-

fications" and engaged in the supervision of the erection of the buildings involved.

The court also relied on the participation of the defendant in the supervision of construction which it considered as not incidental to the authorization to "make plans and erect buildings."

Tenn.   *Tenn. Code Ann.* §§62–201–62–222 (1955). The statute requires any person who practices architecture or engineering to register. It further provides that a person will not be required to register who does not use the appellation "architect" or "engineer" unless the public safety or health is involved. In *State Bd. of Examiners v. Rodgers,* 167 Tenn. 374, 69 S.W. 2d 1093 (1934), an action by the State Board of Examiners to enjoin an individual from practicing without a license, it was held that a contract to furnish plans and specifications for construction of dwellings and for supervising the construction, did involve "the public safety or health." Therefore, the defendant violated the statute whether or not he had represented himself to the public as an architect.

Cantrell v. Perkins, 177 Tenn. 47, 146 S.W. 2d 134 (1941). One transaction, the drafting of plans or specifications for a dwelling house, even where the party did not represent himself to the public as a practicing architect, was sufficient to constitute a violation of the statute, because that one transaction jeopardized the public safety and health.

THE LAWS PERTAINING TO THE LICENSING of engineers, surveyors, and contractors are almost universally directed toward restricting professional practice to licensed persons. The following states have laws licensing professional engineers and land surveyors. (The citations are to the entire statutory sections relating to engineering and surveying.)

Ala.   *Ala. 1958 Code* tit. 46, §§128(1)–128(24) as found in 1963 Supp. (engineers and surveyors).

Alaska   *Alaska Stat. 1962* §§08.48.010–08.48.430 (engineers).

Ariz.   *Ariz. Rev. Stat. Ann.* tit. 32, §§101–145 (1956) (engineers and surveyors).

Ark.   *Ark. Stat. 1943,* 1957 Replacement, §§71–1001–71–1024 (engineers).

Cal.   *Cal. Bus. and Prof. Code* §§6700–6799 (1964) (engineers).
       Cal. Bus. and Prof. Code §§8700–8753 (1964) (surveyors).

Colo.   *Colo. Rev. Stat. Ann. 1963* §§51–1–1–51–1–23 (engineers).
        Colo. Rev. Stat. Ann. 1963 §§51–2–1–51–2–14 (surveyors).

Conn.   *Conn. Gen. Stat. Ann.* §§20–299–20–310 (1960) (Supp. 1964) (engineers and surveyors).

Del. *Del. Code Ann.* §§24–2701–24–2735 (1953) (Supp. 1964) (engineers and surveyors).

Fla. *Fla. Stat. Ann.* §§471.01–471.36 (Supp. 1964) (engineers).
Fla. Stat. Ann. §§472.01–472.14 (Supp. 1964) (surveyors).

Ga. *Ga. Code Ann.* §§84–2101–84–2146 (1955) (Supp. 1963) (engineers and surveyors).

Hawaii *Rev. Laws of Hawaii 1955* c. 166, §§1–14 (Supp. 1963) (engineers and surveyors).

Idaho *Idaho Code* §§54–1201–54–1234 (1957) (Supp. 1963) (engineers and surveyors).

Ill. *Ill. Ann. Stat.* c. 48½, §§32–61 (1950) (Supp. 1964) (engineers).
Ill. Ann. Stat. c. 133, §§34–54 (1964) (surveyors).

Ind. *Ind. Ann. Stat.,* 1961 Replacement, §§63–1501–63–1553 (engineers and surveyors).

Iowa *Iowa Code Ann.* §§114.1–114.25 (1949) (Supp. 1964) (engineers and surveyors). Note exception to employees of non-engineering corporation.

Kan. *Kan. Stat. Ann.* 26a–101–26a–125 (1964) (engineers).

Ky. *Ky. Rev. Stat. Ann.* §§322.010–322.990 (1963) (engineers).

La. *La. Stat. Ann.* tit. 37, §§681–704 (1964) (engineers and surveyors).

Me. *Me. Rev. Stat. Ann. 1964* tit. 32, §§1251–1360 (engineers).

Md. *Md. Ann. Code Gen. Laws 1957* art. 75½, §§1–21 (Supp. 1964) (engineers and surveyors).

Mass. *Mass. Ann. Laws* c. 112, §§81D–81T (1957) (Supp. 1964) (engineers and surveyors).

Mich. *Mich. Stat. Ann.* c. 156, §§18.84(1)–18.84(27) 1957) (Supp. 1963) (engineers and surveyors).

Minn. *Minn. Stat. Ann.* §§326.02–326.16 (1945) (Supp. 1964).

Miss. *Miss. Code 1942 Ann.* §§8791–01–8791–26 (engineers).
Miss. Code 1942 Ann. §§8792–01–8792–18 (Supp. 1964) (surveyors).

Mo. *Mo. Stat. Ann.* §§327.010–327.280 (1949) (Supp. 1964) (engineers).
Mo. Stat. Ann. §§344.010–344.130 (1949) (Supp. 1964) (surveyors).

Mont. *Mont. Rev. Code 1947 Ann.,* 1962 Replacement, §§66–2324–66–2347 (Supp. 1963) (engineers and surveyors).

Neb. *Neb. Rev. Stat. 1943* reissue of 1958, as amended by 1963 Ann. Supp. §§81–839–81–856 (engineers). Same as above for surveying except §§81–8108–81–8127 (not amended as above also).

Nev.   *Nev. Rev. Stat.* §§625.010–625.580 (1963) (engineers and surveyors).

N.H.   *N.H. Stat. Ann. 1955* c. 319.1–319.30 (Supp. 1963) (engineers).

N.J.   *N.J. Stat. Ann.* §§45–8–27–45–8–48 (1963) (engineers and surveyors).

N.M.   *N.M. Stat. 1953* §§67–21–27–67–21–53 (Supp. 1963) (engineers and surveyors).

N.Y.   *N.Y. Educ. Law* §§7201–14 (1961) (Supp. 1964) (engineers and surveyors).

N.C.   *N.C. Gen. Stat.,* 1965 Replacement, §§89–1–89–16 (engineering and surveyors).

N.D.   *N.D. Century Code* §§43–19–01–43–19–25 (1960) (Supp. 1963) (engineers).

   N.D. Century Code §§43–24–01–43–24–15 (1960) (surveyors).

Ohio   *Ohio Rev. Code Ann. 1964* §§4733.01–4733.99 (engineers and surveyors).

Okla.   *Okla. Stat. Ann.* tit. 59, §§411–471 (1963) (engineers).

Ore.   *Ore. Rev. Stat.* §§672.010–672.990 (1963) (engineers and surveyors).

Pa.   *Pa. Stat. Ann.* tit. 63, §§149–158 (1959) (Supp. 1964) (engineers and surveyors).

R.I.   *R.I. Gen. Laws 1956* §§5–8–1–5–8–36 (Supp. 1964) (engineers and surveyors).

S.C.   *S.C. Code of Laws 1962* §§56–701–56–740 (Supp. 1964) (engineers and surveyors). Poor drafting led to unnecessary trouble. See *State v. Montgomery,* 244 S.C. 308, 136 S.E. 2d 778 (1964).

S.D.   *S.D. Code 1939* §§18.0101–18.0116, as amended by 1960 Supp. to S.D. Code of 1939 §§18.0101–18.0119.

Tenn.   *Tenn. Code Ann.* §§62–201–62–222 (1955).

Tex.   *Tex. Rev. Civ. Stat.* art. 3271a, §§1–25 (1952) (engineers).
   Tex. Rev. Civ. Stat. art. 5268–5305 (1962) (surveyors).

Utah   *Utah Code Ann. 1953,* 1963 Replacement, §§58–22–1–58–22–22 (engineers and surveyors).

Vt.   *Vt. Stat. Ann. 1959* tit. 26, §§1051–1152 (engineers).

Va.   *Va. Code 1950* §§54–17–54–41 (Supp. 1964).

Wash.   *Wash. Rev. Code Ann.* §§18.43.010–18.43.920 (1961) (engineers and surveyors).

W.Va.   *W.Va. Code 1961* §§2966–2974(7) (engineers).

Wis.   *Wis. Stat. Ann.* §§101.31(1)–101.31(14) (1957) (Supp. 1965) (engineers).

Wyo.   *Wyo. Stat. 1957* §§33–356–33–368 (Supp. 1963) (engineers and surveyors).

The following states have regulatory laws licensing general contractors:

Ala.   *Ala. Code* tit. 46, §§65–82 (1958) (Supp. 1963).

Ariz.   *Ariz. Rev. Stat. Ann.* §§32–1101–32–1164 (1956) (Supp. 1963).

Ark.   *Ark. Stat. 1947*, 1957 Replacement, §§71–701–71–720 (Supp. 1963).

Cal.   *Cal. Bus. and Prof. Code* §§7000–7150 (1964).

Hawaii   *Rev. Laws of Hawaii 1955* §§166A–1–166A–22 (1963 Supp).

La.   *La. Stat. Ann.* §§2151–2163 (1964).

Mich.   *Mich. Stat. Ann.* §§18.85(1)–18.85(22) (1957) for residential construction only.

Nev.   *Nev. Rev. Stat.* §§624.010–624.340 (1963).

N.M.   *N.M. Stat. 1953* §§67–12–1–67–12–19 (Supp. 1963).

N.C.   *N.C. Gen. Stat.* §§87–1–87–15 (1965).

S.C.   *S.C. Code of Laws 1962* §§56–401–56–428.

Tenn.   *Tenn. Code Ann.* §§62–601–62–622 (1955).

Utah   *Utah Code Ann. 1953*, 1963 Replacement, §§58–23–1–58–23–18.

Va.   *Va. Code 1950* §§54–113–54–145.2 (Supp. 1964).

Wash.   *Laws 1963*, c. 77 H.B. No. 89.

Although formerly the learned professions could not incorporate, the trend in the past few decades has been to liberalize professional organization laws. This is true of the architectural and engineering professions. As of 1960 only nine states completely prohibited the corporate practice of engineering though a somewhat greater number still prohibit the corporate practice of architecture.

In many instances, the legislatures have sought to maintain professional responsibility in the traditional sense while allowing incorporation. To insure that responsibility continues after incorporation, some states have imposed conditions on those choosing the corporate form of organization —one or more of the following being typical:

1. The professional work done is in the responsible charge of a licensed individual and carries the signature of such individual.
2. At least two principals of the corporation are licensed.
3. The corporation does not hold itself out as a licensed architect.
4. The chief executive officer is a licensed architect.
5. The executive director and the owners of a majority of the stock of such corporation are duly registered (Wisconsin).
6. The corporation name does not contain the name of a non-licensed individual.
7. The principal's name appears in the corporation's name.

The professional practice of corporations has been involved in a number of cases:

Ark.	*Ark. State Board of Architects v. Bank Building and Equipment Corp. of America,* 225 Ark. 889, 286 S.W. 2d 323 (1956). Held: A corporation with a staff of 200 persons engaged in designing and supervising the construction and alteration of bank buildings was illegally practicing architecture where only the chief architect was licensed, and he delegated the inspection and supervision functions to subordinates.

Conn.	*Conn. Society of Architects, Inc. v. Bank Bldg. and Equip. Corp. of America,* 151 Conn. 68, 193 A 2d 493 (1963).

Fla.	Under a Florida statute, corporations were not permitted to practice architecture. Nevertheless, it was held that Robert L. Weed, Architect, Inc. could foreclose a lien for services rendered since there was never any question but that Robert L. Weed was the real party in interest.
	Robert L. Weed, Architect, Inc. v. Horning, 159 Fla. 847, 33 So. 2d 648 (1947).

Ga.	Under a Georgia statute which provided that "no person shall . . . use the title 'architect'. . . or any words . . . indicating or implying that he or she is an architect without having qualified . . . ," it was held that the conspicuous absence of the pronoun "it," rendered the statute inapplicable to corporations.
	W. J. Folsom, Sr. v. Summer Locatell & Co. Inc., 90 Ga. App. 696, 83 S.E. 2d 855 (1954).

Ill.	*Continental Paper Grading Co. v. Howard & Fisher & Associates,* 3 Ill. App. 118, 120 N.E. 2d 577 (1954).

N.Y.	*Turner Construction Co. v. 1600 East Ave. Inc.,* 30 Misc. 2d 811, 219 N.Y.S. 2d 677, *aff'd* 15 App. Div. 2d 631, 222 N.Y.S. 2d 688 (1961). Held: the propriety of issuing a license under a "grandfather" clause could be attacked inasmuch as that function of the Education Department is purely ministerial.
	American Stove Equipment & Construction Corp. v. Jack Dempsey's Punch Bowl, Inc. (see citation and summary infra page 26).

Pa.	*Baker v. Chambers,* 183 Pa. Sup. 634, 133 A. 2d 589 (1957).

CHAPTER THREE

Practicing without a license

The failure of an architect, engineer, surveyor, or general contractor to procure a license as required by statute may constitute a misdemeanor subjecting him to criminal prosecution, and render the contracts he has entered into for the performance of professional services illegal and void.

The license laws of most states prescribe penalties for a violation of their provisions, usually terming such violation a misdemeanor punishable by fine or imprisonment or both. These sections have, upon occasion, been made the basis of criminal prosecution.

An evasion of the statutes impresses the stamp of illegality on contracts entered into for the performance of professional services by one not licensed. If the contract is illegal, it will receive no consideration by the courts in the event of its breach, and this will often mean that the unlicensed individual will be unable to collect compensation for his services if the party with whom he contracts refuses payment.

EVASION OF THE LICENSE LAWS has in some instances been made the basis of criminal prosecution by the state.

Ala. *Evans v. State*, 125 Ala. App. 335, 146 So. 287 (1933). Conviction of a person for "practicing the profession of civil engineering" without a license was reversed where the evidence showed he was acting merely as a "surveyor."

Ark. *Arkansas State Bd. of Architects v. Bank Building and Equipment Co.*, 286 S.W. 2d 323 (1956).

Cal. *People v. Wright*, 293 P. 2d 165 (1956).

Howard v. State, 85 Cal. App. 2d 361, 193 P. 2d 11, 14 (1948). In prosecution for evasion of license law pertaining to contractors, the court in applying criminal sanctions said: "The statute in question expresses the judgment of the legislature that the prospect of having to pay damages for incompetence, fraud, and breach of contract, is not an adequate deterrent from wrongful practices in the building trades." *Ex parte McManus,* 151 Cal. 331, 90 Pac. 702 (1907).

N.J.   *N.J. State Bd. of Architects v. Armstrong,* 85 N.J., Super. 22,203 A. 2d 530 (1963). Under a statutory provision exempting those designing and constructing buildings for their "own occupancy" or occupancy by members of their family, defendant was found not to be illegally practicing architecture when he designed plans for and built a dwelling house and tavern, both being integral parts of the same structure.

N.D.   *State v. Gillespie,* 39 N.D. 512, 168 N.W. 38 (1918).

Pa.   *Commonwealth v. Smithgall,* 45 Pa. D. & C. 1, 48 Lanc. Rev. 25 (1943).

Tenn.   *State Bd. of Examiners v. Rodgers,* 167 Tenn. 374, 69 S.W. 2d 1093 (1934); *Ross-Frankel, Inc. v. State,* 179 Tenn. 320, 165 S.W. 2d 590 (1942).

Wyo.   *State v. Butler,* 40 Wyo. 404, 278 Pac. 563 (1929). Information charging that land surveyor was appointed city engineer and that he was not a registered engineer was not sufficiently definite regarding acts constituting offer to practice engineering and surveyor is guilty of no crime unless he offers to practice professional engineering.

WHERE COMPLIANCE WITH LICENSING STATUTES is a prerequisite to validity of the contracts, the cases are not in agreement as to what constitutes a *prima facie* case for recovery. Some states require a license to be pleaded by the plaintiff in order to establish a *prima facie* case; others consider the lack of a license a matter of defense.

Ill.   *Woodly v. Zeman,* 178 Ill. App. 369, 371 (1926). "The question of a license is one collateral to the suit, and it has many times been held that in such circumstances the issuance of a license will be presumed unless proof to the contrary is presented by the other party to the litigation."

Samuel v. Lee–Tex Rubber Products Corp., 340 Ill. App. 220, 91 N.E. 2d 134 (1950). Complaint alleging that plaintiff was a professional engineer and that he agreed to furnish labor and materials to complete project and to furnish plans and specifications did not disclose on its face that plaintiff was an architect practicing without a license, but such matter was an affirmative defense.

Hardy v. Dobler, 248 Ill. App. 361 (1928). Even if plaintiff had contracted to practice architecture without a license, the defendants could not raise the proposition as the issue had not been properly raised.

N.Y. *John V. Dinan Co., Inc. v. Slatter*, 132 Misc. 454, 230 N.Y.S. 145, *aff'd*, 232 N.Y.S. 780 (1928). Corporate plaintiff, suing to recover for engineering services rendered, was not entitled to recover in the absence of pleading and proof that it was licensed as an engineer.

Pa. *McClymont v. La Nasa*, 40 York 25 (1926). In action to recover compensation for preparation of building plans and for superintending work, plaintiff need not allege capacity in which he contracted.

Hildebrant v. Kline, 66 D. & C. 431 (1948). A complaint does not fall because engineer failed to aver that he is a registered engineer, where he was employed only as an estimating engineer, and not as a consulting or active engineer in the actual construction work.

Howarth v. Gilman, 164 Pa. Super. 454, 65 A. 2d 691 (1949). Where it appeared from the pleadings and cross-examination of one of the plaintiffs that plaintiffs were not licensed, and that one of the plaintiffs represented himself as being engaged in industrial engineering, the illegality of the contract sued upon was properly cognizable by the court although such defense had not been previously raised.

Utah *Smith v. American Packing & Provision Co.*, 102 Utah 351, 130 P. 2d 951, 959 (1942). ". . . the general rule is that where a person seeks recovery for professional services for which a license is required as a condition precedent to the rendition of such services for a fee, such person must allege and prove facts which show he was licensed at the time such services were performed or that he was exempted from the class required to have such license."

Olsen v. Reese, 200 P. 2d 733 (1948). Complaint of a general contractor suing for services performed and materials furnished was required to allege that he was a licensed contractor at the time the contract was entered into by the parties.

Wis. *Hickey v. Sutton*, 191 Wis. 313, 210 N.W. 704 (1926). It is not necessary that the pleadings raise the question that the plaintiff has not procured an architectural license. If the objection is not raised by the defendant, it is the duty of the court to make it on its own behalf.

In New York, noncompliance with the architects' licensing act vitiates entirely any contract involving some element of architectural performance (*American Store Equipment & Constr. Corp. v. Jack Dempsey's Punch Bowl, Inc.*, 174 Misc. 436, 21 N.Y.S. 2d 117, *aff'd*, 258 App. Div. 794, 16 N.Y.S. 2d 702, *appeal den.* 258 App. Div. 876, 17 N.Y.S. 2d 220 (1939)), *aff'd*, 283 N.Y. 601, 28 N.E. 2d 23 (1940).

In this case plaintiff construction corporation contracted to remodel defendant's restaurant. The corporation was not licensed to practice architecture but used a licensed architect to prepare the plans, drawings, and specifications. The contract called for architectural services amounting to no more than 10% of the work, 90% relating to materials supplied and installed. In an action to recover compensation pursuant to the contract, the corporation was denied recovery, the court applying the general rule that if any part of the consideration for a contract is contrary to public policy, the whole contract fails. In denying recovery for even those services not pertaining to architecture, the court said:

> "... there is no means of segregating the good from the bad portions of the contract, in this case. The contract was entire and indivisible: to plan, construct, and furnish a complete unit. If the plaintiff had sold the interior furnishings and decorations, the contract could have been separated at least to the extent of permitting recovery for the merchandise sold. Here however were only services, ideas, and supervision. They cannot be separated into different classes—legal and illegal." (21 N.Y.S. 2d 119).

N.Y. *Industrial Installations Corp v. Rosenblatt*, 74 N.Y.S. 2d 197 (1947). Above rule applied in action for recovery for architectural services rendered by corporation.
Industrial Installations Corp. v. Sparer, 74 N.Y.S. 2d 198 (1947). Where recovery was sought for "extras" performed after the work contracted for was fully paid for, and latter agreement involved no architectural services, contract was held separable and recovery allowed to unlicensed corporation.

IN STATES WHICH REQUIRE CERTIFICATION as a prerequisite to the practice of architecture, a contract entered into for the performance of architectural services by an unlicensed person is generally held void and unenforceable. However, due to variations in statutory wording, to liberal judicial construction of statutory language, or of the facts in a given case, contracts of unlicensed persons have upon occasion been held enforceable.

Idaho *Johnson v. Delane*, 77 Idaho 172, 290 P. 2d 213 (1957). The purpose of practice statutes is to safeguard life and health and, in furtherance of this purpose, architects of one state are not permitted to practice in another until they demonstrate in some manner that they would have been able to acquire the license in the other state. In this case a contract was made in Idaho by an architect registered only in Washington for the construction of a building in Idaho. The court held that since plans and payment for the building were to be made in Washington, the plaintiff was not practicing architecture "in the State," and could recover for services performed.

Ill. *Haynes v. East St. Louis Council,* 258 Ill. App. 38 (1930). Co-partnership was entitled to recover for architectural services rendered although one partner was not registered, where it appeared that the licensed partner had supervised the preparation of all the plans. The making of the contract, the court said, did not violate the statute and it was not subsequently violated where a registered architect was the responsible party in drawing the plans.

Kennan v. Tuma, 240 Ill. App. 448 (1926). Individuals, like corporations, may perform architectural services through licensed architects. Where an unlicensed individual employed a licensed architect to draw the plans while he himself supervised the construction, he was not entitled to recover on the contract, since in supervising the work, he undertook the practice of architecture in violation of the statute.

Taheny v. Catholic Bishop of Chicago, 304 Ill. App. 581, 26 N.E. 2d 667 (1940). Oral contract under which unlicensed architect is employed to observe construction of a church and to report any irregularities is not void on the ground that his services constitute the illegal practice of architecture where plans for the building are furnished by a licensed architect who also supervises its construction.

(Recovery denied on another ground).

Ky. *Board of Educ. v. Elliott,* 276 Ky. 790, 125 S.W. 2d 733 (1939). Plaintiff was not entitled to recover for architectural services rendered where he had assumed to act as architect, though unlicensed. The fact that he had the plans and specifications prepared by a licensed architect did not entitle him to recover.

Mich. *Wedgewood v. Jorgens,* 190 Mich. 620, 157 N.W. 360 (1916). Unlicensed architect was not entitled to recover for services rendered in preparing plans and specifications for a building (municipal ordinance construed).

Minn.   *Op. Atty. Gen.* 10–A-3 (May 8, 1950). Where state employed one who was not a registered architect or engineer when he accepted employment to prepare plans and specifications for remodeling of court house, his claim could not be paid in full though his services were satisfactory and reasonably worth the fee claimed.

N.J.   *Lewis v. Collins,* 1 N.J. Misc. 392 (1923). Plaintiff was held not entitled to recover for architectural services rendered under a contract which he entered into prior to procuring a certificate of registration. The court held that since the contract was made prior to plaintiff's licensure (actually nine of the ten months worked), it violated the policy of the statute.

Buechele v. Vogel, 2 N.J. Misc. 738 (1924). Architect who procured a license during the period in which he was preparing plans for defendant was permitted to recover for his services. The court found that he was hired first as a draftsman and later as an architect.

See *Dane v. Brown,* 70 F. 2d 164 (1934), *infra.*

N.Y.   *Bowen v. Schenectady,* 136 Misc. 307, 240 N.Y.S. 784, *aff'd,* 231 App. Div. 779, 246 N.Y.S. 913 (1930). Where a statute requiring a license for the practice of architecture intervenes between the making of the contract and its execution, an unlicensed architect is not permitted to enforce the contract since performance on his part had been made impossible by legislative fiat.

See also *Industrial Installations Corp. v. Sparer,* 74 N.Y.S. 2d 198 (1947).

Ohio   *McGill v. Carlos,* 39 Comm. Pl. 502, 81 N.E. 2d 726 (1947). Contractor was denied recovery for the value of plans and specifications for a dwelling furnished defendant. The court declared that a builder who is not a registered architect may not prepare plans and specifications for a building for another when expert knowledge and skill are required in such preparation. See the case for a summary of the architects' license law as it exists in Ohio.

Op. Atty. Gen. No. 273 (1949). Where an unlicensed person practices architecture, the fact that he is unlicensed precludes recovery by him for architectural services, either on an express contract, implied contract, quasi-contract, or any other type of action.

Maxfield v. Bressler, 55 N.E. 2d 424 (1942). A contract for architectural services covering a building to be erected in Kentucky was not void so as to bar the architect from recovering the agreed compensation because he was not licensed as an architect as required by the Kentucky statute where the contract was drawn up in Ohio and the architect did not supervise the work.

McDonald v. Henderson, 116 Ohio App. 173, 187 N.E. 2d 194 (1962). Architect could recover for services although he did not properly sign his drawings or include the serial number of his certificate, both of which were required by statute.

Pa. *McClymont v. Gitt,* 90 Pa. Super. 395 (1927). An architect who had been engaged in the practice of architecture for one year prior to the enactment of a licensing statute was permitted to recover the value of his services even where he had not filed the required affidavit, stating that he had been in practice for a year. The court found nothing in the act to impose a penalty for this failure and therefore upheld his contract.

Tenn. *State Bd. of Examiners v. Rodgers,* 167 Tenn. 374, 69 S.W. 2d 1093 (1934).

Cantrell v. Perkins, 177 Tenn. 47, 146 S.W. 2d 134 (1941).

Wis. *Wahlstrom v. Hill,* 213 Wis. 533, 252 N.W. 339 (1934). A person hired by an owner to be his agent in transacting the business part of a construction project may, though unlicensed, recover for the services he has rendered. Supervision within the terms of the statute, the court held, means inspection from time to time by an architect to see that his specifications were followed. It is distinct from the business portion of the project, such as the buying of materials, hiring for laborers and mechanics, etc., which an owner may properly do for himself.

Lytle v. Goodfirnon, 241 Wis. 533, 6 N.W. 2d 652 (1942). Where an unlicensed plaintiff sued to recover for architectural services rendered, the case was remanded to the lower court to determine whether plaintiff agreed to furnish the services through another or perform them himself. If he agreed merely to furnish the services and concerned himself with the business end of the transaction, he could recover. Cf. *American Store Equipment & Constr. Corp. v. Jack Dempsey's Punch Bowl, Inc., supra,* where corporation, though it hired licensed architect to perform the architectural services involved in construction contract, was not entitled to recover.

U.S. *Dane v. Brown,* 70 F. 2d 164 (1934). Supervising construction of a building in New Jersey and approving bills in New Jersey by a Massachusetts architect pursuant to preliminary conferences held in Massachusetts and plans and specifications made in Massachusetts, was not "pursuing the practice of architecture" so as to preclude recovery for services on the ground that the contract was illegal. Such a view is not supported by other cases and the New Jersey statute itself now provides: "Any single act or transaction shall constitute engaging in the business of practice of architecture." *N.J. Stat. Ann.* 45 Sec. 45:3–10.

Many cases arose under old "title" statutes requiring the courts to determine whether a non-licensed architect was required to inform the owner of such fact to recover for his services. Because of the present predominance of practice statutes under which disclosure of unlicensed status does not constitute a defense to a claim of unlicensed professional practice, these cases will not be treated in any detail here, and reference may be made to the previous editions of this book. However, a recent case, *David, Brody, Wisniewski v. Barret*, 253 Ia. 1178, 115 N.W. 2d 839, appears to be a departure from precedent. In this case the plaintiff had implied that it was an architect, in clear violation of the Iowa "title" statute. Violation of this statute is a misdemeanor. Nevertheless, the court found that the commission of a misdemeanor did not bar recovery by plaintiffs for their services.

IN STATES WHICH REQUIRE CERTIFICATION as a prerequisite to the practice of engineering, contracts for the performance of engineering services by persons not licensed are not enforceable. Certain activities are common to both architectural and engineering practice. An engineer may not, however, practice architecture, and courts scrutinize the facts as to performance in a given case to determine whether they are properly within the scope of engineering practice.

La.　*Rabinowitz v. Hurwitz-Mintz Furniture Co.*, 19 La. App. Rep. 811, 133 So. 498 (1931). Licensed engineer was entitled to recover for engineering services rendered under a contract which was drawn on a printed form for architects. Use of such form did not amount to a holding out that he was an architect and thus subject to the architect's licensing statute. The determining factor was whether or not the work undertaken was that of an architect or engineer.

N.J.　*Gionti v. Crown Motor Freight Co.*, 128 N.J. L.407, 262 A. 2d 282 (1942). Licensed engineer was not entitled to recover for architectural services rendered where he did not also possess an architect's license. The court rejected the argument that since the professions overlap, they differ in name only.

N.Y.　*Usdin v. Kvatinetz*, 69 N.Y.S. 2d 634 (1947). In action by unlicensed engineer to recover on a contract for engineering services performed in connection with the manufacture of an exerciser for children, the question whether an engineer's license was required as a condition of recovery depended on whether his services involved the safeguarding of life, health, or property within the meaning of the statute. If the designing of the machine involved elimination of risks to the user or others in contact with it, the services would fall within the scope of the statute.

Ohio *Fanning v. College of Steubenville,* 197 N.E. 2d 423, App. Div. 174 Ohio St. 343, 189 N.E. 2d 72 (1961). In an action by a licensed engineer to recover for professional services rendered, the court held the services to be architectural in character and denied recovery. (In so doing the court cited various definitions of architectural and engineering practice, but made no attempt to apply the facts of the case thereto.)

Pa. *Lindholm v. Mount,* 163 Pa. Super. 36, 60 A. 2d 422 (1948). Plaintiff, unlicensed as an engineer, was not entitled to recover for services rendered as a consulting engineer. The act requires one who is to practice engineering in but one isolated transaction to register.

Howarth v. Gilman, 365 Pa. 50, 73 A. 2d 655 (1950). A firm of industrial engineers which engaged in the practice of engineering without registering was barred from recovery of a sum due under a contract for engineering services.

Tex. *Gray v. Blau,* 223 S.W. 2d. 53 (1949). Non-registered engineer could not recover for services where he was employed as consulting engineer though he did other types of non-engineering work also, and he did not show what portion of work he performed as supervising engineer and what portion in non-engineering duties. The fact that a registered engineer supervised erection, was immaterial, where the non-registered engineer was not his "subordinate."

Utah *Smith v. American Packing & Provision Co.,* 102 Utah 351, 130 P. 2d 951 (1942). Licensed professional engineer was entitled to recover for services which included activities common to the field of architecture. A licensee is not required to have a license in each of the fields into which his profession may overlap. The criterion for determining whether a licensed engineer may perform architectural functions without an architect's license is whether such functions are necessarily embraced within the scope of engineering covered by his license.

Wis. *Kuenzi v. Radloff,* 253 Wis. 575, 34 N.W. 2d 798 (1948). Licensed professional engineer was entitled to recover for building plans and specifications prepared by an unlicensed associate, for which the licensed engineer assumed full responsibility.

U.S. *Keller v. Baumgartner,* 153 F. 2d 474 (1946). Unregistered engineer who was employed as a sales agent for the defendant, in giving incidental engineering advice to purchasers, was held not to be practicing engineering and was therefore entitled to an accounting.

IN STATES WHICH REQUIRE CERTIFICATION as a prerequisite to the practice of general contracting, contracts for the performance of general contracting services are held void and unenforceable without such certification.

Ariz.   *Hunt v. Douglas Lumber Co.*, 41 Ariz. 276, 17 P. 2d 815 (1933). Under a statute declaring it unlawful to act as a contractor without having a license and making a violation thereof a misdemeanor, an unlicensed contractor's agreement as to the construction of a building was held unenforceable as against the owner of the premises.

Sobel v. Jones, 96 Ariz. 287, 394 P. 2d 415 (1964). Where plaintiff was under the "control" of defendant and where the latter made the major purchasing decisions, plaintiff was not an independent contractor, but an employee, and was permitted to recover for services rendered.

Ark.   *Arkansas Licensing Bd. v. Rosamond*, 237 S.W. 2d 22 (1951). Where defendant was employed by owner to supervise workers in constructing a building, and owner paid for all the materials and paid all the workmen, and defendant was paid on an hourly basis and worked solely under the direction and orders of the owner, who could nullify his action in employing or discharging workers, the defendant was not a general contractor within the meaning of the license law for general contractors.

Mich.   See *Maciak v. Olejniczak*, 79 F. Supp. 817 (1948) *infra*.

N.M.   *B & R Drilling Co. v. Gardner*, 55 N.M. 118, 227 P. 2d 627 (1951). A contract for drilling a well to produce water for agricultural irrigation purposes falls within category of named occupations as to which the Contractors' License Act does not apply, and therefore the Act does not bar recovery for services rendered under such contract.

Utah   See *Dow v. United States*, 154 F. 2d 707 (1946) *infra*.

Butterfield v. Chaney, 12 Utah 2d 347, 366 P. 2d 607 (1961). The contractors' practice statute exempted those person who contracted for "a job aggregating a fixed sum of less than $1,000." The court affirmed the trial court which had permitted recovery by an unlicensed contractor because his performance was not of one, but three separate jobs, each of which was less than $1,000.

U.S.   *Dow v. United States*, 154 F. 2d 707 (1946). General rule that a contract of an unlicensed person will not be enforced does not apply where an unlicensed contractor seeks to recover from a licensed contractor for services rendered pursuant to a contract entered into between them, especially where the subcontract has been completed and the contractor has received payment in full (Utah statute construed).

Maciak v. Olejniczak, 79 F. Supp. 817 (1948). Plaintiff home owner was entitled to recover for loss sustained resulting from contractor's legal and financial inability to complete performance of a remodeling contract, where the contractor, who was unable to obtain the required state license, made misrepresentations of his ability to perform the contract. The building contract was void for failure of the contractor to obtain the license, and the contractor was guilty of fraud in representing himself as able to perform (Michigan statute applied).

California is the source of most of the reported cases involving application of contractors' licensing statutes. The law in this jurisdiction, which has not significantly changed over the years, expressly provides as follows:

"No person engaged in the business or acting in the capacity of contractor, may bring or maintain any action in any court of this state for the collection of compensation for the performance of any act or contract for which a license is required by this chapter without alleging and proving that he was a duly licensed contractor at all times during the performance of such act or contract. . . ." *Business and Professional Code* §7031.

Cal. *Machinery Eng. Co. v. Nickel,* 226 P. 2d 78 (1951). A large and expensive hay mill intended to be operated as a commercial enterprise is not a construction or operation "incidental to farming" within the statute permitting such construction by an unlicensed contractor, and a contractor constructing a mill without a license could not recover the balance allegedly due for construction.

Oddo v. Hedde, 225 P. 2d 929 (1951). Evidence that when contractor constructed a building, he held a general contractor's license and had no actual knowledge of registrar's rule requiring a supplemental classification, established that he substantially complied with the law, and statute making him subject to "disciplinary action" for ignoring a classification could not be construed to deny him the contract price for his work.

Powell v. Berg, 221 P. 2d 743 (1950). In action to recover reasonable value of services rendered in the construction of a house and garage for defendants, the evidence sustained the finding that one of the plaintiffs did not represent himself to be a licensed contractor and that he performed services as an employee of another with wages as his sole compensation.

Owens v. Haslett, 221 P. 2d 252 (1950). Where building contractor entered into a contract for the construction of a dwelling house and began work on it without a license, his contract was illegal, and procurement of a license during the course of the work did not validate the contract, since the statute requires a license "at all times" during the performance of the work.

Alvarado v. Davis, 115 Cal. App. 782, 6 P. 2d 121 (1931). Unlicensed contractor was not entitled to recover for construction services rendered in an action to foreclose a mechanic's lien.

Phillips v. McIntosh, 124 P. 2d 835 (1942). Plaintiff, unlicensed as contractor, was not entitled to recover for contracting services furnished where she had not procured a license. Plaintiff argued that she was entitled to compensation as an employee of the owner, but where the evidence showed that plaintiff made a profit on the labor of others, charged 15% over and above the cost of materials, and performed no labor herself, the court ruled that she was an independent contractor and as such, needed a contractor's license.

Cash v. Blackett, 87 Cal. App. 2d 233, 196 P. 2d 585 (1948). Plaintiff, unlicensed as contractor, was not entitled to recover for services performed under a written contract reciting that he was not a licensed architect but authorized him to prepare sketches and construct a building. The plaintiff could not gain immunity from the contractors' licensing statute simply by stating he had no architect's license if in fact he performed acts which brought him within the definition "contractor."

Sheble v. Turner, 46 Cal. App. 2d 762, 117 P. 2d 23 (1941). Plaintiff was not entitled to recover for breach of contract entered into with owner of land providing that he was to act as owner's agent in the erection of residences, in procuring loans, and assisting in the sale of property, since plaintiff was held to require a license as contractor and real estate broker before he could lawfully perform the agreed services.

Moon v. Goldstein, 158 P. 2d 1004 (1945). Plaintiff owner was not entitled to enforce contract for the plastering of houses he was constructing for future sale. The court held that he was a contractor and could not escape the licensing requirement by contracting with one licensed contractor to furnish labor or materials for a minor part of the project or by dividing up the project among licensed contractors unless it was substantially carried out by such contractors.

Holm v. Bramwell, 20 Cal. App. 2d 332, 67 P. 2d 114 (1937). Licensed contractor was not entitled to recover from the owner a balance due on the cost of the buildings where he had awarded certain subcontracts to an unlicensed contractor. Since the contract with the unlicensed contractor was void, "the plaintiff who voluntarily paid the illegal demand, either knowing it to be illegal or in ignorance or misapprehension of the law respecting the validity, and not under compulsion or coercion" could not get reimbursement from the owner.

Los Angeles Scenic Studios, Inc., v. Television, Inc., 17 Cal. App. 2d 356, 61 P. 2d 1192 (1936). Unlicensed contractor was entitled to recover for services rendered in construction of an exhibit within an exhibit building under provision exempting from the requirement of a license those engaged in construction or repair work upon personal property "which is not fabricated into and does not become a permanent fixed part of the structure."

Costello v. Campbell, 81 Cal. App. 452, 184 P. 2d 315 (1947). Unlicensed contractor was entitled to recover for services performed in installing two cold storage plants, under the exemption quoted in *Holm v. Bramwell, supra,* where he waived demand for services as a contractor.

Rutherford v. Standard Engineering Corp., 88 Cal. App. 554, 199 P. 2d 354 (1948). Exclusive agency contract for the erection and sale of prefabricated houses did not violate contractors' State License Act, and agent was entitled to recover for breach of contract by defendant manufacturer of prefabricated houses.

Loving & Evans v. Blick, 177 P. 2d (1947), *aff'd,* 191 P. 2d 445 (1948), *aff'd,* 33 Cal. 2d 603, 204 P. 2d 23 (1949). Motion to vacate an arbitration award in favor of contractors was upheld where one partner had no license, and the partnership as such had no license, since the law requires firms of two or more persons acting jointly to procure a firm or joint license before engaging in contracting.

Gatti v. Highland Park Builders, Inc., 27 Cal. 2d 687, 166 P. 2d 265 (1946). Where two individually licensed contractors completed work as a partnership, which only one of them had agreed to do for a corporation, but with the corporation's consent, they could recover against the owner the value of the work performed, although they had no license as partners or joint adventurers.

Steinbrenner v. J. A. Waterbury Construction Co., 28 Cal. Rep. 204 (1963). Cabinet maker could recover as practice statute did not apply to persons who do not themselves fabricate or consume materials in the same manner as contractors.

Culbertson v. Cizek, 37 Cal. 549 (1964). "Although (the contractor) was found not to hold the required contractor's license, the relevant statute and rule of law do not prevent him from offsetting as a defense against sums due the plaintiffs any amounts that would otherwise be due under his contract."

Fairlane Estates Inc. v. Carrico Construction Co., 39 Cal. Rept. 35 (1964) approved principle that owner could recover for breach of contract against joint contractors, some of whom were unlicensed, when he was not in *pari delicto* with them.

CHAPTER FOUR

Power of licensing boards

Licensing boards created by statute may grant and revoke licenses as empowered by statute. Courts will generally overrule their determination only in clear cases of abuse of discretion.

The duty of administering the statutory standards for persons seeking professional licenses is conferred upon a licensing board or similar authority. Where the statutory standards are broad and do not cover the qualifications of applicants in detail, the board generally has its own rules as to the exact nature and scope of the examination. On the other hand, where the issuance of a license is mandatory on the applicant's compliance with a specific statutory condition, the board cannot go beyond the statute to impose other conditions. Examinations are usually required only of those who were not in practice prior to the effective date of the statute, since it is generally considered inequitable to subject a long-standing practitioner to detail examination in order that he be permitted to continue his profession. Accordingly, the statutes generally include a provision known as a "grandfather clause" that specifies a period of prior practice proved by affidavit, or otherwise, as sufficient to qualify one for a license.

Where no statutory provision exists for judicial review of board action, the writ of mandamus is available to compel the board to act upon an application. No damages may be recovered from a board, however, even when a license is unlawfully refused.

The authority of boards to revoke or suspend licenses also stems from legislative mandate, and the courts subject to careful scrutiny an exercise of such authority. A license creates no permanent or vested interest, and as a grant of privilege, it may be withdrawn in the state's discretion. But the courts reason that this privilege to practice a profession, once conferred, becomes a highly valuable one and should be revoked only under

37

circumstances clearly indicating its absolute necessity for the good of public welfare.

A typical statute allows revocation of a license for the following causes:

1. Gross incompetence, dishonesty or gross negligence in the practice of architecture.
2. Affixing his seal or name to any plan, specification or drawing or other related document which was not prepared by him or under his responsible supervision and control.
3. Using his seal or engaging in any other act constituting the practice of architecture at a time when his certificate of registration is suspended.
4. Conviction of a felony.
5. Wilfully misleading or defrauding any person employing him as an architect.
6. Wilfully violating any provision of this chapter or any lawful rule or regulation adopted by the board pursuant to law (*La. Rev. Stat.* tit. 37, §156.1).

The statutes generally provide for the institution of revocation proceedings upon complaint made to the board or other authority charged with administration. Provision is also made for notice and a hearing at which the defendant licensee is given an opportunity to present evidence in his behalf. Procedure for judicial review on the basis of the record of such hearing may also be outlined. Even in the absence of statutory authorization, for appeal, recourse to the courts is available to a person aggrieved by reason of the suspension or revocation of his license.

A BOARD CANNOT IMPOSE CONDITIONS not found in the statute or exercise its own discretion with respect to issuance of a license. The conditions set forth in the statute may not, however, be waived by the board.

Under those sections which do vest discretion in the board in the issuance of licenses, the courts will not interefere to control the board's discretion unless it is grossly abused or illegally or arbitrarily exercised.

Cal.   *Andrews v. State Bd. of Registration for Civil and Professional Engineers*, 267 P. 2d 352 (1954). When on the face of his application plaintiff may have been able to demonstrate that he was entitled to registration, the board could not refuse to register him without at least giving him the benefit of a hearing.

Ill.   *State Bd. of Architects v. People*, 93 Ill. App. 436 (1901). Licensing Board was upheld in denying architect's license to an applicant whom it found to be a builder and contractor.

Ky.   *Baker v. Commonwealth*, 272 S.W. 2d 803 (1954). Where the Board is required to evaluate an applicant's qualifications to determine whether, without taking and passing the usual examination, he is entitled to registration, it cannot insist that he take the examination on the grounds that it cannot otherwise measure his professional skill.

La. *Charbonnet v. Board of Architectural Examiners*, 205 La. 232, 17 So. 2d 261 (1944). Under a statute authorizing the issuance of an architect's license on presentation of a diploma from an architectural college of good standing, the Board did not have authority to prescribe an additional requirement that the applicant seeking license without examination must complement his course of study with three years' practical experience.

Md. *Stark v. Christie*, 179 Md. 276, 19 A. 2d 716 (1941). Where applicant applied for mandamus for issuance of engineer's license, held that the procedure was an appeal, as provided in section of the statute.

Mich. *Waier v. State Bd. of Registration*, 303 Mich. 360, 6 N.W. 2d 545 (1942). Under Michigan statute requiring the Board, at any time within 5 years following its enactment, to accept as conclusive evidence of qualification, a record of at least 12 years of active practice as an architect prior to the act, Board was held to have acted arbitrarily in refusing applicant an architect's license where such proof had been submitted to it.

Green v. State Bd. of Registration, 307 Mich. 285, 11 N.W. 2d 891 (1943). Mandamus to compel the Board to issue the plaintiff a professional engineer's license was denied by the court where it found that actual practice by the plaintiff for 12 years had not been established.

Marino v. State Bd. of Registration, 307 Mich. 438, 12 N.W. 2d 437 (1943). Where applicant had actively practiced as a professional engineer for more than the required 12 year period, the fact that he was in high school, from which he graduated at the age of 24, for two years during that period, should not deprive him of registration.

Kaufmann v. State Bd. of Registration, 313 Mich. 258, 21 N.W. 2d 122 (1946). A college degree in engineering could not be required of one qualifying under the "grandfather clause," in the absence of its requirement by the terms of the act.

Op. Atty. Gen., No. 25011 (Dec. 16, 1942). It is not permissible to apply toward the 12 year period of practice required, years spent in professional schools.

Op. Atty. Gen., No. 0–730 (May 18, 1943). Isolated occasions of engaging in land surveying should not be considered as "engaging

in the active practice of land surveying," but the fact that surveying work did not occupy a major portion of applicant's time would
not negative active practice. The extent to which his services were
required in his community and whether he at all times held himself out as a surveyor willing to accept available employment as
such, could be material on the question.

Minn.   *Malm v. Shepard,* 229 Minn. 425, 40 N.W. 2d 72 (1950). Evidence sustained finding that petitioner applied to licensing board
for permission to take an examination to obtain architect's certificate and not for a certificate without examination, as authorized
by statute under certain conditions, so that board properly withheld certificate on his inability to pass the examination.

N.J.   *Cardiff v. State Bd. of Architects,* 69 N.J.L. 173, 54 Atl. 294
(1903). Where evidence indicated that applicant was a practicing
architect, by a writ of certiorari, the Board was compelled to grant
him a license.

N.Y.   *Siegel v. Mangan,* 258 App. Div. 448, 16 N.Y.S. 2d 1000, *aff'd,*
283 N.Y. 557, 27 N.E. 2d 280 (1940). Board of Regents could reconsider application for architect's license after it had previously
passed a resolution to grant the license, since reconsideration is an
administrative act and subject to review. The action of the Board
in reconsidering the application is not reviewable until it has become final.

Ohio   *Op. Atty. Gen.,* No. 4313 (1932). Where a person, employed
as a draftsman by a firm of architects, is known in the profession
and to the public only as a draftsman, and has rendered services
outside his employment as a draftsman, he is not engaged in the
practice of architecture so as to entitle him to exemption from
examination.

Okla.   *Garman v. Meyers,* 182 Okla. 141, 80 P. 2d 624 (1938). Where
in action to compel the issuance of an engineer's license, plaintiff
alleged that while he was in high school he was in charge of construction work, it was held that this experience did not require
the application of engineering principles and data so as to entitle
him to an engineer's license without examination.

Pa.   *Cronheim v. State Registration Bd.,* 53 Dauph. 171 (1942). Since
registration act refers to "engineering in any of its branches" the
Board acted illegally and unconstitutionally in recognizing only
mechanical, mining, electrical, and civil engineering, inasmuch as
there are other generally recognized branches, as "architectural
engineering."

S.C. *State v. Wilson*, 130 S.C. 326, 125 S.E. 572 (1924). Board of Architectural Examiners will not be compelled by mandamus to issue license to individual where its action on the application had been deferred pending an extended investigation as to facts which it is the Board's prerogative to determine.

Tenn. *Simm v. Dougherty*, 210 S.W. 2d 486 (1948). Held: The board acted reasonably in denying registration to appellant on the statutory ground of lack of "good character and repute." The court relied on the fact that appellant had stated in his application that he had completed four years of an engineering school, when, in fact, he had completed but one.

THE MOST COMMON GROUNDS SPECIFIED in the statutes for revocation of professional licenses are (1) the practice of fraud or deceit in obtaining a certificate of registration, and (2) gross negligence, incompetency, or misconduct in professional practice.

Ariz. *Lee Moor Contracting Co. v. Hardwicke*, 56 Ariz. 49, 106 P. 2d 332 (1940). Contractor's license was not subject to revocation where "alleged" violation of state law by employment of three workmen not citizens on a federally aided highway project was permitted by federal statute.

Cal. *Coffman v. State Bd. of Architectural Examiners*, 130 Cal. App. 343, 19 P. 2d 1002 (1933). Where dishonest practice is made the ground for revocation of a license, "the dishonest acts should be found with certainty, making the dishonesty apparent to all."

O'Neil v. Department of Professional and Vocational Standards, 1 Cal. App. 2d 395, 46 P. 2d 234 (1935). Under a statute authorizing a registrar to initiate investigations looking to the suspension or revocation of a contractor's license, a proceeding of this nature must be taken at the time the contractor is licensed, not after his license has expired.

Barry v. Contractors' State License Bd., 85 Cal. App. 2d 600, 193 P. 2d 979 (1948). Revocation of contractor's license upheld where contractor violated municipal laws in construction projects.

Karz v. Department of Professional & Vocational Standards, 11 Cal. App. 2d 554, 54 P. 2d 35 (1936). Revocation of contractor's license upheld where contractor abandoned without legal excuse a construction project he had undertaken and failed in a material respect to complete the project for the agreed price, since these were acts and omissions mentioned in the statute as grounds for suspension of a license.

West Coast Home Improvement Co. v. Contractors' State License Bd., 68 Cal. App. 2d 1, 155 P. 2d 863 (1945). By statutory provision, the stay of an order or judgment revoking an occupational license, pending determination of an appeal, is a matter of judicial discretion.

Fla. *Everett v. Gillespie,* 63 So. 2d 903 (1953). Inaccuracies were not of sufficient magnitude to constitute "malfeasance" or "malpractice" on which statutory grounds the Board had previously revoked appellant's certificate of registration.

Ill. *Klafter v. State Examiners,* 259 Ill. 15, 102 N.E. 193 (1913). Case upheld constitutionality of provision authorizing revocation of license by state board of examiners. Statute was held not void for uncertainty in having grounds for revocation.

Kalseberg v. Ricker, 177 Ill. App. 527 (1917). In proceeding to revoke license for dishonest practices, a single dishonest act on the part of an architect held not to constitute dishonest "practice" or "practices" within meaning of the statute. Complaint must allege a fraudulent intent and set forth facts from which it may be inferred.

Pa. *In Re Scott,* 46 Dauph. 196 (1938). Revocation of a professional engineer's certificate was upheld where in his application for registration, the engineer had made untrue statements relating to his education and practical experience.

Texas *State Bd. of Registration v. Hatter,* 139 S.W. 2d 169 (1940). A letter signed by the Secretary of the State Board of Registration stating that applicant might practice as a professional engineer until final action was taken on his application, did not constitute a certificate of registration, and a suit to compel the Board to issue a certificate could not be construed as a suit to vacate an order revoking the certificate.

Wis. *Kuehnel v. Wisconsin Registration Bd.,* 243 Wis. 188, 9 N.W. 2d 630 (1943). Where architect sought to have vacated an order of the Board revoking his license, he could not defend on the ground that the work was done on a one-family dwelling for which no architect's registration was necessary. Plaintiff's services had been engaged in reliance on his representations that he was an architect.

22 Op. Atty. Gen., 479 (1933). The Board has no power to revoke a certificate for an offense which does not pertain to the practice of architecture or civil engineering, as for the making of an unauthorized bank loan.

CHAPTER FIVE

Doing business in a foreign state

A license to practice architecture or engineering or engage in the business of contracting, authorizes the holder thereof to practice only within the territory of the state issuing such license. If a licensed person, firm or corporation wishes to practice in another state, it must secure a license from that state as well.

Corporations wishing to do business in states other than that of incorporation must "qualify" in such other states. The procedures, terms and conditions upon which a foreign corporation will be permitted to qualify to do business in a state other than that of its incorporation are prescribed by the statute of that state.

A foreign corporation, within the meaning of these laws, is a corporation which has obtained its charter or articles of incorporation in a state other than the one into which it comes to do business. For example, a corporation incorporated in New York wishing to do business elsewhere would be called a domestic corporation in New York and a foreign corporation in every other state.

A corporation is purely a creature of state law and has no existence beyond the boundaries of the state of its incorporation. Therefore, when it seeks to go into some other state to do part or all of its business, it must arrange to secure the consent of that state. The making of such arrangements is generally termed qualifying to do business.

The state may, within constitutional limitations, subject the corporation to such terms and conditions as in its discretion it sees fit to impose. The requirements of the various states, though varying somewhat in content and application, are based on a common policy of protecting citizens of the state against the imposition of insolvent and unreliable corporations and of placing the corporations within reach of the legal process of state courts in favor of its residents who may have cause to sue them.

The states generally require a foreign corporation, as a prerequisite to doing business within them, to do one or more of the following: To appoint and designate a resident agent upon whom process may be served in suits against it (some statutes may require that the agent be a designated public officer); to maintain and designate one or more places of business within the state; to take out a license, permit, or certificate from the Secretary of State or other named official giving it authority or permission to do business; to file designated reports, such as a statement of its financial condition, assets, capital, and other information; to pay all necessary taxes and license fees.

Not all business contacts in a state will subject a foreign corporation to the statutes requiring the obtaining of authority to engage in business. The corporation will be required to qualify if it is "doing business" in the state. The statutes do not specify particular transactions that will constitute doing business, and the determination necessarily devolves upon the courts. In most cases the decision must be made upon the facts of the particular case. The general rule applied by the courts is that a foreign corporation must transact a substantial part of its business in a state, continuous in character, as distinguished from merely casual or occasional transactions, in order to be "doing," transacting, or engaging in business.

A corporation which engages in performing but a single construction contract is generally held to be doing business in the state. The nature of construction work is such that it extends over an appreciable length of time and is accordingly not construed as a single transaction although it may involve performance of but one contract or project.

A closely related problem concerns the question whether an agreement by a foreign corporation to sell and install an article in the state constitutes doing business in the state. It is generally held that if the agreement to install or assemble an article or structure is incidental to the sale made outside the state, it retains the character of an interstate transaction immune from state control. On the other hand, if the sale of the article shipped into the state is merely incidental to or in aid of a contract for labor or construction work in the state, the transaction falls within the "doing business" category, making the corporation amenable to state regulation.

A FOREIGN CORPORATION WHICH UNDERTAKES to perform a single construction contract in a state is generally deemed to be doing business in the state requiring it to comply with the statutory requirements therefor.

   Ala.   *Alabama W. R. Co. v. Talley-Bates Constr. Co.*, 162 Ala. 396, 50 So. 341 (1909). A foreign corporation which contracted outside the state to construct a railroad within the state was held to be doing business within the state, notwithstanding that it employed independent contractors to do the actual work and did no part of the actual work itself.

Ariz. *National Union Indemnity Co. v. Bruce Bros., Inc.*, 44 Ariz. 454, 38 P. 2d 648 (1934). A foreign corporation which secured a contract for the construction of a highway within the state, moved a large portion of its equipment into the state, and maintained an office in the state from which its operations were conducted, was held to be doing business in the state.

Ark. *E. E. Morgan Co., Inc. v. State*, 202 Ark. 404, 150 S.W. 2d 736 (1941). A foreign corporation engaged in the construction of a levee in Arkansas under a federal contract negotiated outside the state was held to be doing business within the state. See *Kansas City Structural Steel Co. v. Arkansas*, 269 U.S. 148 (1925), *infra*.

Fla. *Hague v. D. N. Morrison Constr. Co., Inc. of Virginia*, 156 So. 377 (1934). Foreign corporations, furnishing materials and performing labor as general contractors in the construction of a hotel building were held to be doing business in the state.

Ill. See *National Carbon Paint Co. v. Fred Bredel Co.*, 193 Fed. 897 (1911), *infra*.

Ind. *United States Constr. Co. v. Hamilton Nat. Bank of Fort Wayne*, 73 Ind. App. 149, 126 N.E. 866 (1920). A contract by a construction company under which it was to equip a manufacturing plant with a sprinkler system, requiring the employment of labor for several weeks, and involving the building of a tower, a tank, and other carpentry work, was held to be the transaction of local business within the state.

La. *Harnischfeger Sales Corporation v. Sternberg Co., Inc.*, 179 La. 317, 154 So. 10 (1934). A foreign corporation making only one contract to build a levee in the state, necessitating numerous subsidiary contracts, was held to be doing business within the state.

Mich. See *In re Springfield Realty Co.*, 257 Fed. 785 (1919), *infra*.

Miss. *Newell Contracting Co. v. State Highway Comm'n.*, 195 Miss. 395, 15 So. 2d 700, 703 (1943). Foreign construction company doing contract work on a highway project was held to be doing business within the state. The court stated that the test applied to a foreign corporation doing business within the meaning of the statutes is "whether or not it is doing such acts as are within the function of its corporate powers, and where the business so performed is substantial in scope, such corporation is held to be doing business."

Mo.   *Hanson & Willadsen Co. v. Creason,* 222 Mo. App. 880, 5 S.W.
2d 1105 (1928). A foreign corporation in the business of constructing drainage ditches, sewers, and systems for carrying water and engaged in performing a contract for the construction of a sewer in
the state, was held to be doing business therein.

Mont.   *Greene Plumbing and Heating Co. v. Morris,* 305 P. 2d 252
(1964). In a suit by a subcontractor against an owner to foreclose
a mechanics lien, the court denied recovery, relying on the non-
qualification of both the subcontractor and the principal contractor. At one point in the opinion, the court asserted that the
latter's non-qualification alone would operate to defeat a subcontractor's claim.

N.Y.   *Berkshire Engineering Corp. v. Sealt-Paine,* 217 N.Y.S. 2d 919.
Where plaintiffs activities in New York were substantial, and ex-
tended over a two-year period, plaintiff was "doing business" in
New York and could not recover for services rendered.

Ohio   *National Sign Corp. v. Maccar Cleveland Sales Corp.,* 33 Ohio
App. 89, 168 N.E. 758 (1929). Foreign corporation erecting and
maintaining signs under contract along the highways was held to
be doing business within the state.

Pa.   See *Pittsburgh Constr. Co. v. West Side Belt R. Co.,* 151 Fed. 125
(1907), *infra.*
Hoffman Constr. Co. v. Erwin, 331 Pa. 384, 200 Atl. 579 (1938).
A foreign corporation which entered into a contract involving a
continuing project within the state for at least 4 months and in
the performance of which the corporation's agents and employees
were in the state to supervise and to do work, employ labor, and
purchase materials, was held "to be doing business" in the state.
The court stated that the acts done in the state were not a mere
incident of corporate existence but were the performance of the
function for which the corporation was organized.
Glenn Mitchell Construction Co. v. Russell, Pa. Com. Pl. Ct., 14
Bucks Co. L. Rep. 203 (1952).

Tenn.   *Davis & Rankin Bldg. & Mfg. Co. v. Caigle,* 53 S.W. 240 (1899).
A foreign corporation which entered into a contract for the erection of a single plant was not doing business in the state in which
the plant was to be located. The court held this to be a transaction of interstate commerce.
See *Consolidated Indemnity & Ins. Co. v. Salmon & Cowin, Inc.,*
64 F. 2d 756, 757 (1933), *infra.*

Tex.   *State Bank of Chicago v. Holland,* 103 Tex. 236, 126 S.W. 564
(1910). A foreign corporation which entered into a contract to

construct and equip a co-operative canning factory in the state was held to be doing business therein.

Anthony Miller, Inc., v. Taylor-Fichter Steel Constr. Co., Inc., 139 S.W. 2d 657 (1940). Where a foreign corporation made a contract in New York to do certain work on a bridge in Texas, the effort of such corporation to execute the contract in Texas constituted doing business therein.

St. Louis Expanded Metal Fire-Proofing Co. v. Beilharg, 88 S.W. 512 (1905). A foreign corporation which through a resident agent makes a contract in the state to furnish labor and material for construction of a portion of a large building and sends large quantities of materials, a number of laborers, employees, and a superintendent into the state for the performance of its contract over a period of 12 months, engages in business within the state.

Va.   *F. S. Bowen Elec. Co. v. Foley*, 194 Va. 92, 72 S.E. 2d 388 (1952).

Wis.   See *In re Bell Lumber Co.*, 149 F. 2d 980 (1945), *infra*.

Wyo.   *Interstate Constr. Co. v. Lakeview Canal Co.*, 31 Wyo. 191, 224 Pac. 850 (1924). A foreign corporation which undertook to perform in the state a contract to enlarge and extend a canal and furnish all the labor and material therefor, was held to be transacting business within the state.

U.S.   *Kansas City Structural Steel Co. v. Arkansas*, 269 U.S. 148 (1925). A foreign corporation contracting to construct a bridge within the state, was held to be doing intrastate business when it made the contract within the state, shipped structural materials to itself within the state, and delivered them to the subcontractor which used them in its part of the work.

In re Bell Lumber Co., 149 F. 2d 980 (1945). Where foreign corporation, after contracting to furnish a Wisconsin lumber company plans, designs, and services for houses to be prefabricated by the lumber company, moved its principal office into the state, hired architects, draftsmen, and clerical help in the state, and took an essential part in the manufacture of prefabricated houses by the lumber company, it was transacting business in the state.

Consolidated Indemnity & Ins. Co. v. Salmon & Cowin, Inc., 64 F. 2d 756, 757 (1933). A foreign corporate subcontractor who obtained a subcontract to do portions of road work contract was held not to be doing business in the state. The court stated, "While considerable time was required to perform the subcontract, it was an isolated transaction, and appellee had not entered the state for the purpose of continuously doing business."

In re Springfield Realty Co., 257 Fed. 785 (1919). A contract by a foreign corporation for the installation of an automatic fire sprinkler system called for the doing of business within the state; and the fact that some material and labor used were brought into the state was immaterial.

National Carbon Paint Co. v. Fred Bredel Co., 193 Fed. 897 (1911). The court was inclined to take the view that a contract by a foreign corporation to furnish materials and perform labor in the construction of a plant did not constitute doing business within the state. It took the position that statutes like the one under consideration applied to the carrying on of a permanent business in the state and not to the performance of a single contract. However, it did not directly pass upon the question as it was not raised by the pleadings.

Pittsburgh Constr. Co. v. West Side Belt R. Co., 151 Fed. 125 (1907). A foreign corporation which contracted within the state to construct a railroad therein was held to be doing business within the state.

A FOREIGN CORPORATION WHICH CONTRACTS to sell and install or assemble articles or materials shipped into the state will be deemed to be doing business in the state if the sale is incidental to or made in aid of a construction project in such state.

Ala.   *Geo. W. Muller Mfg. Co. v. First Nat. Bank*, 176 Ala. 229, 57 So. 762 (1912). A contract to furnish materials and construct certain fixtures in a bank building, involving construction of brick walls, putting on finished plaster, and furnishing and construction of different articles making up the furniture and fixtures of the bank, constituted doing business and was more than an ordinary sale.
Times Bldg. Co. v. Cline, 233 Ala. 600, 173 So. 42 (1937). A foreign corporation which by one inseparable contract sold and installed marble in an Alabama building was doing business in the state. The court rejected the corporation's argument that the setting of the marble was merely an installation incident to and in furtherance of interstate commerce, and held the contract to be one for the erection of a part of a building.

Mich. See *A. H. Andrews Co. v. Colonial Theatre Co.*, 283 Fed. 471 (1922), *infra*.

Mo.   *National Refrigerator Co. v. Southwest Missouri Light Co.*, 288 Mo. 290, 231 S.W. 930 (1921). Where a foreign corporation entered into and executed a contract to furnish and install ice-making plant in Missouri, it was held to be doing business therein. The court, in distinguishing this from a sale in interstate commerce, stated: "... this contract bound the appellant to sell the ice-making machine to respondent, and in addition thereto, to furnish material and labor which was necessary to erect the plant upon which the machine was to be erected, which required the furnishing of a considerable amount of material and much labor. The doing of the two latter things brings the case at bar within our statutes which requires a foreign corporation to take out a license in this state before it can do business herein (p. 938).

Pa.   *Alcorn Combustion Co. v. M. W. Kellog Co.*, 295 Pa. 232, 145 Atl. 125 (1929). Contracts by a foreign corporation erecting chimneys and plants within the state containing machinery made outside the state, requiring the corporation to furnish all necessary materials and perform all necessary work, were held to be construction contracts rather than agreements of sale.

Tex.   *S. R. Smythe Co. v. Ft. Worth Glass and Sand Co.*, 105 Tex. 8, 142 S.W. 1157 (1912). A foreign corporation which entered into a builder's contract to furnish all the material and labor to erect a gas producer in a glass factory, contemplated from 6 to 8 weeks for the performance, was held to be transacting business within the state.

Va.   *Western Gas Constr. Co. v. Commonwealth of Virginia*, 147 Va. 235, 136 S.E. 646 (1927), *aff'd*, 276 U.S. 597 (1928). A foreign corporation undertaking to erect for a municipality a water-gas generating set and connecting it with other units of the city gas plant, which required the furnishing of labor and materials over a period of several months, was doing business within the state.

U.S.   *A. H. Andrews Co. v. Colonial Theatre Co.*, 293 Fed. 471 (1922). Where a foreign corporation contracted to manufacture in Illinois, ship, and install seats in a theatre in Michigan, the part of the contract for installation concerned the doing of purely local business in the state after completion of the interstate part of the transaction.

CHAPTER SIX

Violation of laws in a foreign state

The failure of a foreign corporation to comply with the statutory conditions precedent to doing business in a state may render its contracts entered into within the state void or unenforceable and subject it to the imposition of criminal penalties. Some states will not permit enforcement of such contracts even when the corporation subsequently qualifies to do business. Another category of states will permit enforcement upon subsequent compliance by the corporation with or without payment of a penalty.

A majority of the statutes which require foreign corporations doing business within them to comply with certain conditions include provisions imposing criminal penalties for violations of these conditions. These provisions have been enforced upon occasion and constitute an obvious risk to the corporation which disregards them. The greater financial hazard lies in the fact that the contracts of such a foreign corporation may prove unenforceable in the courts of the state should a dispute concerning them subsequently arise.

No general rule may be formulated on this subject as the decisions of the various states are in conflict, in large part due to differences in the language of the various provisions. In most of the states a corporation which is doing business in the state without complying with the local requirements may not maintain an action in the state courts on contracts it has entered into within the state. In the absence of express statements in the statutes to the effect that a contract entered into by a non-complying corporation is void, there is no one simple rule which may be adopted in all cases to distinguish the void contract from the voidable or merely unenforceable contract.

The states may be placed roughly into four categories on this question.

1. Those states where the contracts are not enforceable even if the foreign corporation subsequently qualifies.
2. Those states where the contracts are enforceable only if the foreign corporation does subsequently qualify.
3. Those states where the contracts are enforceable after qualification but the payment of a penalty is required before the corporation is permitted to qualify.
4. Those states in which the right to sue is not covered by statute, where the courts usually hold that a foreign corporation is not prohibited from enforcing its contracts.

Where a contract is entered into by a foreign corporation in a state in which it is not licensed to do business, several jurisdictions have deemed such contract void and unenforceable. States falling into this category are Alabama, Arkansas, Idaho and Vermont. However, many states will deny enforcement of a contract made by a foreign corporation not licensed to do business in the state only until that corporation qualifies. Falling into this classification are such jurisdictions as Alaska, Colorado, Connecticut, District of Columbia, Hawaii, Illinois, Iowa, Louisiana, Massachusetts, Minnesota, Missouri, Nebraska, Nevada, New Hampshire, New Mexico, New York, North Carolina, North Dakota, Oklahoma, Oregon, Rhode Island, South Carolina, Tennessee, Utah, Virginia, Washington, West Virginia and Wyoming. In a few states, such as Arizona, Mississippi and South Dakota, contracts made by foreign corporations not licensed in the state in which a suit is instituted are deemed void and unenforceable even if the contract was made outside the state.

California, Florida, Maryland, Ohio, Pennsylvania and Wisconsin permit the enforcement of a contract entered into by a foreign corporation not licensed in their respective states only after said corporation has qualified and paid a penalty. In Florida a corporation can qualify during the progress of a suit, and in Illinois the courts make a distinction between the right to file a suit and the right to maintain a suit, permitting the former without qualification and denying the latter until qualification is secured. In Delaware the restrictions which are imposed upon Delaware corporations in other states are reciprocally applied in respect to foreign corporations instituting suit in Delaware.

The state laws denying the use of the courts to non-complying corporations cannot be evaded by resort to the federal courts. The Supreme Court of the United States in *Woods v. Interstate Realty Co.* 337 U.S. 535 (1949) held that the federal courts will follow the state rule in their decisions.

PART TWO

RELATIONS AMONG ARCHITECTS AND ENGINEERS

CHAPTER SEVEN

Partnership

A partnership is an association of two or more persons to carry on as co-owners a business for profit. If the association is formed to carry on a single specific enterprise or transaction, rather than a general and continuing business, it will be termed a joint venture. Where the agreement of the parties is ambiguous as to whether or not a partnership exists, the receipt by a person of a share of the profits establishes a presumption that he is a partner in the business.

Since many states prohibit the formation of corporations to engage in the practice of architecture or engineering, the most frequently employed form of business association for this purpose is the partnership. As defined in the *Uniform Partnership Act* §6 (1), a partnership is an association of two or more persons to carry on as co-owners, a business for profit. It is, in other words, a voluntary contract between two or more persons to place their money, property, labor, and skill in business, and to divide the profits and share the losses in certain proportions.

Two or more persons or firms may associate together to carry on a single specific enterprise, such as the performance of a contract with a third party to render architectural or engineering services for a single construction project. This type of association, closely akin to the partnership, is the joint venture. The only distinction between the two is that a joint venture is formed to carry on a single specified enterprise or transaction, whereas a partnership is formed for the transaction of a general and continuing business of a particular kind. While they are not identical, the rules and principles applicable to partnership govern the rights and duties of parties to a joint venture. Consequently, no distinction will be made in the treatment of the partnership and the joint venture in the following pages.

The continuance of the partnership relation rests upon the voluntary consent of the partners. The rights, duties, privileges, and responsibilities which the parties contemplate as to their relations are generally set forth in the partnership agreement. A partnership may be informally created and proved by the acts and declarations of the parties, but in the interests of certainty and for the purpose of modifying certain incidents implied by law, it is highly desirable to embody the terms of association in a written instrument known as articles of partnership. The rights and duties of the parties among themselves are regulated by the express contract, except as to those matters not provided for where the general principles of partnership law govern.

Unlike a corporation, a partnership is not recognized for all purposes as a legal entity, subject to rights and obligations as a distinct unit. It has often been said to have no existence distinct from the persons who compose it. The growing tendency has been for the courts to treat a partnership as a legal entity for a number of purposes, such as the maintenance of legal action against it, the keeping of partnership accounts, conveyance of property, and marshaling of assets.

As a general rule, any person who is capable of entering into a contract may become a partner. Restrictions are placed upon the rights or obligations of certain persons to contract to become partners. An infant who enters into a partnership may repudiate the contract of partnership and also personal liability to partnership creditors. But his capital contribution to the partnership may not be restored to him until the claims of creditors of the partnership are satisfied. The contract of an insane person to be a partner, like that of an infant, is voidable. Although at common law a married woman was incapable of entering into a contract, most states have enacted legislation permitting her to exercise such a right. Corporations may become partners when specific authority is conferred by corporation laws or corporate articles. It has been held that a corporation may be a partner within the *Uniform Partnership Act.*

Since the partnership relation is created by contract, a person cannot be made a member of a partnership without his consent or by operation of law. Nor can he become a member without the consent of all the other associates. In certain instances, persons who are not partners may be liable to a third person as partners on the ground that by their acts and conduct they represented themselves as partners and created the appearance of a partnership relation upon which the third person relied.

It is often important for the purpose of ascertaining the rights and duties of the parties concerned to distinguish the relation of partnership or joint venture from employment. In every case the intention of the parties governs. If ambiguously expressed, it may raise future disputes which can be resolved only by litigation. The courts have settled upon no single test by which it is possible to distinguish between partnership and employment. Under the general rule and the provisions of the *Uniform Partnership Act* a profit sharing agreement creates a presumption that a partnership is in existence, but this may be rebutted and outweighed by other circumstances, such as a showing that the profits were received as wages. Generally, if it is shown that the profits were received under agreement for the rendition of services, the presumption no longer operates.

There are many situations where an employer and employee are associated in business and in lieu of wages the employee shares in the profits of such business. Such associations are not partnerships. The factors of co-ownership and power of control are lacking. The question as to whether the parties intended a partnership often arises where the contribution to the business by one of the parties is that of skill only. The rendition of personal services is characteristic of the association of architects and in the absence of specific agreement, the question of partnership will be squarely posed.

The prevailing view is that sharing profits or compensation for services rendered does not establish a partnership, but sharing "profits as profits" or "profits as principal" or sharing a "property interest in the profits" is conclusive of a partnership. The above language of itself does not clarify the problem but the courts, in using it, indicate that in addition to profit sharing, other factors evidencing an intent to form a partnership are necessary. These may include one or more of the following: 1. participation in net profits as distinguished from gross profits—if small risk is imposed on the person rendering the services, the courts tend to view it as an employment relation; 2. agreement to share both profits and losses —this implies an agreement to pay losses beyond the capital contribution made; 3. agreement to share expenses; 4. joint property rights in real and personal property used to produce the profits; 5. equal rights in management and control; 6. right of the parties to bind one another within the scope of the business.

In order to avoid future disputes as to the existence of a partnership and to preclude judicial inquiry into intention, the parties who become associated as partners to engage in the profession of engineering or architecture should express in writing their intention to form a partnership.

U.P.A. §7.

"IN DETERMINING WHETHER A PARTNERSHIP exists, these rules shall apply:
  1. "Except as provided by section 16 [creating appearance of partnership by acts and conduct of the parties] persons who are not partners as to each other are not partners as to third persons.

2. "Joint tenancy, tenancy in common, tenancy by the entireties, joint property, common property, or part ownership does not of itself establish a partnership, whether such co-owners do or do not share any profits made by the use of the property.

3. "The sharing of gross returns does not of itself establish a partnership, whether or not the persons sharing them have a joint or common right or interest in any property from which the returns are derived.

4. "The receipt by a person of a share of the profits of a business is prima facie evidence that he is a partner in the business, but no such inference shall be drawn if such profits were received in payment:
   a. As a debt by installments or otherwise,
   b. As wages of an employee or rent to a landlord,
   c. As an annuity to a widow or representative of a deceased partner,
   d. As interest on a loan, though the amount of payment vary with the profits of the business,
   e. As the consideration for the sale of a good-will of a business or other property by installments or otherwise."

CASES HOLDING PARTNERSHIPS NOT ESTABLISHED.

Wis.   *Kuenzi v. Radloff,* 253 Wis. 575, 34 N.W. 2d 798 (1948). Where professional engineer agreed, for a stipulated fee, to draw plans for a proposed bowling alley and was aided by others who were paid for their services whether the engineer collected on the contract or not, the relationship between the engineer and his associates was not a partnership, and he could properly maintain an action on the contract without joining his associates as parties plaintiff. The court said that to constitute a partnership, profits which a partner is to share must be real profits, not wages.

Utah   See *Johanson Brothers Builders v. Board of Review, Industrial Commission,* 222 P. 2d 563 (1950) for list of factors which compelled the conclusion of no partnership in that case.

U.S.   *City of Wheeling v. Chester,* 134 F. 2d 759 (1943). So-called "junior members" of engineering firm who received a share of the profits as wages but were expressly excluded from co-ownership, were not "partners," but merely "employees."

CHAPTER EIGHT

Partnership contracts

The rights, privileges, duties, and responsibilities of partners are determined by the intention of the parties as expressed in the articles of partnership. Situations which the partnership agreement fails to cover are governed by the law of partnership. It is therefore important for the parties to express their intention in the articles of partnership on the following matters: 1. duration of the partnership; 2. property rights of the parties; 3. financial arrangements among the partners; 4. rights of the partners in control and management; 5. authority of the partners to bind the firm; 6. method of liquidation of partnership on dissolution by death of a partner or otherwise.

Once parties have determined to enter into a partnership to practice architecture or engineering, it becomes important for them to draw up a complete written agreement delineating their rights, privileges, duties, and responsibilities in the prosecution of the enterprise. It is well established that the relations of the members of a partnership among themselves are determined by the intention of the parties.

So far as this intention is clearly expressed, the courts find little difficulty in giving it effect when called upon to do so. However, concerning those aspects of the relationship which have been treated equivocally or not covered at all, the courts must resort to general principles of partnership law to resolve future differences. This can result in the imposition of legal responsibility not contemplated by one or more of the partners, and the result may differ materially from the relation which the parties had in mind when they entered into the agreement. Further, the law concerning the partnership relation is in many instances uncertain, due to conflict between the decisions of various states and to inconsistent legal theories. In such case, in the absence of partnership agreement, even the decision of the courts cannot be anticipated with any degree of certainty.

To obviate these hazards of judicial interpretation, the parties should cover as completely as possible every phase of their relationship. The following aspects of their association should be carefully regulated by the articles of the partnership.

DURATION OF THE PARTNERSHIP.

The partnership contract should set forth the length of time the partnership is to endure. If the agreement sets a definite date for termination, the relation ends when that date arrives. If the association is formed to engage in an enterprise of limited duration or purposes, the partnership or joint venture will terminate when that purpose has been accomplished. In the absence of a provision as to duration, it will be inferred that the partnership is terminable at will.

A partnership may be terminated by any partner who so elects although the term of the partnership has not expired or the particular undertaking has not been accomplished. If it is a partnership at will, the partner who chooses to dissolve it does not breach the contract, however injurious his action may be to the other members who neglected to protect themselves by specifying a definite term for its duration. But if the partnership is terminated by one of the partners in violation of the contract, he is responsible for damages suffered by the remaining partners through his breach.

U.P.A. §31.

Dissolution is caused:
1. "Without violation of the agreement between the partners,
    a. by the termination of the definite term or particular undertaking specified in the agreement,
    b. by the express will of any partner when no definite term or particular undertaking is specified,
    c. by the express will of all the partners. . . .
2. "In contravention of the agreement between the partners, where the circumstances do not permit a dissolution under any other provision of this section, by the express will of any partner at any time."

U.P.A. §38.

2. a. II. When dissolution is caused in contravention of the partnership agreement, each partner who has not caused dissolution wrongfully shall have the right, as against each partner who has caused the dissolution wrongfully, to damages for breach of the agreement.

PROPERTY RIGHTS OF THE PARTNERS.

The intention of the parties determines what property belongs to the firm and what property belongs to the individual partners. In the absence of express agreement, there is no restriction on the type or source of property which may become that of the firm. It may initially be owned by the individuals who later become partners, or it may be acquired by the members subsequent to the formation of the partnership, or it may be acquired by the partnership by purchase or otherwise in the course of partnership transactions.

Partnership property is applied for partnership purposes during the continuance of the business and in the course of liquidation. A partner's separate property, although used by the partnership in the course of its business, may nevertheless be claimed by him as his individual property. It often becomes necessary to distinguish firm property from that owned by individuals in determining the rights of the partners to specific items of property while the business continues and after its dissolution. The rights of creditors are also affected by the determination made.

At common law it is held that a partnership as such cannot hold title to real property although such ownership is completely recognized in equity. Under the *Uniform Partnership Act* much of the confusion resulting from this rule has been obviated by the provision that any real estate may be acquired in the partnership name and that property so acquired can be conveyed only in the partnership name. The prevailing view with regard to firm ownership of real property is that the intention of the parties at the time the property was acquired and the attitude of the parties toward the property following purchase, are determinative in any questions arising over ownership.

Where the conduct of the parties at the time of acquisition does not clearly evidence their intent, other factors may be considered to determine the question, as the partnership books, use of partnership funds in the purchase of the property, purchase of the property for partnership purposes, use to which the property is put following its purchase, and source of funds used to make improvements on the property.

In many cases the presumption still exists that real property is not partnership property unless a different intention is clearly shown. In order to avoid doubt on this subject, if the parties intend the partnership to own real property, they should specifically so provide. The partnership contract may also place restrictions upon the type of property which the partnership may subsequently acquire. There is no restriction on the right of a partnership to own personal property and almost any type may be included in the partnership assets.

Each partner is said to be a co-owner with the other partners of the specific partnership property. Under the *Uniform Partnership Act* he has no power to dispose of his share in specific partnership property. In some states where the act has not been adopted, he may do so, but the other partners are protected by their right to have it applied in payment of debts and in adjustment of their accounts. In most states creditors of the individual partner may not subject his right in specific partnership property to attachment or execution unless they are also creditors of the partnership.

A partner's interest in the partnership includes his share of the profits and capital, and he may transfer this interest to a third person. In states which have not enacted the *Uniform Partnership Act*, mere assignment of such interest dissolves the partnership. Such transfer does not make the assignee a partner in the firm without the consent of the other partners, but it does entitle him to receive the transferor's share in the profits during the continuance of the partnership business and his share in the capital on dissolution. Such assignment may be made to a co-partner and if fairly made and in good faith will be upheld by the courts. The partnership agreement may itself provide for the exercise by one of the partners of an option to purchase another partner's interest and may further provide the method by which such partner's interest in the firm is to be evaluated.

U.P.A. §8.

1. "All property originally brought into the partnership stock or sub-sequently acquired by purchase or otherwise, on account of the partnership, is partnership property.
2. "Unless the contrary intention appears, property acquired with part-nership funds is partnership property.
3. "Any estate in real property may be acquired in the partnership name. Title so acquired can be conveyed only in the partnership name.
4. "A conveyance to a partnership in the partnership name, though without words of inheritance, passes the entire estate of the grantor unless a contrary intent appears."

U.P.A. §25.

1. "A partner is co-owner with his partners of specific partnership property holding as a tenant in partnership.
2. a. A partner has an equal right with his partners to possess specific partnership property for partnership purposes.

b. A partner's right in specific partnership property is not assignable except in connection with the assignment of rights of all the partners in the same property.

c. A partner's right in specific partnership property is not subject to attachment or executions, except on a claim against the partnership. . . ."

U.P.A. §27.

1. "A conveyance by a partner of his interest in the partnership does not of itself dissolve the partnership, nor, as against the other partners in the absence of agreement, entitle the assignee, during the continuance of the partnership, to interfere in the management or administration of the partnership business or affairs, or to require any information or account of partnership transactions, or to inspect the partnership books; but it merely entitles the assignee to receive in accordance with his contract the profits to which the assigning partner would otherwise be entitled.

2. "In case of a dissolution of the partnership, the assignee is entitled to receive his assignor's interest and may require an account from the date only the last account agreed to by all the partners."

FINANCIAL ARRANGEMENTS.

An important provision in the articles of partnership relates to the nature and extent of the partners' share in the income of the firm. This will frequently be expressed in terms of the proportion that profits and losses are to be shared by the partners. In the absence of express agreements, the courts will assume that profits and losses are to be shared equally among the partners.

The claim of each partner to a share in the profits rests on his contribution of capital, property, or skill to the business. In many instances these contributions are not of equal value and the partners therefore do not intend that the profits be distributed equally. If they do not specifically state their intention, the courts will not interfere to adjust their equities.

They may agree to pay salaries to some or all of the members above and beyond their share in the profits. In such event the parties should consider the effect on salary payments of such contingencies as a lack of profits in a given year, illness or absences of a partner from the firm business. The courts uniformly hold that unless a different intention is expressed, a partner is not entitled to additional compensation for services he has rendered even though they may be greater in extent and value than those contributed by other members. If the parties themselves do not provide additional compensation to a managing partner or to one who devotes his time and energies exclusively to the partnership business, the courts decline to intervene. They point out that it is impossible to determine or evaluate the relative knowledge, skill, and effort which each partner has contributed to the conduct of the business. The law will imply a contract for payment for services only in special circumstances where they are contributed by a partner in a different capacity and outside the scope of the partnership business.

Inasmuch as the matter is left entirely to the voluntary agreement of the parties, it is essential that they recognize inequalities in contribution either in the arrangement for sharing profits and losses or by specific provision for additional compensation such as salary payments. This problem is particularly vital in a professional association where the partners render personal services which by their nature cannot be readily gauged, and will not be reviewed by the courts.

U.P.A. §18.

   a. "Each partner shall share equally in the profits and surplus remaining after all liabilities, including those to partners, are satisfied, and each must contribute towards the losses, whether of capital or otherwise, sustained by the partnership according to his share of the profits.

   f. "No partner is entitled to remuneration for acting in the partnership business, except that a surviving partner is entitled to reasonable compensation for his services in winding up the partnership affairs."

   Ky.   *Weinedel v. Ward*, 211 Ky. 687, 277 S.W. 1010 (1925). In plaintiff architect's action for a portion of the fees secured by defendant architect for architectural work on a lodge building, evidence supported the finding that the contract was obtained through the parties' joint efforts for their joint use and benefit although in the name of the defendant.

RIGHTS IN CONTROL AND MANAGEMENT.

The articles of partnership should declare the rights of each partner in the management and conduct of the business and duties of each partner including services he is to render. In the absence of express agreement on the subject, the law confers on each partner equal rights in the management of the partnership business. Whenever a difference of opinion arises as to ordinary partnership matters, a majority vote will control. A dissenting member is therefore bound by the decisions of the majority on any policy or act which is not violative of the agreement between the partners.

The application of the above rules to a given partnership may prove ill suited to its needs and such problems of internal management are more appropriately left to the agreement of the parties concerned. The partners may wish to place restrictions on equality in control and management; if they so elect, they may confer unlimited power of control over the business of the firm upon one or more of the partners.

The law implies that each partner will devote a reasonable time to the partnership business in the interests of and for the mutual benefit of all. It does not prohibit a partner from engaging in a separate enterprise in his own behalf during the time he is a member of a partnership provided it is not a connected or competing business. Where participation in a separate enterprise is contemplated by a partner at the time the partnership is formed, the parties should consider this in their contract. A limitation upon the right of equal control and management of the enterprise, and an agreement permitting participation in another business may be desirable. If careful and full consideration is given to this subject, future misunderstandings and disputes with regard to the expected contribution of each member to the business will be averted. Where such intangible values as personal services are concerned, and where the courts are ill equipped and unwilling to interfere, the partnership contract should explicity state the intention of the partners and leave nothing to inference.

The parties may also wish to provide for the expulsion of a member on stated terms and conditions, such as misconduct, breach of the partnership agreement, acts and conduct prejudicial to the successful conduct of the business, inability or refusal to perform duties, among others. In the absence of an express agreement to that effect, the members have no power to expel or eliminate another member of the firm at will, even by action of the majority. Further, the members cannot forfeit the share or interest of a member or compel him to withdraw from the firm by offering him what is due him.

U.P.A. §18.

e. "All partners have equal rights in the management and conduct of the partnership business.

h. "Any differences arising as to ordinary matters connected with the partnership business may be decided by a majority of the partners; but no act in contravention of any agreement between the partners may be done rightfully without the consent of all the partners."

U.P.A. §31.

1. d. "Dissolution is caused without violation of the partnership agreement by the expulsion of any partner from the business bona
fide in accordance with such a power conferred in the partnership agreement."

AUTHORITY OF PARTNERS TO BIND THE FIRM.

The relationship of partners to third persons should be considered at
the time the partnership agreement is drawn and the powers and limitations of partners to bind the firm expressly declared.

The partnership creates a relation of agency among the members of the
firm. Each partner is not only a principal but also a general agent of
the firm and its members for all purposes within the scope and objects of
the partnership business. The co-partners may therefore be legally liable
for the act of every partner done within the scope of the firm's business,
although it may not actually have been authorized.

To determine what is within the scope of the partnership business, the
courts refer to the past course of dealing of the firm or to the general
custom and usage of parties and firms conducting similar enterprises in
the locality. The implied power of a partner includes whatever is reasonably necessary to carry on the firm's business in the ordinary and usual
manner. Persons dealing with a firm may rely on partnership responsibility for the acts of any partner which are apparently conducted in the
business of the partnership. It is therefore desirable to set forth in the
partnership contract the exact scope of the partnership business.

By provision in the articles of partnership, the parties may restrict the
authority of each as agent for the firm, and third persons dealing with
the firm who have notice of the restrictions are bound by them. It should
be noted, however, that if the parties restrict their powers by secret
limitations, third persons dealing with them who rely on the apparent
authority of the partners are not affected by the limitations.

In the absence of specific provisions in the partnership agreement, a
number of limitations are placed upon the authority of partners to bind
the partnership. In this respect it is important to distinguish between a
trading and a non-trading partnership since members of the former have
greater implied powers. The association of architects is designated as a
non-trading partnership, while a partnership engaged in buying and
selling as a business is known as a trading partnership. A member of a
non-trading partnership has no implied authority to borrow money or
give a promissory note on the credit of the firm. In the case of a commercial partnership it is presumed that a member has authority to do so

since it may be an ordinary or necessary incident of the business. Many partnership contracts, in order to protect each partner from ill-advised activities of any other partner, provide for the necessity of more than one signature on checks made on the partnership accounts.

Unless expressly authorized, a partner has no authority to assign the partnership property in trust for creditors, transfer the good will of the firm, confess a judgment, submit a partnership claim or liability to arbitration, sell or execute a mortgage on partnership real estate, dispose of the personal property of a non-trading firm, or do any other act which would prevent the partnership from carrying on its ordinary business.

U.P.A. §9.

1. "Every partner is an agent of the partnership for the purpose of its business, and the act of every partner, including the execution in the partnership name of any instrument, for apparently carrying on in the usual way the business of the partnership of which he is a member binds the partnership unless the partner so acting has in fact no authority to act for the partnership in the particular matter, and the person with whom he is dealing has knowledge of the fact that he has no such authority.

2. "An act of a partner which is not apparently for the carrying on of the business of the partnership in the usual way does not bind the partnership unless authorized by the other partners.

3. "Unless authorized by the other partners or unless they have abandoned the business, one or more but less than all the partners have no authority to:
   a. Assign the partnership property in trust for creditors or on the assignee's promise to pay the debts of the partnership,
   b. Dispose of the good will of the business,
   c. Do any other act which would make it impossible to carry on the ordinary business of a partnership,
   d. Confess a judgment,
   e. Submit a partnership claim or liability to arbitration or reference.

4. "No act of a partner in contravention of a restriction on authority shall bind the partnership to persons having knowledge of the restriction."

METHOD OF LIQUIDATION ON DISSOLUTION BY DEATH OF PARTNER OR OTHERWISE.

The dissolution of a partnership, as defined by the *Uniform Partnership Act* §29 is the change in the relation of the partners caused by any partner ceasing to be associated in the carrying on as distinguished from the winding up of the business. Dissolution of a partnership may be effected in a number of ways. The parties should provide for such contingency in the partnership contract by setting forth the manner in which the business is to be liquidated. The importance of using exact and clear language in describing the manner in which the business is to be liquidated cannot be overemphasized.

A partnership may be dissolved by the acts of parties, by operation of law, or by decree or order of a court. The death of a partner, by operation of law, dissolves the partnership and compels the surviving partners to wind up the affairs of the firm unless a specific agreement to the contrary has been entered into.

Under the principles of partnership law, a partnership business must be liquidated upon the death of a partner even though the terms of the partnership contract has not expired or its specific undertaking has not been accomplished. On dissolution a partnership has a limited existence for the purpose of settling all the accounts, collecting all the property and assets of the partnership, and winding up its affairs. All authority of the partners to act for the firm is terminated except for the purpose of completing transactions begun before dissolution.

However, immediate liquidation of the business may be financially detrimental both to the surviving partner and to the estate of the deceased partner. To obviate this result, the partnership agreement may provide that the partnership be liquidated over a period of time in order to assure the surviving partner the maximum benefit from liquidation. Or it may be desirable for the parties to provide a method for disposing of the interest of the deceased partner without disrupting the continuity of the business. Any number of possible provisions may be decided upon to accomplish this purpose.

The partnership contract may provide that the heirs or personal representatives of the deceased partner shall carry on the operation of the partnership business together with the surviving partners. Such a provision is usually binding upon the survivors but is optional with the representative. Many partnership agreements provide that upon the death of one of the partners the surviving partner will have a preferential right to purchase the interest of the deceased partner on stated terms and conditions. If a workable formula determining the interest of the deceased partner is detailed in the partnership agreement, future disputes will be avoided. It should be specifically provided in the partnership contract whether good will is to be considered in determining the value of the deceased partner's interest, or whether good will shall become the sole property of the surviving partner. It is also permissible for the agreement to specify a definite sum to be paid for the deceased partner's interest.

It has often been deemed advisable for the contract of partnership to provide that mutual life insurance policies be taken out on the lives of each of the partners in order to enable the surviving partner to have sufficient funds to purchase the deceased partner's interest. The partnership agreement may provide that the interest of the deceased partner shall continue in the business and that the surviving partner shall have the business. Such a provision, if supported by sufficient consideration, will be binding upon all of the parties. In the absence of contract stipulation, a surviving partner, though permitted to purchase a deceased partner's interest, enjoys no priority as purchaser and the courts will closely scrutinize such a transaction to determine whether the terms of the purchase are fairly made.

The last will and testament of each of the partners should be in conformity with whatever plan is evolved to cover the contingency of the death of one of the partners. A mere direction in a partner's will as declaratory of his intent on the disposition to be made of the partnership business on his death will not be binding on the other partners without their express assent. For example, a direction in his will to the effect that the surviving partners be required to allow the executors of his estate to claim his interest and participate in a continuation of the business will not be enforceable as against his co-partners. If they have not agreed to this or some other arrangement, they may insist on a dissolution of the firm following the death of a partner.

Where the interest of the deceased partner is to be purchased by the survivor by means of insurance provided for that purpose or otherwise, the estate will be the recipient of a large cash sum. It may be advisable to provide for a testamentary trust for the protection of the widow and children of the deceased partner and for sound investment of such money. If the partners intend that after the death of one of them his legal representative continue to operate such business, the wills of the partners should include provisions sufficiently broad to empower the executors to carry on the business without the necessity of constant application to court for authorization to perform acts relating to the firm business after the death of one of the partners.

The partnership interest may be the most important asset of the estate. If a man dies intestate his assets may not go exclusively to his wife, but may be shared by other heirs. Only a valid will can provide for a different result or prevent a number of heirs from exercising their divergent views on the operations of the surviving partnership. It is apparent that in the absence of a will or with one poorly drawn, the financial protection afforded to those whom the partner seeks to provide for may prove wholly inadequate.

Under the *Uniform Partnership Act* the surviving partner is entitled to reasonable compensation for his services in winding up the partnership affairs. In states which have not adopted legislation on the subject, the prevailing view is that a surviving partner is not entitled to such compensation unless his services are unusual and such as could not have been reasonably contemplated. Under this rule, liquidation of the business by the surviving partner is regarded as a duty incident to the contract of partnership. An express agreement by the parties as to compensation will supersede whatever rule of compensation is applicable in their state.

With regard to the accountability of a surviving partner for profits made after dissolution, the courts are not in agreement where the profits earned are attributable to the skill or services of the partners carrying on the business. One court has held that a contract for the rendition of architectural services was of such a nature as to admit of only a personal performance and was therefore dissolved by the death of one of the parties. In another case decided in the same state, the court held that on the death of one of the parties to a joint venture, his legal representatives were entitled to share in the profits of unfinished business completed subsequent to his death. It may be said generally that the courts are more inclined to decree accountability where personal services are not the controlling consideration. On this point, as on the many other aspects of the partnership relation, the agreement of the parties will be determinative.

U.P.A. §33.

"Except so far as may be necessary to wind up partnership affairs or to complete transactions begun but not then finished, dissolution terminates all authority of any partner to act for the partnership."

U.P.A. §36.

1. "The dissolution of the partnership does not of itself discharge the existing liability of any partner."
4. The individual property of a deceased partner shall be liable for all obligations of the partnership incurred while he was a partner but subject to the prior payment of his separate debts.

U.P.A. §37.

"Unless otherwise agreed the partners who have not wrongfully dissolved the partnership or the legal representative of the last surviving partner, not bankrupt, has the right to wind up the partnership affairs; provided, however, that any partner, his legal representative or his assignee, upon cause shown, may obtain winding up by the court."

U.P.A. §38.

1. "When dissolution is caused in any way, except in contravention of the partnership agreement, each partner, as against his co-partners and all persons claiming through them in respect of their interests in the partnership, unless otherwise agreed, may have the partnership property applied to discharge its liabilities, and the surplus applied to pay in cash the net amount owing to the respective partners."

Cal. *Galich v. Borkich*, 229 P. 2d 89 (1951). An alleged partnership or joint adventure in contracting business had no license. An associated corporation, of which one of the members was president and sole stockholder with the exception of one share, had such a license. It was held no defense to a suit for dissolution of the partnership that it had no license and that the contractual relation was therefore illegal, since the contract itself was not *per se* contrary to any statute, and public welfare and safety were not threatened by denying one partner relief against the other.

Norwood v. Judd, 93 Cal. App. 2d 276, 209 P. 2d 24 (1949). Partner of contracting firm was permitted to maintain an action for dissolution and accounting though only one of the partners was licensed, since the licensing statutes were passed primarily for the protection of the public, not for the benefit of a partner who seeks to retain the fruits of the partnership enterprise to the exclusion of another partner entitled to share therein.

Mass. *Rutan v. Coolidge*, 241 Mass. 584, 136 N.E. 257 (1922). In a proceeding for a partnership accounting against a surviving partner, whether the architectural firm had any good will with respect to the possibility of future business was held to be a question of fact. The court found that where the surviving partner had done the designing and artistic work and dealt with the clients and the deceased partner for more than two years took no part in the business of the firm, the good will of the firm was of only nominal value.

Stearns v. Blevins, 262 Mass. 577, 160 N.E. 417 (1928). Where two architects were associated as joint adventurers to furnish architectural services in the erection of an apartment house, it was held that on the death of one, the contract was dissolved, and the survivor was held accountable for one-half the value of the work done at the time the joint adventure ended by death.

N.Y. *Stern v. Warren*, 227 N.Y. 538, 125 N.E. 811 (1920). Where two architectural firms became joint adventurers in the performance of a contract for architectural services for a specific project, on the death of a partner of one of the firms it was held that his legal representative was entitled to a share of the profits of the unfinished business completed subsequent to his death.

Tenn.   *Hunt v. Street*, 182 Tenn. 167, 184 S.W. 2d 553 (1945). On voluntary dissolution of an architectural partnership, a former member could not enjoin another former member from continuing to use the firm name since the good will of the partnership terminated upon its voluntary dissolution.

PART THREE

ARCHITECT, ENGINEER, AND OWNER— THE EMPLOYMENT RELATION

CHAPTER NINE

Agreements with owners

The employment relation between architect or engineer and owner is entered into by a voluntary agreement between the parties; its creation and existence is governed by the general principles of contract law.

The employment of an architect or engineer is a matter of voluntary agreement between the parties. To determine whether such an agreement has been made or is binding, the general rules of contract law apply. Every binding contract contains four essential elements: 1. two or more parties with capacity to contract; 2. a lawful consideration; 3. a lawful purpose; 4. mutuality—a mutual assent, a mutual understanding, sometimes described as a meeting of the minds of the parties. Without these necessary elements, an agreement will not be recognized as binding.

The law protects certain classes of persons whom it deems incapable of properly guarding their interests by permitting them to void, or repudiate, at their option contracts into which they have entered. These classes include insane persons, intoxicated persons, and infants. Generally, infants are persons under 21 years of age, although in some states women are held to attain legal age at 18 years instead of at 21 years.

The capacity of a corporation to enter into binding contracts is limited to those powers granted by the state. Its express powers are set forth in the charter or articles of incorporation, while its implied powers are those reasonably necessary or incidental to the accomplishment of the powers expressly granted. A person dealing with a corporation is chargeable with notice of the limitation on its powers. If those limits are exceeded, the contract is deemed to be *ultra vires* and void.

A contract must be supported by consideration in the absence of a statutory exception. The term consideration imports something of value exchanged for its legal equivalent. Consideration may take the form of promises exchanged, the forbearance from taking action, or the giving up of certain rights. Another requisite of a valid contract is that it must be entered into for a lawful purpose. If the agreement contravenes rules of law or public policy, it is not acceptable. Illegal purposes may include violation of civil laws, like building codes, or ordinances governing public construction contracts.

The courts also speak of mutuality as an essential element. Since a contract is a voluntary relationship, there must be a meeting of the minds or a mutual assent to create an agreement. This is generally accomplished by the tender of an offer by one party and an unconditional acceptance of the offer by the second party, manifested by some overt act. A mutual assent is lacking, however, where the consent of one of the parties is the result of mistake, fraud, duress, or undue influence.

The offer cannot be accepted after it is effectively withdrawn. It will continue in effect until withdrawal by the offeror, rejection by the offeree, the destruction of the subject matter or the death of either party before acceptance. If the offer provides that it will be open for a specified time, it will be deemed withdrawn at the end of such time, or if no time is specified, at the end of a reasonable period of time, determined in each instance by the circumstances of the particular case.

The contract under which the architect or engineer is employed need not be in writing to be valid unless it is such that it cannot be performed within a year. An oral contract which embodies fully the terms upon which the parties have agreed to proceed is valid even though they agree that a written contract will be executed thereafter and this is not done. If the understanding is that a written contract is a condition precedent to a completed agreement, then the oral agreement is not binding until it has been reduced to writing.

A contract, whether oral or in writing, must be certain and definite as to the terms upon which the parties agree. Where, for example, an owner agrees in writing to employ a named architect if the owner should build at some future time, no binding contract results since the terms are too uncertain to express the parties' intent. The writing fails to state what the terms of the employment are to be, and amounts to no more than an agreement to do something which will require a further meeting of the minds. A valid contract under which an architect or engineer agrees to furnish professional services, once entered into, cannot be arbitrarily canceled by the owner. Such a contract is not generally regarded as a personal satisfaction contract, terminable at the pleasure of the owner.

A person who assumes to act as agent for another in hiring an architect or engineer, must be authorized to enter into such contract by his employer, or principal. A person may properly appoint an agent to enter into contracts with third persons in his behalf, but unless such authority is expressly or impliedly given or is within the agent's apparent authority, the principal will not be bound. Unauthorized acts of the agent do not bind the principal unless he has by his own acts, words, or conduct, given the agent the appearance of authority to act for him, or has subsequently ratified the agent's action expressly or by implication after full knowledge of the facts. Therefore, an architect or engineer who enters into a contract with a purported agent without inquiring into his authority, does so at his peril.

The principle that a person dealing with an agent assumes the risk of lack of authority in the agent applies as well to his dealings with officers or agents of a public corporation or other public bodies. Contracts by public officers or agents must be strictly within the authority delegated by the charter, ordinance, or other law. All limitations on the authority of the officer acting for the public must be read into and made a part of the contract entered into with the architect or engineer. If the officer does not have the requisite power to enter into the contract, it is invalid; and no liability is incurred for work done under a void contract. In some instances a public body may enter into contracts without specific approval, as where the employment of an architect or engineer is necessary to accomplish a purpose specifically authorized, or where it has discretionary power to employ. It is also essential to the validity of a public contract that it be entered into in the manner and upon the conditions specified in the legislative authorization.

Municipal ordinances often provide that a municipal corporation cannot execute a contract unless an appropriation has previously been made for the purpose which the contract seeks to accomplish. Or there may be a limitation precluding the municipality from entering into contracts for projects because the cost of the proposed project would exceed the municipality's constitutional debt limitation.

Other requirements may pertain to the holding of proper meetings of the designated authorities, required percentages of votes necessary to authorize a contract, and the execution of a written agreement signed by the proper officials. Contracts which have been entered into by unauthorized subordinates employing architects or engineers may be ratified by the proper public body or official where the intent to ratify is unequivocal and ratification is executed in the manner prescribed.

The validity of a contract entered into with a public body is of controlling importance with respect to the architect's or engineer's right to recover for services rendered under such contract. Even though it may be within the power of the governmental body to enter into the contract, the architect's or engineer's right to be paid for his work may depend on whether there has been strict adherence to the mode and form of execution of the contract. Although the work has been performed by the architect and the benefits accepted by the governmental unit, it may not be obliged to pay for the work if there had been a deviation from the prescribed method for execution of the contract. Not only will the architect be unable to recover under the contract, but he will also be barred from recovering in *quantum meruit* for the reasonable value of the services actually rendered. In a few recent cases the courts have modified the harshness of this rule by permitting a recovery in *quantum meruit* where the public body had the power to execute the given contract but where the statutory requirements as to mode of execution were not followed. This rule will be considered again in the subsequent chapter on compensation. It should be noted, however, that it is a rule of limited application, and does not hold true in all jurisdictions.

In the awarding of public contracts, statutes which require competitive bidding have been generally held not to apply to contracts for engineering or architectural services. Such contracts contemplate services of a professional nature which demand a high degree of skill and technical knowledge. An award on a competitive basis to the lowest bidder, it is felt, would tend to encourage underbidding by persons not capable or experienced. The reason for the rule has been thus stated:

> "An architect is an artist. His work requires taste, skill, and technical learning, ability of a high and rare kind. Advertising might bring many bids, but it is beyond peradventure that the lowest bidder would be least capable and most inexperienced and absolutely unacceptable. As well advertise for a lawyer or civil engineer for the city and intrust its vast affairs and important interest to the one who would work for the least money." *Miller v. Boyle,* 43 Cal. App. 39, 184 Pac. 421, 423 (1919).

Where contracts are awarded by selection of plans submitted in competition in response to a notice or advertisement, the rights of the parties who enter the competition depend upon the terms of such notice. If the terms of the competition specify that the designer of the accepted plan will be employed to supervise construction of the proposed building, an enforceable contract exists between the sponsors of the competition and the winning architect, and he has a right of action for any failure of the sponsors to carry out their part of the contract. It has even been held that where under the terms of the competition, an architect will be selected as winner, a contract exists between the architects who entered the competition and the promoters, and failure of the promoters to select a winning contestant is a breach of the contract which the court will specifically enforce by requiring that a selection be made.

However, where the notice expressly reserves the right to reject any and all plans submitted, and this right is formally exercised, no contract may be claimed by any architect who has entered the competition. Furthermore, in the absence of a special provision to that effect, there is no obligation to employ the architect, whose plans have been selected, to supervise construction of the proposed buildings.

Ordinarily, where the competition provides for an award to the winner, the contract is fulfilled by paying to the winner the amount of the award. To establish a contract employing an architect where the competition makes no provision therefor, there must be an offer made to the architect and accepted by him. Statutes and resolutions adopting particular plans do not result in a contract employing the designer of such plans but are merely expression of intention and may be rescinded.

The architect's or engineer's employment may be rightfully terminated in any of several ways. Ordinarily the employment relation ceases on completion of performance. It may also be terminated by mutual consent, or if there is no provision to the contrary, the employer may terminate the contract but will be responsible for the resultant loss.

Frequently the parties include stipulations in the contract providing for termination under certain contingencies. An example of such stipulation is the provision for abandonment of the project at the owner's option. The parties are free to agree also that the owner may arbitrarily discharge the architect if he is not satisfied with his performance. If the contract specifies the grounds upon which the architect may be discharged or evidences an intent that reasonable grounds must exist as a condition to discharge, then the owner may not arbitrarily terminate the employment.

As in the case of any other relation of a professional character, the contract between owner and architect or engineer is personal in nature and where the architect or owner dies before performance has been completed, the employment relation is terminated. The estate of the owner will not be liable for any services rendered by the architect following death of the owner. Similarly on the death of the architect, his right to complete the work does not survive to his executors, although recovery may be had for work performed prior to his death. The personal nature of the relationship is also the basis of the rule that an architect may not delegate to another his duties under a contract for professional services. Thus, in *Huggins v. Atlanta Tile and Marble Co.,* 106 S.E. 2d 191 (1958), the court stated that:

> "An architect is selected and agreed upon to exercise his personal skill, discretion and judgment, and his duty to exercise such skill, judgment and discretion cannot be delegated."

GENERAL PRINCIPLES OF THE LAW OF CONTRACTS and agency determine the creation, termination, and incidents of the employment relation between owner and architect or engineer.

Ariz. *Litchfield v. Greene*, 43 Ariz. 509, 33 P. 2d 290 (1934). Contract employing an architect made by an agent was not binding on the principal because he did not have full knowledge of the facts and did not subsequently ratify the contract.

Mass. *Rhodes v. Green*, 264 Mass. 295, 162 N.E. 305 (1928). Whether owners really agreed to employ plaintiff as architect of contemplated building, subsequently erected, held to be a question for jury.

Benton v. Springfield YMCA, 170 Mass. 534, 49 N.E. 928 (1898). No contract to employ architect was made where vote of committee appointing architect was rescinded before official notice of his appointment was given.

Mich. *Baily v. Goldberg*, 236 Mich. 29, 209 N.W. 805 (1926). Failure of one of the owners to sign contract employing architect does not invalidate contract which represented the intent of all the parties. Contract for performance of architectural services is not a personal satisfaction contract and cannot therefore be arbitrarily cancelled by the owners.

Minn. *Lamoreaux v. Wiesman*, 136 Minn. 207, 161 N.W. 504 (1917). Where jury could find that contract with architect was fully agreed to and that architect was to proceed under it, and that a written contract was to be executed thereafter, there was a present enforceable contract although a written contract was never executed.

Neb. *Berlinghof v. Lincoln County*, 128 Neb. 28, 257 N.W. 373 (1934). Where architect was employed to render architectural services with respect to construction of courthouse and paid a commission therefor on its completion, the contract was completely fulfilled and architect was not entitled to further commissions for use of his plans some years later.

N.Y. *Pope v. Hoyt*, 200 App. Div. 475, 193 N.Y.S. 179 (1922), *aff'd*, 235 N.Y. 526, 139 N.E. 720 (1923). Husband's contract with a landscape architect entitling architect to certain percentage of the purchase price on sale of wife's land, for services in improving the land, was not ratified by wife by permitting the architect to work on the property, unless she knew of the contract or understanding.

Pa. *Lippincott v. Warren Apartment Co.*, 307 Pa. 320, 161 Atl. 330 (1932). Where contract provides that work shall be done to the satisfaction of the owner, his dissatisfaction, to defeat recovery for the architect's services, must be real and genuine, not prompted by caprice or bad faith.

Wash. *Ryan v. Hanna,* 89 Wash. 379, 154 Pac. 436 (1916). Written contract whereby owner agreed to employ architect to draw plans and specifications and supervise construction of building if the owner should build in the future, was too uncertain and indefinite to entitle architect to recover thereon.

Wis. *Fernekes v. Nugent Sanitarium,* 158 Wis. 671, 149 N.W. 393 (1914). Where the general manager of corporation and former owner of sanitarium conducted by it was in control of business, the corporation was bound by his act employing architects for addition to sanitarium.

A PUBLIC CONTRACT UNDER WHICH an architect or engineer is employed to furnish professional services is invalid unless the public or governmental body has power to make it, and the contract is entered into by the proper public official in the manner prescribed. The proper public body may ratify unauthorized contracts employing architects or engineers if the intent to ratify is shown by unequivocal action properly taken.

Ala. *Board of Revenue v. Merrill,* 193 Ala. 521, 68 So. 971 (1915). County Board of Revenue was held to have discretionary power to employ an architect with respect to the construction of a courthouse.

Ark. *Dierks Special School Dist. v. Van Dyke,* 152 Ark. 27, 237 S.W. 428 (1922). Contract of school board employing architect was held not binding because not executed pursuant to authority given or legally ratified.

Klingensmith v. Logan County, 116 Ark. 65, 171 S.W. 1191 (1914). Contract of county judge employing architect held invalid in absence of a court order appointing the architect and an appropriation therefor.

Ga. *Spalding County v. W. Chamberlin Co.,* 130 Ga. 649, 61 S.E. 533 (1908). Where statute required contracts with county to be in writing and entered on minutes, contract employing architect which did not specify compensation in minutes though compensation was agreed upon in contract, held not binding since material portion was not in writing as provided by statute.

Savannah v. Kops, 28 Ga. App. 713, 113 S.E. 99 (1922). Under city resolution authorizing committee to employ architect, architect was not entitled to recover for plans and specifications prepared by oral direction of the committee chairman.

Ill. *Hall v. Cook County,* 359 Ill. 528, 195 N.E. 54 (1935). Employment of an architect to prepare plans for auditorium prior to enabling act does not relieve county of liability for services rendered because enabling act was thereafter declared unconstitutional since employment of architect was "necessary."

Ind. *Gaddis v. Barton School Tp.*, 89 Ind. App. 369, 164 N.E. 499 (1929). Contract employing architect held void as not created with the proper body and in the manner prescribed by statute. *Barringer v. Guilford School Tp.*, 100 Ind. App. 445, 194 N.E. 651 (1935). Specific appropriation of an amount for architectural fees held not necessary to the validity of a contract employing architect since such services were payable out of the appropriation for the school building.

Ky. *Goin v. Board of Educ. of Frankfort*, 298 Ky. 645, 183 S.W. 2d 819 (1945). Board of Education can ratify any contract it can make but ratification must be in the same manner and with the same formality that is required to bind the Board in making contracts, and their action must be unequivocal.
Jameison v. City of Paducah, 195 Ky. 71, 241 S.W. 327, 329 (1922). "... persons dealing with a municipal corporation are bound, at their peril, to know that contracts made by the officials of such corporation are executed in the mode pointed out by its charter and ordinances, and if such persons fail to inform themselves as to whether the official has power to contract, they must suffer the consequences."

Me. *Bunker v. City of Old Town*, 130 Me. 510, 153 Atl. 441 (1931). Architect could not recover payment for preliminary sketches prepared for school committee and school superintendent where city did not ratify and had no knowledge of dealings between the parties.

Mass. *Vinal v. Town of Nahant*, 232 Mass. 412, 122 N.E. 295 (1919). Contract employing an architect for a public purpose must be reasonably definite in order to be binding, and such a contract cannot be made by a resolution that a specified plan for a building be adopted.
William S. Drummey, Inc. v. Cambridge, 282 Mass. 170, 184 N.E. 458 (1933). City school committee held to have power to employ an architect to give expert advice when necessary, without the approval of the Mayor.
McGovern v. Town of Southbridge, 264 Mass. 578, 163 N.E. 175 (1928). Town vote on repairing and enlarging sewage disposal works held not a ratification of agreement to pay engineer additional compensation for preparing plans.

Mich. *Stratton v. Detroit*, 246 Mich. 139, 224 N.W. 649 (1929). City held not liable to architect for commissions in excess of sum in original contract where a subsequent modification by the board of health was unauthorized.

Mo.　*Barnett v. St. Louis,* 198 S.W. 452 (1917). A building committee of a board of trustees empowered to examine and report on the expediency of erecting buildings, has no power to employ an architect.

Bonsack & Pearce, Inc. v. School Dist of Marceline, 226 Mo. App. 1238, 49 S.W. 2d 1085 (1932). School board was estopped to repudiate a contract legally authorized where the architect had partly performed before the attempted repudiation.

Neb.　*Helleberg v. City of Kearney,* 139 Neb. 413, 297 N.W. 672 (1941). No contract employing architect was held to exist where not created by official action of the city council.

N.J.　*DeMuro v. Martini,* 137 N.J.L. 640, 61 A. 2d 230 (1948). Valid contract employing architect was held to exist where member of board of commissioners of city pursuant to board's resolution wrote to architect engaging him and setting forth details of employment and architect agreed to terms thereof and thereafter work was commenced on project and architect placed in charge.

Sleight v. Board of Educ. of Paterson, 112 N.J.L. 422, 170 Atl. 598 (1934). Board of Education held vested with implied power to incur reasonable expense for obtaining expert information, such as architectural plans, necessary for accurate estimate of cost of proposed school building.

N.Y.　*Curran v. Board of Estimate,* 173 Misc. 1022, 19 N.Y.S. 2d 624 (1939), *aff'd,* 259 App. Div. 712 (1940). Section of New York City Charter authorizing Department of Public Works to employ architects in private capacity as consultants in connection with buildings costing in excess of $100,000 did not intend to differentiate between architectural services generally and consulting services in a technical and limited sense.

Vermuele v. Corning, 186 App. Div. 206, 174 N.Y.S. 220 (1919), *aff'd,* 230 N.Y. 585, 130 N.E. 903 (1920). Common Council adopted unauthorized act of board in hiring engineer, where on three different occasions it audited bills rendered by the engineer and made payments on account thereof.

Wooley v. Schenectady, 226 App. Div. 383, 236 N.Y.S. 104 (1929). Contract employing architect held void when not executed in accordance with statutory requirement.

Pierce v. Board of Educ. of Union Free School Dist., 125 Misc. 589, 211 N.Y.S. 788 (1925), *aff'd,* 216 App. Div. 787, 214 N.Y.S. 904 (1926). Architect dealing with municipality is bound to know

that his right to recover for services is conditioned on the expense
of construction coming within appropriation.

Brown v. Mt. Vernon Housing Authority, 109 N.Y.S. 2d 392, 2/9
App. Div. 794 (1952). Where approval by the State Division of
Housing was required by a state statute to validate agreements
between architects and defendants, plaintiffs could not recover
under an unapproved agreement for the value of their services.

Okla.   *City of Muskogee v. Senter*, 186 Okla. 174, 96 P. 2d. 534 (1940).
Under City Charter authorizing Mayor to "sign" contracts, Mayor
was not authorized to contract for architectural services in connection with repair of public building independently of any action
on part of council.

Blumenauer v. Kaw City, 182 Okla. 409, 77 P. 2d 1143 (1938).
Contract employing architect entered into by Mayor pursuant to
resolution of City Council held void because council had no power
to delegate to Mayor right to incur financial obligation by contract
not approved or ratified by council.

Ore.   *Forrester v. City of Hillsboro*, 156 Ore. 89, 66 P. 2d 496 (1937).
Engineer who performed engineering services for city held not
entitled to recover for services though contract had been fully
executed and services accepted by the city where charter requirements as to execution of such contracts were not complied with.

Ore.   *White v. City of Seaside*, 107 Ore. 330, 213 Pac. 892 (1923).
Where an architect performed services for city under a contract
which was not executed in the manner provided by charter, the
city was not liable for his services though work was accepted by it.

Pa.   *Kline v. School Dist. of Longswamp*, 35 Berks 181, 35 Mun. 17
(1943). At common law, school districts as bodies corporate were
capable of entering into valid contracts either orally or in writing
and it is presumed that this common law principle remains un-
altered in absence of express declaration by statute.

Innes v. School Dis., 342 Pa. 433, 20 A. 2d 225 (1941). Architect
entering into contract with city agency must ascertain limits of
agency's permitted indebtedness, and if contract creates indebtedness exceeding limitation, contract is void.

Altman v. School Dist. of Uniontown, 334 Pa. 336, 5 A. 2d 896
(1939). Fact that cost of building designed by architect would
have exceeded school district's constitutional debt limitation, was
immaterial with respect to validity of architect's separate contract
to furnish plans.

Osterling v. Allegheny County, 272 Pa. 458, 116 Atl. 385 (1922).
Failure of County Commissioners to follow procedure required by

statute in contracting for architect's services defeats his claim for services.

Tex.   *City of Big Spring v. Ward,* 140 Tex. 609, 169 S.W. 2d 151 (1943). Engineer entering into contract with city was bound to know extent of city's powers and hence could not complain of city's termination of his services where city might disregard contract as *ultra vires.*

Eldorado Indep. School Dist. v. Becker, 120 S.W. 2d 476 (1938). Architect was entitled to fees for architectural services although there were no school funds available when the contract was entered into because, although the contract depended on bonds being voted and sold and the erection of the building that was erected, all such conditions had been fulfilled and school board had set aside funds for payment.

Harlingen Indep. School Dist. v. C. H. Page & Bro., 48 S.W. 2d 983 (1932). School board was without authority to contract for architect's services and bind the proceeds to be derived from schoolhouse bonds not voted at the time the contract was made, notwithstanding that the contract was conditioned on bonds being voted and sold.

Wash.   *State v. Pratt,* 31 Wash. 2d 725, 198 P. 2d 814 (1948). Architect contracting with County Commissioners is put on notice of their authority and county's debt limit and if he prepared plans for building, estimated cost of which would exceed county's debt limit, he imperils his right to compensation.

Pehrson v. School Dist., 694 Wash. 334, 77 P. 2d 1022 (1938). Architect could not recover for services prepared at unauthorized request of superintendent of school district where authority of district to enter into such contract must be exercised through its board.

COMPETITIVE BIDDING among architects and engineers has been condemned in recent formulations of the code of ethics of the two professions. Statutes which require competitive bidding as a basis for awarding public contracts are generally held not to apply to the services of architects, engineers, or surveyors.

Cal.   *Kennedy v. Ross,* 28 Cal. 2d 569, 170 P. 2d 904 (1946); *Miller v. Boyle,* 43 Cal. App. 39, 184 Pac. 421 (1919).

Colo.   *Cf. Johnson-Olmsted Realty Co. v. Denver,* 89 Colo. 250, 1 P. 2d 928 (1931). Contract with corporation for architectural services must be let to lowest bidder because corporation cannot render personal services so as to come within rule that services of personal nature are not subject to competitive bidding.

La. *Louisiana v. McIlhenny*, 201 La. 78, 9 So. 2d 467 (1942).

Minn. *Krohnberg v. Pass.*, 187 Minn. 73, 244 N.W. 329 (1932).

Mo. *Contracting Plumbers' Ass'n v. Board of Educ.*, 238 Mo. App. 1096, 194 S.W. 2d 731 (1946). Charter provision requiring all contracts for public improvements to be let to lowest responsible bidder does not prohibit city from constructing improvements under the direction of its own engineers and officers.

N.Y. *Vermeule v. Corning*, 186 App. Div. 206, 174 N.Y.S. 220 (1919), *aff'd*, 230 N.Y. 585, 130 N.E. 903 (1920); *People v. Board of Educ. of Utica*, 198 App. Div. 476, 190 N.Y.S. 798 (1921); *Horgan & Slattery v. New York City*, 114 App. Div. 555, 100 N.Y.S. 68 (1906); *People v. Flagg*, 17 N.Y. 584 (1858). City could make contract with surveyor without first calling for bids.

N.D. *Rosatti v. Common School Dist.*, 52 N.D. 931, 204 N.W. 833 (1925).

Ohio *Lurie v. Board of Educ. of City School Dist.*, 2 Ohio Supp. 292 (1938).

Pa. *Kline v. School Dist. of Longswamp*, 35 Berks 181, 35 Mun. 17 (1943).

Tenn. *State v. Brown*, 159 Tenn. 591, 21 S.W. 2d 721 (1929).

Tex. *Stephens County v. J. N. McCammon, Inc.*, 40 S.W. 2d 67 (1931); *Hunter v. Whiteaker & Washington*, 230 S.W. 1096 (1921); *Houston v. Glover*, 40 Civ. App. 177, 89 S.W. 425 (1905).
Cf. Ashby v. James, 226 S.W. 732 (1920). Contract with architect held to fall within letter of statute providing for competitive bidding when expenditure of $2000 or more required.

WHERE PLANS ARE SUBMITTED IN COMPETITION in response to an advertisement, the rights of the parties are governed by the terms of the competition.

Ill. *Hood v. Polish Nat. Alliance*, 246 Ill. App. 137 (1927). In contest to select architect where first prize was cash sum, employment of architect, and usual commission on cost of building, wherein one of competing architects was awarded first prize and paid cash portion of award, mutual contract was effected under which both society and architect could be compelled to perform or pay damages.

Mass. *Benton v. Springfield YMCA*, 170 Mass. 534, 49 N.E. 928 (1898). Where committee reserved right to reject all plans submitted in competition and did so but appointed one competitor as architect, his appointment was not made pursuant to terms of the competition, and the committee could rescind the appointment before official notice to him.

See *Edge Moor Bridge Works v. Bristol County*, 170 Mass. 528, 49 N.E. 918 (1898). Where County Commissioners advertised for proposals for bridge specifying that person awarded contract would be required to execute contract within 6 days, and Commissioners voted that a given architect's bid was accepted and a contract be awarded to him, it was held that their vote was not agreement to enter into contract with him.

Mo.   *Walsh v. St. Louis Exposition & Music Hall Ass'n*, 101 Mo. 534, 14 S.W. 722 (1890). Where, according to the terms of a competition, the designer of the accepted plan was to be made superintendent of construction subject to certain conditions, the architect selected did not have a right of action for refusal to employ him as superintendent where he refused to accede to the condition imposed.

N.Y.   *Higgins v. General Electric Co.*, 258 App. Div. 606, 17 N.Y.S. 2d 596 (1940). Where architectural competition was held under conditions requiring that names and addresses of competitors be annexed to designs, after awards were made other persons had no right to make any use of unsuccessful competitors' designs except in accordance with the agreement governing competition.

Pa.   *Palmer v. Central Bd. of Educ.*, 220 Pa. 568, 70 Atl. 433 (1908). Where terms of competition were that committee would examine each plan until one was selected meeting board's approval and board rejected one plan submitted by committee and no further plans were examined, competing architects had a right of action against the board for failure to select a winning design and specific performance of the contract would be enforced.

Cope v. Hastings, 183 Pa. 300, 38 Atl. 717 (1897). Architects who submitted designs whose cost would exceed appropriation therefor and thus violated terms of contract had no cause for complaint when sponsors refused to consider their designs.

Tex.   *Flanders v. Wood*, 83 Tex. 277, 18 S.W. 572 (1892). Where architects entering competition agreed that they would each submit plans but agreed to share equally in remuneration for accepted plan, the agreement was not against public policy and would be enforced.

U.S.   *Lord & Hewlett v. United States*, 217 U.S. 340 (1909). Act of Congress which appropriates money for competition for plans of proposed building, successful plans to be transmitted to Congress, and which does not appropriate money for the building itself, creates no obligation on the part of the government to use plans of successful competitor.

Tilley v. Cook County, 103 U.S. 155 (1880). Where an architect who submitted plans in competition was awarded prize specified for the best design, the city was not required to appoint him superintendent of construction.

Audsley v. New York, 74 Fed. 274 (1896). Where architect sues to compel award of prize submitted in competition, terms of which provided for award to six best plans, he is not entitled to compensation in absence of evidence showing his plans were chosen as one of six best.

THE ARCHITECT'S OR ENGINEER'S AUTHORITY may be terminated in accordance with the terms of the contract between the parties by mutual consent or by the death of one of the parties.

Ariz. *Sitkin v. Smith,* 35 Ariz. 226, 276 Pac. 521 (1929). Where dispute arises on facts as to whether architect's authority has been terminated, question of termination may be one for jury to decide.

Cal. *Fitzhugh v. Mason,* 2 Cal. App. 220, 83 Pac. 282 (1905). Where owners employed architect to perform architectural services, they were entitled to discontinue work at their option in absence of contract to contrary, on paying architect for services and expenses incurred.

Mass. *Stearns v. Blevins,* 262 Mass. 577, 160 N.E. 417 (1928). Contract for architectural services being personal in nature will be considered dissolved by death of one of the parties.

N.Y. *Rockart v. Mt. Vernon,* 140 Misc. 270, 251 N.Y.S. 514 (1931). Contract for employment of consulting architect in erection of proposed city hall was held abandoned by mutual consent where project was abandoned and no further steps taken until 12 years later when a building resolution was adopted and a different building was erected at far greater cost.

Wash. *Gould v. McCormick,* 75 Wash. 61, 134 Pac. 676 (1913). Where contract provides that architect must superintend construction to entire satisfaction of owner, and certain requirements are attached to his performance, the owner has option to discharge architect only where there is good cause for dissatisfaction.

CHAPTER TEN

Architect's or engineer's authority

An architect or engineer generally acts as the limited agent of his client; his powers and authority are restricted to those expressly conferred by the contract or reasonably implied from the nature of his undertaking.

A client is ordinarily bound by the acts of an architect or engineer employed to prepare plans and specifications or to supervise the construction of a building or other structure because of the principal-agent relationship, although in a few situations he has been held not to be so bound. In the latter situations the architect or engineer was considered an "independent contractor."

An agency is created by contract, either express or implied, whereby one person (the principal) confers on another (the agent) authority to manage some business or transaction in his behalf and subject to his control. The principal-agent relationship differs from the ordinary employer-employee (master-servant) relationship in that the agent is not only employed by the principal, but has authority to represent him and affect his legal relations with third parties as well.

The principal can be bound only by those acts of the agent done within his actual or apparent authority. Actual authority is that intentionally conferred by the principal either expressly or by implication. Apparent authority is the appearance of authority which the employer, by his own conduct or acts, holds his agent out as possessing, although he may not actually have empowered the agent to act.

There is a distinction between the power of a general agent and that of a special agent to represent the principal. A general agent is empowered to do all acts relative to the business in which he is employed. A special agent, however, is only authorized to do the specific acts conferred or implied from the specific act to be done. An architect or engineer generally falls within the category of a special agent having limited powers. When employed to superintend the construction of a building or other structure, his authority, in the absence of provisions enlarging it, extends only to insuring that the work is done in conformity with the plans and specifications. However, the owner may constitute the architect or engineer his general agent for all purposes connected with the construction by express stipulation, or by clothing him with the appearance of authority. The general principles of agency determine the extent of the architect's or engineer's authority, but these are subject to limitation in the contract of employment, since the parties may restrict or entirely remove the powers.

While in most instances an architect or engineer who is employed to furnish plans and specifications or to supervise construction by an independent contractor, acts in the capacity of an agent, he may himself in performing such services occupy the position of an independent contractor. Whether in a given case he is an agent or an independent contractor depends upon the particular facts and circumstances. It is important to ascertain whether he acts as agent or independent contractor, since different legal incidents attach to each capacity. An independent contractor does not act as a representative of the owner. He exercises an independent calling and is not subject to the control of the person employing him in the performance of the contract, but only as to the results. On the other hand, the principal has the right to control the conduct of the agent as to those matters entrusted to him. The test often applied to differentiate an agent from an independent contractor is whether the employed person is subject to or free from the control of the employer with regard to details of the work.

Those cases where the architect has been held to be an independent contractor have generally involved the question of the liability of the owner for negligence of the architect.

Although the general rule is that the owner is liable for the negligence of his architect or engineer, a few cases have stated the rule that an architect in preparing plans and specifications acts as an independent contractor for whose negligence the owner is not liable. In those cases it was held that the owner was relieved of responsibility by a showing that he delegated the preparation of the plans and specifications to a competent architect or engineer upon whose judgment and skill he relied. In such cases the negligence of the architect was not imputed to the owner unless it was such that he by ordinary care could have anticipated or known it. The reason was thus stated in *White v. Green*, 82 S.W. 329 (1904):

> "Comparatively few men are skilled in the science of building houses and of necessity they have to depend upon those who have made it a study. So when an owner has used due care to employ an architect to

prepare plans and specifications and build accordingly, he should not be held liable for the plans unless the defects were such that he should know of them."

An architect is regarded as an independent contractor when he undertakes to build as well as to prepare plans and specifications. In other cases, however, the courts generally hold the owner responsible for the architect's negligence even if he has exercised reasonable care in selecting a competent architect. Where the owner has been held liable to third persons for damage sustained as a result of the architect's negligence either in preparing plans and specifications or in supervising construction, the courts have generally held that the architect was acting within the scope of his agency. Since he is in such case subject to the control of his employer, his negligence can be imputed to the employer. As between owner and architect in the absence of waiver there is little question that the architect is responsible for his own negligent performance of the contract.

The architect is employed upon the basis of the personal trust and confidence which the owner places in his honesty, ability, and skill. He therefore cannot delegate his authority to another without his client's consent. The rule does not apply to duties of a purely ministerial or clerical character which often must be delegated to insure efficiency in operation and to make available the architect's time for duties to which his particular aptitude and skill are suited. While the architect may properly delegate such duties, the responsibility for proper performance remains his, and the owner has a right to look to him for proper execution of the entire project committed to him.

If the parties mutually consent to a delegation of the architect's authority, such delegation is permissible, since they may waive conditions in the contract which cannot be varied individually by either. Delegation of authority with respect to the issuance of certificates and arbitration of disputes between owner and contractor will be discussed in a subsequent chapter. The reasons underlying the rule that delegated authority cannot be redelegated also form the basis for the rule that such a contract of employment cannot be assigned to another person without the consent of the employer, and where such unauthorized assignment is attempted, it will not under any circumstances be enforceable against the owner.

Every delegation of authority to the architect or engineer as agent includes by implication all incidental authority necessary, usual, or proper to effectuate the main object of his undertaking. Where in supervising the construction of a building or other structure, he is authorized to determine proper workmanship and fit materials, he has implied authority to reject unfit materials and improper workmanship. In certain cases he has been held to have authority to direct the manner of doing the work. Where the specifications are ambiguous, he has authority to determine what materials shall be used.

In the absence of specific elaboration of the architect's or engineer's power in the contract of employment, the principle universally applied is that he is an agent with limited authority. Thus, where he is employed to supervise construction, his authority and duty are confined to seeing that the work is done in accordance with the plans and specifications agreed upon. However, such express powers as the architect or engineer is given in addition to the authority to superintend construction must be given a strict interpretation. Thus, an architect who is told to "get other bids" has no implied authority to enter into a contract for performance of the work. An authority conferred on the superintending architect to demand the removal of undesirable workmen does not empower him to require that non-union men be discharged. He has a right to discharge only those workmen who are incompetent or refuse to work in harmony with the other workmen on the project.

A provision in the contract that the contractor shall furnish all materials and perform all the work under the direction and to the satisfaction of the architect generally goes no further than to make the architect the agent of the owner in deciding whether the work done fulfills the requirements of the specifications and drawings. Such a stipulation does not include the power to direct the manner in which the work is to be done or the time when it is to be done.

In supervising construction the architect or engineer has no power to approve a material departure from the plans of a building. He may not accept a class of work or material inferior to or different from that called for by the contract. He cannot relieve the contractor from complying with his undertaking in order to make it easier for him, or for any other purpose that might be detrimental to the owner. Further, he has no authority to change materials used in the construction although the materials provided by the contract may be difficult to obtain and consequently lead to delaying construction.

It is a well established rule that the architect has no authority to vary the terms of the contract or create new obligations binding on the owner. Contracts with respect to the work done or materials furnished are included in this prohibition. He is not authorized to increase the owner's liability by promising subcontractors that they will be paid when the principal contractor is found to be in financial difficulties.

The architect cannot substitute a subcontractor for the principal contractor, after his failure to perform or make changes in the method of payment for construction work. Further, the architect has no authority over the employment of workmen or their payment except where he is so authorized by his client. As a limited agent, he generally has no authority to receive notice of liens for his employer.

Stipulations commonly inserted in construction contracts provide that no extra work or alteration shall be performed by the contractor without a written order therefor by the architect or engineer. These are intended to protect the owner against unwarranted claims or unfair charges and are uniformly upheld. An architect or engineer who waives such provisions or alters their terms is deemed to exceed his authority.

Any contractor who relies on the architect's oral assurance that he will be paid for such extra work will not be permitted to recover for it without a written order. It has been held that such a contract provision is fully complied with if at any time during the progress of the work, the architect gives the written order after first approving and ordering it. However, a written approval of the contractor's bill for extra cost after the installation of extras has been held insufficient since it was the intention of the parties that the work be approved before it is undertaken by any of the parties.

Stipulations in contracts with public authorities which require that alterations or additions are to be specified in writing are likewise upheld; the strict observance of these is required for the protection of the public. Where an oral order for extras is made by a governmental officer, architect or engineer, it is generally held to be insufficient to bind the public body to pay for such extras.

There is a conflict in the decisions as to whether a plan or drawing of the proposed alteration or extra work constitutes an "order in writing" within the meaning of the contract. One line of authorities holds that it does not meet the requirement, while another line of cases takes the position that if the plans and drawings are complete and definite enough, they sufficiently meet the requirement.

If an architect or engineer exceeds the limits of his authority, his unauthorized acts may be ratified by his employer either expressly or by implication. But where subsequent ratification of the principal is sought to be established, it must be shown that the principal had knowledge of all the material facts. The owner who permits the architect to exceed his powers without objecting or calling the attention of the third party to his lack of authority, will be bound by the agent's acts.

AN ARCHITECT OR ENGINEER ACTS AS THE GENERAL AGENT of the employer only when he is vested with such authority, or is put in the position of having apparent authority.

Cal. *Hornlein v. Bohlig*, 37 Cal. App. 646, 174 Pac. 697 (1918). Architect held agent of owner for purposes of lien law.

Mo.   *Fairbanks, Morse & Co. v. Merchants' & Consumers' Market House Ass'n*, 199 Mo. App. 317, 202 S.W. 596 (1918). Although in general an owner is not liable for the architect's failure to return guaranty checks on rejection of bids, it may be shown that the architect was acting for the owner in such a way as to bind him.

N.Y.   *Thomas v. Stewart*, 132 N.Y. 580, 30 N.E. 577 (1892). Employer found to have constituted an architect his agent for all purposes connected with the erection of the building.

Pa.   *American Mailing Device Corp. v. Widener*, 260 Pa. 375, 103 Atl. 875 (1918). One claiming rights under construction contract made with architect has burden of proving architect had authority to make such contract.

Howard P. Foley v. Barnett, 303 Pa. 218, 154 Atl. 391 (1931). Where one, employed as lodge's supervising contractor and agent to supervise work on theatre, was placed in apparent position of authorized agent to place orders and direct work as general agent, lodge was liable for services and materials ordered by him.

Wash.   *Union High School Dist. v. Pacific Northwest Constr. Co.*, 148 Wash. 594, 269 Pac. 809 (1928). Delegation of authority to architect to represent school board in construction of building was not complete surrender of all powers of board and it could waive provisions in contract with builder made for its benefit.

IN CERTAIN CASES THE ARCHITECT OR ENGINEER has been termed an independent contractor for whose negligence the employer is not liable to third persons if he has exercised reasonable care in selecting the architect or engineer.

Ala.   *Looker v. Gulf Coast Fair*, 203 Ala. 42, 81 So. 832 (1919). Owner sued by employee of contractor for injuries sustained by collapse of partially completed grandstand on ground he negligently accepted defective plans of architect held not liable where he employed competent architect to prepare plans and there was nothing to put him on notice that plans were defective.

Cal.   *Boswell v. Laird*, 8 Cal. 469, 68 Am. Dec. 345 (1857). Contractors, and not employers, are liable for injuries caused by bursting of dam before its completion and acceptance by employers where contractors are also skilled architects and undertake to execute entire work, as well as plans, and no control or supervision is exercised by employers.

N.Y.   *Uggla v. Brokaw*, 117 App. Div. 586, 102 N.Y.S. 857 (1907). It is a good defense in an action against the owner of a building for injury to a third person caused by portion of roof to building blown into street during windstorm, that preparation of plans for building had been delegated to skilled architect and workmen and owner relied on the skill of such persons.

Burke v. Ireland, 166 N.Y. 305, 59 N.E. 914 (1901). Architect in supervising construction of building was not agent or servant of owner but exercised an independent calling and his personal negligence in supervising construction could not be imputed to owner.

Fox v. Ireland, 46 App. Div. 541, 61 N.Y.S. 1061 (1900). When building falls by reason of defective foundation injuring workman, owner to be relieved of liability must show architect was skilled and competent and owner relied on him both for plans and supervision and did not interfere with him in the discharge of his duties.

Pa.   *Mackay v. Benjamin Franklin Realty & Holding Co.*, 288 Pa. 207, 135 Atl. 613 (1927). Where architect in preparing plans, misappropriates the ideas or plans of another architect, his employer is not responsible since the architect is an independent contractor and has no power to obligate the owner.

Tex.   *Hamblen v. Mohr*, 171 S.W. 2d 168 (1943). Where owner employed reputable architect to draft plans for department store and to supervise its construction, and had employed reputable contractor to construct it, he was not liable to third person for injuries sustained in falling on stairs which did not provide reasonably safe footing for ordinary person.

McDaniel v. City of Beaumont, 92 S.W. 2d 552 (1936). Architect is not agent of owner so as to impose liability on owner for extra costs caused by contractor by his acts where architect was agent of owner only to extent provided in contract documents.

White v. Green, 82 S.W. 329 (1904). Owner of building is not liable for injury to property of another through its fall caused by defects in plans and specifications of architect, where architect and builder were independent contractors, owner used ordinary care in their selection, and their negligence was not such as owner by ordinary care could have known.

WHERE THE ARCHITECT OR ENGINEER ACTS AS THE AGENT of the owner, or where an absolute duty is imposed on the owner to protect third persons or where control over construction is retained by owner, the owner is liable for negligence of the architect or engineer acting within the scope of his employment.

Ala.   *Campbell v. Lunsford*, 83 Ala. 512, 3 So. 522 1888). Owner is responsible for negligent supervision of architect where architect is subject to control of owner notwithstanding discretion given to architect in directing manner of doing work.

Ill.   *Claffy v. Chicago Dock & Canal Co.*, 249 Ill. 210, 94 N.E. 551 (1911). Architect acting as owner's agent in supervising construction bound owner by his acts in failing to comply with statutory requirement for inclosing elevator shafts used in construction of building.

Iowa   *Mortrude v. Martin,* 185 Iowa 1319, 172 N.W. 17 (1919). Where firm of architects and engineers employed by owner to supervise construction of building are negligent while acting within the scope of their employment, the owner is liable.

Manton v. H. L. Stevens & Co., 170 Iowa 495, 153 N.W. 87 (1915). Where architects prepared plans and entered into subcontracts for materials and labor and owner paid workmen on approval of architects, architects were not independent contractors and owner was responsible for not providing workmen safe place to work.

Connolly v. Des Moines Invest. Co., 130 Iowa 633, 105 N.W. 400 (1905). The duty of exercising reasonable care for safety of the public is an absolute duty resting on owner and he cannot escape responsibility by delegating to architect duty to inspect building, even though he uses care in selection of architect.

Mass.   *Morgan v. Burlington,* 316 Mass. 413, 55 N.E. 2d 758 (1944). Architect held town's agent so as to render town liable to contractor for damages caused by architect's unreasonable delay in drafting plans and by architect's unauthorized decision to let the contract for installation of a new drainage system on bids to another contractor.

Mo.   *Fairbanks, Morse & Co. v. Merchants' & Consumers' Market House Ass'n,* 199 Mo. App. 317, 202 S.W. 596 (1918). Although owner is not generally liable for architect's failure to return guaranty checks on rejection of bids, it may be shown that architect was acting in such a way as to bind owner.

Neb.   *Erskine v. Johnson,* 23 Neb. 261, 36 N.W. 510 (1888). The owner is liable to the contractor for the increased cost of the project incurred by charges owing to mistake in architect's plans.

W.Va.   *Voeckler v. Stroehmann's Vienna Bakery,* 75 W.Va. 384, 83 S.E. 1025 (1914). Though owner, in improving his property, employs competent architect and skilled contractor, if work remains in his control he cannot escape liability for injury to adjoining property caused by their negligence.

U.S.   *Hudgins v. Hann,* 240 Fed. 387 (1917). Though architect employed to supervise work is an independent contractor, employer will be liable for his negligence where he has absolute duty to so use his property as not to injure another.

SINCE THE EMPLOYMENT OF AN ARCHITECT or engineer is based upon the trust and confidence placed in his personal integrity and skill, he cannot delegate his authority or assign his contract to another unless the employer consents to such delegation or assignment.

Cal. *American Trust Co. v. Coryell*, 3 Cal. 2d 151, 43 P. 2d 1102 (1935). Engineer may delegate some of work of supervision to qualified subordinates without being guilty of fraud against owner, especially where he is frequently at place of work.

Conn. *Johnson & Burns Inc. v. Hayden*, 98 Conn. 185, 119 Atl. 50 (1922). Contract for architectural services is a personal one and undelegable, entire and indivisible.

Ill. *Monahan v. Fitzgerald*, 164 Ill. 525, 45 N.E. 1013 (1897). Where by contract work is to be done under immediate supervision of architect and payments to be made on architect's certificate, owner is not bound by certificates issued in the absence of architect, by one to whom he attempted to delegate his authority.

Ind. *Weatherhogg v. Board of Comm'rs of Jasper County*, 158 Ind. 14, 62 N.E. 477 (1902). Where County Commissioners employed architect to prepare plans and thereafter consented to his transfer of contract to another, they could not thereafter object that contract was unassignable because one of trust and confidence.

Kan. *Smith v. Board of Educ. of Liberal*, 115 Kan. 155, 222 Pac. 101 (1924). Contract for professional services of firm of two architects is contract for personal services requiring special knowledge, skill, and taste, and involving element of personal confidence, and change in personnel in firm whereby one of architects is not available renders employment contract unenforceable.

THE SPECIFIC AUTHORITY DELEGATED to the architect or engineer includes by implication all incidental authority to accomplish the specified purpose.

Ala. *Lafayette Ry. Co. v. Tucker*, 124 Ala. 514, 27 So. 447 (1900). Where civil engineer, superintending construction of railroad, has no actual authority to contract for extra work, such action may fall within his implied authority.

Ind. *Gibson County v. Motherwell Iron & Steel Co.*, 123 Ind. 364, 24 N.E. 115 (1890). Where County Commissioners gave architect full supervision of construction, and he ordered a change in the work without complying with terms of contract, Commissioners were held liable for price of extra work.

Ky.   *Nick Warisse Baking Co. v. National Concrete Constr. Co.*, 218 Ky. 422, 291 S.W. 356 (1927). Evidence held to support finding that supervising architect was authorized to make changes in the contract for construction.

Mass.   *Dahlstrom Metallic Door Co. v. Evatt Constr. Co.*, 256 Mass. 404, 152 N.E. 715 (1926). Architect's authority to make changes in the work with the approval of the owner authorizes him to require the contractor to omit elevator doors and fronts.

N.J.   *Drummond v. Hughes*, 91 N.J.L. 563, 104 Atl. 137 (1918). Where building contract required contractor to remove material condemned by the architect, specifications calling for an approved brand of lime, contemplated a brand approved by the architect.

Tex.   *Hewitt v. Buchanan*, 4 S.W. 2d 169 (1927). Where building contract empowers architect to determine what was proper workmanship and fit material, his directions as to manner of doing the work and his approval as to the material used, are binding on the owner.

Buchanan & Gilder v. Gibbs, 156 S.W. 914 (1913). A provision in a building contract that wainscoting, lavatories, and stairs, when shown, should be of marble authorizes the architect to require marble wainscoting in the basement.

Wash.   *Stimson Mill Co. v. Feigenson Engineering Co.*, 100 Wash. 172, 170 Pac. 573 (1918). Superintending architect has implied authority to reject unfit materials.

EXPRESS POWERS GIVEN TO THE ARCHITECT or engineer, have been given limited interpretation. It has been held that their authority does not extend beyond matters necessarily implied from the duty to prepare plans or superintend construction.

Cal.   *Albert Steinfeld & Co. v. Broxhlome*, 59 Cal. App. 623, 211 Pac. 473 (1922). Architect who was told "to get other bids" for certain work to be done was not authorized to enter into contract for such work.

D.C.   *Fontano v. Robbins*, 22 App. D.C. 253 (1903). Provision that contractor will provide materials and perform work under direction of and to satisfaction of architect means only supervision according to terms of contract and does not permit architect to change plans of work.

Ga.   *Cannon v. Hunt*, 113 Ga. 501, 38 S.E. 983 (1901). Where work of contractor is by contract "under the personal and direct supervision" of named person, owner's right to have contract complied with is not affected by agent's acceptance of class of work and material different from that named in contract.

Mass.   *Leverone v. Arancio,* 179 Mass. 439, 61 N.E. 45 (1901). Provision that contractor shall provide material and labor under direction and to satisfaction of architect acting as agent of owner makes architect agent of owner in matter of deciding whether work done fulfilled requirements of specifications and drawings, and he cannot waive any condition of contract.

Mo.   *Burke v. Kansas City,* 34 Mo. App. 570 (1889). Where contract provided that pipe was to be placed according to directions of city engineer, it did not authorize him to change depth at which pipe was to be placed but merely to give directions to have work completed according to plans and specifications.
Lewis v. Slack, 27 Mo. App. 119 (1887). Architect employed to supervise construction had no authority to supervise letting of subcontracts and employment of men.

N.Y.   *Slater v. Mersereau,* 64 N.Y. 138 (1876). Provision requiring work to be done to satisfaction and under direction of architect contemplated direction simply as to fitness of materials and manner in which work was done, not as to time in which it should be done.

Ore.   *Hayden v. City of Astoria,* 74 Ore. 525, 145 Pac. 1072 (1915). Power of engineer under contract permitting him to increase or diminish quantity of work to be done, in his discretion, is limited to such changes as are within contemplation of parties at time contract is made.

Pa.   *American Mailing Devise Corp. v. Widener,* 260 Pa. 375, 103 Atl. 875 (1918). Powers ordinarily given supervising architect do not include power to contract for installation of mail chutes in building.

Tex.   *Funk v. House,* 168 S.W. 481 (1914). Contract providing owner could retain a percentage of sum due contractor on contractor's failure to complete building, and if necessary apply it in liquidating damages under direction of architect, did not make architect the arbiter of damages due under contract, but implied that if owner completed building, completion should be under direction of architect and damages determined by amount required to complete it.

Wash.   *Columbia Security Co. v. Aetna Accident & Liability Co.,* 108 Wash. 116, 183 Pac. 137 (1919). Authority given architect to interpret plans and specifications and condemn material as unsound did not empower him to recast drawings and specifications upon a matter already clear, thereby increasing total cost of building.

U.S.   *Gerhard Bldg. Co. v. Dallas,* 298 Fed. 264 (1924). Contract
authorizing architect to require removal of undesirable workmen
does not permit him to demand removal of non-union men.

THE ARCHITECT OR ENGINEER SUPERVISING construction of a building has
no power to approve a material departure from the plans as to design,
workmanship, or materials.

N.Y.   *People v. Lewis,* 159 App. Div. 612, 145 N.Y.S. 862 (1913).
Architect employed by individual owner for erection of building
has not, by virtue of his employment, authority to consent to
change or substitution of materials.

W.Va.   *Smith v. Board of Educ. of Parkersburg,* 76 W.Va. 239, 85
S.E. 513 (1915). Architect supervising construction had no authority to change plans and dispense with vitrolite wainscoting
shown on drawings without consent of owner.

U.S.   *United States v. Walsh,* 115 Fed. 697 (1902). Engineers could
not bind government by consenting to deviation from requirements
of specifications.

THE ARCHITECT OR ENGINEER HAS NO AUTHORITY to waive or vary the terms
of the contract or create new obligations binding on the owner with
respect to the work done or materials furnished.

Conn.   *Starkweather v. Goodman,* 48 Conn. 101, 40 Am. Rep. 152
(1880). Architect employed to supervise construction may not
change the plans and specifications by ordering extra work.

Ill.   *Campbell v. Day,* 90 Ill. 363 (1878). Architect employed to supervise work done by contractor has no authority to employ another
to do work on building which contractor has undertaken to do.
Bouton v. McDonough County, 84 Ill. 384 (1877). Action of supervising architects in making arrangement under which subcontractor was to continue work, after contractor's bankruptcy and
abandonment of work, and to receive payment directly from county
held not binding on county because architects had no authority to
vary terms of agreement in any respect.

Ind.   *Wm. R. Jungclaus Co. v. Ratti,* 67 Ind. App. 84, 118 N.E. 966
(1918). Architect has no power to waive provision of contract requiring that extension of time for contractor to complete work
must be granted on contractor's written request for such extension.

Kan.   *Cuthbert v. Rickey,* 119 Kan. 233, 237 Pac. 883 (1925). Architect had no authority to substitute subcontractor for principal
contractor either in performance or payment of work.

Ky. *Watts v. Metcalf,* 23 Ky. L.R. 2189, 66 S.W. 824 (1902). Architect, being owner's agent to see that contract with builder was performed, had no authority to alter contract or make new one, and therefore could not bind owner by contract to pay subcontractor.

La. *Hatchitoches Motor Co. v. Campbell,* 17 La. App. 425, 136 So. 133 (1931). Assistant engineer of contractor had no authority to bind contractor by accepting order without express authority.

Mass. *Morgan v. Town of Burlington,* 316 Mass. 413, 55 N.E. 2d 758 (1944). Under contract authorizing architect to change plans on discovering subsoil required revision in drainage system, architect's decision to let contract for installation of new drainage system on bids to another than building contractor not binding on town or contractor.

Gaffey v. United Shoe Machinery Co., 202 Mass. 48, 88 N.E. 330 (1909). A contract authorizing the engineer to change the grade at which a ledge is to be levelled does not authorize him to change the grade to an impracticable level so as to abrogate the contract, but only to make such reasonable changes as will render the removal of the ledge more satisfactory to the owner.

Mich. *Harrigan & Reid Co. v. Hudson,* 291 Mich. 478, 289 N.W. 222 (1939). Architect rendering general architectural services in construction of house did not have authority to bind employer to pay plumbing and heating concern for services and materials furnished in construction of house.

Finnigan v. Worden-Allen Co., 201 Mich. 445, 167 N.W. 930 (1918). Practice of engineer in measuring value of work performed which he claimed to be a practical construction of the contract cannot affect subcontractor's right to payment under the contract where there is no ambiguity and therefore no question of construction involved.

Miss. *Union Indemnity Co. v. Acme Blow Pipe & Sheet Metal Works,* 150 Miss., 332, 117 So. 251 (1928). Architect's agreement with materialmen to withhold funds due principal contractor to amount of their claims held not binding on employer.

N.Y. *Dillon v. Syracuse,* 5 Silv. Cup. Ct. 575, 9 N.Y.S. 98 (1890). Engineer had no authority to give contractors stone owned by city where contract provided certain sum for stone used by contractors should be allowed by engineer and deducted from their account.

Pa. *Reifsnyder v. Dougherty,* 301 Pa. 328, 152 Atl. 98 (1930). Architect cannot impose on principal additional liability of paying subcontractors unless he had specific authority to do so.

Tenn.   *Alexander v. Grenada Bank*, 2 Tenn. App. 580 (1926). Person
employed as architect is not entitled to change, alter, or modify
contract entered into by builder and his employer or bind owner
by contracts for any work done or materials furnished for structures concerning which he is employed.

Tex.   *J. Kennard & Sons Carpet Co. v. Houston Hotel Ass'n*, 197 S.W.
1139 (1917). Architect had no authority to purchase for owner
hotel fixtures which were not in accordance with or called for by
contract.

Danovant v. Taylor, 40 S.W. 326 (1897). Where owner authorizes
architect to let contract for sanding job and owner pays price for
sanding, third person with whom architect thereafter makes contract and who does sanding cannot recover from owner.

Wash.   *Schanen-Blair Co. Marble & G. Works v. Sisters of Charity*,
77 Wash. 256, 137 Pac. 468 (1914). Supervising architect has no
authority to bind owner by statement to subcontractor that he
would lose no legal remedy if subcontract was performed with
principal contractor on latter's default.

W.Va.   *Charleston Lumber Co. v. Friedman*, 64 W.Va. 151, 61 S.E.
815 (1908). Architect has no authority to waive contract provision
making contractor liable to owner for liquidated damages if work
is not completed at certain date, and extension of time is not
secured on written certificate of architect.

Wis.   *Dodge v. McDonnell*, 14 Wis. 600 (1861). Where architect is
employed to perform usual architectural services and is given
money to be paid to contractor when due, he is not general agent
of owner so as to bind him by new contracts with other persons
for materials furnished.

U.S.   *Davies v. Kahn*, 251 F. 2d 324 (4th Cr. 1958).

AN ARCHITECT GENERALLY HAS NO AUTHORITY to receive notice of liens or
assignments on behalf of the owner.

Cal.   *Renton v. Monnier*, 77 Cal. 449, 19 Pac. 820 (1888). Architect
employed to perform usual architectural services has no authority
to accept notice of assignment of payments due under building
contract so as to charge owner with notice thereof.

Tex.   *Burns & Hamilton Co. v. Denver Inv. Co.*, 217 S.W. 719 (1919).
Architect has no authority to receive notice on behalf of owner of
materials furnished in absence of express or implied authority to
that effect.

Wash.   *Ellis-Mylroie Lumber Co. v. St. Luke's Hospital*, 119 Wash.
142, 205 Pac. 398 (1922). Notice of intention to claim lien ad-

dressed to owner in care of architect is sufficient where architect received notice and delivered it to owner's president.

Wis. *Bates Expanded Steel Truss Co. v. Sisters of Mercy of Janesville,* 208 Wis. 457, 243 N.W. 456 (1932). Architect as special agent of owner is not authorized to receive notice of intention to claim mechanic's lien.

WHERE A BUILDING CONTRACT PROVIDES that no extra work or alterations shall be performed by the contractor without a written order therefor by the architect, engineer, or other designated agent, an architect or engineer who attempts to waive such provision or alter its terms exceeds his authority, and his action does not bind the owner to pay for such work.

(a) Private Contracts

Cal. See *Bavin & Burch Co. v. Bard,* 81 Cal. App. 733, 255 Pac. 200 (1927).

Gray v. La Societe Francaise de Bienfaisance Mutuelle, 131 Cal. 566, 63 Pac. 848 (1901).

See *White v. San Rafael & S.K.R. Co.,* 50 Cal. 417 (1875).

Wilson v. Keefe, 150 Cal. App. 2d 178, 309 P. 2d 516 (1957).

Iowa *Iowa Electric Light & Power Co. v. Hopp,* 221 Iowa 680, 266 N.W. 512 (1936).

Des Moines Plumbing and Heating Co. v. Magarian, 201 Iowa 647, 207 N.W. 750 (1926).

Benson & Marxer v. Brown, 190 Iowa 848, 179 N.W. 81 (1921).

Volquardsen v. Davenport Hospital, 161 Iowa 706, 141 N.W. 432 (1913).

Chicago Lumber & Coal Co. v. Garner, 132 Iowa 282, 109 N.W. 780 (1906).

Md. *McNulty v. Keyser Office Bldg. Co.,* 112 Md. 638, 76 Atl. 1113 (1910).

Baltimore Cemetery Co. v. Coburn, 7 Md. 202 (1854).

Mass. *Crane Constr. Co. v. Commonwealth,* 290 Mass. 249, 195 N.E. 110 (1935).

Burns v. Thorndike, 228 Mass. 552, 117 N.E. 799 (1917).

Mo. See *Hunt v. Owen Bldg. & Inv. Co.,* 219 S. W. 138 (1920).

Neb. *Carter v. Root, Inc.,* 84 Neb. 723, 121 N.W. 952 (1909).

But see *Erskine v. Johnson,* 23 Neb. 261, 36 N.W. 510 (1888). Architect could bind owner by oral order necessitated by his own mistake in plans and specifications.

N.Y. *National Bank v. City of Watervliet,* 97 Misc. 121, 160 N.Y.S. 1072 (1916), *aff'd,* 178 App. Div. 944, 164 N.Y.S. 1103 (1917).

Traitel Marble Co. v. Brown Bros., Inc., 159 App. Div. 485, 144 N.Y.S. 562 (1913).

Kelly v. St. Michael's Roman Catholic Church, 148 App. Div. 767, 133 N.Y.S. 328 (1912).

L'Homme dieu v. Winthrop, 59 App. Div. 192, 69 N.Y.S. 381 (1901); *Langley v. Rouss,* 185 N.Y. 201, 77 N.E. 1168 (1906).

Ohio   *Baltimore & O.R. Co. v. Jolly Bros. & Co.,* 71 Ohio St. 92, 72 N.E. 888 (1904).

Okla.   See *Hunt v. Tulsa Terrazzo & Mosaic Co.,* 157 Okla. 174, 11 P. 2d 521 (1932). Waiver of stipulation by owner.

Pa.   *Gillison v. Wanamaker,* 140 Pa. 358, 21 Atl. 361 (1891).

Tenn.   *Bannon v. Jackson,* 121 Tenn. 381, 117 S.W. 504 (1891).

Utah   *Salzner v. Jos. J. Snell Estate Corp.,* 81 Utah 111, 16 P. 2d 823 (1932). Contract provision forbidding alterations in work without art architect's order stating the amount payable by the owner was held inapplicable to contractor's extra work necessitated by new plans and specifications complying with city building inspector's requirements.

Vt.   *Wanderwerker v. Vermont C.R. Co.,* 27 Vt. 130 (1854).

Wis.   See *McGrath Constr. Co. v. Waupaca-Green Bay R. Co.,* 148 Wis. 372, 134 N.W. 824 (1912). Where stipulation was deemed waived.

U.S.   *Baton Rouge v. Robinson,* 127 F. 2d 693 (1942).

Coal & Iron R. Co. v. Reherd, 204 Fed. 859, *cert. den.,* 231 U.S. 745 (1913).

Cf. *Sartoris v. Utah Constr. Co.,* 21 F. 2d 1 (1927), *cert. den.,* 278 U.S. 651 (1929).

But see *Jefferson Hotel Co. v. Brumbaugh,* 168 Fed. 867 (1909). Architects held to be agents of company with power to waive stipulation.

(b) Public Contracts

Cal.   *Contra Costa Constr. Co. v. Daly City,* 48 Cal. App. 622, 192 Pac. 178 (1920).

J. M. Griffith Co. v. Los Angeles, 54 Pac. 383 (1898).

Ga.   *Heard v. Dooley County,* 101 Ga. 619, 28 S.E. 986 (1897).

Ill.   *Joliet Bridge & Iron Co. v. East Side Levee & Sanitary Dist.,* 210 Ill. App. 575 (1918).

Ind.   See *Alsmeier v. Adams,* 62 Ind. App. 219, 105 N.E. 1033 (1914). Ratification by owner of unauthorized order changing method of construction.

Kan.   *Dolman v. Kingman County,* 116 Kan. 201, 226 Pac. 240 (1924).

La.   *O'Leary v. New Orleans,* 150 La. 649, 91 So. 139 (1921).

Mass.   *Millen v. Boston,* 217 Mass. 471, 105 N.E. 453 (1914); *Stuart v. Cambridge,* 125 Mass. 102 (1878).

Mich.   See *Schneider v. Ann Arbor,* 195 Mich. 559, 962 N.W. 110 (1917); *Rens v. Grand Rapids,* 73 Mich. 237, 41 N.W. 263 (1889); But cf. *Moran v. Schmitt,* 109 Mich. 282, 67 N.W. 323 (1896).

N.J.   *Van Buskirk v. Board of Educ. of Passaic Tp.,* 78 N.J.L. 650, 75 Atl. 909 (1910).

N.Y.   *Stanton v. State,* 103 Misc. 221, 175 N.Y.S. 568 (1918); *People v. Snedeker,* 106 App. Div. 89, 94 N.Y.S. 319, *aff'd,* 182 N.Y. 558, 75 N.E. 1133 (1905); see *O'Brien v. New York,* 139 N.Y. 543, 35 N.E. 323 (1893); and *Abells v. Syracuse,* 7 App. Div. 501, 40 N.Y.S. 233 (1896).

Okla.   *State Highway Comm'n v. Green-Boots Constr. Co.,* 199 Okla. 477, 187 P. 2d 209 (1947).

Pa.   But see *Stewart v. Pennsylvania State Sons of America,* 122 Pa. Super. 30, 184 Atl. 476 (1936). Owner bound by changes ordered by architect in work required under contract or necessary thereto. See also *Willis Bancroft, Inc. v. Millcreek Tp.,* 235 Pa. 529, 6 A. 2d 916 (1939).

  Gibbs v. School Dist. of Girardville, 195 Pa. 396, 46 Atl. 91 (1900).

Utah   *Campbell Bldg. Co. v. State Road Comm'n,* 95 Utah 242, 70 P. 2d 857 (1937).

Wash.   *Ambaum v. State,* 80 Wash. 122, 141 Pac. 314 (1914).

Wis.   Cf. *First Savings & Trust Co. v. Milwaukee County,* 158 Wis. 207, 148 N.W. 22 (1914). Waiver of provision requiring written order.

THERE IS A CONFLICT IN THE CASES as to whether a plan or drawing of the proposed alteration or extra work constitutes a sufficient compliance with the stipulation in a contract requiring an "order in writing" for such extra work or alterations.

(a) A plan or drawing of the proposed alteration held not to constitute an "order in writing."

N.J.   *Condon v. Jersey City,* 43 N.J.L. 452 (1881).

N.Y.   *Fetterolf v. S. & L. Constr. Co.,* 175 App. Div. 177, 161 N.Y.S. 549 (1916).

U.S.   *McIntyre v. United States,* 52 Ct. Cl. 503 (1917).

(b) A plan or drawing of the proposed alteration held sufficient to meet the requirement of an "order in writing."

Kan.   *Lantry Contracting Co. v. Atchison, T. & S.F. R. Co.,* 102 Kan. 799, 172 Pac. 527 (1918).

Ohio   *Expanded Metal Fireproofing Co. v. Noel Constr. Co.,* 78 Ohio
       St. 428, 101 N.E. 348 (1913).
U.S.   *Sartoris v. Utah Constr. Co.,* 21 F. 2d 1 (1927), *cert. den.,* 278
       U.S. 651 (1929).

THE EMPLOYER WILL BE BOUND BY THE UNAUTHORIZED acts of the architect
or engineer if they are ratified by him, or are done within the apparent
scope of the agent's authority.
   Ala.   *Lafayette R. Co. v. Tucker,* 124 Ala. 514, 27 So. 447 (1900). En-
          gineer, who surveyed and staked out route of railroad and who
          personally supervised construction of road with authority to change
          and modify grade, may bind company to pay for extra work, al-
          though not expressly authorized to do this, where such acts are
          within his apparent authority.
   Cal.   *Albert Steinfeld & Co. v. Broxholme,* 59 Cal. App. 623, 211 Pac.
          473 (1922). Owner cannot enforce contract entered into without
          his authority by architect and contractor where contractor with-
          drew from it prior to owner's ratification of such contract.
   Ga.   *Employer's Liab. Assurance Corp. v. Sheftell,* 97 Ga. App. 398,
          103 S.E. 2d 143 (1958). The ratification of a number of changes
          in plans by the architect was held to create apparent authority
          for the latter to bind the principal to a price above that stipulated
          in the contract.
   Ind.   *Gibson County v. Motherwell Iron & Steel Co.,* 123 Ind. 364, 24
          N.E. 115 (1890). Where commissioners gave architect full super-
          vision of construction they were bound to pay for extra work
          ordered by architect after acceptance of building by them, though
          cost of such changes was not reduced to writing as provided in
          the contract.
   Iowa   *Birdsall v. Perry Gas Works,* 181 Iowa 1268, 161 N.W. 304
          (1917). Where building contract required use of brick "picked for
          evenness of color," and owner's manager saw brick used without
          objecting and architect approved the brick, the owner was es-
          topped to rely on non-compliance with specifications as to even-
          ness of color.
   N.Y.   *Hall v. Whitney,* 165 N.Y.S. 838 (1917). The fact that architects
          bought and paid for a saluting gun for their employer's yacht
          showed no real or apparent authority in architects to exchange
          gun for one costing five times as much, and employer did not
          ratify purchase by failing to return gun or personally notifying
          seller because the architects notified seller in a few days that em-
          ployer didn't want it.

Woodruff v. Rochester & P. R. Co., 108 N.Y. 39, 14 N.E. 832 (1888). Acceptance of road by railroad after its completion did not amount to ratification of contract for extra work entered into by supervising architect unless railroad had knowledge of such contract.

Ore. *Davis v. Bush & Lane Piano Co.*, 124 Ore. 585, 265 Pac. 417 (1928). Where owner of building knew that architect was supervising alterations and repair work and made no objection and did not call contractor's attention to architect's lack of authority, he was bound by acts of the architect done within apparent scope of his authority.

Wash. *Sando v. Kalberg*, 138 Wash. 247, 244 Pac. 576 (1926). Owners who directed contractors to negotiate with architect for building contract and who failed to object promptly to architect's modification of proposed contract by provision for extra work were held to have ratified his acts.

Wis. *Dodge v. McDonnell*, 14 Wis. 600 (1861). Where agency is to be proved by subsequent ratification of principal, there must be evidence of knowledge on part of principal of all material facts.

CHAPTER ELEVEN

Relationship to owner

A principal-agent relationship exists between owner and architect or engineer imposing upon the architect or engineer a fiduciary duty to the owner.

Since an architect or engineer generally acts in the capacity of agent, the relationship created between him and the owner is one of trust and confidence. Good faith and loyalty are the primary obligations imposed upon the architect or engineer in the transaction of business entrusted to him. It is his duty to make a full disclosure of all matters upon which he has information which it is desirable or important for his principal to know. He should have no pecuniary interest in the performance of the contract, nor be in the employ of both the owner and builder, receiving compensation from both, unless the owner knows and consents to such employment.

Cal. *Palmer v. Brown,* 273 P. 2d 306, 316 (1954). "As a trusted agent of the owner, and to avoid conflict of loyalties, he should not 'at the same time be employed by the owner and the builder and receive pay from both, except with the knowledge and consent of the owner.'"

Ind. *Rice v. Caldwell,* 87 Ind. App. 616, 161 N.E. 651 (1928). Action of architect in advising owner who placed confidence in him to hire contractor with whom architect worked in collusion amounts to a fraud on the owner.

Me. *Lane v. Town of Harmony,* 112 Me. 25, 90 Atl. 546 (1914). Good faith should characterize management by architect of business entrusted to him.

Mich. *Zannoth v. Booth Radio Stations,* 333 Mich. 233, 52 N.W. 2d 678 (1952) where an architect was repeatedly requested to keep costs below a specified amount, it was improper for him to proceed in disregard thereof.

THE ARCHITECT OR ENGINEER OWES to his client a fiduciary duty to act loyally and in good faith.

Cal.   *Edward Barron Estate Co. v. Woodruff Co.,* 163 Cal. 561, 126 Pac. 351 (1912). Architect has duty to make full disclosure of all matters of which he has knowledge which it is desirable or important that the owner should learn.

Hall v. County of Los Angeles, 74 Cal. 502, 16 Pac. 313 (1888). If architect secures adoption of his plans through the advocacy of an agent who pretends to be an unbiased expert, his action is fraudulent and justifies employer in rescinding the contract.

Orlandi v. Gray, 125 Cal. 372, 58 Pac. 15 (1899). Architect may act as architect and subcontractor where owner has knowledge of such dual capacity and there is no fraud or deception.

Gate-Way, Inc. v. Wilson, 94 Cal. App. 2d 706, 211 P. 2d 311 (1949). In action to enjoin consulting engineer from disclosing trade secrets relating to patented process for coating metal objects, evidence sustained the finding that the engineer had not entered into an agreement to keep such process secret, and that such process was not in fact secret, but in the public domain.

Havens v. Donohue, 111 Cal. 297, 43 Pac. 962 (1896). Architect is under no duty to keep secret fact that owner intends to build a new building.

Mo.   *Atlee v. Fink,* 75 Mo. 100, 42 Am. Rep. 385 (1881). Where person employed to supervise erection of building for employer had secret arrangement with lumber dealer to pass upon accounts for materials for commission on sales made to employer through his influence, contract was void as tending to induce fraudulent conduct toward employer.

N.Y.   *Higgins v. G. Piel & Co.,* 208 App. Div. 729, 202 N.Y.S. 874 (1924). Architect who makes plans upon which owner makes a contract with builder is not liable to owner for remaining silent when builder gave his estimate of the cost, the owner at the time having no legal right to an opinion from the architect.

Wash.   *Taft v. Whitney Co.,* 85 Wash. 389, 148 Pac. 43 (1915). If approval or condemnation of work by architect is arbitrary, it amounts to constructive fraud on person injured.

PART FOUR

THE DECISION OR CERTIFICATE
OF THE ARCHITECT OR ENGINEER

CHAPTER TWELVE

When architect's or engineer's decision or certificate is final

Provisions in building contracts that the decision of the supervising architect or engineer with respect to execution of the work, and his estimate, certificate, or approval of performance of the contract shall be final and conclusive, are valid and will be sustained.

The parties to a building contract may stipulate that the decision of some third person, such as the architect or engineer, will be conclusive on all questions or disputes as to the execution of the work and satisfactory performance. Conclusiveness of the arbiter's determination will not be implied but it will be given that effect where it plainly appears that the parties intended that his determination of the sufficiency of performance be final and binding on all parties to the agreement.

The rights, powers, and duties of the arbiter under such stipulation are defined and limited by the contract, but an implied condition of the validity of any determination is that it be rendered without fraud or such gross neglect or mistake on his part as would necessarily imply bad faith or a failure to exercise an honest judgment. The reason underlying this rule is that under such stipulations the architect or engineer acts in the capacity of an arbitrator and his determination can be attacked only in the same manner as that of any other arbitrator.

Various forms of contract provisions are in use by which the architect or engineer is given the authority to make a final determination on one matter or another. The same principle of conclusiveness applies to all, however, viz., where the contract plainly indicates that his decision shall be final, such decision in the absence of fraud or mistake binds both parties to the contract. The contract may designate the architect or engineer the final arbiter of questions or disputes relating to its execution.

It may provide that the work shall be done to the satisfaction, approval, or acceptance of the architect or engineer and in such case he is constituted sole arbiter between the parties.

If the contract provides that the certificate or approval of the architect is a condition to payment, or that compensation shall be made upon estimates or certificates of the architect or engineer in charge of the work, such approval, estimates, or certificates are conclusive. Other stipulations under which the parties constitute the architect or engineer a final arbiter may authorize him to determine such questions as the amount, classification, sufficiency, price or completion of the work.

However, contract provisions making the architect the arbiter of disputes or permitting him to determine the price of extra work have been held invalid where, unknown to the contractor, the architect has guaranteed to keep the cost of the building below a certain sum. Under such circumstances, bias and prejudice on the part of the architect may be presumed to exist, particularly where the contractor has no knowledge of the guaranty made to the owner. The provisions designating the architect as a judge between the parties in such a situation are held invalid.

A clause sometimes included is one giving the owner the right to terminate the contract on certification by the architect that the contractor failed to supply sufficient workmen or materials, or failed to use due diligence to complete the work within the time specified. Whether alleged extra work is within the meaning of the plans and specifications is another matter upon which the arbiter often makes the final decision.

It may therefore be stated that most stipulations whereby the parties constitute the architect or engineer a final arbiter as to a matter relating to the execution of the contract are valid and make his decision conclusive.

The one state which does not recognize the rule that the decision of an architect or engineer can be made final by contract, is Indiana. In that jurisdiction the rule is that parties cannot, by an agreement in advance, deprive the courts of jurisdiction and make conclusive the estimate, certificate or decision of the arbiter. In Indiana any decision of the engineer or architect may be controverted, and at the instance of either party such determination will be reviewed by the court to ascertain its correctness. While the decision or estimate of the arbiter is not conclusive in that state it is regarded as prima facie correct, and the burden rests on the party seeking to impeach it to prove fraud or mistake.

WHERE AN ARCHITECT OR ENGINEER IS AUTHORIZED to make final and conclusive determinations on questions regarding the execution of a building contract his determination is binding on the parties in the absence of fraud or gross mistake.

Ariz.　*United States v. Ellis,* 2 Ariz. 253, 14 Pac. 300 (1887).

Ark.　*Trinity Universal Ins. Co. v. Willbanks,* 201 Ark. 386, 144 S.W. 2d 1092 (1940).

American Surety Co. v. Kinnear Mfg. Co., 185 Ark. 959, 50 S.W. 2d 586 (1932).

Boston Store v. Schleuter, 88 Ark. 213, 114 S.W. 242 (1908).

Carlile v. Corrigan, 83 Ark. 136, 103 S.W. 620 (1907).

Cal.　*Monson v. Fischer,* 118 Cal. App. 503, 5 P. 2d 628 (1931).

Brown v. Aguilar, 202 Cal. 143, 259 Pac. 735 (1927).

American-Hawaiian Eng. & Constr. Co. v. Butler, 165 Cal. 497, 133 Pac. 280 (1913).

Rialto Const. Co. v. Reed, 17 Cal. App. 29, 118 Pac. 473 (1911).

Haggenwood Sanitary Dist. v. Dawner Corp., 179 Cal. App. 2d 756, 3 Cal. Rptr. 873 (1960).

Colo.　*Platte Valley Ditch & Reservoir Co. v. H. C. Laltier Constr. & Eng. Co.,* 91 Colo. 317, 14 P. 2d 1079 (1932).

Dutton K. Co. v. Hoffman, 83 Colo. 305, 264 Pac. 1092 (1928).

Elliott v. Wolfer, 78 Colo. 213, 240 Pac. 694 (1925).

Ferguson v. Christensen, 59 Colo. 42, 147 Pac. 352 (1915).

Empson Packing Co. v. Clawson, 43 Colo. 188, 95 Pac. 546 (1908).

Conn.　*Beattie v. McMullen,* 82 Conn. 484, 74 Atl. 767 (1909).

Del.　*Crumlish v. Wilmington & W. R. Co.,* 5 Del. Ch. 270 (1879).

Ga.　*State Highway Dep't v. MacDougal Constr. Co.,* 189 Ga. 490, 6 S.E. 2d 570 (1939).

Morris v. Peachtree Heights Park Co., 38 Ga. App. 303, 143 S.E. 909 (1928).

Royal Indem. Co. v. Batson-Cook Co., 37 Ga. App. 797, 142 S.E. 210 (1928).

Green v. Jackson, 66 Ga. 250 (1880).

Idaho　*Nelson Bennett Co. v. Twin Falls Land & Water Co.,* 14 Idaho 5, 93 Pac. 789 (1908).

Ill.　*Cerny Pickas & Co. v. Dallch,* 249 Ill. App. 424 (1928).

Johnson v. Hogg, 202 Ill. App. 253 (1916).

B. J. Regnell Co. v. Meiswinkel, 191 Ill. App. 238 (1915).

Concord Apartment House Co. v. O'Brien, 228 Ill. 360, 81 N.E. 1038 (1907).

Iowa　*Granette Products Co. v. Arthur H. Newmann & Co.,* 208 Iowa 24, 221 N.W. 197 (1928).

Ross v. McArthur Bros., 85 Iowa 203, 52 N.W. 125 (1892).

Jemmison v. Gray, 29 Iowa 537 (1870).

Kan.   *Edwards v. Hartshorn,* 72 Kan. 19, 82 Pac. 520 (1905).

La.   *C. G. Kershaw Contracting Co. v. Crowley,* 149 So. 181 (1933).
American Heating & Plumbing Co. v. West End Country Club,
171 La. 482, 131 So. 466 (1930).
Fritz Jahncke v. Fidelity & Deposit Co., 166 La. 593, 117 So. 729
(1928).

Me.   *Kerr v. State,* 127 Me. 142 Atl. 197 (1928).

Md.   *Seventh Baptist Church v. Andrew & Thomas,* 115 Md. 535, 81
Atl. 1, 82 Atl. 452 (1911).

Mass.   *Hathaway v. Stone,* 215 Mass. 212, 102 N.E. 461 (1913).
C. W. Hunt Co. v. Boston Elev. Pr. Co., 199 Mass. 220, 85 N.E.
446 (1908).
White v. Abbott, 188 Mass. 99, 74 N.E. 305 (1905).
Norcross v. Wyman, 187 Mass. 25, 72 N.E. 347 (1905).

Mich.   *Banbrook-Gowan Co. v. Ainger Printing Co.,* 290 Mich. 95, 287
N.W. 392 (1939).

Minn.   *St. Paul & N. P. R. Co. v. Bradbury,* 42 Minn. 222, 44 N.W. 1
(1889).
Leighton v. Grant, 20 Minn. 345 (1874).

Miss.   *Mississippi Fire Ins. Co. v. Evans,* 153 Miss. 635, 120 So. 738
(1929).

Mo.   *United Constr. Co. v. St. Louis,* 334 Mo. 1006, 69 S.W. 2d 639
(1934).
Eldridge v. Fuhr, 59 Mo. App. 44 (1894).

Mont.   *Clifton, Applegate & Toole v. Big Lake Drain Dist.,* 82 Mont.
312, 267 Pac. 207 (1928).

Neb.   *Anderson v. Imhoff,* 34 Neb. 335, 51 N.W. 854 (1892).
Fuchs v. Parsons Const. Co., 111 N.W. 2d 727 (1961).

N.H.   *J. H. Ferguson Co. v. City of Keene,* 89 N.H. 410, 200 Atl. 396
(1938).

N.J.   *Landstra v. Bunn,* 81 N.J.L. 680, 80 Atl. 496 (1911).
Cf. Atlantic & Suburban R. Co. v. Atlantic County, 84 N.J. Eq.
618, 94 Atl. 602 (1915).

N.M.   *Odell v. Colmor Irrig. & Land Co.,* 34 N.M. 277, 280 Pac. 398
(1912).

N.Y.   *Elizabeth Sash, Door & Supply Co. v. St. Vincent's Hospital,*
241 App. Div. 751, 270 N.Y.S. 195 (1934).
Butts v. Randall, 145 Misc. 708, 260 N.Y.S. 713 (1932).
Chas. S. Wood & Co. v. Alvord & Swift, 232 App. Div. 603, 251
N.Y.S. 35 (1931), *aff'd,* 258 N.Y. 611, 180 N.E. 354 (1932).
Kuhs v. Flower City Tissue Mills Co., 104 Misc. 243, 171 N.Y.S.
688 (1918), *aff'd,* 189 App. Div. 539, 179 N.Y.S. 450 (1919).

Midtown Contracting Co. v. Goldsticker, 165 App. Div. 264, 150 N.Y.S. 809 (1914).

Neidlinger v. Onward Constr. Co., 44 Misc. 555, 90 N.Y.S. 115 (1904), *aff'd,* 107 App. Div. 398, 95 N.Y.S. 1148 (1905), *aff'd,* 188 N.Y. 572, 80 N.E. 1114 (1907).

Burke v. New York, 7 App. Div. 128, 40 N.Y.S. 81 (1896).

N.C.   *Shepard's Chemical Co. v. O'Brien,* 173 N.C. 618, 92 S.E. 594 (1917).

Ohio   *Cleveland v. Griffen,* 27 Ohio C.C. 167 (1904).

Okla.   *City of Lawton v. Sherman Machine & Iron Works,* 77 P. 2d 567 (1938).

Ore.   *Friberg v. Elrod,* 136 Ore. 186, 296 Pac. 1061 (1931).

Mayer v. East Side Logging Co., 130 Ore. 341, 278 Pac. 957 (1925).

Pa.   *Ruch v. York,* 233 Pa. 36, 81 Atl. 891 (1911).

Wiggins v. Columbian Fireproofing Co., 227 Pa. 511, 76 Atl. 742 (1910).

Conneaut Lake Agric'l Ass'n v. Pittsburgh Surety Co., 225 Pa. 592, 74 Atl. 620 (1909).

Brown v. Decker, 142 Pa. 640, 21 Atl. 903 (1891).

Drhew v. Altoona, 121 Pa. 401, 15 Atl. 636 (1888).

Tex.   *Uvalde Rock Asphalt Co. v. Fantham,* 210 S.W. 2d 646 (1948).

State v. Martin Bros., 138 Tex. 505, 160 S.W. 2d 58 (1942).

Neyland v. State, 151 S.W. 2d 331 (1941).

Austin Bridge Co. v. Teague, 137 Tex. 119, 152 S.W. 2d 1091 (1941).

Croft v. H. M. Cohen Lumber & Bldg. Co., 107 S.W. 2d 1040 (1937).

Schoenfeld v. DePuy, 58 S.W. 2d 574 (1933).

Taub v. Woodruff, 63 Civ. App. 437, 134 S.W. 750 (1910).

Wash.   *McKivor v. Savage,* 60 Wash. 135, 110 Pac. 811 (1910).

Ilse v. Aetna Indem. Co., 55 Wash. 487, 104 Pac. 787 (1909).

W.Va.   *Vaughan Constr. Co. v. Virginian R. Co.,* 86 W.Va. 440, 103 S.E. 293 (1920).

Berry v. Huntington Masonic Temple Ass'n, 80 W.Va. 342, 93 S.E. 355 (1917).

U.S.   *Central Nebraska Public Power & Irrig. Dist. v. Tobin Quarries, Inc.,* 157 F. 2d 482 (1946).

S. J. Groves & Sons Co. v. Warren, 135 F. 2d 264 (1943).

United States v. Madsen Constr. Co., 139 F. 2d 613 (1943).

H. W. Zweig Co. v. United States, 92 Ct.Cl. 472 (1941).

General Contracting Corp. v. United States, 92 Ct.Cl. 5 (1940).

W. Horace Williams Co. v. United States, 85 Ct.Cl. 431 (1937).

Wenzel & Henoch Constr. Co. v. Metropolitan Water Dist., 18 F.
Supp. 616 (1937).

McCullough v. Clinch-Mitchell Constr. Co., 71 Fed. 17, cert. den.,
293 U.S. 582 (1934).

Southern Shipyard Corp. v. United States, 76 Ct.Cl. 468 (1932),
cert. den., 290 U.S. 640 (1933).

Southern New England R. Corp. v. Marsch, 45 F. 2d 766 (1931).

Cranford Co. v. New York, 38 F. 2d 52, cert. den., 281 U.S. 760
(1930).

Memphis Trust Co. v. Brown-Ketchum Iron Works, 166 Fed. 398,
cert. den., 214 U.S. 515 (1909).

Arkin Constr. Co. v. Reynolds Metal Co., 310 F. 2d 11 (1962).

In *Kyburg v. State*, 108 N.W. 2d 645, a contractor sued the state of
South Dakota for $1687.50 which the state had deducted from its pay-
ments to the contractor as the value of bedsprings which the state argued was included in the plans which were the basis of the construction
contract. The contract contained the following provision:

> "In case any question shall arise between the parties hereto relative
> to said contractor specification, the determination or decision of the
> State Engineer shall be a condition precedent to the right of the con-
> tractor to receive any money or payment for work under this contract
> affected in any manner or to any extent by such question."

The State Engineer felt that the plaintiff should have supplied bedsprings under the contract.

The court held that "The power to construe and define the intent and
meaning of plans and specifications made a part of a contract is one
thing ... and may be properly left to arbiters selected by the parties;
the power to construe the contract itself and to determine what is within
and what without such contract is a different and independent question,
and belongs primarily to the courts."

The determination of the State Engineer was found to fall into the
latter classification so the court felt at liberty to, and did, overturn it.

WHERE THE CONTRACT PROVIDES THAT THE WORK shall be done to the
satisfaction of the architect or engineer, or shall be accepted or approved
by him, his decision is binding and conclusive on the parties in the absence of fraud or gross mistake.

Cal.   *American Trust Co. v. Coryell*, 3 Cal. 2d 151, 43 P. 2d 1102
(1935).

Dingley v. Greene, 54 Cal. 333, 33 Am. Rep. 80 (1880).

Fla.   *Wilcox v. Stephenson*, 30 Fla. 377, 11 So. 659 (1892).

Ill.   *Davidson v. Provost,* 35 Ill. App. 126 (1889).

Iowa   *Edwards v. Louisa County,* 89 Iowa 499, 56 N.W. 656 (1893).

Kan.   *Board of Educ. of Paola v. Shaw,* 15 Kan. 35 (1875).

Md.   *Baltimore & O.R.R. Co. v. Brydon,* 65 Md. 198, 3 Atl. 306 (1886).
   Lynn v. Baltimore & O.R.R. Co., 60 Md. 404, 45 Am. Rep. 741 (1883).

Mass.   *Evans v. Middlesex County,* 209 Mass. 474, 95 N.E. 897 (1911).
   Robbins v. Clark, 129 Mass. 145 (1880).

Mo.   *Myers v. Union Electric Light & Power Co.,* 334 Mo. 622, 66 S.W. 2d 565 (1933).
   Nofsinger v. Ring, 71 Mo. 149, 36 Am. Rep. 456 (1879).

Neb.   *State v. Commercial Casualty Ins. Co.,* 125 Neb. 43, 248 N.W. 807 (1933).
   School Dist. of Sarpy County v. Randall, 5 Neb. 408 (1877).

N.J.   *Jose Naples, Inc. v. Great Notch Dev. Co.,* 8 N.J. Mis. 135, 149 Atl. 33 (1930).
   See, *MacKinson v. Conlon,* 55 N.J.L. 564, 27 Atl. 930 (1883).

N.M.   *Odell v. Colmor Irrig. & Land Co.,* 34 N.M. 277, 280 Pac. 398 (1929).

N.Y.   *Kausen v. Leonhardt Realty Co.,* 79 Misc. 621, 140 N.Y.S. 493 (1913).
   McManus v. Annett, 101 App. Div. 6, 91 N.Y.S. 808 (1905).
   Graves Elevator Co. v. John H. Parker Co., 92 App. Div. 456, 87 N.Y.S. 156 (1904).
   Brady v. New York, 132 N.Y. 415, 30 N.E. 757 (1892).
   Wyckoff v. Meyers, 44 N.Y. 143 (1870).

Ohio   *Kane v. Stone Co.,* 39 Ohio St. 11 (1883).

Ore.   See, *Williams v. Mt. Hood Rr. & Power Co.,* 57 Ore. 251, 110 Pac. 490, 111 Pac. 17 (1910).

Pa.   *Stierheim v. Bechtold,* 158 Pa. Super. 107, 43 A. 2d 916 (1945).
   See, *Bizet v. Smith,* 272 Pa. 31, 115 Atl. 868 (1922).
   Kennedy v. Poor, 151 Pa. 472, 25 Atl. 119 (1892).

Tex.   *McKenzie Constr. Co. v. Chanowsky,* 86 S.W. 2d 480 (1935).
   Eckert-Fair Construction Co. v. Glabiano 342 S.W. 2d 629 (1961). The court held that a provision requiring a subcontractor to perform "to the complete satisfaction" of the architect did not render the latter's determination of unsatisfactory performance binding on the subcontractor because of the vagueness of the wording of that provision.

Utah   *Midgley v. Campbell Bldg. Co.,* 38 Utah 293, 112 Pac. 820 (1911).

Va. See, *Southgate v. Sanford & Brooks Co.*, 147 Va. 554, 137 S.E. 485 (1927).

Wash. *Bavaria Inv. Co. v. Washington Brick, Lime & Sewer Pipe Co.*, 82 Wash. 187, 144 Pac. 68 (1914).

Taft v. Whitney Co., 85 Wash. 389, 148 Pac. 43 (1915).

Eastham v. Western Constr. Co., 36 Wash. 7, 77 Pac. 1051 (1904).

Wis. *Wauwatose v. Jacobus & Winding Concrete Constr. Co.*, 223 Wis. 401, 271 N.W. 21 (1937).

Ashland Lime, Salt & Cement Co. v. Shores, 105 Wis. 122, 81 N.W. 136 (1899).

Tetz v. Butterfield, 54 Wis. 242, 11 N.W. 531 (1882).

U.S. *M. DeMatteo Const. Co. v. Maine Turnpike Authority*, 184 F. Supp. 907 (1960). The contract between the owner and the contractor provided in part as follows: "The Engineer shall decide any and all questions which may arise as to the quality or acceptability of materials furnished . . .". And further on "The Engineer shall determine the amount and quantity of the several kinds of work performed . . . and his decisions shall be final." The court held that by necessary implication the former category of determinations was also final.

Steacy-Schmidt Mfg. Co. v. United States, 64 Ct.Cl. 499 (1928).

United States v. Hurley, 182 Fed. 766 (1910).

Crane Elevator Co. v. Clark, 80 Fed. 705 (1897).

Sheffield & Birmingham Coal, Iron & R. Co. v. Gordon, 151 U.S. 285 (1894).

WHERE THE CONTRACT PROVIDES THAT COMPENSATION shall be payable upon the estimate or certificate of the architect or engineer, or that his certificate is a condition of payment, such estimate or certificate is conclusive on the parties in the absence of fraud or mistake.

Ariz. *Gillespie Land & Irrig. Co. v. Hamilton*, 43 Ariz. 102, 29 P. 2d 158 (1934).

Guarantee Title & Trust Co. v. Willis, 38 Ariz. 33, 297 Pac. 445 (1931).

Fla. *Duval County v. Charleston Eng. & Contracting Co.*, 101 Fla. 341, 134 So. 509 (1931).

Ill. *Gilmore v. Courtney*, 158 Ill. 432, 41 N.E. 1023 (1895).

Bournique v. Arnold, 33 Ill. App. 303 (1889), rev'd on another point, 144 Ill. 132, 33 N.E. 530 (1893). Decision of surveyor held final.

Classen v. Davidson, 59 Ill. App. 106 (1895).

Iowa *Mitchell v. Kavanagh*, 38 Iowa 286 (1874).

Ky. *Henderson Bridge Co. v. O'Connor,* 88 Ky. 303, 11 S.W. 18 (1889).

Me. *Seretto v. Rockland, S. T. & O. H. R.,* 101 Me. 140, 63 Atl. 651 (1906).

Mass. *Sikora v. Hogan,* 315 Mass. 66, 51 N.E. 2d 970 (1943).
Loftus v. Jorjorian, 194 Mass. 165, 80 N.E. 235 (1907).
Herbert v. Dewey, 191 Mass. 403, 77 N.E. 822 (1906).

Mich. *Otto Misch Co. v. E. E. Davis Co.,* 241 Mich. 285, 217 N.W. 38 (1928).
Rens v. Grand Rapids, 73 Mich. 237, 41 N.W. 263 (1889).

Mo. *Massman Constr. Co. v. Lake Lotawana Ass'n, Inc.,* 240 Mo. App. 469, 210 S.W. 2d 398 (1948).
Spitcaufsky v. State Highway Comm'n, 349 Mo. 117, 159 S.W. 2d 647 (1941).
Mackler v. Mississippi River & Bonne Terre R.R. Co., 62 Mo. App. 677 (1895).

N.J. *Sisters of Charity v. Smith,* 46 Atl. 598 (1899).

Okla. *Fuqua v. Tulsa Masonic Bldg. Ass'n,* 129 Okla. 106, 263 Pac. 660 (1928).

Pa. *John Conti Co. v. Donovan,* 358 Pa. 566, 57 A. 2d 872 (1948).
Phillips v. American Liability & Surety Co., 309 Pa. 1, 162 Atl. 435 (1932).

Tenn. *Bannon v. Jackson,* 121 Tenn. 381, 117 S.W. 504 (1908).

Tex. *American Surety Co. v. Shaw,* 69 S.W. 2d 47 (1934).
American Employer's Ins. Co. v. Huddleston, 123 Tex. 285, 70 S.W. 2d 696 (1934).
Alexander v. Good Marble & Tile Co., 4 S.W. 2d 636 (1928).
Southern Surety Co. v. Sealy Indep. School Dist., 10 S.W. 2d 786 (1928).

U.S. *Henegan's Case,* 17 Ct.Cl. 273 (1881).
Cf. *Central Trust Co. v. Louisville St. L. & T. R. Co.,* 70 Fed. 282 (1895). Estimate of engineer held not to be conclusive by terms of contract.

OTHER PROVISIONS MAKING THE ARCHITECT OR engineer a final arbiter as to the amount, sufficiency, classification, or completion of the work, default of contractor, liquidated damages, or other matters, operate to make his decision binding in the absence of fraud or gross mistake.

Ala. *Shriner v. Craft,* 166 Ala. 146, 51 So. 884 (1910). Provision that expenses incurred by owner and damages sustained through contractor's default shall be audited and certified by architect.

Cal. *C. J. Wood, Inc. v. Sequoia Union High School Dist.*, 199 Cal.
App. 433, 18 Cal. Rptr. 647 (1962).

Ill.   *Weld v. First Nat. Bank*, 255 Ill. 43, 99 N.E. 72 (1912). Provision
authorizing architect, in event work is unfinished after designated
date, to determine what period of delay was chargeable to contractor for which a specified deduction was to be made.

Andrew Lohr Bottling Co. v. Ferguson, 223 Ill. 88, 79 N.E. 35
(1906). Provision submitting all questions to decision of architect
and authorizing payment upon his certificate of performance.

Brownell Improv. Co. v. Critchfield, 197 Ill. 61, 64 N.E. 332 (1902).
Provision authorizing architect to decide all questions as to proper
performance of work.

Iowa *Ross v. McArthur*, 85 Iowa 203, 52 N.W. 125 (1892). Where
subcontractor agreed to grade land, the work to be done under the
supervision of the railroad company's chief engineer, whose classifications and measurements of the work performed was to be conclusive on all parties, the parties are bound by the estimates,
unless they were fraudulently made.

Mass. *Handy v. Bliss*, 204 Mass. 513, 90 N.E. 864 (1910). Provision
making decision of architect final as to true construction of drawings and specifications is binding.

National Contracting Co. v. Commonwealth, 183 Mass. 89, 66
N.E. 639 (1903). Provision authorizing engineer to make any
changes he deemed necessary.

Minn. *Langdon v. Northfield*, 42 Minn. 464, 44 N.W. 984 (1890). Provision authorizing owner to declare contract abandoned or to
employ others to execute work and to charge same to contractor,
if in engineer's opinion work was not progressing rapidly enough
to be completed within time specified in contract.

Trainor v. Worman, 33 Minn. 484, 24 N.W. 297 (1885). Provision
that arbiter is to decide when work is completed.

N.Y. *Wilson v. Curran*, 190 App. Div. 581, 180 N.Y.S. 337 (1920),
aff'd, 323 N.Y. 587, 134 N.E. 582 (1922). Provision that on contractor's default in proper performance and architect's certification
to that effect, owner could terminate contract and complete work
on contractor's account.

New York State Nat. Bank v. Whitehall Water Power Co., 161
App. Div. 304, 146 N.Y.S. 769 (1914). Where contract provided
that architect's explanation of any discrepancy between the specifications and plans should be final and binding on the contractor,
the architect's decision that certain work was not extra work but

was required by the contract under the plans and specifications was binding.

Mahoney v. Oxford Realty Co., 133 App. Div. 656, 118 N.Y.S. 216 (1909). Provision authorizing owner to terminate contract and complete building himself if architect should certify that contractor had failed to supply sufficient workmen or materials or to use due diligence.

Ore. *Leiter v. Dwyer Plumbing & Heating Co.,* 66 Ore. 474, 133 Pac. 1180 (1913). Provision authorizing architect to suspend work whenever in his opinion it was necessary or advantageous.

Pa. *Kann v. Bennett,* 234 Pa. 12, 82 Atl. 1111 (1912). Provision authorizing architect to decide preliminary question of contractor's default, and ultimate determination of account between owner and contractor.

Ruch v. York, 233 Pa. 36, 81 Atl. 891 (1911). Provision authorizing architect to make conclusive determination of rights of parties to liquidated damages under terms of contract.

Tenn. *East Tennessee V. & G.R. Co. v. Central Lumber Mfg. Co.,* 95 Tenn. 538, 32 S.W. 635 (1895). Provision that all allowances and differences that were not agreed upon before work was begun were to be referred to chief engineer for settlement.

Tex. *Brin v. McGregor,* 45 S.W. 923 (1898). Provision making supervising architect judge of proper performance of contract.

Wright v. Meyer, 25 S.W. 1122 (1894). Provision authorizing architect to pass on fitness of labor and material and to reject same if unfit.

City of San Antonio v. Meader, 326 S.W. 2d 557 (1959). In an action against a contractor for damages, held that city engineer's determination of cause of damage was final and conclusive in the absence of fraud or gross mistake.

U.S. *Lippert Bros. Inc. v. City of Atoka,* 94 F. Supp. 630 (1950). Where parties to a construction contract designate an engineer as arbiter of the amount and character of the work done and the amount due the contractor, his decision is binding in the absence of actual fraud or gross mistake constituting constructive fraud.

Mittry v. United States, 73 Ct.Cl. 341 (1931). Provision authorizing "head of the department" to determine whether there was unavoidable delay arising from causes beyond the control of the contractor. If this were found to be true, an extension of time for completion would be allowed the contractor.

Kennedy v. White Bear Lake, 39 F. 2d 608 (1930). Provision authorizing engineers to decide all questions as to compliance or non-compliance with specifications of contract.

Driscoll v. United States, 34 Ct.Cl. 508 (1899). Provision authorizing named officer or inspector to reject any part of work which is not in his opinion strictly in accordance with drawings and specification.

Pauly Jail Bldg. & Mfg. Co. v. Hemphill County, 62 Fed. 698 (1893). Where contract provides that owner's inspector shall inspect work and notify contractor of any insufficiency, and that if work is completed without such notice it shall be accepted by the owner, the action of inspector "should be conclusive except upon clear and distinct proof of fraud."

PROVISIONS REFERRING CERTAIN QUESTIONS TO the decision of the architect or engineer are invalid where, unknown to the contractor, the arbiter has guaranteed to keep the cost of the construction within a specified sum.

Tex. *Manett, Seastrunk & Buckner v. Terminal Bldg. Corp.,* 120 Tex. 374, 39 S.W. 2d 1 (1931). Where contract provides that architect is to issue certificates for work done under the contract and for extra work, and the architect, unknown to the contractor, has a financial interest in keeping down costs because of his guaranty to keep the cost of the building within the estimate, the contractor is relieved from the obligations of the contract and may recover for his work on a *quantum meruit* basis.

Wash. *Long v. Pierce County,* 22 Wash. 330, 61 Pac. 142 (1900). Where contractor had agreed to construct a building for $270,000 claimed additional sum of $73,000 for extras and, unknown to him, the architects had guaranteed to keep the cost of the building below $300,000, a provision referring disputes to them was annulled, since under such circumstances bias and prejudice on their part would be implied.

INDIANA DOES NOT RECOGNIZE THE RULE that the determination of the architect or engineer may by contract be made conclusive on the ground that the parties cannot agree in advance to "oust the courts of jurisdiction."

Ind. See *Wacker v. Essex,* 67 Ind. App. 584, 119 N.E. 466 (1918). Architect's certificate reciting that it is an expression of his opinion and shall not be considered as an acceptance, is not conclusive on owner.

Indianapolis Northern Traction Co. v. Brennan, 174 Ind. 1, 87 N.E. 215 (1909). Provision in construction contract that engineer shall determine classification of excavated matter and that his decision shall be conclusive contemplates honest judgment by engineer and does not prevent resort to courts to obtain correct construction of agreement, though his decision is prima facie correct and to that extent binding in absence of showing of fraud or gross or obvious mistake by him.

Maitland v. Reed, 37 Ind. App. 469, 77 N.E. 290 (1906). Provision of building contract which assumes to make decision of architect or arbitrator final, is void, inasmuch as it is not competent for parties, in advance of dispute, to oust courts of jurisdiction.

Board of Comm'rs of Fulton County v. Gibson, 158 Ind. 471, 63 N.E. 982 (1902). Provision in construction contract that disputes as to construction or what is extra work shall be conclusively determined by county commissioners and architect is not binding on contractor, as a party to the contract cannot be made arbitrator of differences arising therefrom.

Baltimore & O. & C. R. Co. v. Scholes, 14 Ind. App. 524, 43 N.E. 156 (1896). Contract provision that final estimate of engineer as to guaranty of work, etc. shall be conclusive on parties does not prevent estimates from being attacked for mistake or fraud but merely makes them prima facie correct, as parties cannot agree to oust courts of jurisdiction.

McCoy v. Able, 131 Ind. 417, 30 N.E. 528, 31 N.E. 453 (1892). Though contract provides that estimates of county engineer as to cost of work are to be conclusive, they are not such but are merely prima facie correct and the burden is on the party attacking them to show fraud or mistake.

Supreme Council, O. C. F. v. Forsinger, 125 Ind. 55, 25 N.E. 129 (1890).

Louisville E. & St. L. R. Co. v. Donnegan, 111 Ind. 179, 12 N.E. 153 (1887).

CHAPTER THIRTEEN

When architect's or engineer's decision or certificate is not final

The certificate or decision of the architect or engineer is conclusive only as to those matters within the scope of the submission to him and which he determines without exceeding his authority. It is binding only upon those persons who are parties to the contract. It may be impeached for fraud or gross error of the arbiter in rendering it.

Only those disputes which by stipulation between the parties are referable to the architect or engineer for final determination may be submitted to him. Unless a given dispute clearly falls within the terms of the submission the arbiter has no authority to decide it. The general rule is that contract provisions cannot be extended by implication. For example, where there is a stipulation for submission of disputes as to fulfillment of the contract, the arbiter is not given the authority under such a provision to pass on a claim for damages for breach of the contract. A dispute which arose before the contract was entered into and is settled by the contract as made, may not be raised again under the contract provision for settlement of disputes.

The architect or engineer is generally not authorized to determine the question of his own negligence. Closely related to his limitation is the requirement that the arbiter must not exceed his authority. The architect or engineer may be authorized to decide as to performance or non-performance of the work within the terms of the contract, but he cannot require the performance of additional work which is not within the contract's terms. Similarly, in determining disputes with regard to the use of proper materials or the quality of work called for by the contract, he has no authority to change the plans and specifications, or waive provisions in the contract requiring proper performance or provisions holding the contractor liable for defective work or material or delay in completion. Nor can he make a new contract for the parties by interpreting the contract differently from its proper meaning, or by giving it an arbitrary construction.

Where the arbiter is authorized to determine responsibility for delay in performance, and the amount of the loss thereby caused, the damage to which he may certify has been held to be only that resulting from matters with which he is familiar, such as damage relating to extra expense for labor and materials. One case held that he cannot determine the loss of rent suffered by the owner on account of the contractor's delay.

The inclusion in the certificate of matters not left to the determination of the architect or engineer does not void the whole certificate. The certificate is invalid only as to those matters which the architect or engineer did not have the power to determine.

The certificate of an architect or engineer approving the contractor's work is not conclusive against the owner as regards latent defects which could not have been discovered by him at the time he gave his certificate. It has been held that where the defects might have been discovered by the architect by the application of well-known tests, the contractor will not be liable for defects of which he had no knowledge and which are discovered after the work has been accepted and paid for.

The decision of the architect or engineer, when made final, is binding on the owner, the contractor, and any other parties to the contract. It does not have conclusive effect on third persons who do not agree to be bound by such stipulation. Frequently, subcontracts entered into between the general contractor and subcontractors or materialmen make the specifications in the main contract a part of the subcontract. In that event, any provision making certificates or decisions of the arbiter final, will be conclusive on the parties to the subcontract. However, any such agreement between the parties to the subcontract, if not made specific, will not be implied from the mere statement in the main contract that the decisions of the arbiter as to disputed questions will be final and binding.

The decision, certificate, or estimate of the architect or engineer may be impeached for fraud on his part. Therefore, if the arbiter fails to exercise his honest judgment, acts arbitrarily or capriciously, or makes such gross mistakes as would imply bad faith, his decision is not binding on either party to the contract. Every contract providing for the architect's or engineer's decision or certificate is subject to the implied condition that his decision be an honest one. If he knowingly and wilfully disregards his duty in this respect, either party may attack his determination for fraud or bad faith. Collusion between the architect and owner or contractor will constitute a fraud against the other party. However, it is not neces-sary, in order to prove a fraudulent determination, to establish that either party had knowledge of such improper conduct on the part of the arbiter, or acted collusively with him.

An architect or engineer who issues a certificate of performance when he knows that the work has not been fully performed acts fraudulently. Likewise, an arbiter who does not know whether the contractor's work conforms to the plans and specifications, yet gives a certificate, is not acting on his own knowledge and is guilty of acting arbitrarily. On the other hand, the unreasonable refusal of the architect or engineer to certify work which has been properly done makes his action fraudulent and not conclusive on the contractor. Mere errors of judgment or com-putation which are not made wilfully do not constitute fraud and are insufficient to avoid a certificate. Mistakes justifying impeachment have been called "palpable mistakes," "gross mistakes," or "mistakes so clear as to imply bad faith." Likewise, gross negligence on the part of the arbiter in certifying the execution of work may justify the inference of fraud or bad faith.

To avoid a certificate it is enough to show conduct and circumstances from which the jury may infer that it was made capriciously, arbitrarily, in a grossly negligent manner, or without any reason.

A DECISION, ESTIMATE, OR CERTIFICATE of an architect or engineer is not conclusive where the contract does not specifically or impliedly so provide.

Colo. *Shore v. Wallace,* 117 Colo. 301, 186 P. 2d 581 (1947). Esti-mates of engineer were not conclusive where contract did not so provide.

Conn. *West v. Suda,* 69 Conn. 60, 36 Atl. 1015 (1897). Contract pro-vision that all work must be done to architect's satisfaction has no application to question of damages caused by the owner in break-ing contract.

Whitney Co. v. Church, 91 Conn. 684, 101 Atl. 329 (1917). Archi-tect's valuation of extra work was held not conclusive where the contract provided for arbitration if his valuation was not agreed to.

Idaho *Maney v. Idaho Constr. Co.,* 30 Idaho 111, 163 Pac. 297 (1917). Provision in contract that work was to be paid for "as per engi-neer's estimate sheet" did not make his estimates final.

Ind. *Warren v. State,* 208 Ind. 526, 196 N.E. 710 (1935). Under a statutory provision that county commissioners must "inform" them-selves as to whether money is due, architect's certificate is not binding on them.

Wacker v. Essex, 67 Ind. App. 584, 119 N.E. 466 (1919). Architect's certificate as to the amount due for labor and materials, reciting that it is an expression of the architect's opinion and shall not be considered as an acceptance, is not conclusive on the owner.

Ky. *Kanawha-Knox Coal Co. v. Jackson,* 213 Ky. 199, 280 S.W. 926 (1926). Contract provision that engineer's measurements should be basis of settlement did not make such measurements conclusive.

La. *American Heating & Plumbing Co. v. West End Country Club,* 171 La. 482, 131 So. 466 (1930). Contract requiring contractor to make good injury occurring before acceptance of work did not impliedly make decision of architect final on sufficiency of performance.

Garrett v. Verlander, 9 La. App. 317, 120 So. 492 (1928). Certificate of supervising architect that contractor has substantially complied with the plans and specifications cannot be lightly disregarded.

Mass. *Morgan v. Murdough,* 216 Mass. 502, 104 N.E. 455 (1914). Contract stipulates that architect should be referee in all cases to decide upon the quality and fitness of work and material does not entitle him to settle a dispute over the construction of the contract as to whether the plans or written contract should control.

Minn. *P. M. Hennessy Constr. Co. v. Hart,* 141 Minn. 449, 170 N.W. 597 (1919). Architect's allowance of contractor's preliminary estimates does not fix the actual but only the approximate value of materials covered by the estimate.

Miss. *Mississippi Fire Ins. Co. v. Evans,* 153 Miss. 635, 120 So. 738 (1929). Contract provision making decisions of architect subject to arbitration held not to provide that decisions should be final or conclusive.

Neb. *State v. Commercial Casualty Ins. Co.,* 125 Neb. 43, 248 N.W. 807 (1933). Final certificate of engineers constitutes prima facie evidence that the work has been performed according to contract requirements.

N.J. *Gerisch v. Herold,* 82 N.J.L. 605, 83 Atl. 892 (1912). Architect's certificate that contractor was entitled to final payment did not bind owner where contract provided that final payment should be made when all of the work was completed according to the plans and specifications, to the satisfaction of the owner or his representative.

N.Y. *Delamater v. Folz,* 50 Hun. 528, 3 N.Y.S. 711 (1889). Disputes referable to the engineer are only those relating to performance of the contract.

Kausen v. Leonhardt Realty Co., 79 Misc. 621, 140 N.Y.S. 493 (1913). Architect's certificate was held not conclusive in absence of provision to that effect in the contract.

Kelly v. Ferguson, 205 App. Div. 591, 200 N.Y.S. 86 (1923). City controller has power and duty to question architect's certificate because of inclusion of an item not authorized under the contract.

Okla.   *Smith v. Goff,* 325 P. 2d 1061 (1958). In an action for damages by an owner against a contractor, the court held the acceptance of the work by the architect was inconclusive where the contract did not provide for the conclusiveness of his determination.

Ore.   *Halvorson v. Blue Mtn. Prune Growers Co-op,* 188 Ore. 661, 214 P. 2d 986 (1950). Provision authorizing architect to compute proper value of alterations in event of disagreement between owner and contractor, constituted a limited arbitration agreement under which the architect's decisions were not conclusive in the absence of unequivocal language making them so.

Lovell v. Potts, 112 Ore. 538, 226 Pac. 1111 (1924). Architect's certificate was held not conclusive as to alleged abandonment of contract by contractor.

Seaside v. Randles, 92 Ore. 650, 180 Pac. 319 (1919). Where contract provides that work and materials are subject to the approval of the engineer and are to be in strict accordance with the plans and specifications, acceptance by the engineer is not thereby made final and conclusive.

Rogue River Fruit & Produce Ass'n v. Gillen-Chambers Co., 85 Ore. 113, 165 Pac. 679 (1917). Right of inspection reserved to owner's engineer does not make his acceptance binding upon owner.

Pa.   *Kann v. Bennett,* 234 Pa. 12, 82 Atl. 1111 (1912). Certificate of architect stating that certain items of materials, as to which mechanics' liens had been filed, were excluded is incomplete and cannot be sued upon under the rule that an award of an arbitrator that is not final is void altogether. Also, where contract provides that on contractor's default owner may complete contract at his expense, and that decision of architect as to disputed matters shall be final, architect cannot allow owner rental value of building from date specified by contract for completion, to date of actual completion, but he may allow amount for supervision of completion of building.

Reilly v. Rodef Sholem Congreg., 243 Pa. 528, 90 Atl. 345 (1914). Architects were held not authorized to pass on the question whether or not they themselves were at fault.

Shoemaker v. Riebe, 241 Pa. 402, 88 Atl. 662 (1913). Architect was not authorized to determine compensation due subcontractor after his discharge by architect, where the legality of such discharge was in dispute.

Tex.   *Fort Worth Nat. Bank v. State,* 158 S.W. 2d 885 (1942). Acts done by the state in clear violation of its own contract do not come within the purview of matters delegated to the engineer for decision.

Black v. Acers, 178 S.W. 2d 152 (1943). Provision requiring dwelling to be "built to meet the requirements of the Federal Housing Administration" did not constitute such agency final arbiter of all matters touching substantial performance of the building contract.

Va.   *Mills v. Norfolk & W. R. Co.,* 90 Va. 523, 19 S.E. 171 (1894). It is competent to show that engineer's estimate and certificate are not within the terms of the submission, but are in violation of the contract and are therefore void and inconclusive.

Wash.   *Bavaria Inv. Co. v. Washington Brick, Lime & Sewer Pipe Co.,* 82 Wash. 187, 144 Pac. 68 (1914). Where contract provides that either party, if dissatisfied with the architect's decision may appeal to arbitrators, the architect's decision is conclusive unless such an appeal is duly taken.

Weiffenbach v. Smith, 97 Wash. 391, 166 Pac. 613 (1917). Where carpentry and masonry specifications differed and the principal contractor, before letting the subcontract, told subcontractor which to follow, there was no dispute between the principal contractor and subcontractor, the dispute having been settled before drawing of the contract.

Wis.   *Formann v. Walsh,* 97 Wis. 356, 72 N.W. 881 (1897). Where contract provides that the work is to be done to the entire satisfaction of the superintendent and owner, the owner may refuse to pay part of the price, although the superintendent has issued a certificate, where the builder has not reasonably performed his part of the contract.

Wyo.   *School Dist. v. Howard,* 49 Wyo. 41, 52 P. 2d 421 (1935). Certificate of substitute architect allowing claim against contractor for defective work is not binding where contract stipulates that all decisions of the architect are subject to arbitration.

U.S.   *Dyker Bldg. Co. v. United States,* 182 F. 2d 85 (1950). Decision of engineer as to measurement of quantities was held not final where the contract did not provide to that effect, where the "final" computation was not deemed final even by the engineer himself, and where the engineer regarded himself and was regardd by the parties as no more than an informed expert.

Franklinville Realty Co. v. Arnold Constr. Co., 120 F. 2d 144 (1941). Where contract provided that the decision of the architect should be final on matters relating to artistic effect, the architect's certificate was not conclusive in other regards.

Glades County v. Detroit Fidelity & Surety Co., 57 F. 2d 449 (1932). Architect's monthly certificates of work done and material furnished by contractor, where his decisions were subject to arbitration, were not conclusive of amount owed by city under the contract.

J. A. La Porte Corp. v. Baltimore, 13 F. Supp. 795 (1936). Contract provision that chief engineer's certificate of completion should be condition precedent to contractor's recovery and that city should not be estopped from showing correct amount and character of work, was held to mean that certificate was conclusive in the absence of fraud or gross mistake.

Dock Contractor Co. v. New York City, 296 Fed. 377 (1924). Where parties to contract determined that underpinning was necessary to the construction, the engineer could not determine question whether underpinning was necessary.

Northwestern Terra Cotta Co. v. Caldwell, 234 Fed. 491 (1916). Fact that architect would decide a dispute in a particular way is not equivalent to its submission to him and his actual decision thereon.

Jefferson Hotel Co. v. Brumbaugh, 168 Fed. 867 (1909). Where contract provided that architects act as the owner's supervising agents, an architect's final certificate was only prima facie evidence of its contents.

Freygang v. Vera Cruz P. R. Co., 154 Fed. 640 (1907). Although the contract did not provide that the engineer's estimate should be conclusive, acceptance and payment of 44 out of 49 estimates without question on the part of the railroad company made his estimates prima facie evidence of the work done.

THE ARCHITECT'S OR ENGINEER'S DECISION OR CERTIFICATE is not conclusive if he exceeds his authority in rendering it.

Ark.   *Boston Store v. Schleuter*, 88 Ark. 213, 114 S.W. 242 (1908). Provision on contract that architect's certificate shall be conclusive "on all matters" renders such certificate conclusive only as to those matters which by specific terms of the contract are within the powers and duties of the architect.

Cal. *Van Doren v. Burns,* 106 Cal. App. 224, 288 Pac. 1107 (1930). Architect in conferring with contractor and acting as arbitrator in agreeing on claims in accordance with provisions of contract was held not to have exceeded his authority.

Smith v. Empire Sanitary Dist., 273 P. 2d 37 (1954) held that the court's finding that the owner acting through its engineer had unreasonably and arbitrarily refused to certify proper payments because of insufficient funds, was tantamount to finding of bad faith which renders the engineer's decision inconclusive and which constitutes a material breach. The court further indicated that the assignment of false reasons for the withholding of monies was itself a breach of duty which might justify the contractor's ceasing further performance under the contract.

Colo. *Elliott v. Wolfer,* 78 Colo. 213, 240 Pac. 694 (1925). Where contract provides that architect's certificate is final in matters relating to artistic effect, his decision is final only as to such matters.

Ga. *Mallard v. Moody,* 105 Ga. 400, 31 S.E. 45 (1898). Where owner-builder contract provided that contractor was to install certain heating apparatus and made architect's decision as to meaning of drawings and specifications final, architect could not abrogate contract's terms by decision that contractor was not required to install such apparatus.

Iowa *F. E. Marsh & Co. v. Light & Power Co. of St. Ansgar,* 196 Iowa 926, 195 N.W. 754 (1923). Architect authorized to determine disputes relating to performance of the contract had no authority to change plans and specifications and approve inferior materials and workmanship.

Van Dyck Heating & Plumbing Co. v. Central Iowa Bldg. Co., 200 Iowa 1003, 205 N.W. 650 (1925). Architect cannot issue a certificate waiving express provisions in the contract holding the contractor liable for defective work or material.

Me. *Jacques v. Otto Nelson Co.,* 119 Me. 388, 111 Atl. 515 (1920). Architect may decide as to performance of the work but he cannot require performance of additional work within the terms of the contract.

Tex. *Harrell v. City of Lufkin,* 280 S.W. 174 (1926). Architect may not make a new contract for parties by interpreting the original contract differently from its proper meaning and intention.

Eastman Bros. v. Blanchette, 42 Civ. App. 205, 94 S.W. 441 (1906). Under contract authorizing architect to decide any disagreement between owner and contractor, architect has no power to make a final decision on whether he himself fulfilled the contract.

Travis-Williamson County Water Control and Improvement Dist. No. 1 v. Page, 358 S.W. 2d 158 (1962), modified 367 S.W. 2d 307. The court held the decision of the engineer inconclusive because "(we) believe the refusal of the engineer to issue the certificate of completion, in the light of the jury finding, was arbitrary as being without legal warrant in the sense that it was contrary to the terms of the contract which defined his authority and by which he and the parties were bound."

Wash.   *Bavaria Inv. Co. v. Washington Brick, Lime & Sewer Pipe Co.*, 82 Wash. 187, 144 Pac. 68 (1914). Although contract authorized architect to determine responsibility for delay and amount of loss occasioned thereby, his determination as to loss of rent suffered by owner on account of contractor's delay was not binding, since this particular decision did not relate to a matter with which he, as an architect, would necessarily be familiar and, consequently, he could not form a fair opinion.

W.Va.   *Parke v. Pence Springs Co.*, 94 W.Va. 382, 118 S.E. 508 (1923). Where contract does not authorize architect to waive claim of owners for delay in completion of the contract, architect's final statement which does not include such damage is not conclusive against the owners.

U.S.   *M. De Matteo Const. Co. v. Maine Turnpike Authority*, 184 F. Supp. 907 (1960). "If the engineer exceeded the powers given it in the Contract or disregard the ground rules specified in the Contract, its decision was not final...". In this case judgment was refused because it was not clear that the engineer had rendered an honest judgment on the suitability of the materials proposed by the plaintiff as required in the contract.

THE CERTIFICATE OF AN ARCHITECT OR ENGINEER approving the contractor's work is not conclusive as regards latent defects. Invalidity of a portion of the arbiter's certificate does not void the certificate in its entirety.

(a) Latent defects

Mo.   *Standard Stamping Co. v. Hemminghaus*, 157 Mo. 23, 57 S.W. 746 (1900). Contractor held not liable for warping of flooring, due to insufficient seasoning, occurring after building had been paid for where contractor had no knowledge of such defect which might easily have been discovered by the architect by the application of a well-known test.

N.C.   *Shepard's Chemical Co. v. O'Brien*, 173 N.C. 618, 92 S.E. 594 (1917). Guaranty clause in contract whereby builder was to correct all defects arising or discovered in work within two years refers to defects appearing after architect's certificate was given and not to defects then observable.

Okla.   *City of Lawton v. Sherman Machine & Iron Works*, 182 Okla. 254, 77 P. 2d 567 (1938). Certificate of approval is not conclusive against owner as regards latent defects in performance of the work, which could not have been discovered by the architect or engineer.

Tex.   *American Employers' Ins. Co. v. Huddleston*, 123 Tex. 285, 70 S.W. 2d 696 (1934). Under contract requiring contractor to correct faulty workmanship and materials discovered after final payments, owners were held entitled to recover against the surety on the contractor's bond although defects were discovered after owners made final payment on architect's final certificate.

(b) Certificate held void in part

Ill.   *Snead & Co. Iron Works v. Merchants' Loan & Trust Co.*, 225 Ill. 442, 80 N.E. 237 (1907). Where architect departed from authority conferred upon him by contract, and his award was an entirety, it was not binding and was wholly ineffectual.

N.Y.   *Neidlinger v. Onward Constr. Co.*, 44 Misc. 555, 90 N.Y.S. 115 (1904), *aff'd*, 107 App. Div. 398, 95 N.Y.S. 1148 (1905), *aff'd*, 188 N.Y. 572, 80 N.E. 1114 (1907). Where architect certifies that contract is completed, that contractor is entitled to certain payments and also that there were damages because of delay, the part of the certificate pertaining to payments is insufficient if it does not specify a definite amount to be paid and the award is void *pro tanto*.

Wash.   *Bavaria Inv. Co. v. Washington Brick, Lime & Sewer Pipe Co.*, 82 Wash. 187, 144 Pac. 68 (1914). Inclusion in the certificate of matters not left to the architect's determination does not void the whole certificate, it being invalid only as to those matters which the architect did not have power to determine.

A CERTIFICATE OR DECISION IS NOT CONCLUSIVE on either party where the contract contains a stipulation that the certificate or decision shall not constitute acceptance of the work, or shall not relieve the contractor of responsibility for defective material or work.

Idaho   *Nelson Bennett Co. v. Twin Falls Land & Water Co.*, 14 Idaho 5, 93 Pac. 789 (1908). Measurements and classifications made by engineer, which contract permits owner to dispute and question, will not be enforced as final and conclusive on the contractor. A stipulation, in order to be binding on one party, must be made obligatory on the other.

Ill.   *Snell v. Evans,* 55 Ill. App. 670 (1894). Where a contract provides
that the architect's certificate shall not exempt the contractor from
liability to make good the work afterward found not in accord
with plans and specifications, the contractor is responsible for
defects even though he may have obtained a certificate covering
such work.

Mich.   *Benjamin v. Wm. Hillger Land Co.,* 225 Mich. 613, 196 N.W.
191 (1923). Where the contract provides that the architect's certificate shall not be considered as an acceptance of any work done
or material furnished, the certificate is not conclusive on the
owner.

But see: *Pratt v. Van Rensselaer,* 235 Mich. 633, 209 N.W. 807
(1926). Court's instruction to the jury that the owner was bound
by architect's certificate given to the carpenter was not incorrect
where it was modified to make compliance with the contract necessary before the certificate was binding.

N.Y.   *Condict v. Onward Const. Co.,* 210 N.Y. 88, 105 N.E. 886
(1913). Where there is no conflict between the provision for a
final certificate and a provision of an express warranty, a final
certificate is not conclusive of the right to recover for a breach of
the warranty.

Farrell v. Levy, 139 App. Div. 790, 124 N.Y.S. 439 (1910). Where
contract provides that payment is not an acceptance of defective
work or that no certificate given or payment made, except the
final certificate or payment, shall be conclusive evidence of performance, an intermediate certificate is not conclusive.

Olsen v. Schwarzwaelder, 109 App. Div. 282, 95 N.Y.S. 651 (1905).
A provision that the architect's certificate shall not lessen the final
responsibility of the contractor, nor exempt him from liability to
replace defective work, does not make the architect's certificate
conclusive on the parties.

O'Brien v. New York, 139 N.Y. 543, 35 N.E. 323 (1893). Where
one portion of a contract provided that the decision of the engineer should be final, and another portion provided that the
commissioners should not be precluded by any certificate of the
engineer from showing the true amount of work done, the engineer's decision did not bind the commissioners.

Glacius v. Black, 50 N.Y. 145, 10 Am. Rep. 449 (1872). Where contract stipulated for materials of the best quality and performance
of work in the best manner, to be paid for when done completely
and accepted, acceptance by the architect of a different class of

work or of inferior materials will not bind the owner to pay for them.

N.D. *Hatchinson v. Bohnsack School Dist.*, 51 N.D. 165, 199 N.W. 484 (1924). Where a contract provides that neither the final certificate nor payment shall relieve the contractor of responsibility for faulty materials or workmanship, a final certificate of the architect certifying completion is not conclusive upon the owner as against failure of the contractor to comply with the specifications.

Okla. *National Surety Co. v. Board of Educ. of Hugo*, 62 Okla. 259, 162 Pac. 1108 (1917). Where contract provided that no payment should be construed to be an acceptance of defective work and an architect's final certificate was issued and the building accepted and paid for, an action for damages for latent defects could be maintained within a reasonable time after the discovery of such defects.

U.S. *United Constr. Co. v. Haverhill*, 223 F. 2d 256 (1927). Where a contract provided that assistant engineer's approval of improper work should not entitle the contractor to payment, the contractor was liable for failure to excavate to required depth though engineer's assistant may have approved work.

Mercantile Trust Co. v. Hensey, 205 U.S. 298 (1907). Under contract providing that architect's installment certificate should not lessen the contractor's final responsibility, or exempt him from liability to replace defective work, owner could show that the contractor had not in fact complied with his contract.

PROGRESS CERTIFICATES OR PERIODIC ESTIMATES upon which installment payments are made are generally not conclusive as to the matters certified unless there is a clear provision to that effect in the contract.

Ark. *Parker v. Stephens*, 157 Ark. 89, 247 S.W. 393 (1923). Monthly settlements based upon estimates which did not include all the work done were held not conclusive.

Cal. *Coplew v. Durand*, 153 Cal. 278, 95 Pac. 38 (1908). Progress certificates of approval were not conclusive that work therein certified was properly performed.

N.Y. *Hyers v. Victorian Realty Co.*, 213 App. Div. 658, 211 N.Y.S. 218 (1925). Use of term "estimates" in contract signified that estimates were not to be precisely accurate but were simply to afford practical means of making payments as work progressed.

Pa. *Gonder v. Berlin Branch R. Co.*, 171 Pa. 492 33 Atl. 61 (1895). Under contract providing for monthly estimates and a final estimate (the latter to be conclusive) an estimate made after completion of the work, in the form of a monthly estimate and intended to show only the work done during the preceding month, is not the final estimate.

W.Va. *Twentieth Street Bank v. Summers,* 90 W.Va. 90, 110 S.E. 478 (1922). Architect's progress estimates do not create an absolute liability on the owner to pay if the contract provides for retention of any amount which may become due for liens or claims, and such claims exist.

Vaughan Constr. Co. v. Virginian R. Co., 86 W.Va. 440, 103 S.E. 293 (1920). Where the contractor acquiesces in the monthly estimates of the egineer and receives payments thereon, he is estopped, on the final estimate and award, from putting a different construction on the contract and from impeaching such estimates for fraud or mistake.

U.S. *Glades County v. Detroit Fidelity & Surety Co.,* 57 F. 2d 449 (1932). Architect's monthly certificates were to fix tentatively the proportionate value of work performed for the purposes of installment payments and not to fix final liability for work and material upon the premature ending of the contract.

Warner Constr. Co. v. Louis Hanssen's Sons, 20 F. 2d 483 (1927). Where right of final inspection is reserved, the owner is not bound by partial settlements and acceptances made during the progress of the work.

Blanchard v. Sonnefield, 116 Fed. 257 (1902). Progress certificates of architects were not conclusive where contract provided that the work was to be at the contractor's risk until accepted by the owner as a whole.

THE DECISION OR CERTIFICATE OF AN ARCHITECT OR ENGINEER is binding on the subcontractor, materialmen, and the third parties only if they are parties to the main contract or otherwise agree to be bound by such decision or certificate.

Ark. *Trinity Universal Ins. Co. v. Willbanks,* 201 Ark. 386, 144 S.W. 2d 1092 (1940). The decision of the architect when made final is binding in its legal operation and effect on the owner, the contractor, and other parties to the contract, including those guaranteeing its faithful performance.

La. *Fritz Jahncke, Inc. v. Fidelity & Deposit Co.,* 166 La. 593, 117 So. 729 (1928). Architect's decisions were not binding on subcontractor under provision in original contract making architect's decisions on disputes final in view of a stipulation in the subcontract for arbitration of disputes.

Md. *Hughes v. Model Stoker Co.,* 124 Md. 283, 92 Atl. 845 (1915).
Where specifications of the principal contract provide they shall
be binding on the subcontractor, the subcontractor, who has
knowledge thereof, is bound by a provision making the determination of a certain officer conclusive as to the amount, quality, and
acceptability of work.

Mo. *Berger Mfg. Co. v. Crites,* 178 Mo. App. 218, 165 S.W. 1163
(1914). Where specifications, made part of the contract between
materialman and contractor, require all work to meet the approval of the school board and its architect, their decision is binding as between the contractor and materialman.

Neb. *Central Nebraska Millwork Co. v. Olson & Johnson Co.,* 111
Neb. 396, 196 N.W. 707 (1923). Materialman held not bound by
decision of architect as to whether materials were in conformity
with plans and specifications.

N.J. *Atlantic & S. R. Co. v. Atlantic County,* 84 N.J. Eq. 618, 94 Atl.
602 (1915). Engineer's certificates, under contract between county
and its contractor that pavement as constructed was an established
grade were not conclusive on a trolley company, which had agreed
to pay one-third the cost of repairing the highway.

N.Y. *Patrizio & Hendrickson v. McDermott & Hannigan, Inc.,* 97
Misc. 670, 162 N.Y.S. 302 (1916). General contractor cannot defend action on his guaranty of compensation to a subcontractor on
the ground of unsatisfactory work, where the subcontractor has
received the architect's certificate of approval.

Ore. *Wallace v. Oregon Eng. & Constr. Co.,* 90 Ore. 31, 174 Pac. 156
(1918). Engineer was held not authorized to determine the validity
of a contract between contractor and subcontractor.

Pa. *Foundation & Constr. Co. v. Franklin Trust Co.,* 307 Pa. 10, 160
Atl. 711 (1932). Under an agreement permitting payments only on
the architect's certificate, the subcontractor not having such certificate could not recover the sum alleged due it.

Tex. *Austin Bridge Co. v. Teague,* 137 Tex. 119, 152 S.W. 2d 1091
(1941). Where subcontractor claims rights under a contract executed by contractors and highway department, he is bound by
the terms of that contract as to the determination of disputes and
claims by the engineer.
McKenzie Constr. Co. v. Chanowsky, 86 S.W. 2d 480 (1935).
Where contractor contracts for materials subject to the engineer's
approval, if the engineer acts fraudulently in condemning materials, the contractor is bound by his acts and is not responsible
to the owner of the materials.

Schoenfeld v. De Puy, 58 S.W. 2d 574 (1933). Where parties agreed that stone to be furnished by subcontractor should be subject to government inspector's approval, the subcontractor was held not liable to the contractor for failure to furnish stone which the inspector had rejected arbitrarily.

Deal v. Craven, 277 S.W. 1046 (1925). Where contractor and sub-contractor agreed that county engineer's acceptance of the work should be conclusive as to performance, such acceptance bound them in absence of fraud.

Olson v. Burton, 141 S.W. 549 (1911). Where subcontract provided that contractor was to pay subcontractor when work was accepted by architect, such provision merely fixed time when payments were to become due and did not mean that architect was to determine whether work was performed as between contractor and subcontractor.

Wis.   *Modern Steel Structural Co. v. English Constr. Co.*, 129 Wis. 31, 108 N.W. 70 (1906). Subcontractor was held not bound by a certificate of the superintendent as to the amount of damages when there was no provision to that effect in the subcontract.

A CERTIFICATE, ESTIMATE, OR DECISION CAN BE IMPEACHED for gross error or fraud on the part of the architect or engineer issuing it. Unintentional errors of judgment or computation are not sufficient to impeach a certificate.

Ark.   *American Surety Co. v. Kinnear Mfg. Co.*, 185 Ark. 959, 50 S.W. 2d 586 (1932). Where architect granted a final certificate when he knew the contract had not been fulfilled, the binding character of his decision was destroyed.

Boston Store v. Schleuter, 88 Ark. 213, 114 S.W. 242 (1908). Decisions of architect are not conclusive where he fails to exercise honest judgment or makes such gross mistakes as necessarily imply bad faith.

Cal.   *American Trust Co. v. Coryell*, 3 Cal. 2d 151, 43 P. 2d 1102 (1935). Fact that work constructed is later found in bad condition does not necessarily imply that architect issued his certificate fraudulently or was so grossly negligent as to be guilty of constructive fraud.

Rialto Constr. Co. v. Reed, 17 Cal. App. 29, 118 Pac. 473 (1911). Whether erroneous estimate made by chief engineer was mere error of figures or of judgment or such neglect or careless mistake as to indicate bad faith, was held a question for the jury.

Colo.   *Ferguson v. Christensen,* 59 Colo. 42, 147 Pac. 352 (1915). It
is competent for either party to allege and prove, for purpose of
avoiding certificate, that architect did not exercise honest judgment, or that he acted arbitrarily, capriciously, and in bad faith.

Conn.   *George S. Chatfield Co. v. O'Neill,* 89 Conn. 172, 93 Atl. 133
(1915). Architect's decision cannot be impeached for negligence
not amounting to bad faith or fraud.

Ga.   *Royal Indem. Co. v. Batson-Cook Co.,* 37 Ga. App. 797, 142 S.E.
210 (1928). Where contracting officer rendered his decision upon
a report made to him by the engineer of the construction division,
something more than mere absence of a personal inspection was
required to impeach his judgment.

Ill.   *Edward Edinger Co. v. Willis,* 260 Ill. App. 106 (1931). If architect, without any reason therefor, arbitrarily decides against a
party upon questions in dispute, such action constitutes constructive fraud and impeaches architect's decision to the same extent
as actual fraud.

Davis v. Gibson, 70 Ill. App. 273 (1897). Fraud or mistake in the
architect's decision cannot be proved by evidence of the quality of
the work, but by evidence concerning the architect himself to
show that he did not exercise his best judgment.

Dore v. Northwestern Elev. R. Co., 67 Ill. App. 137 (1896). Mere
fact that architect allowed contractor full contract price although
the building was not completed at the agreed time, does not
establish that his certificate was fraudulently issued.

Snell v. Brown, 71 Ill. 133 (1873). A mistake or error of judgment
by an architect in condemning some of the work affords no ground
to impeach his estimate.

Ind.   *James I. Barnes Const. Co. v. Washington Township of Starke
County,* 184 N.E. 2d 763 (1962). The court held that the evidence
was sufficient to sustain a jury finding of gross error or non-exer-
cise of honest judgment. The court went on to say "(whether or
not there was such gross mistake of fact) ... was a matter to be
determined by the jury."

Iowa   *F. E. March & Co. v. Light & Power Co.,* 196 Iowa 926, 195
N.W. 754 (1923). Where building contract provided that approval
and acceptance of structure by the designing engineer should be
binding on both parties, but both engineer and contractor were
guilty of gross mistake in the use of materials and in workmanship,
the owner was not bound by the engineer's acceptance and approval of the building.

Edwards v. Louisa County, 89 Iowa 499, 56 N.W. 656 (1893).
Where plaintiff agreed to construct a levee and to receive payment
on the estimates of the engineer who was made sole judge as to
quality and quantity of work performed, he cannot recover more
than the estimates in the absence of fraud or mistake by the engineer making them.

Kan. *Edwards v. Hartshorn,* 72 Kan. 19, 82 Pac. 520 (1905). Where
evidence warranted inference that estimates were not fairly and
honestly made and discrepancies were such as to show palpable
mistakes and utter disregard of contractor's rights, estimates were
not binding.

Mich. *Frolich v. Klein,* 160 Mich. 142, 125 N.W. 14 (1910). Issuance
of a final certificate by the architect before the building was completed was held to be a fraud on the owner and not binding on him.
Guthat v. Gow, 95 Mich. 527, 55 N.W. 442 (1893). Where building
contract provides that the work shall be done to the satisfaction
of the architect and that any dispute as to claims for extra work
shall be referred to him for final decision, in an action by the
builder on the contract, it is error to refer to the jury questions as
to extra work and the performance of the contract if there is no
evidence of fraud or if the question of fraud is not submitted to the
jury.

Mo. *Lund v. McClinton,* 205 S.W. 240 (1918). Evidence held to
sustain finding that architect did not act in fair, impartial manner
in giving many orders to contractor relative to removal of work
and in issuing final certificate, but that his actions were arbitrary,
oppressive, and not in good faith.

Neb. *Anderson v. Imhoff,* 34 Neb. 335, 51 N.W. 854 (1892). Whether
architect wilfully disregarded his duty, was partial in performance
thereof, or made a mistake, is a question for the jury.

N.M. *O'Dell v. Colmor Irrig. & Land Co.,* 34 N.M. 277, 280 Pac. 398
(1929). A mistake in the engineer's final estimate, involving no
fraud and separable from the remainder of the estimates may be
corrected by the appellate court.

N.Y. *Elizabeth Sash, Door & Supply Co. v. St. Vincent's Hospital,* 241
App. Div. 751, 270 N.Y.S. 195 (1934). Mere error in computation
or judgment of the architect in estimating the sum due contractor
when the work is partly completed, does not justify abandonment
of the work for non-payment of the full amount which the subcontractor deems due.
O'Hehir v. Central New England R. Co., 152 App. Div. 677, 137
N.Y.S. 627 (1912). An error in judgment of the engineer in pre-

paring an estimate, which is not wilful, does not constitute fraud. *Farrell v. Levy,* 139 App. Div. 790, 124 N.Y.S. 439 (1910). Where contract did not provide that architect's certificate was to be final, owner did not need to allege fraud as an affirmative defense to an action by the contractor since full performance is part of the contractor's burden of proof.

Neidlinger v. Onward Constr. Co., 44 Misc. 555, 90 N.Y.S. 115 (1904), *aff'd,* 107 App. Div. 398, 95 N.Y.S. 1148 (1904), *aff'd,* 188 N.Y. 572, 80 N.E. 1114 (1907). In the absence of proof of fraud or a palpable mistake apparent on the face of the architect's award, neither party can show that he decided wrongly on the law or facts.

Dorwin v. Westbrook, 86 Hun. 363, 33 N.Y.S. 449 (1895), *aff'd,* 158 N.Y. 742, 53 N.E. 1124 (1899). Where fraud is alleged to invalidate the decision of the engineer it is not necessary that plaintiff connect the other party with fraud.

N.C.   *Shepard's Chemical Co. v. O'Brien,* 173 N.C. 618, 92 S.E. 594 (1917). Where there was a dispute as to whether the building was complete, and a new agreement was made, whereupon the final certificate was given, there was no fraud so as to permit impeachment of the certificate by the building owner.

McDonald v. MacArthur Bros. Co., 154 N.C. 122, 69 S.E. 832 (1910). Where certificate given by engineer was not only erroneous, but the error was so gross as to amount to a legal fraud, the contractor could sue for work done without relying on the certificate.

Ohio   *Fred R. Jones Co. v. Fath,* 101 Ohio St. 47, 126 N.E. 878 (1920). Mere fact of disagreement between representative of subcontractor and city engineer, and settlement on basis to relieve the city from liability to suit, is not evidence of fraud or bad faith on the part of city engineer.

Ore.   *Mayer v. East Side Logging Co.,* 130 Ore. 341, 278 Pac. 957 (1929). When the parties entered into a contract making the decision of the engineer final, they agreed to be bound by any honest mistake made by him that did not amount to "gross mistake."

Okla.   *National Surety Co. v. Board of Educ. of Hugo,* 62 Okla. 259, 162 Pac. 1108 (1917). Any fraud or want of good faith on the part of the architect destroys the force of the certificate and renders it subject to impeachment.

Pa.   *Zimmerman v. Marymor,* 290 Pa. 299, 138 Atl. 824 (1927). Where there is evidence of collusion between the architect and contractor, whose interests the architect serves in disregard of the owner's rights, the owner is not concluded by the architect's certificate that final payment is due.

Bowman v. Stewart, 165 Pa. 394, 30 Atl. 988 (1895). Allegations of mistake and negligence on the part of the engineer are not sufficient to impeach his certificate, since by agreeing that his certificate should be final and conclusive, the parties impliedly assumed the risk of negligence and mistakes.

Gonder v. Berlin Branch R. Co., 171 Pa. 492, 33 Atl. 61 (1895). Fact that the engineer was in the employ of the owner does not make his award conclusive on the owner where such award was the result of collusion with the contractor.

Tenn.   *Chandler v. Wheeler*, 49 S.W. 278 (1898). Owner is not bound by architect's approval of work where such approval is the result of either bad faith, collusion, or negligence.

Tex.   *Uvalde Rock Asphalt Co. v. Fantham*, 210 S.W. 2d 646 (1948). Where engineer did not know whether contract was performed in accordance with plans and specifications at the time he accepted the work, he was not acting upon his own knowledge and judgment and so was acting arbitrarily.

Southern Surety Co. v. Sealy Indep. School Dist., 10 S.W. 2d 786 (1928). Fraudulent concealment of material defects in a building, where the contract provided only for architect's inspection at intervals, was held sufficient to invalidate architect's acceptance.

Daniels v. Franklin, 233 S.W. 380 (1921). Architect's certificate, to be conclusive, must be made without such gross ignorance, carelessness, or indifference as will amount to a fraud upon the builder.

Garrett v. Dodson, 199 S.W. 675 (1917). Defective judgment of the architect in determining whether the work meets the specifications, does not justify abandonment of the work by the contractor.

Wash.   *Hurley v. Kiona-Benton School Dist.*, 124 Wash. 537, 215 Pac. 21 (1923). Where architect certified that contractor had complied with the contract, when all parties knew the work had not been performed, such certificate was a fraud and not binding.

Bavaria Inv. Co. v. Washington Brick, Lime & Sewer Pipe Co., 82 Wash. 187, 144 Pac. 68 (1914). Fact that architect, before certifying damages caused by contractor's delay, consulted with the owner's president and its foreman in charge of the work, does not show his certificate to be collusive.

Ilse v. Aetna Indemnity Co., 55 Wash. 487, 104 Pac. 787 (1909). The making of a certificate without proper knowledge of a fact, which on investigation is found to be untrue, is equivalent to the making of a certificate known to be false and operates as a fraud in law.

U.S. *H. W. Zweig Co. v. United States,* 92 Ct.Cl. 472 (1941). Where contracting officer's decision is not fair and impartial, such decision is not final under the terms of the contract.

Southern New England R. Corp. v. Marsch, 45 F. 2d 766 (1931). Where engineer during progress of work knowingly withheld sums from monthly estimates to which the contractor was entitled and in other particulars acted in violation of the terms of the contract, his findings were not binding on the contractor.

Thompson-Starret Co. v. La Belle Iron Work, 17 F. 2d 536, *cert. den.,* 274 U.S. 748 (1927). Fact that arbiter was self willed and prejudiced did not show lack of good faith in his dissatisfaction with contractor's performance.

Lewis v. Chicago, S. F. & C. R. Co., 49 Fed. 708 (1891). Court will relieve against mistakes in measurement and calculations apparent on the face of estimates or clearly proven, or from a wrong construction put upon the provisions of the contract by the engineer.

CHAPTER FOURTEEN

Duties of architect or engineer as arbiter

The architect or engineer, in determining disputes or issuing certificates of performance, is required to act impartially and in good faith and in accordance with the terms of the contract. It is his duty to determine all disputes properly submitted to him, and to give his certificate or estimate when the contractor is entitled to it. The determination must be made by the person designated in the contract, and must be based on his personal knowledge, unless the parties to the contract agree to substitute another person in his place.

The architect or engineer who is authorized to determine disputes or issue certificates generally acts in a dual capacity. In furnishing plans, drawings and specifications, and in supervising construction of the project, he acts as agent of the owner and binds him by those acts done within the scope of his authority. As the arbiter charged with the task of determining disputes or issuing certificates upon the execution of the work (insofar as his decisions are conclusive), he acts for and binds both parties.

The fact that he is in the employ of but one of the parties does not in itself disqualify him from acting in the second capacity. However, in such case, both parties to the contract are entitled to an honest judgment, and he must act impartially and in good faith in performing his duties. If other factors in his relationship toward the parties make it impossible for him to act in an impartial manner, or if his conduct indicates that he is biased and unfair toward one of the parties, his determination will not have conclusive effect. Thus, if the architect or engineer, under his contract with the owner, is required to keep the building cost within a guaranteed maximum his estimates or certificates are presumably biased. Where the acts of the arbiter throughout the performance of the contract are biased and unfair, and his attitude hostile to the contractor, he is clearly an improper person to construe the contract or approve performance, and such conduct will disqualify him. Gross incompetency amounting to fraud or bad faith will disqualify the arbiter or avoid his decision.

However, it has been held that the architect or engineer is not disqualified because he is interested in the ownership of the building being erected, or because he has been a witness in an action between the owner and contractor involving the same matter referred to him for decision. In certain cases he has been held qualified to pass on questions of his own default.

Not only is it the duty of the architect or engineer to act honestly and in good faith when making his decision, but it is likewise his duty to pass on all matters in dispute properly submitted to him, and to give his estimate, certificate, or approval when the contractor is entitled to it. He cannot withhold a certificate arbitrarily or capriciously. Nor can he refuse his decision or certificate on grounds which it is not within the scope of his authority to determine. Thus, he is not justified in refusing a certificate because the building will cost more than the contract price, or because he thinks the contractor's claim cannot be sustained. As a general rule, he is permitted to refuse his certificate or approval only where the contractor has substantially failed to perform the contract.

Furthermore, the determination of the arbiter must be made in accordance with the terms of the contract. Provisions in the contract that notice be given to the contractor, that an estimate be furnished the contractor, that a certificate be furnished at a certain stage of the work, require strict compliance. If the arbiter disregards or violates the contract provisions, by making his certificate or estimate on a different basis than that contemplated in the contract, his determination can be avoided.

Where the manner in which a decision is to be made is not specified in the contract, it has been held that the arbiter may make it by whatever proper method he chooses and on such evidence as he chooses to receive. As a general rule, whatever action he takes is required to be based upon his personal knowledge. The guiding consideration for the architect or engineer, then, is that he act honestly and impartially, and proceed in accordance with such requirements as may be set forth in the contract.

Once the architect has made his decision or final certificate, he may not subsequently modify, revoke, or annul it or make a new award upon the same issues. Likewise, after approval of materials or work he cannot later withdraw his approval and substitute new materials or require different workmanship. The courts uniformly hold that the power of the engineer or architect to issue a certificate or estimate is exhausted by issuance of such certificate or estimate, and any attempted re-exercise of such power is not binding.

A related question is the period of time during which the decision of the architect or engineer will be found to be conclusive where acceptance of the contractor's work does not necessarily resolve the issue. In one case, the court seemed to hold that, in the absence of a clear intention to the contrary, as to issues which could have been presented to the architect for his determination, before the acceptance of the work, determinations of those issues subsequent to the final acceptance lose their conclusive effect. The justification given for this position was that the purpose of vesting the architect with the powers of an arbiter is to keep control over the work *as it progresses* in the hands of a qualified person who can make decisions quickly. See *Fred McClean Heating Supplies, Inc. v. Jefferson Const. Co.*, 159 N.E. 2d 95 (1959).

Where the architect has given no proper certificate, as required by the contract, his testimony as a witness in a suit based on the contract will not be conclusive. If the contract provides for the decision, certificate, or estimate of a *designated* architect or engineer, the person named is required to make the determination unless both parties have agreed upon a substitution.

A stipulation for the certificate or decision of two architects requires action by both. Thus, where the certificate or judgment of two architects is called for, it has been held that where the certificate of one only is given, or where the judgment of one is based solely upon information given him by the other, such certificate or judgment is insufficient.

By the terms of some contracts a person other than the named architect has been permitted to issue a certificate, as where the term "architect" was defined to include the architect and his associate, or where provision was made for the certificate of another in the alternative. In a number of circumstances, the parties may agree to a substitute architect, thus impliedly authorizing him to issue the required certificate. On the inability of the original architect to act, the building contract may authorize the substitution of another in his place. Even without a specific contractual provision to that effect, where the architect named in the contract dies or is removed, and is replaced by another architect whom the contractor accepts, the certificate of the new architect will be required. It has been held that where the owner, by dismissing the architect named, makes it impossible for the contractor to secure his certificate, the contractor sufficiently complies with the contract if he secures the certificate of the architect in charge of the project.

If the person agreed upon by the parties attempts to delegate his authority to another, the latter's decision will not be conclusive on the parties. Since such authority is considered to be personal in nature, it is non-delegable, unless the parties impliedly or specifically assent to it. It has been held, however, that where it is impractical for one engineer to supervise all of the work, he may appoint expert agents for the purpose and issue certificates on their reports. It has also been held that an engineer may seek information from his superior officer upon which to base his decision, provided only that the decision is his own.

To QUALIFY AS AN ARBITER, the architect or engineer must act honestly, impartially, and in good faith. The fact that he is employed by one of the parties does not in itself disqualify him.

Cal. *Bacigalupi v. Phoenix Blds. & Constr. Co.*, 14 Cal. App. 632, 112 Pac. 892 (1910). Architect issuing certificate need not be a professional arbiter.

Conn. *George S. Chattfield Co. v. O'Neill*, 89 Conn. 172, 93 Atl. 133 (1915). Incompetency or negligence of an architect does not void his decision unless it is so gross as to amount to fraud or bad faith.

Ill. *Chicago Athletic Ass'n v. Eddy Electric Mfg. Co.*, 77 Ill. App. 204 (1900). An architect is not disqualified because he is interested in the ownership of the building under construction.

Ind. *Louisville E. & St. L. R. Co. v. Donnegan*, 117 Ind. 179, 12 N.E. 153 (1887). Contract implies that railroad company will furnish a competent and honest engineer.

Kan. *State v. Massachusetts Bonding & Ins. Co.*, 91 Kan. 74, 136 Pac. 905 (1913). Architect was not disqualified by reason of the fact that he was a state officer, since in making estimates he was not acting as a state architect but as an individual.

Edwards v. Hartshorn, 72 Kan. 19, 82 Pac. 520 (1905). Arbiter of disputes is not disqualified because he is employee of owner but law requires of him utmost diligence and good faith.

Mass. *Marsch v. Southern New England R. Corp.*, 230 Mass. 483, 120 N.E. 120 (1918). Allegations that engineer was under absolute control and direction of owner and owner could at any time dismiss him and appoint another person to act in his stead, are not sufficient allegations of bias, fraud, or prejudice to show collusion or fraud.

Mo. *Lund v. McClinton*, 205 S.W. 240 (1918). Architect's belief that contractor is not complying with the plans and specifications as to one particular does not justify him in acting arbitrarily, or maliciously with respect to other particulars.

N.Y. *Elizabeth Sash, Door & Supply Co. v. St. Vincent's Hospital*, 241 App. Div. 751, 270 N.Y.S. 195 (1934). In making periodic estimates, architect must act in a judicial manner and apply reasonable care and good judgment.

Atlantic, Gulf & Pacific Co. v. Woodmere Realty Co., 156 App. Div. 351, 142 N.Y.S. 953, *appeal dismissed,* 209 N.Y. 557, 103 N.E. 1120 (1913). Where contract provided for determination of disputes by city surveyor in locality of harbor project, subsequent employment of surveyor to represent interests of employer disqualified him from acting as arbiter.

Pa.   *Barclay v. Deckerhoof,* 171 Pa. 378, 33 Atl. 71 (1895). Architect was not disqualified because he had previously been a witness in an action between the owner and contractor involving the same matter referred to him for decision.

Tex.   *American Surety Co. v. Shaw,* 69 S.W. 2d 47 (1934). Subcontractors who could obtain compensation from contractor only upon estimates of the architect, were not bound by the architect's arbitrary refusal to approve payments where he was disqualified because financially interested.

Manett, Seastrunk & Buckner v. Terminal Bldg. Corp., 120 Tex. 374, 39 S.W. 2d 1 (1931). Estimates made by architect primarily liable for keeping building cost within guaranteed maximum are presumably biased.

Wash.   *Bavaria Inv. Co. v. Washington Brick, Lime & Sewer Pipe Co.,* 82 Wash. 187, 144 Pac. 68 (1914). Where certificate of architect was attacked on ground of his incompetency, mere showing that he did not understand method of manufacturing terra cotta, to be used in building, although he could judge whether completed product was defective, did not show him to be incompetent.

W.Va.   *Berry v. Huntington Masonic Temple Ass'n,* 80 W.Va. 342, 93 S.E. 355 (1917). Agency of architect is separable, and insofar as he is made arbiter between owner and contractor, he acts for and binds both.

U.S.   *Northern Pac. R. Co. v. Twohy Bros. Co.,* 95 F. 2d 220 (1938). Evidence that railroad's chief engineer was biased against contractor made him an improper person to construe the contract and his decision concerning the meaning of certain terms was not binding on the contractor.

Southern New England R. Corp. v. Marsch, 45 F. 2d 766 (1931). Railroad engineer held disqualified to make up final certificates where his acts throughout performance of contract were clearly biased and deliberately unfair and hostile to the contractor.

Firestone Tire & Rubber Co. v. Riverside Bridge Co., 247 Fed. 625 (1918). Owner's engineers in determining claim for extension of time construction, could pass on the question whether their own default caused the delay which under the contract would entitle the contractor to an extension of time.

Memphis Trust Co. v. Brown-Ketchum Iron Works, 166 Fed. 398, *cert. den.,* 214 U.S. 515 (1909). Architects authorized to determine disputes could properly determine whether the delay on account of which damages were asked by contractors was their fault or that of contractors, there being nothing to indicate that the architects would become liable to the owner in case they were at fault as between them and contractors.

IT IS THE DUTY OF THE ARCHITECT OR engineer to render a decision when any dispute provided for in the contract is properly submitted to him and to issue a certificate or estimate when the contractor is entitled to it.

Ariz. *Gillespie Land & Irrig. Co. v. Hamilton,* 43 Ariz. 102, 29 P. 2d 158 (1934). Engineer is justified in refusing final certificate only when there is a real and substantial failure on the part of the builder to fulfill his contractual duty.

Cal. *Kling v. Bucher,* 32 Cal. App. 679, 163 Pac. 871 (1917). Where the work has been completed, there can be no legal ground upon which architect's certificate can be refused.

Mich. *Hart v. Reid,* 243 Mich. 175, 219 N.W. 692 (1928). Certificate cannot legally be withheld because the owner is without funds to pay the contractor.

Kunze v. Jones, 200 Mich. 453, 166 N.W. 904 (1918). Evidence held to show reasonably satisfactory performance of contract by contractor and arbitrary refusal of architect to give certificate for part payment.

N.J. *Central Union Stock Yards Co. v. Uvalde Asphalt Pav. Co.,* 82 N.J. Eq. 246, 87 Atl. 235 (1913). Certificate cannot be refused where the work has been fully performed.

N.Y. *Borup v. Von Kokeritz,* 162 App. Div. 394, 147 N.Y.S. 832 (1914). Contractor was held not entiled to a partial payment where the architect refused certificate because the work was defective, although he stated as additional ground, the refusal of the superintendent of construction to approve the work.

People v. Craven, 210 N.Y. 443, 104 N.E. 922 (1914). Under contract authorizing engineer to decide disputes, it was his duty to pass on contractor's claim for extra work, though he thought it could not be sustained.

Pa. *Sgarlat v. Griffith,* 349 Pa. 42, 36 A. 2d 330 (1944). It was held the duty of the architect and the general contractor to present to the owner a certificate of performance by the subcontractor within a reasonable time after his completion of the work.

Hunn v. Pennsylvania Inst. for Instruction of Blind, 221 Pa. 403, 70 Atl. 812 (1908). Every matter of dispute included in the contract and referred to the architects must be determined by them.

THE ARCHITECT OR ENGINEER MUST COMPLY with the terms of the contract in determining disputes or issuing estimates by whatever method he chooses where none is specified in the contract.

Ariz.   *Guarantee Title & Trust Co. v. Willis,* 38 Ariz. 33, 297 Pac. 445 (1931). The decision of the engineer is binding where so provided in the contract, except that he cannot change the terms of the contract.

Ill.   *Bloomington Hotel Co. v. Garthwait,* 227 Ill. 613, 81 N.E. 714 (1907). Where the architect's certificate is to be issued upon completion of the work, a certificate issued by him prior thereto is not binding on the parties.

Mass.   *Benjamin Foster Co. v. Commonwealth,* 318 Mass. 190, 61 N.E. 2d 147 (1945). Decisions of engineers are not to be controlled by any extrinsic standard of reasonableness or necessity for that would merely substitute the judgment of the court or jury for that of the engineers.

Norcross v. Wyman, 187 Mass. 25, 72 N.E. 347 (1904). Architects may make their decisions on such legal principles as they deem applicable and on such evidence as they choose to receive.

Minn.   *Benson v. Miller,* 56 Minn. 410, 57 N.W. 943 (1894). Where building contract stipulated for the decision of two named architects with respect to delay or default of contractor and the judgment of one architect was based solely on what the other had informed him and not upon his own examination and inquiry, the decision was not binding.

Schwerin v. De Graff, 21 Minn. 354 (1875). Where engineers' estimate is to be furnished to the contractor and is to be conclusive as to the quantity of work done, an estimate made by the engineers but not furnished to the contractor, is not conclusive upon him.

Kausen v. Leonhardt Realty Co., 79 Misc. 621, 140 N.Y.S. 493 (1913). A certificate of approval is not conclusive when it is obtained from the architect upon a mere statement made to him by the contractor and is subsequently revoked.

Neidlinger v. Onward Constr. Co., 107 App. Div. 398, 95 N.Y.S. 1148 (1905), *aff'd,* 188 N.Y. 572, 80 N.E. 1114 (1907). Architect is not required to take the testimony of witnesses in determining whether the contract has been completed.

Tex. *Perkins v. Locke,* 88 Tex. 66, 29 S.W. 1048 (1895). Where engineer's certificate did not comply in essential particulars with contract requirements, it was not evidence of completion according to the contract.

Va. *Mills v. Norfolk & W. R. Co.,* 90 Va. 523, 19 S.E. 171 (1894). It is competent to show that engineer's estimates and certificate are in such gross violation of the contract as to amount to a fraud.

W.Va. *Parr v. Howell,* 74 W.Va. 413, 82 S.E. 126 (1914). Certificate showing cost of completion of work by owner, on contractor's default, in order to be conclusive must be founded on thorough audit of such expense.

U.S. *Hall v. Union Indemnity Co.,* 61 F. 2d 85 (1932). Where the contract requires payments on invoices approved by architect, he must procure contractor's statement of labor, materials, and values, not merely estimates, since an invoice calls for statement of facts while estimates call for opinion or approximation.

Gearing v. United States, 48 Ct.Cl. 12 (1912). Where the contractor appeals from decision of the local engineer to the engineer in charge, the latter cannot refer the dispute back to the local engineer for decision.

Kimball v. United States, 24 Ct.Cl. 35 (1888). Where the contract provides that the contractor shall be informed of defects in his work and given an opportunity to perfect it, the refusal of the engineer in charge to accept the work does not bind the contractor in the absence of a notice of defects, although engineer's decision, according to the contract, is to be final.

THE POWER OF AN ARBITRATOR IS EXHAUSTED AFTER HIS FINAL DECISION, certificate, or approval is given, and he may not subsequently modify, revoke, or annul it or make a new award upon the same issues. Where he has given no proper certificate as required by the contract, his testimony as a witness will not be conclusive.

Iowa *Granette Products Co. v. Arthur H. Newmann & Co.,* 208 Iowa 24, 221 N.W. 197 (1928). Where artificial stone had been delivered by subcontractor, approved by architect, and a portion used in construction, architect could not thereafter reject the material pursuant to a change in the entire construction plan by arrangement with the principal contractor.

Mo. *Boteler v. Roy,* 40 Mo. App. 234 (1890). Where no proper certificate has been given by the architect, his decision on the witness stand will not be conclusive but will be received on the same terms as that of any other witness with equal knowledge and opportunity.

Fitzgerald v. Beers, 31 Mo. App. 356 (1888). Where subcontractor was allowed to proceed with work on building without being informed of changes which required extra work and there was a later refusal to enter into an agreement with him as to the amount and price of extra work, he could not be bound by estimates of the architect delivered on the witness stand.

Tex. *Wright v. Meyer,* 25 S.W. 1122 (1894). Where the architect is present and has knowledge of the character of materials being used and does not object at the time, his conduct will be deemed an approval which cannot be reversed to the injury of the contractor.

U.S. *City of St. Charles v. Stookey,* 154 Fed. 722 (1907). Power of the engineer to make a final estimate certifying the amount due was exhausted by his first estimate and a second estimate made some months later was not binding.

THE CERTIFICATE, DECISION, OR APPROVAL must be given by the architect or engineer designated in the contract.

Ark. *J. E. Hollingsworth & Co. v. Leachville Special School Dist.,* 157 Ark. 430, 249, S.W. 24 (1923). Where term "architect" in contract referred expressly to a designated architect and his associate and partner, the partner had authority to pass on the work.

Cal. *Rialto Constr. Co. v. Reed,* 17 Cal. App. 29, 118 Pac. 473 (1911). Chief engineer need not personally make measurements or estimates, but estimates made by an assistant and forming the basis for a final estimate by the chief engineer are sufficient.

Ga. *Hilton v. Taylor,* 18 Ga. App. 647, 90 S.E. 223 (1916). Although contract sued on does not name an architect, where an architect is named in the specifications attached thereto, the contractor must allege approval by the architect specified.

Huggens v. Atlanta Tile and Marble Co., 106 S.E. 2d 191 (1958). "The person agreed upon by the parties to pass upon the work has no right to delegate his authority to another, and if he attempts to do so, the decision of such other person is not conclusive on the parties, unless they agree to such substitution."

Ill. *Costello v. Delano,* 274 Ill. 426, 113 N.E. 689 (1916). Where contract stated that chief engineer should make final estimate, railroad company was not concluded by the final estimate of a subordinate engineer.

Vermont St. M. E. Church v. Brose, 104 Ill. 206 (1882). Where contract provided that work should be done to the satisfaction of the architect or his assistant superintendent, the approval of either was sufficient.

Lull v. Korf, 84 Ill. 225 (1876). Where payments are to be made on the certificate of two architects who are partners, a certificate signed by one in the firm name is sufficient where no objection is made to the certificate but payment is refused on another ground.

Iowa   *McNamara v. Harrison*, 81 Iowa 486, 46 N.W. 976 (1890). A payment by contractors to subcontractors on the final estimate of a subordinate engineer is not a waiver of contract provision that amount due subcontractors shall be paid them only on certificate of the engineer and subcontractors cannot recover alleged deficiency due them without such certificate.

Minn.   *Benson v. Miller*, 56 Minn. 410, 57 N.W. 943 (1894). Where the judgment of two named architects was required, and the judgment of one was based solely upon the other's information, and not upon his own examination, it was not conclusive.

N.J.   *Wallis Iron Works v. Monmouth Park Ass'n*, 55 N.J.L. 132, 26 Atl. 140 (1893). Engineer authorized by contract to make certain decisions was intended to be the incumbent at time the decision was due and after work was finished party who had been owner's engineer but had left his employ was not the party intended.

N.Y.   *McEntyre v. Tucker*, 36 App. Div. 53, 55 N.Y.S. 153 (1898). Contractor cannot produce certificate signed by another party for the architect named in the contract unless there has been a modification of the contract, and he pleads and proves such modification.

Tex.   *Wright v. Meyer*, 25 S.W. 1122 (1894). Although an architect cannot delegate his power to make decisions to his partner, if the latter is mutually accepted by the parties, they are precluded from denying his authority.

Va.   *Richmond College v. Scott-Nuckols Co.*, 124 Va. 333, 98 S.E. (1919). Where it is impractical for the engineer to personally inspect all the work, he may appoint expert agents for that purpose and issue certificates on their report.

Johnson & Grommett Bros. v. Bunn & Monteiro, 108 Va. 490, 62 S.E. 341 (1908). Contractor may not employ a third person to make a final estimate of the work, in the absence of any unreasonable delay of the designated engineer in making estimates or of any mistake or fraud on his part.

Wash.   *Lavanway v. Cannon*, 37 Wash. 593, 79 Pac. 1117 (1905). Where two architects whose certificate is required dissolve their partnership and the owner refuses to allow one architect access to the work and accepts progress certificates signed by the other, a final certificate by such architect is sufficient.

Van Hook v. Burns, 10 Wash. 22, 38 Pac. 763 (1894). Chief engineer's decision on disputed point was not conclusive if he paid no personal attention to the matter but acted solely on the statement of his subordinates.

U.S.   *Warner Constr. Co. v. Louis Hanssen's Sons,* 20 F. 2d 483 (1927). Where the right of final approval is reserved, the arbiter at the time of final inspection is the person authorized to make the final decision.

Eyre-Shoemaker, Inc. v. Buffalo R. & P. R. Co., 193 Fed. 387 (1912). Contract providing for final decision of chief engineer did not mean the person who filled the position when contract was entered into, but the person who was chief engineer when the decisions contemplated were made.

Bowers Hydraulic Dredging Co. v. United States, 41 Ct.Cl. 214 (1906). Engineer may seek information from his superior officer upon which to base his decision, provided only that the decision rendered by him is his own.

THE CERTIFICATE OR DECISION OF ANOTHER ARCHITECT may be substituted for that of the architect named where the parties to the contract agree upon such substitution.

Cal.   *Griffith v. Happersberger,* 86 Cal. 605, 25 Pac. 137 (1890). Where the owner, by discharging the architect named, makes it impossible for the contractor to procure his certificate, the contractor may obtain the certificate of the architects in charge.

Me.   *Seretto v. Rockland S. T. & O. H. R. Co.,* 101 Me. 140, 63 Atl. 651 (1906). Where railroad company substitutes, with contractor's acquiescence, another engineer for the engineer named, certificates made by the substitute engineer are binding upon the parties, and the railroad is estopped from denying the authority of the substituted engineer.

N.Y.   *Beecher v. Schuback,* 4 Misc. 54, 23 N.Y.S. 604 (1893), *aff'd,* 158 N.Y. 687, 53 N.E. 1123 (1899). If the architect named in the contract dies and another is substituted by the owner and accepted by the contractor, the certificate of the substituted architect is necessary.

U.S.   *Memphis Trust Co. v. Brown-Ketchum Iron Works,* 166 Fed. 398, *cert. den.,* 214 U.S. 515 (1909). Building contract may authorize substitution of another architect in place of the original person designated on his inability to act.

CHAPTER FIFTEEN

The right of the architect or engineer to interpret the construction contract

Under a stipulation that the decision of an architect or engineer with respect to disputes arising during the performance of the contract or his certificate at the conclusion thereof is final, the architect or engineer may not have authority to determine questions of law.

Prior to the decision of the U.S. Supreme Court in *United States v. Moorman*, 342 U.S. 98 (1951), the courts were in general agreement that an architect or engineer who is authorized under the terms of a construction contract to issue a final certificate of completion or determine disputes between the owner and contractor does not have the authority to interpret the contract itself. While the decisions are almost unanimous that he may not construe the contract, the courts have had difficulties in deciding what is a dispute within the competence of the arbiter to decide, and what is a question involving a construction of the contract. Since any decision on a dispute arising under a building contract entails in some degree a construction of the contract itself, the courts have attempted to clarify this principle by distinguishing between questions of fact, which are within the peculiar competence of the arbiter as an expert to determine, and questions of law.

The Supreme Court decision in *United States v. Moorman* has had the effect of superseding many of the decisions which previously denied to the arbiter authority to determine questions of law in rendering a decision on a disputed question. It clearly indicates that the arbiter will not in all cases be prevented from determining questions of law. The Court specifically held that, under a stipulation in a government construction contract that the decision of the Secretary of War should be final, a decision rendered by the Secretary on the specific point at issue was final whether or not it involved a determination of a question of fact or a question of law.

The agreement provided that, if the contractor considered any work demanded of him to be outside the requirements of the contract and the governmental contracting officer, charged with determining that question, ruled against him, an appeal from the contracting officer's decision could be taken to the Secretary of War "whose decision or that of his duly authorized representative shall be final and binding upon the parties to the contract."

The subcontractor had entered into the usual government contract to grade a plant site. A controversy arose as to whether the contract required the contractor to grade a particular portion of the site shown on the drawings but not located within the plant as described by the specifications. On demand of the Government, the contractor did the grading and then filed a claim for extra compensation. It was rejected by the government engineer and on appeal, by the authorized representative of the Secretary of War.

The contractor brought an action in the Court of Claims contending that he had a right there to challenge the findings of the Secretary of War because his findings were based on issues of law while the contract only stated that the findings as to questions of fact "should be final and conclusive on the parties." The Court of Claims reconsidered the dispute and, on the basis of its new findings, entered judgment for the contractor.

The Supreme Court reversed this decision stating that, since the parties had by the terms of the contract intended to authorize final determinations by the Secretary of War, he was clearly enpowered to make a determination on the question of work outside the requirements of the contract, whether or not his decision was one of fact or law.

The Court found that such provision was neither in conflict with nor limited by another provision as to determination of questions of fact, which read as follows:

"Except as otherwise specifically provided in this contract, all disputes concerning questions of fact arising under this contract shall be decided by the contracting officer subject to written appeal by the contractor within 30 days to the head of the department concerned or his duly authorized representative, whose decision shall be final and conclusive upon the parties thereto."

While the decision involves a disputes clause in a government contract, no valid reason appears why it should not apply also to a similar clause included in private contracts. The impact of the Moorman decision may be felt in states where courts previously held to the contrary.

In the citations and discussion that follow this should be kept in mind. It must also, however, be pointed out that in many situations, the Moorman decision may not be controlling.

Certain questions have been readily classified as concerning themselves with factual or legal determinations. Others required interpretation by the court as to whether they fall within one or the other category. Many courts, while determining that a particular decision was within the authority conferred, did not discuss the question as to whether the decision amounted to a construction of the contract. The discussion, therefore, will be limited to cases which have considered the question as to whether the decision was a construction of the contract.

There can be found in a number of cases on this point statements to the effect that the arbiter has power to construe the meaning of the contract. However, such statements have not been given strict interpretation and it is not certain whether they were intended to stand for the proposition that a legal construction of the contract on the part of the architect or engineer is permissible.

In a number of government contracts which have come before the courts, the government contracting officer was authorized to make certain final decisions with regard to questions of fact. The determination as to whether the decision of the contracting officer involved a question of fact or construction of law depended upon the contract stipulation and the particular dispute presented. If it was found that the decision involved a construction of the contract, such decision was held not binding and the court reconsidered the whole question and determined the controversy. Even in some of the earlier cases where the government contract did not restrict the decision of the contracting officer to questions of fact, the Court of Claims took the position that such decision should have been limited to factual determinations. The principle relied upon has been thus stated:

"... the competency of the parties to so stipulate (that the determination of the contracting officer shall be final), as the courts have many times pointed out, is limited to the decision of questions of fact arising under the contract, such as the quantity and quality of materials delivered, whether the work performed meets contract requirements, causes of delay in the performance of the work, etc. These are questions of fact, the correct solution of which is usually largely dependent on professional knowledge and skill. They are questions which the parties to a contract may properly submit to the determination of the contracting officer or head of the department, and lawfully agree to be bound by his decision." *Davis v. United States,* 82 Ct.Cl. 334, 346–7 (1936).

Certain construction contracts have given the architect or engineer specific authority to construe the contract or, most commonly, the true intent and meaning of the drawings and specifications. The courts have in many instances upheld determinations of the arbiter where the specifications were ambiguous and difficult of interpretation. In most cases there arose a dispute with respect to the technical requirements of drawings or specifications, and the courts simply determined that the architect's or engineer's decision was binding. In a few cases, however, the courts determined whether a specific decision was authorized by the stipulation giving the right to construe the papers made part of the contract by reference.

Thus under such stipulations, architects have been permitted to determine whether alleged additional work was work within the meaning of the contract, the type of material required for the construction, whether the drawings or specifications governed in a conflict between them.

However, while the right of the architect or engineer, under stipulations to that effect, to construe the specifications, was generally recognized, some courts limited this authority to the drawings or specifications and refused to extend it to include interpretation of the contract itself. Thus there have been excluded from the purview of the arbiter's authority such questions as arise after the completion of the contract with respect to the legal rights of the parties; decisions as to whether a contractor is required to do certain work not expressly or impliedly within the language of the contract or specifications and the liability of the owner for payment for certain work performed by the contractor.

Where the architect or engineer is charged with the duty of determining disputes under the contract or issuing a certificate of performance, many cases have held that a *misconstruction* of the contract on his part did not make his decision or certificate binding on the parties. The courts in such cases did not determine whether he had authority to construe the contract, thus implying that a proper construction of the contract, though involving a legal determination, would be permissible.

Among the specific issues on which engineers or architects have made decisions is included the determination of the basis for measurement of work performed. It has been almost uniformly held that the architect or engineer could properly measure the work done, and his decision would be binding. But where the method of measurement required a construction of the contract, or where the method was not specified, or if he did not measure the work in accordance with the terms of the agreement, or where the contract was ambiguous as to what was to be measured, the arbiter's measurement or decision based on his measurement was not binding on the parties. In these cases it was held not within the province of the architect or engineer to determine the intent of the parties since it involved an interpretation of the contract.

Ordinarily the determination as to the type and quality of materials and specific work required under the contract would appear to be within the special competence of the architect or engineer since he is a person skilled in that field. While many courts have left such determinations to the architect or engineer, others have held that such a determination involved a construction of the contract and was therefore not intended to be left to the architect or engineer and a decision by him was not binding. Thus, where the terms of the contract were doubtful, or where a particular term had a well-defined meaning, or where the engineer sought to modify the terms of the contract, it was held that his decision would not be final.

Building contracts have frequently included clauses authorizing the architect or engineer to determine all disputes submitted to him under the contract. Where the clause was specifically considered, the courts, prior to the Moorman decision, generally limited the arbiter's power to decide only those questions which did not involve a legal interpretation. The position has been taken that the parties cannot by such an agreement oust the courts of jurisdiction and where it was found that the arbiter in reaching his decision construed the contract, it was held that his decision did not preclude the court from reconsidering the question.

The law in this area has developed in rather unique fashion since *Moorman*. First, in *United States v. Wunderlich*, 342 U.S. 98 (1951), the Court extended the principle of *Moorman*, at least as to questions of fact, by holding that a clause making the "contract officer's" decision "final and conclusive" was binding although found to be "arbitrary," "capricious," or "grossly erroneous" where no actual fraud is proved.

The reaction of the business community to this turn of events prompted Congress in 1954 to adopt Public Law 356 which provided in substance that no government contract should contain a provision making the decision of a government official final on a question of law. It further provided that the decision of a contracting officer in respect to a question of fact shall not be final and conclusive if that decision is fraudulent, capricious, arbitrary, so grossly erroneous as necessarily to imply bad faith, or is not supported by substantial evidence.

Subsequent cases have demonstrated a reluctance on the part of some state courts to subscribe to the rule of *Moorman*. In *Kyburg v. State*, 108 N.W. 2d 645, the Supreme Court of South Dakota had the following to say on the issue of the finality of the State Engineer's decision that the contractor was required to provide bedsprings under the contract:

"The power of the architects under the contract was unquestionably binding where deciding questions arising as to the meaning of the provisions of the plans and specifications concerning all work that was within the contract, but they were not given the power expressly, nor may we give it to them by implication, to either add to or take away from the contractual rights or liabilities of either party under the contract itself. The power to construe and define the intent and meaning of plans and specifications made a part of the contract is one thing, and may properly be, as it was in this instance, left to arbiters selected by the parties; the power to construe the contract itself and to determine what is within and what is without such contract is a different and independent question, and belongs primarily to the courts."

The language of this case has been approved in at least one other case. See *Eickhof Construction Co. v. City of Grafton,* 123 N.W. 2d 580 (1963).

However, the New York Court of Appeals, in the case of *Board of Education of Union Free School District No. 1 v. Barbaresi & Son, Inc.,* 4 N.Y. 2d 812, ruled that a construction contract which provides for the final determination of all disputes between owner and contractor to be made by the architect is valid, even though the dispute involves the construction and interpretation of the architect's own plans and specifications. The dispute in question concerned the installation of a certain type of ceiling in the auditorium of a school under construction. The general contractor contended that such installation was not part of his contract, but was the responsibility of the electrical contractor and demanded arbitration of this issue under Article 39 of the General Conditions of the American Institute of Architects. The architect, however, ruled that his plans and specifications required installation of the ceiling by the general contractor. The owner's refusal to arbitrate the issue was sustained by the Court under an express provision of the contract which stated that the architect shall "determine whether the . . . plans and specifications have been fully complied with by the contractor" and that his determination "shall be final and binding."

It has been generally held that an architect or engineer empowered by the construction contract to determine disputes or issue certificates of performance has no authority to construe the contract.

Ariz. *Guarantee Title & Trust Co. v. Willis,* 38 Ariz. 33, 297 Pac. 445 (1931). Legal interpretation of a building contract is always a matter for the courts.

State v. Kisselburg, 27 Ariz. 336, 233 Pac. 580 (1925). A provision that all disputes arising under the contract were to be finally determined by the state engineer was held not to make his decision binding on questions of law, such as the meaning of the contract terms, since the provision referred only to issues of fact, such as the quantity and quality of the work.

Ark. *Connelly v. Parkes,* 160 Ark. 496, 255 S.W. 22 (1923). A contract between a road district and a contractor, providing that the decision of an engineer as to the meaning of all specifications shall be final, refers to disputes between the parties as to the meaning of the specifications in the contract, and has no reference to the interpretation of the contract or the determination of any issue between the contractor and engineer growing out of their respective contracts with the district, that being a question for the courts.

N.Y. *E. H. Smith Contracting Co. v. New York City,* 240 N.Y. 491, 148 N.E. 655 (1925). Where contractor brought action to recover difference between amount certified to by engineer to be paid for alterations and amount contractor thought was due, whereas to one of the items the decision of the engineer was entirely arbitrary or based on a broader interpretation of the contract than was permissible, contractor would recover despite provisions in contract making engineer's decision final on all questions arising under the contract.

Ohio *State v. Tracy,* 129 Ohio St. 550, 196 N.E. 650 (1935). A provision authorizing the director of highways to make final decisions does not authorize him to construe the contract.

Ore. *Wallace v. Oregon Eng. & Constr. Co.,* 90 Ore. 31, 174 Pac. 156 (1918). A provision in the main contract empowering the engineer to settle disputes was held not to authorize him to determine the validity of the contract between contractor and subcontractor nor oust the courts of jurisdiction in an action for its breach.

Wis. *Joint School Dist. v. Bailey-Marsh Co.,* 181 Wis. 202, 194 N.W. 171 (1923). Under contract providing for monthly payments to contractor for work and material furnished, as assessed by architect, architect could not arbitrarily determine what material had been furnished and his determination was not conclusive so far as it involved an interpretation of the contract terms.

U.S. *Stiers Bros. Constr. Co. v. Broderick,* 60 F. Supp. 792 (1945). Subcontractor's right to recover an amount due to the elimination of work provided for by the contract depends on the terms of the contract which is a question of law for the court, respecting which the parties could not provide for finality of the arbiter's determination.

S. J. Groves & Sons Co. v. Warren, 135 F. 2d 264, *cert. den.*, 319 U.S. 766 (1943). Parties to a construction contract including the United States may designate a person finally to determine disputes arising under the contract, but he cannot make conclusive determinations on questions of law since the rights of the parties are fixed by the contract, the interpretation of which is a question exclusively for the courts.

Cf. United States v. Moorman, considered *supra*.

United States v. John Kerns Constr. Co., 140 F. 2d 792 (1944). Where government engineers changed and delayed work called for by prime contract which in turn necessitated change and delayed work under sub-contract requiring performance by a specified time, sub-contractor was not liable to general contractor for liquidated damages for the delay. Where sub-contract contained penalty clause differing materially from penalty clause contained in prime government construction contract, sub-contractor was not bound to follow procedure provided in prime contract for obtaining extension of time to avoid liability for liquidated damages for delay. Where situation of parties to sub-contract changed after signing thereof, agreement whereby general contractor under government construction contract waived claim against sub-contractor for liquidated damages for delay was binding.

A FEW COURTS, ALTHOUGH STATING THAT THE ARCHITECT OR ENGINEER had no authority to vary the terms of the contract, have indicated that under a particular stipulation the architect or engineer did have the authority to construe the meaning of the contract.

Ga.   *Mallard v. Moody*, 105 Ga. 400, 31 S.E. 45, 47 (1898). "He (the architect) could construe the contract, and decide what it meant or determine the nature and character of the work or materials required, but he could not eliminate or abrogate any of its terms."

Wash.   *De Honey v. Gjarde*, 134 Wash. 647, 236 Pac. 290, 297 (1925). "There was (sic) elsewhere in the contract, it is true, recitals to the effect that the architect was the agent of the owner, and that his interpretation of the contract should be final, but these provisions referred to instances of repugnant provisions of the contract, or to instances where the contract did not speak; it gave the architect no power to modify provisions capable of but one interpretation."

Dyer v. Middle Kittitas Irrig. Dist., 40 Wash. 238, 82 Pac. 301, 302 (1905). "The contract provides that the engineer shall define the meaning, intent, and purport of the plans and specifications and that his decision in all cases shall be final; but this, it is plain, refers to the interpretation of doubtful and uncertain terms of the contract, not to the question of law presented by the language of the contract or specifications."

U.S.   See *United States v. Moorman*, considered *supra*.

THE FINALITY OF DECISIONS MADE BY A GOVERNMENT CONTRACTING officer, under a stipulation authorizing him to make certain determinations, has been held limited to specific issues of fact and, where the court found that such decisions amounted to a legal construction of the contract, it would reconsider the issue and determine the controversy. This rule was applied whether or not the contract itself specifically limited the officer's decision to issues of fact.

U.S.   *Tobin Quarries v. Central Nebraska Public Power and Irrig. Dist.*, 157 F. 2d 482 (1946). Controversy with regard to type of gravel required under contract presented not question of fact but question of law, which engineer was not authorized to decide.
W. E. Callahan Constr. Co. v. United States, 91 Ct.Cl. 538 (1940). Decision with regard to claims of contractor for compensation for extra work held to be based upon construction of the contract and not binding.
Schmoll v. United States, 91 Ct.Cl. 1 (1940). Decision that contractor was not required to furnish certain materials and work was held to be one construing the contract and therefore not binding.
Rust Eng. Co. v. United States, 86 Ct.Cl. 461 (1938). Decision that extra cost was not payable to the contractor was held to be one construing the contract and not binding. *Davis v. United States*, 82 Ct.Cl. 334 (1936). Decision that contractor was required to furnish certain material held to be a question of law and outside the province of the contracting officer.
Albina Marine Iron Works, Inc. v. United States, 79 Ct.Cl. 714 (1934). Decision of officer as to cause and extent of contractor's delay was binding as a point of fact, but the delay so determined was not subject to reduction of one day per month of the contract period on the ground that the contractor should have anticipated that amount of delay each month. This was a finding as to a principle of law and therefore not binding.
United States v. Mason & Hanger Co., 260 U.S. 323 (1922). Decision that contractor was to be reimbursed for a premium paid on a contractor's bond for government work was held conclusive. No discussion as to whether it constituted a construction of the contract.

Collins & Farwell v. United States, 34 Ct.Cl. 294 (1899). Where the engineer in charge proceeds upon a wrong theory of the contract the court will grant relief, notwithstanding provision that engineer's decision shall be final, since this provision refers only to his measurement and not to the principle of law on which it is made.

Lyons v. United States, 30 Ct.Cl. 352 (1895). Decision of engineer as to basis of measurement of earth filling was held to be improper. Stipulation that decision of engineer as to quality should be final referred only to his measurement in point of fact and not to the principle of law on which it was made. For cases on the decision of a government officer on the interpretation of the drawings and specifications see pages 222–223.

Cf. United States v. Moorman, considered *supra.*

Cf. John J. Harte Co. v. United States, 91 F. Supp. 753 (1950). Where government contract provided that "all disputes" thereunder should be decided by the contracting officer subject to timely appeal to the Secretary of War, and the contracting officer determined that he was without authority to determine the question of duress raised by the plaintiff, failure of the plaintiff to make a timely appeal to the Secretary of War precluded him from suing for breach of the contract in the Court of Claims, and it was immaterial whether the questions involved were those of fact or law.

WHERE THE CONTRACT PROVIDED THAT AN ARCHITECT OR ENGINEER determine conclusively the true intent and meaning of the drawings and specifications, the courts in some cases decided whether a particular decision was authorized by such a provision.

Ark.   *Brashears v. Garland School Dist.,* 133 Ark. 599, 202 S.W. 234 (1918). Where specifications did not indicate whether three-ply or four-ply roofing was to be used, it was held to be a question for the decision of the architect under a stipulation referring to him decisions on true meaning of the specifications.

Colo. *Stewart v. Breckenridge,* 69 Colo. 108, 169 Pac. 543 (1917). Architect was held authorized to decide whether drawings or specifications should govern in case of a conflict between them.

Ga.   *Mallard v. Moody,* 105 Ga. 400, 31 S.E. (1898). Where the specification as to heating apparatus was agreed to by the parties, it was held that the architect had no authority to decide that the contractor was not bound to install the heating apparatus.

Mass. *Norcross v. Wyman,* 187 Mass. 25, 72 N.E. 347 (1904). Architect was held authorized to determine that specifications relating to excavation were not inserted with intent that expense of work made necessary by quicksand encountered in the excavation should be borne by the contractor, and for purposes of his determination was free to adopt such legal principles as he honestly believed to be applicable.

Mich. *Kelly v. Muskegon Public Schools,* 110 Mich. 529, 68 N.W. 282 (1896). Where builder before entering into contract could have examined plans and specifications and found apparent discrepancies in them, he was bound by contract provisions that if discrepancies were found to exist, the architect's decision as to the full content and meaning of the plans, drawings, and specifications should be final.

N.Y. *Chas. S. Wood & Co. v. Alvord & Swift,* 232 App. Div. 603, 251 N.Y.S. 35 (1931), *aff'd,* 258 N.Y. 611, 180 N.E. 354 (1932). Where specifications provided "all concealed heating risers and radiator connections . . . shall be covered," the architect was held authorized to decide that the contractor was required to cover only the concealed radiator connections.

W. B. Armstrong Co. v. State, 111 Misc. 297, 181 N.Y.S. 185 (1920). Architect was held authorized to determine that "piping" under the contract should be "extra heavy pipe."

Pa. *Ruch v. York,* 233 Pa. 36, 81 Atl. 891 (1911). Architect was held authorized to determine whether alleged additional work was within the contract.

Barclay v. Deckerhoof, 171 Pa. 378, 33 Atl. 71 (1895). Architect held authorized to determine whether the contractor and sureties were bound to refund to the owner an amount paid on a mechanic's lien where the contract provided that the contractor was to deliver the building free from all claims.

Va. *Rosenberg v. Turner,* 124 Va. 769, 98 S.E. 763 (1919). Architect was held authorized to determine whether extra compensation was payable to the contractor in interpreting the word "excavation."

Wash. *Northwestern Marble & Tile Co. v. Megrath,* 72 Wash. 441, 130 Pac. 484 (1913). Where the specifications provided that pipe was to be "galvanized, wrought iron, or mild steel," the architect was held without authority to order the removal of mild steel pipe and installation of galvanized iron pipe.

U.S. *Consolidated Engineering Co. v. United States,* 35 F. Supp. 980 (1940). Engineer was held authorized to determine type of manhole required under the contract.

Merrill-Ruckgaber Co. v. United States, 241 U.S. 387 (1916). Architect was authorized to require contractor to underpin two buildings where the specifications were ambiguous.

McBride Electric Co. v. United States, 51 Ct.Cl. 448 (1916). Architect was held authorized to determine what work was contemplated by the contract where the specifications were ambiguous.

WHERE THE CONTRACT PROVIDED THAT AN ARCHITECT OR ENGINEER determine conclusively the true intent and meaning of the drawings and specifications, some courts have ruled that his authority could not be extended to include construction of the contract also.

Ark. *Drainage Dist. v. Kochtitzky*, 146 Ark. 495, 226 S.W. 172 (1920). Decision of engineer requiring excavation of a narrower ditch than required by the contract was held to be unauthorized since it involved a construction of the contract.

Ga. *State Highway Dep't v. MacDougald Constr. Co.*, 189 Ga. 490, 6 S.E. 2d 570 (1939). Engineer was held authorized to construe the contract together with the specifications for the incidental purpose of determining the kind or class of material required.

Md. *Aetna Indem. Co. v. Waters*, 110 Md. 673, 73 Atl. 712 (1909). Decision of architect that a provision for construction of "roof slabs" required the contractor to construct a ceiling over upper floor of the building was held without authority as involving a construction of the contract.

Mass. *Derby Desk Co. v. Conners Bros. Constr. Co.*, 204 Mass. 461, 90 N.E. 543 (1910). Decisions as to whether contractor was required to furnish iron frames on certain windows and doors or only to complete the necessary woodwork was held not within authority of the architect as involving a construction of the contract.

N.J. *Welch v. Hubschmitt Bldg. & Woodworking Co.*, 61 N.J.L. 57, 38 Atl. 824 (1897). Where contract provided that architect was to decide disputes as to the true meaning of the drawings and specifications, and the work was to be done to the satisfaction of the architect and owner, the architect's certificate was held conclusive only as to the plans, style, measurements, and way in which the building was constructed, but the character and quality must have the approval of both owner and architect.

N.Y. *Fowler v. Bushby*, 69 Misc. 341, 125 N.Y.S. 890 (1910). That portion of architect's letter dealing with the construction of the contract with respect to the owner's liability for certain work performed by the contractor was held to have no force or effect whatever.

Pollock v. Pennsylvania Iron Works Co., 13 Misc. 194, 34 N.Y.S. 129 (1895), *aff'd*, 157 N.Y. 699, 51 N.E. 979 (1898). Under stipulation providing that the interpretation of the drawings should be given by the engineer, the contract did not authorize him to determine the meaning of the specifications, but only the drawings.

Pa. *Ruch v. York*, 233 Pa. 36, 81 Atl. 891 (1911). Engineer was held without authority to determine contractor's right to damages where such determination required a construction of the whole contract.

Wisc. *Tomlinson v. Ashland County*, 170 Wis. 58, 173 N.W. 300 (1919). Decision of architect that contractor was required to furnish certain earth fillings held without authority where contract reasonably construed did not require such performance.

U.S. *Gammino v. Dedham*, 164 Fed. 593 (1908). Architect was held without authority to determine the question arising after completion of the contract as to whether or not the contractor had received the compensation to which he was entitled.

WHERE CONTRACTS PROVIDED THAT THE ARCHITECT OR ENGINEER determine certain questions during the execution of the contract or issue certificates upon performance of the work, a number of courts have held that his erroneous construction of the contract was not binding.

Ariz. *State v. Kisselburg*, 27 Ariz. 336, 233 Pac. 580 (1925). Misconstruction as to method of measurement.

Mo. *Scott v. Parkview Realty & Improv. Co.* 241 Mo. 112, 145 S.W. 48 (1912). Misconstruction of contract as to method of measurement.

N.Y. *Oscar Daniels Co. v. New York City*, 196 App. Div. 856, 188 N.Y.S. 716 (1921). Misconstruction as to basis of measurement for payment of work performed.

Croton Falls Constr. Co. v. New York City, 168 App. Div. 261, 154 N.Y.S. 76 (1915). Misconstruction as to payment for work performed.

Merrill-Ruckgaber Co. v. New York, 160 App. Div. 513, 147 N.Y.S. 577 (1914). Misconstruction as to work included.

Burke v. New York City, 7 App. Div. 128, 40 N.Y.S. 81 (1896). Misconstruction as to work included in contract and performed by contractor.

Uvalde Contracting Co. v. New York City, 160 App. Div. 284, 145 N.Y.S. 604 (1914). Misconstruction as to calculation for payment of work performed.

R. G. *Packard Co. v. New York City*, 151 App. Div. 941, 137 N.Y.S. 9 (1912), *aff'd*, 210 N.Y. 590, 104 N.E. 1139 (1914). Misconstruction as to mode of measurement of excavation.

Molloy v. Village of Briarcliff Manor, 145 App. Div. 483, 129 N.Y.S. 929 (1911), *aff'd*, 217 N.Y. 577, 112 N.E. 729 (1916). Misconstruction as to work included.

Ohio   *State v. Tracy*, 129 Ohio St. 550, 196 N.E. 650 (1935). Architect was not authorized to construe the contract to determine the basis of measurement for payment for work performed.

U.S.   *Dock Contractor Co. v. New York City*, 296 Fed. 377 (1924). Misconstruction as to work included.

Lewis v. Chicago S. F. & C. R. Co., 49 Fed. 708 (1891). Court will correct error of classification by engineer resulting from an erroneous interpretation of contract, but will not correct slight discrepancies of measurement.

WHERE CONTRACTS PROVIDED THAT AN ARCHITECT OR ENGINEER determine disputes arising under the contract, some courts have held that his determination as to the materials or work required in the performance of the contract was not binding where it amounted to a construction of the contract.

Ariz.   *Guaranty Title & Trust Co. v. Willis*, 38 Ariz. 33, 297 Pac. 445 (1931).

Ark.   *Drainage Dist. v. Kochtitzky*, 146 Ark. 495, 226 S.W. 172 (1920).

Cal.   *McGillivray Constr. Co. v. Hoskins*, 54 Cal. App. 636, 202 Pac. 677 (1921).

Ga.   *State Highway Dept. v. MacDougald Constr. Co.*, 189 Ga. 490, 6 S.E. 2d 570 (1939).

Mass.   *Morgan v. Murdough*, 216 Mass. 502, 104 N.E. 455 (1914).

N.H.   *N.E. Redlon Co. v. Franklin Square Corp.*, 89 N.H. 137, 195 Atl. 348 (1937).

N.Y.   *Isaacs v. Dawson*, 70 App. Div. 232, 75 N.Y.S. 337, *aff'd*, 174 N.Y. 537, 66 N.E. 1110 (1903).

BUILDING CONTRACT CLAUSES REFERRING to the architect or engineer all matters in dispute have been generally held not to empower the arbiter to determine the legal rights of the parties under the contract.

N.Y.   *Meachem v. Jamestown F. & C. R. Co.*, 211 N.Y. 346, 105 N.E. 653 (1914). Where contract provided that engineer should determine finally and conclusively all matters in dispute arising out of the contract, but each party waived all right of action or other legal remedies to enforce any claim, except as determined by the engineer, the court held such clause invalid as tending to oust the courts of jurisdiction.

Wis. *Keachie v. Starkweather Drainage Dist.*, 168 Wis. 298, 170 N.W. 236 (1919). Contract provision making decision of arbiter final in interpreting specifications and contract and upon all questions concerning execution of the work held to be usual and customary provision and enforceable.

U.S. *McCullough v. Clinch-Mitchell Constr. Co.*, 71 F. 2d 17, *cert. den.*, 297 U.S. 592 (1934). Part of arbitration clause in contract providing submission of disputes to chief engineer held effective notwithstanding invalidity of part of clause waiving all judicial remedies for determination of questions coming within arbitration clause.

Robert Grace Contracting Co. v. Chesapeake & O. N.R. Co., 281 Fed. 904 (1922). Provision in contract that engineer's decision is to be final on all controversies is invalid as ousting court's jurisdiction unless it can be limited to questions as to manner of construction.

Mitchell v. Dougherty, 90 Fed. 639 (1898). Parties to building contract may not stipulate that any dispute arising between them, including questions of value or character of work done and of legal rights under contract, be submitted to architect for final decision and such stipulation will not oust court's jurisdiction.

King Iron Bridge & Mfg. Co. v. St. Louis, 43 Fed. 768 (1890). Provision that state commissioner was to decide conclusively all questions relative to execution of contract, does not give him jurisdiction to determine whether contractor has incurred penalty, provided for in contract, for delayed completion of work.

CHAPTER SIXTEEN

When certificate is prerequisite to suit

Whether a contractor may sue the owner to recover his compensation in the absence of a certificate of completion or a submission of the question to arbitration depends upon whether the parties by the terms of the contract intended such certificate or arbitration to be a prerequisite to the contractor's right to payment.

The terms of the contract entered into between owner and contractor determine whether the certificate, estimate, or approval of the supervising architect or engineer must be obtained before the contractor may sue the owner for the compensation provided in the contract. Where the contract provides that the work performed is subject to acceptance or approval by the architect or engineer before the contractor is entitled to payment, or his certificate, decision, or estimate is required for this purpose, then the contractor is required to produce such certificate or prove acceptance before he may sue to recover compensation. Such requirement may be stated expressly but often it is implied from the wording of the contract.

The same principle applies to progress payments made at certain stages of the work. Where the contract provides for installment payments to the contractor to be made on certificate of the architect, a certificate is necessary as to each of the payments, including the final installment, to entitle the contractor to compensation for each installment.

In the absence of any provision requiring the contractor's claim to be passed on by a third party arbiter, the contractor is not bound to prove acceptance of his work before suing for his compensation.

Where contracts provide for arbitration of disputes and the decision of the arbitrator is to be final, arbitration is not regarded as a condition precedent to the contractor's right to recover compensation unless such an intention appears in the contract either expressly or by necessary

172

implication. The covenant to arbitrate and the covenant to pay for work performed are each regarded as distinct and independent.

Under contracts providing that the decision of an architect is to be binding except in certain cases as to which "either party may appeal from the architect's decision to arbitration" or providing that all questions should be submitted to arbitration "at the choice of either party," arbitration is a matter of choice and is therefore not a condition precedent to suit on the contract.

Where the agreement entered into between subcontractor and contractor adopts all the terms and requirements of the original contract made between owner and contractor, the subcontractor is bound by a stipulation in the original contract requiring the certificate or approval of the architect with respect to the subcontractor's performance. Thus where final payment to a subcontractor is dependent upon payment to the contractor on final estimates of the engineer in charge, the subcontractor has no right of action against the contractor until the latter has been paid the full amount due.

The contract also determines whether the contractor may recover damages against the owner for breaching the contract in the absence of a certificate or submission to arbitration. Generally, a provision requiring a certificate as a condition precedent to payment does not require the contractor to produce a certificate before he sues the owner for breaching the contract. Where the provision for arbitration of disputes is not mandatory, the contractor is not compelled to submit the question of a breach to arbitration before seeking a remedy in the courts. The intention of the parties wherever it is discernible in the contract will determine whether specific remedies must be exhausted before legal action may be commenced. Thus, when the parties agree to arbitrate differences arising under the contract, in order to prevent litigation and disputes, a suit by the contractor before the arbitrator has had an opportunity to act, has been held to be premature and not to affect the arbitrator's powers.

Similarly, whether the owner may sue the contractor in damage where there has been no submission to arbitration and no certificate is determined by the contract. If the contract provides for a certificate of the architect as to expenses incurred by the owner in completing the work after default by the contractor, the owner must produce the certificate in order to recover on the contract. But where the owner does not complete the work himself, such certificate is not necessary. A clause requiring work to be done to the satisfaction of the building inspector has been held not to require the owner to show that the work was not satisfactory to the inspector where another provision requires the work to be performed in accordance with the plans and specifications and in a manner acceptable to the owner.

Another problem concerns the contractor's right to recover compensation if he has not complied with the plans and specifications so as to entitle him to the certificate or approval of the architect or engineer in charge. It is undisputed that he may not sue on the contract itself if he has not completed it according to its terms. Under such circumstances, however, he may recover in *quantum meruit*. Such a suit is based on the right to recover for value received by the other party. In the contractor's suit, he would be entitled to recover the value of the materials and services furnished to the owner. The contractor who defaults in some particular will generally not recover the full contract price but he will be assured of some payment for the value of material furnished and labor expended in performing the contract, unless the damage suffered by the owner through improper performance is greater than the value of the work properly done. It has been held, however, that where by the terms of the contract, the contractor's right to recover depends upon an architect's certificate and he fails to obtain it, he cannot recover even on a *quantum meruit* basis.

It should be pointed out, however, that in all cases where a certificate, estimate, or approval is required as a condition precedent to recovery, the contractor may recover without it if compliance with such requirement is waived or excused. The circumstances under which it will be deemed waived or excused will be discussed *infra*.

A BUILDING CONTRACTOR CANNOT RECOVER COMPENSATION unless he secures the certificate, estimate, or approval of the architect or engineer, where the contract makes that a condition precedent to payment. In the absence of such a provision in the contract, he may recover without such evidence of approval. The same principle applies to progress payments and stipulations for submission to arbitration.

(a) Final certificate, estimate, or approval

Cal. *Thomas Haverty Co. v. Jones*, 185 Cal. 285, 197 Pac. 105 (1921). Where contract required work to be performed to the satisfaction of named architects, and they were discharged and another architect employed without any agreement for his substitution, architect's certificates were not required as a condition precedent to the contractor's right to recover.

Fla. *Duval County v. Charleston Eng. & Contracting Co.*, 101 Fla. 341, 134 So. 509 (1931). Unjust refusal of parties to submit matters in dispute to arbitration, as agreed upon, or failure to procure engineer's final estimate, as condition precedent to payment, operates as a bar to suit involving matters within the arbitration provision or the engineer's certificate.

Ga. *Morris v. Peachtree Heights Park Co.*, 38 Ga. App. 303, 143 S.E. 909 (1928). Where grading contract made estimates of engineer binding, and estimates included both kind and amount of materials, they were a condition precedent to the contractor's right to recover.

Ill. *Hegeman-Harris Co. v. Tebbetts & Garland Co.*, 262 Ill. App. 524 (1931). Contractor need not prove acceptance of work in order to recover on contract where contract does not require it.

Kan. *Neale Constr. Co. v. Topeka Township Sewage Dist.*, 178 Kan. 359, 285 P. 2d 1086 (1955). Where the construction contract provided that a certificate by the engineer was a condition precedent to recovery under the contract, the court held that judgment was properly rendered for the owner and against contractor, when the latter failed in his opening statement to state sufficient facts demonstrating compliance with condition or supporting excuse from condition.

Mass. *Hennebique Constr. Co. v. Boston Cold Storage & Terminal Co.*, 230 Mass. 456, 119 N.E. 948 (1918).
Ordway v. City of Newburyport, 230 Mass. 306, 119 N.E. 863 (1918). Under statute requiring copy of plans for a public building to be filed with building inspector by owner or achitect, failure of contractor to file plans does not deprive him of his right to recover for work.

Minn. *St. Paul Sash, Door & Lumber Co. v. Berkner*, 137 Minn. 402, 163 N.W. 668 (1917). Contractor may not recover final payment where his pleading does not allege issuance of a final certificate or the furnishing of a guaranty by him, as provided by the building contract.

Mo. *Bruton v. Sellers & Marquis Roofing Co.*, 237 Mo. App. 451, 168 S.W. 2d 101 (1943). Subcontractor could not recover for work in re-laying roof where he had warranted that it would be watertight and acceptable to the state and the state refused to accept the roof, in the absence of a waiver of his warranty or fraud or misconduct preventing him from complying with the contract.
Meyers v. Union Electric Light & Power Co., 334 Mo. 622, 66 S.W. 2d 565 (1933). Contractors could not recover amount they claimed for work which they had done where they had accepted the final estimates of the engineers and payment thereunder without impeaching the estimates for fraud or mistake.

N.J. *Hasson v. Bruzel*, 104 N.J. Eq. 95, 144 Atl. 319 (1929). Compensation to contractor for "extra work" is payable only on presentation of architect's certificate, under a contract making such sums for labor and materials so payable.

N.Y. *Kuhs v. Flower City Tissue Mills Co.*, 104 Misc. 243, 171 N.Y.S. 688 (1918), *aff'd*, 189 App. Div. 539, 179 N.Y.S. 450 (1919). Absence of architect's final certificate does not bar recovery by principal contractor, and certificate issued to subcontractor is conclusive as to complete performance of the contract and entitles both to recover for money due them under the contract.
Barth v. Gatto, 165 N.Y.S. 213 (1917). Where contractor took over a building contract requiring architect's certificate before payment, by a supplemental contract providing for final payment when the requirements were met, architect's certificate remained necessary for payment.
Empire Lighting Fixture Co. v. Browning, 93 Misc. 489, 157 N.Y.S. 284 (1916). Where contractor is required by contract to furnish certificates from the board of fire underwriters for all fixtures furnished and installed, such certificates are required before he may sue on the contract.
Pneumatic Signal Co. v. Texas & P. Ry., 200 N.Y. 125, 93 N.E. 471 (1910). Where by contract work must be accepted by state railroad commission as a condition to the contractor's right to payment, the commission's refusal to accept work because the railroad company failed to comply with requirements, is no defense to his recovery where he had complied with requirements.

Mont. *McClauflin v. Wormser*, 28 Mont. 177, 72 Pac. 428 (1903). Where final certificate is required and not furnished and no excuse given for its non-production by contractor in action to recover compensation, motion for non-suit will be sustained.

Pa. *Foundation & Constr. Co. v. Franklin Trust Co.*, 307 Pa. 10, 160 Atl. 711 (1932). Under contract making engineer's certificate a condition precedent to final payment, the contractor, after engineer had withdrawn and no other appointed in his place, was not required to attempt to obtain any certificate as a condition to final payment.

U.S. *Utah Constr. Co. v. St. Louis Constr. & Equip. Co.*, 254 Fed. 321 (1916). Provision of a railroad construction contract requiring a final certificate of the chief engineer as a condition precedent to a right of action by the contractor cannot be ignored by the court, and where the contractor has not procured such certificate his petition must be dismissed.

(b) Installment payments

Cal. *Ahlgren v. Walsh*, 173 Cal. 27, 158 Pac. 748 (1916). Where contract provided that if building under construction were totally destroyed the loss would be borne by the owner to the extent installments "may be due," the contractor could recover the installments "due" at the time the building was destroyed though no installment certificate had been issued, as required by the contract.

Hettinger v. Thiele, 15 Cal. App. 1, 113 Pac. 121 (1911). Provision requiring architect's certificate of progress before owner may be liable to contractor for payments, does not apply where the building under construction is destroyed by an earthquake before its completion; particularly where contract requires, in such event, that owner pay what is due contractor.

Ill. *Michaelis v. Wolf*, 136 Ill. 68, 26 N.E. 384 (1891). Where contract requires certificates as condition precedent to payment, fact that some payments are to be made after completion of building does not avoid necessity of obtaining certificate for each payment.

N.Y. *Clark v. Fleischmann Vehicle Co., Inc.*, 187 N.Y.S. 807 (1921). Where by terms of a building contract an installment is not due until the architect's certificate is obtained, nothing is due where such certificate is not produced or waived.

Oberlies v. Bullinger, 75 Hun. 248, 27 N.Y.S. 19 (1894). Provision for payments of installments on architect's certificates that work has been done in accordance with terms of contract does not require certificate as condition precedent to final payment.

(c) Arbitration

Ill. *Foster v. McKeown*, 192 Ill. 339, 61 N.E. 514 (1901). Where contract provided that valuation of extras should be made by architect, and if not agreed to, the matter should be submitted to arbitration, offer to arbitrate as to such extras was not a condition precedent to a right of action where the architect's certificate was refused not because of any disagreement as to valuation, but by the order of the owner.

Ind. *Maitland v. Reed*, 37 Ind. App. 469, 77 N.E. 290 (1906). Where contract provides that decision of architect is to be binding except in cases where "either party may appeal ... to arbitration," appeal from architect's decision is not a condition precedent to action.

N.H. *N.E. Redlon Co. v. Franklin Square Corp.*, 89 N.H. 137, 195 Atl. 348 (1937). Contract providing for submission of disputes to arbitration "at the choice of either party" did not require arbitration as condition precedent to suit on contract, unless demanded by one party.

N.M.   *O'Neal v. Geo. E. Bruce Lumber Co.,* 38 N.M. 492, 35 P. 2d
314 (1934). Where contract contains no covenant indicating intention that arbitration of disputes shall be condition precedent to
right of action, covenant to pay and covenant to arbitrate are
distinct and collateral.

Tenn.   *Cole Mfg. Co. v. Collier,* 91 Tenn. 525, 19 S.W. 672 (1892).
Contract held not to require submission to arbitration as condition
precedent to suit, either expressly or by necessary implication.

Wis.   *Quast v. Guetzkow,* 164 Wis. 197, 159 N.W. 810 (1916). Where
contract for furnishing labor and materials provided that questions
in dispute should be arbitrated but did not provide that arbitration
should precede action thereon, arbitration, unless requested, was
not a condition precedent to the maintenance of an action.

U.S.   *Oregon Short Line R. Co. v. Teton Coal Co.,* 35 F. 2d 919
(1929). Where contract contains covenant to pay and covenant to
arbitrate, they are distinct and collateral and covenant to arbitrate
is not a condition precedent to maintenance of suit.

Eyre-Shoemaker, Inc. v. Buffalo, R. & P. R. Co., 193 Fed. 387
(1912). Suit instituted before arbitration was held to be premature
where parties agreed to arbitrate differences to prevent litigation
and disputes.

WHERE THE SUBCONTRACT ADOPTS THE PROVISIONS and requirements of the
main contract, the subcontractor is bound by a stipulation in the main
contract with respect to production of a certificate as a condition precedent to recovery.

Mich.   *Bolt v. Nelson,* 257 Mich. 610, 241 N.W. 896 (1932). Where
final payment to a subcontractor is due on the contractor's receipt
of final estimates of the engineer in charge, the contractor has no
duty to pay in absence of a final estimate.

Minn.   *Breen Stone Co. v. W. F. T. Bushnell Co.,* 117 Minn. 283, 135
N.W. 993 (1912). Where the original contract is not made a part
of the subcontract, the subcontractor is not bound by a stipulation
in the original contract requiring a certificate.

Pa.   *Foundation & Constr. Co. v. Franklin Trust Co.,* 307 Pa. 10, 160
Atl. 711 (1932). Under agreement permitting payments only on
the architect's certificate, the subcontractor not having a certificate
cannot recover the sum alleged due it.

Brown v. Decker, 142 Pa. 640, 21 Atl. 903 (1891). Where the subcontract adopts all the terms of the original contract, the subcontractor is bound by a stipulation contained in original contract
requiring a certificate.

S.C. *Guimarin v. Southern Life & Trust Co.*, 106 S.C. 37, 90 S.E. 319 (1916). Although materialman's contract provided for final payment after acceptance of the work by an architect, where the contractor abandoned the work before completion and before time for the architect to act, the materialman was not required to show the architect's acceptance in an action for the balance.

Tex. *Herry v. Benoit*, 70 S.W. 359 (1902). Failure of the contractor to comply with a provision requiring the consent of the architect to the subcontract and submission to him of all material is not a defense in an action against contractor by subcontractor, although such defense would be available to the owner as against the subcontractor.

U.S. *Geo. A. Fuller Co. v. B. P. Young Co.*, 126 Fed. 343 (1903). Where subcontract provided that the final certificate should be conclusive evidence of performance, such provision was held not to make production of a final certificate a condition precedent to the subcontractor's right to recover on the completion of the contract.

THE RIGHT OF THE OWNER OR CONTRACTOR TO RECOVER damages for breach of contract by the other without a submission to arbitration or a certificate of the architect or engineer depends upon the terms of the contract.

(a) Damages to contractor

Mich. *Maurer v. School Dist.*, 186 Mich. 223, 152 N.W. 999 (1915). Where contract does not provide for arbitration of disputes on the question of liquidated damages, the contractor's failure to submit such dispute does not defeat recovery of the final installment due, although the contract provides for arbitration of disputes.

Tex. *Linch v. Paris Lumber & Grain Elevator Co.*, 80 Tex. 23, 15 S.W. 208 (1891). Contract provision requiring production of architect's certificate as condition precedent to recovery of compensation was held not to require certificate in order to entitle the contractor to sue for breach of the contract by the owner.

U.S. *Sumner Sollitt Co. v. First Nat. Bank*, 22 F. 2d 620 (1927). Where contract required the decision of arbitrators or of the architect as a condition precedent to legal action by either party, contractor who did not seek arbitration or obtain a decision of the architect could not recover damages against the owner for a breach of the contract.

Robert Grace Contracting Co. v. Chesapeake & O. N. R. Co., 281 Fed. 904 (1922). Failure of contractors to secure engineer's estimates as required by contract does not prevent them from re-

covering damages for failure of the railroad company to provide
a right of way in due time, since engineer's certificates were not
intended to cover that matter.

(b) Damages to owner

Ill.   *Brighton Theatre Co. v. Graf*, 248 Ill. App. 140 (1928). Certificate
of architect as to expenses incurred by owner in completing work
after contractor's default is essential to recovery against the contractor, where the contract provides for such certificate.

Mass.   *Walsh v. Cornwell*, 272 Mass. 555, 172 N.E. 855 (1930). Where
architect's certificate of damages for contractor's default is applicable when owner terminates contractor's employment and
completes the contract himself, and owner does not pursue such
remedy, such certificate is not necessary to his recovery of damages.
Feldman v. Desantis, 260 Mass. 173, 156 N.E. 868 (1927). Where
contract requires work to be done to satisfaction of building inspector, owner who sues for damages for breach of contract need
not show that the work was not satisfactory to the inspector in
view of the provision that work must be performed "in accordance
with the plans and specifications . . . and in a manner acceptable
to the owner."

N.Y.   *Kuhs v. Flower City Tissue Mills Co.*, 104 Misc. 243, 171 N.Y.S.
688 (1918), aff'd, 189 App. Div. 539, 179 N.Y.S. 450 (1919). Architect's certificate is conclusive proof of completion but does not
preclude claim for damages by the owner for breach of an express
warranty.

Wash.   *School Dist. of Pierce County v. Qualis*, 95 Wash. 247, 163
Pac. 761 (1919). Where contract provides that damages to the
owner incurred through the default of the contractor must be
audited and certified by the architect, owner cannot recover
damages without such audit and certification.

UNDER SOME CIRCUMSTANCES A CONSTRUCTION CONTRACTOR who has not
fully performed the contract so as to entitle him to a certificate or approval of the supervising architect or engineer may recover on a *quantum
meruit* basis.

Ga.   *Southern Mfg. Co. v. R. L. Moss Mfg. Co.*, 13 Ga. App. 847, 81
S.E. 263 (1905). Where engineer gives a certificate stating that
the contract has not been complied with, the contractor cannot
recover under contract but may sue in *quantum meruit* to recover
the value of services and materials furnished.

Ill.   *Hart v. Carsley Mfg. Co.*, 221 Ill. 444, 77 N.E. 897 (1906). Where
the contract fails to obtain the architect's certificate upon which

his right to recover under the contract depends, he cannot recover in *quantum meruit* for the value of his services.

Ind. *Everroad v. Schwartzkopf*, 123 Ind. 35, 23 N.E. 969 (1890). Where complaint seeks to recover for services and materials furnished under one paragraph in special contract, and for services and materials in *quantum meruit* in another, answer setting up a breach of the special contract is no defense to the entire complaint.

Mass. *Gillis v. Cobe*, 177 Mass. 584, 59 N.E. 455 (1901). Where building contract provided that the order of the architect for final payment should be considered acceptance of work, but did not negative any recovery in case the architect refused to grant order, failure to secure it was not a bar to plaintiff's recovery in *quantum meruit*.

Mo. *Craig v. McNichols Furniture Co.*, 187 S.W. 793 (1916). Where plaintiffs contracted to plaster a building in a workmanlike manner and replace defective work in two years, and did replace some which was accepted, they could recover in *quantum meruit* the balance of the contract price due, subject to deductions for failure fully to perform the contract, although the architect refused his certificate.

CHAPTER SEVENTEEN

When certificate of performance may be waived

The issuance of a certificate of performance by the architect or engineer as a condition of the contractor's right to payment for his services may be waived by the owner, or its production may be excused by some happening beyond the control of the contractor, as accident, the disability of the arbiter to act, or the arbitrary or unreasonable refusal of the arbiter to issue it.

A provision in a building contract which requires the architect's or engineer's certificate or approval of the work before the contractor is entitled to payment is generally included for the benefit of the owner. He may therefore waive such requirement as a condition to payment. The waiver may be in express terms or it may be implied from his acts, conduct, or declarations which are inconsistent with the purpose of the requirement. If the owner and contractor in their relations with each other proceed without regard to the provision, a waiver may be implied. When the owner bases his refusal to pay the contractor in the first instance on some ground other than failure to procure the requisite approval or certificate he will be deemed to have waived the provision.

Where the work is to be paid for in installments on certificates or estimates, and the owner makes such payments without requesting their production, he has waived the requirement. However, the payment of installments without requiring certificates is generally not construed as a waiver of the final certificate of completion, and a waiver of one progress certificate is likewise not interpreted as a waiver of the right to demand certificates for subsequent installments.

The fact that the owner takes possession of the building in the absence of the arbiter's approval or certificate does not necessarily mean that he has dispensed with the requirement that the work be approved. However, a waiver of approval may be implied from other circumstances, as where he accepts the building as if under a completed contract or promises to pay for it without requiring a certificate.

Aside from waiver, situations exist in which production of the certificate by the contractor may be excused. If the contractor is prevented by some excuse beyond his control from obtaining the required approval, he may be entitled to payment without it. Under such circumstances he will be able to recover for his services if he can establish that the work has been done in a proper manner and substantially according to the contract.

The owner himself may make it impossible for the contractor to produce the necessary approval, as by discharging the contractor or the architect before the work is completed, by failing to employ an architect, or by refusing to permit the architect to issue the necessary certificate.

The death, resignation, or other disability of the architect during the progress of the work will excuse production of the certificate unless another architect is substituted in his place and accepted by the contractor. Disqualification of the architect for any reason will dispense with the necessity of obtaining his certificate. The mere fact that the architect or engineer is a stockholder or director of the corporate owner has been held insufficient to disqualify him.

Accidental causes, such as destruction of the building by fire during construction, will also excuse production of an estimate or certificate. The failure to obtain a certificate must be for valid cause beyond the contractor's control. Hence, a failure to apply for a certificate because the contractor believed the architect to be prejudiced against him has been held to be no excuse.

A certificate is also unnecessary where the architect or engineer wrongfully refuses to issue it. A wrongful refusal, according to the circumstances, has variously been termed malicious, arbitrary, capricious, unreasonable, or fraudulent. It has been held that a refusal is unreasonable where the contractor has at least substantially complied with his contract and there is no apparent reason for the refusal. An arbitrary refusal has been said to involve bad faith and a failure to exercise honest judgment.

However, where the architect or engineer acts in good faith in refusing his certificate because the contract has not been complied with, the contractor cannot recover for his services without such certificate. It has been held that the refusal of an architect to give a certificate of completion is at least *prima facie* evidence that the building was not completed in accordance with the provisions of the contract.

It may generally be said that where work has been properly performed, the arbitrary or unreasonable refusal of the architect or engineer to give a certificate amounts to such fraud as will excuse its nonproduction as a condition to payment. Presentation of the certificate will also be dispensed with where the architect mistakenly refuses to certify work properly done where the mistake is such as would imply bad faith or arbitrary action.

A CONTRACT PROVISION REQUIRING THE APPROVAL or certificate of an architect or engineer as a condition precedent to the contractor's right to payment is for the benefit of the owner and may be waived either in express terms or by such acts, conduct, or declarations of the owner as negative the intention to require it.

(a) Certificate or approval waived

Cal. *Collins v. Ramish,* 182 Cal. 360, 188 Pac. 550 (1920). Where refusal of owner to pay is based upon grounds other than the failure to produce a certificate, and such objection is not raised until trial.

Kling v. Bucher, 32 Cal. App. 679, 163 Pac. 871 (1917). Where owner paid all previous installments without requiring certificate and did not refuse payment on such ground in the first instance.

Conn. *Healy v. Fallon,* 69 Conn. 228, 37 Atl. 495 (1897). Where owner pleaded that contract was not properly performed and yet did not plead a failure to obtain the necessary certificate.

Fla. *Summerlin v. Thompson,* 31 Fla. 369, 12 So. 667 (1893). Where in suit owner interposed pleas involving consideration of entire merits of the controversy by the jury.

Ky. *Green River Steel Corp. v. Alabe Erection Co.,* 294 S.W. 2d 507 (1956). The court in this case recognized that provisions making the decision of the architect or engineer conclusive are generally given effect. It stated, however, that "where the parties to the contract proceed throughout the performance of the contract without reference to the provisions of the contract, (the owners) . . . may be held to waive the provision for some one to decide what is extra work." In this case the court found that the owner "did not recognize the engineer as having the power to bind the parties as to what constituted extra work. The appellant's (owner's) engineer himself did not reply to appellee's (contractor's) letter concerning the alleged extra work. Therefore, the engineer's decision given *for the first time* as a witness at trial was not conclusive, but was received to be considered by the jury on the same basis as the other qualified witnesses." In other words, the jury was entitled to determine in the first instance the scope of the contract with respect to the nature of the work agreed upon therein.

Mass. *James Elgar, Inc. v. Newhall,* 235 Mass. 373, 126 N.E. 661
(1920). Where the court found that the architect's certificate had
in fact been waived, but did not give the basis for waiver.

N.J. *MacDonnell v. Vitella,* 111 N.J. Eq. 502, 162 Atl. 738 (1932).
Where building had been occupied and architect's testimony had
disclosed that the building had been substantially completed and
that he promised to furnish a certificate.

Sargeant Bros., Inc. v. Brancati, 107 N.J.L. 84, 151 Atl. 843 (1930).
Where no architect had been employed and there was evidence
from which waiver of the production of a certificate could be
inferred.

Hasson v. Bruzel, 104 N.J. Eq. 95, 144 Atl. 319 (1929). Owner
waiving production of a certificate in advance was held liable to
lien claimants serving notice before issuance of certificate, to the
extent of the advance payments made.

N.Y. *Hoisting Machinery Co. v. Federal Terra Cotta Co.,* 179 App.
Div. 653, 167 N.Y.S. 85 (1917). Where owner used and accepted
materials and engineer did not disapprove, especially since workmanship and materials were substantially in conformity with the
contract.

Abramson-Engesser Co. v. McCafferty, 86 N.Y.S. 185 (1904).
Where all but a part of the last payment was made without certificates.

Duell v. McCraw, 86 Hun. 331, 33 N.Y.S. 528 (1895). Where
satisfaction with building was expressed by the owner and a promise made to pay the balance of the contractor's compensation upon
his proper completion of the building.

Weeks v. O'Brien, 141 N.Y. 199, 36 N.E. 185 (1894). Where
owner completed the construction work himself under a provision
of the contract, it was unnecessary for the contractor to procure
architect's certificate to recover the difference between the last
installment and the amount expended in completing the work.

Flaherty v. Miner, 123 N.Y. 382, 25 N.E. 418 (1890). Where owners promised to pay for the work and did not require that an
architect's certificate be produced.

Ohio *Creith Lumber, Inc. v. Cummins,* 163 Ohio St. 264, 126 N.E.
2d 323 (1955). A condition to the contractor's recovery of a
balance due under the construction contract was the issuance by
the mortgage lender of a certificate of approval. This the latter
did not do. The court alternatively held, however, that the owner
by taking possession of and occupying the premises as his property and permanent residence, though knowing of deficiencies,

had waived the condition and was entitled only to a deduction for the deficiencies.

Pa. *McKenna v. Vernon,* 258 Pa. 18, 101 Atl. 919 (1917). Where provision requiring payments on certificates was repeatedly disregarded and owner supervised work almost daily and made no complaint as to deviations in the work made at the request of the architect.

Mayer Bros. Constr. Co. v. American Sterilizer Co., 258 Pa. 217, 101 Atl. 1002 (1917). Where nine out of ten payments were made without engineer's certificate, the jury was warranted in finding that the owner had waived such provision.

Tex. *American Surety Co. v. Shaw,* 69 S.W. 2d 47 (1934). If owner waived provisions of building contract requiring architect's certificates as conditions precedent to payments, then contractor likewise waived condition so far as subcontractor's right to payments was concerned.

Wash. *Sweatt v. Bonne,* 60 Wash. 18, 110 Pac. 617 (1910). Provision for final certificate does not apply where plans and specifications are substantially changed under a subsequent contract without any reference to the first contract or certificate.

Wis. *Quast v. Guetzkow,* 164 Wis. 197, 159 N.W. 810 (1916). Where owner without a final certificate accepted the work and settled accordingly.

(b) Certificate of approval not waived

Ill. *Expanded Metal Fireproofing Co. v. Boyce,* 233 Ill. 284, 84 N.E. 275 (1908). Procurement of final certificate was not waived by making partial payments without certificates during the progress of the work.

Gilmore v. Courtney, 158 Ill. 432, 41 N.E. 1023 (1895). Failure of contractor to apply for architect's certificate because he believed the architect to be fraudulently prejudiced against him does not dispense with necessity of procuring the certificate.

Mich. *Fisher v. Burroughs Adding Mach. Co.,* 166 Mich. 396, 132 N.W. 101 (1911). Where owner and contractor agreed as to the amount due on the contract on items which the architect had passed on, owner did not waive production of the architect's certificate for other items before making payments on them.

Hanley v. Walker, 79 Mich. 607, 45 N.W. 57 (1890). Owner's taking possession of premises after contractor's completed work was not a waiver of the condition requiring production of the architect's certificate before they were entitled to payment.

N.Y. *Watson v. McAuliffe,* 176 App. Div. 810, 163 N.Y.S. 914 (1917). Building contractor cannot rely on a subsequent agreement as a waiver of the requirements of the original contract for an architect's certificate unless he performs the conditions of that agreement.

Sherman v. George Backer Constr. Co., 144 N.Y.S. 9 (1913). Where the contractor failed to produce a certificate or allege excuse or waiver therefor, he could not recover although he proved that the architect seldom came to the building and that previous payments had been made without production of certificates.

Tex. *Alexander v. Good Marble & Tile Co.,* 4 S.W. 2d 636 (1928). Building contract was held not to waive the owner's right to insist on the architect's certificate preliminary to making payments.

A CONTRACTOR IS NOT REQUIRED TO OBTAIN the certificate, estimate, or approval of the architect or engineer when he is prevented from doing so by an event beyond his control, as an accident, act of the owner, or discharge, death or disqualification of the architect or engineer.

Ala. *Catanzano v. Jackson,* 198 Ala. 302, 73 So. 510 (1916). Owner by discharging architect and assuming personal control of the work, could not place it beyond the architect's power to give a final certificate and thereby defeat the contractor's recovery for substantial performance.

Cal. *American-Hawaiian Eng. & Constr. Co. v. Butler,* 165 Cal. 497, 133 Pac. 280 (1913). Where the architect on the owner's order refused to approve and certify the work, although the work was well done, the owner breached the contract and the contractor could rescind and sue in *quantum meruit.*

Fla. *Clement v. Pensacola Builders Supply Co.,* 138 Fla. 629 189 So. 852 (1939). Where contract made contractor's final payment dependent upon an architect's final certificate and the owner discharged the first two architects and proceeded without such advice for two or three months, and the third architect felt unqualified to give a final certificate because of his unfamiliarity with the construction throughout its progress, the owner waived production of the final certificate as a condition precedent to payment.

Ill. *St. Louis & P. R. Co. v. Kerr,* 153 Ill. 182, 38 N.E. 638 (1894). Railroad company cannot resist payment for work done because no estimates were furnished by the engineer as provided by the contract, when the company did not permit the engineer to issue them.

Rawson v. Clark, 70 Ill. 656 (1873). Architect's estimate was not required where the building was destroyed by fire before ironwork manufactured for the building could be put up.

Iowa   *C. T. Fitts & Co. v. Reinhart,* 102 Iowa 311, 71 N.W. 227 (1897). Discharge of architect who is to issue a certificate excuses the contractor from furnishing such certificate previously obligatory.

Ky.   *Pleasant J. Potter College v. George A. Collett & Bros.,* 142 Ky. 322, 134 S.W. 173 (1911). Where payment was to be made on warrants of the architect, and the architect, after issuing warrants for three amounts, died, warrants for balance of uncontradicted claims were not condition precedent to recovery.

Mich.   *Hart v. Reid,* 243 Mich. 175, 219 N.W. 692 (1928). Where assignee became insolvent and was unable to pay his obligations under the contract, the contractors were not bound to complete the contract, and the architects could not legally withhold certificates for work done on account of the assignee's inability to pay.

Mo.   *Williams v. Chicago S. F. & C. R. Co.,* 112 Mo. 463, 20 S.W. 631 (1892). The fact that the engineer was a stockholder of the corporate owner did not render a submission to him invalid.

N.Y.   *Walter v. Horwitz,* 60 N.Y.S. 2d 327, *aff'd,* 271 App. Div. 802, 65 N.Y.S. 2d 672 (1946). Where the architect refused a final certificate of completion to the contractors unless they would accept the figures and claim of owner's husband, which were not justified, the certificate was unreasonably withheld and the contractors were not required to obtain it.

Wilson v. Curran, 190 App. Div. 581, 180 N.Y.S. 337 (1920), *aff'd,* 232 N.Y. 587, 134 N.E. 582 (1921). Where the owner took the decision of completion out of the architect's hands by refusing to pay unless the road constructed was plowed up and rebuilt, the certificate was wrongfully withheld and the contractor could recover without it.

Feldman v. Goldblatt, 75 Misc. 656, 133 N.Y.S. 945 (1912). If the owner fails to employ a supervising architect, the contractor need not furnish a certificate as required by the contract.

Abramson Engesser Co. v. McCafferty, 86 N.Y.S. 185 (1904). Where the architect is one of the owners, a demand and refusal to pay compensation on the completion of the work, is held equivalent to a demand and refusal of the certificate of approval, which excuses non-production of the certificate.

Ocorr & Rugg Co. v. Little Falls, 77 App. Div. 592, 79 N.Y.S. 251 (1902), *aff'd,* 178 N.Y. 222, 70 N.E. 1104 (1903). Architect's certificate was held to be unnecessary when the owner had declared the contract voided and taken possession of the building for the purpose of completing it himself.

Beecher v. Schuback, 4 Misc. 54, 23 N.Y.S. 604 (1893), *aff'd*, 158 N.Y. 687, 53 N.E. 1123 (1899). If the architect named in the contract dies, and another is substituted by the owner and accepted by the contractor, the certificate of the substitute is necessary.

Pa. *Mayer Bros. Constr. Co. v. American Sterilizer Co.*, 258 Pa. 217, 101 Atl. 1002 (1917). Where the contract made the engineer's certificate a condition precedent to payment but the engineer had withdrawn and no other had been appointed in his place, the contractor was not required to make the attempt to procure a certificate.

S.C. *Guimarin v. Southern Life & Trust Co.*, 106 S.C. 37, 90 S.E. 319 (1916). Although materialman's contract provided for final payment after the work was accepted by the architect but the contractor abandoned work before completion, it was not necessary for the materialman in a suit for the balance of the account to show the architect's acceptance.

Sullivan v. Byrne, 10 S.C. 122 (1878). Where contractor could show that written order of architects was unreasonably withheld and that work was performed substantially in accordance with the contract, he could recover without their certificate.

Tex. *American Surety Co. v. Shaw*, 69 S.W. 2d 47 (1934). Architect's arbitrary refusal to issue a certificate cannot prejudice the subcontractor where the architect is disqualified because he is financially interested in the project.

U.S. *Hart v. American Concrete Steel Co.*, 278 Fed. 541 (1921). Failure to obtain the architect's certificate does not bar recovery provided the contractor is not at fault.

THE CONTRACTOR'S FAILURE TO PRODUCE A CERTIFICATE of performance as a condition to payment is excused where the arbiter wrongfully or mistakenly refuses to give it.

Cal. *Philbrook v. Mercantile Trust Co.*, 84 Cal. App. 187, 257 Pac. 882 (1927). Parties to a building contract are not presumed to intend that money rightfully due for services should be forfeited by the contractor on the caprice of the architect in withholding a certificate.

Needham v. Sisters of Mercy, 59 Cal. App. 341, 210 Pac. 830 (1922). Unreasonable, arbitrary, or capricious refusal of the architect to give the required certificate excused contractor from pro-

ducing it as a condition precedent to recovery of the payment due
him.

Roebling Constr. Co. v. Doe Estate Co., 33 Cal. App. 397, 165
Pac. 547 (1917). Contractor was entitled to compensation where
the specifications were followed and the architect's monthly certificates were obtained although the flooring subsequently proved
inadequate and the architect refused a final certificate on account
of such defect.

Coplew v. Durand, 153 Cal. 278, 95 Pac. 38 (1908). Refusal of the
architect to issue a certificate is unreasonable where the contractor
has at least substantially complied with his contract and therefore
is entitled to a certificate since there is no apparent reason for
refusal.

Ill.   *Cerny Pickas & Co. v. Dallach*, 249 Ill. App. 424 (1928). Where
a certificate was withheld by collusive and fraudulent agreement
between the owner and architect, recovery could be had by the
contractor without its issuance.

Ind.   *Wm. P. Jungclaus Co. v. Ratti*, 67 Ind. App. 84, 118 N.E. 966
(1918). Where no fraud is shown on the part of architect in refusing a certificate, the contractor cannot recover compensation
without producing the certificate.

La.   *Mahoney v. St. Paul's Church*, 47 La. Ann. 1064, 17 So. 484
(1895). Where the architect's only objection to issuing a certificate
is that the full amount due the subcontractors and materialmen
has not been paid, although the same has been provided for by
the contractor to be paid out of the amount due, the contractor
may sue for the balance due without a certificate after putting the
architects in default by demanding one.

Mass. *Sikora v. Hogan*, 315 Mass. 66, 51 N.E. 2d 970 (1943). Where
the evidence established that the architect in bad faith refused to
give the contractor a certificate for further payment for extras, the
contractor was excused from complying with the provision requiring the architect's certificate.

Mich. *Maurer v. School Dist.*, 186 Mich. 223, 152 N.W. 999 (1915).
Where the only condition attached to issuing a certificate was the
completion of the work, and the architect's refusal to issue a certificate was on the ground that there was a question of liquidated
damages arising out of delayed completion of the building, the
contractor could recover the final installment in the absence of
the certificate.

Miss. *Standard Millwork & Supply Co. v. Mississippi Steel & Iron
Co.*, 205 Miss. 96, 38 So. 2d 448 (1949). Refusal of the architect to

issue a final certificate that the completed work complied with the contract did not preclude the contractor from suing to recover the contract price on ground he had substantially complied with contract.

N.Y. *Walter v. Horwitz*, 60 N.Y.S., 2d 327, *aff'd*, 271 App. Div. 802, 65 N.Y.S. 2d 672 (1946). Where the architect refused to give a final certificate to the contractors unless they accepted the figures and claim of the owner which were not justified, certificate was unreasonably withheld and contractors were not required to procure such certificate as a condition to recovery.

Hevenor v. Union R. Co., 208 App. Div. 610, 204 N.Y.S. 40 (1924). If the jury finds that the work has been substantially performed and that a certificate ought to have been given, the contractor may recover compensation notwithstanding the engineer's persistent refusal to issue the certificate.

Fuchs v. Saladino, 133 App. Div. 710, 118 N.Y.S. 172 (1909). Architect's certificate was not arbitrarily or unreasonably withheld where the contractor's failure to perform amounted to 15% of the value of the work contracted for.

Kuhs v. Flower City Tissue Mills Co., 104 Misc. 243, 171 N.Y.S. 688 (1918), *aff'd*, 189 App. Div. 539, 179 N.Y.S. 450 (1919). Where an architect unreasonably refuses to issue a certificate, there may be recovery for the work performed despite its absence.

Meulenbergh v. Coe, 160 N.Y.S. 581 (1916). Where the architect, under instructions of owner, refused to issue a certificate after substantial completion of the work, the production of a certificate as a condition of payment was excused.

Murdock v. Jones, 3 App. Div. 221, 38 N.Y.S. 461 (1896). Where the architect refuses to give the materialman certificate on the ground that it is unnecessary, such refusal is unreasonable and the materialman need not procure it to recover from the contractor.

Pa. *Fay v. Moore*, 261 Pa. 437, 104 Atl. 686 (1918). Where the architect's refusal to issue a certificate on completion of the work was based on the dictation of the owners and not on the architect's judgment, the contractor was not precluded from recovering the balance due.

Pittsburgh Terra-Cotta Lumber Co. v. Sharp, 190 Pa. 256, 42 Atl. 685 (1899). Where the architect, in collusion with the owner, wrongfully refuses his certificate, the contractor may recover for work properly done.

Tenn.   *P. & M. J. Bannon v. Jackson,* 121 Tenn. 381, 117 S.W. 504
(1908). Contractor could not rely on a certificate obtained subsequent to the institution of suit, unless he brought it forward by
supplemental pleading.

Tex.   *Goodrum v. State,* 158 S.W. 2d 81 (1942). Word "arbitrary,"
with respect to the type of conduct which will prevent the arbiter's decision from becoming final, means bad faith and failure
to exercise honest judgment.

Wash.   *Colby v. Interlaken Land Co.,* 88 Wash. 196, 152 Pac. 994
(1915). Architect's refusal to issue a certificate of completion is at
least *prima facie* evidence that the building was not completed
according to the contract, where the contract provides that completion of the house is to be evidenced by a certificate of the
architect.

Windham v. Independent Telephone Co., 35 Wash. 166, 76 Pac.
936 (1904). Where the architect's refusal to furnish a certificate
was whimsical, such refusal was no defense to an action by the
contractor for the balance due on the contract.

Hangen v. Ranpoch, 260 P. 2d 340 (1953). The lower court had
held that the contractors had a legal excuse for not obtaining the
certificate. It relied partially on findings that they were har-
assed with objections and demands by the owner that were trivial,
unreasonable and capricious. On appeal it was held that the architect was really satisfied with the performance of the contractor,
and refused to issue the certificate only because of collusion with
the owner or opposition from him, all of which excused the contractor from the condition.

Wis.   *Tomlinson v. Ashland County,* 170 Wis. 58, 173 N.W. 300
(1919). Where failure of the architects to give a certificate was
based on their mistaken view of the law, it was no bar to the
contractor's right to recover.

Shine v. Hagemeister Realty Co., 169 Wis. 343, 172 N.W. 750
(1919). Refusal to award a certificate because of matters entirely
outside of the submission is a mistaken and arbitrary refusal, even
though made in good faith, and excuses the contractor from producing a certificate.

Coorsen v. Ziehl, 103 Wis. 381, 79 N.W. 562 (1899). A finding of
the referee that the contractor had substantially completed the
work according to the contract is not equivalent to a finding that
the architect acted in bad faith or under mistake in refusing a
certificate, and the contractor could not recover in the absence of
a certificate.

U.S.   *Lippert Bros., Inc. v. City of Atoka,* 94 F. Supp. 630 (1950). Non-approval by the city's engineer of repair work completed by the contractor within the provision of the plans and specifications, without evidence of defective workmanship or materials, was constructive fraud on the contractor and did not bar the contractor from recovering for such work.

CHAPTER EIGHTEEN

Formal requirements of the certificate

Where no special form of final certificate is required by the contract, a writing which expressly or impliedly states that the work has been fully performed is generally given the legal effect of a final certificate. Where the certificate is not final in content or does not comply with the formal requirements of the contract, where the courts require strict adherence to the contract provisions, it has been held insufficient.

Certificates or estimates as to partial or final performance are intended for the protection of the owner. They evidence the fact that the sum specified has been earned by the contractor and that his work has been properly and fully performed. Many contracts do not make any provision as to the form of the certificate beyond requiring that full performance or the approval of the architect or engineer be certified to in writing. It is generally held that any writing which carries out that purpose is sufficient. It is not required that the certificate recite the language of the contract so long as it conveys the meaning that the work has been fully performed to the satisfaction of the architect or engineer directly responsible for the work.

It has been held that a certificate which states that the last payment is due according to the contract is in effect the same as if it stated that the work had been done to the satisfaction of the architect, where the contract makes the latter a condition of payment. Likewise, a recital that the work has been accepted is equivalent to the statement that the contract has been fully completed.

Where a contract required installment payments to be made on the estimates of the architect, it was held that a bill presented by the contractor, which the architect certified to by the endorsement "o.k." with his initials, was a sufficient compliance with a contract provision for a final certificate of completion. Similarly, a final certificate, in the form of a final bill with the notations "o.k." and the architect's initials, has been held to fulfill the purpose of the contract. A letter written by the architect or engineer may also serve as a certificate provided it certifies satisfactory completion in substance.

There have been cases, however, which have construed the form of the certificate more strictly and have required that averments in the certificate be more or less in exact conformity with the language of the contract. In one case it was stated that since the effect of the architect's certificate is to deprive a party of a trial by jury, it must be construed strictly. In that case a certificate which recited that the contractor was entitled to a certain sum as final payment for construction work was held not to be in conformity with the contract since the certificate made no averment of the satisfactory completion of the work. It has also been held that a mere order of the architect requesting the owner to pay a certain sum on account does not comply with a contract provision requiring a certificate to the effect that the work was done in strict accordance with drawings and specifications, and that the architect has no right to consider the payment properly due until he has fully complied.

A requirement that the certificate be in writing and signed by the architect is not satisfied by the production of an unsigned, uncertified instrument, which is in fact nothing more than a memorandum. It has also been held that where a written instrument is required, oral acceptance of the contractor's work is not sufficient.

WHERE NO SPECIAL FORM OF CERTIFICATE IS REQUIRED by the construction contract, a certificate which shows expressly or by implication that the work was performed to the satisfaction of the architect or engineer is sufficient, and it need not be in the exact language of the contract.

Iowa   *Getchell & Martin Lumber & Mfg. Co. v. Peterson & Sampson,* 124 Iowa 599, 100 N.W. 550 (1904). Where bill presented by contractor was indorsed by architect with notations "o.k." together with his initials, this was held to be a sufficient compliance with contract stipulation requiring a written certificate as a condition to payment.

N.J.   *Jose Naples, Inc., v. Great Notch Dev. Co.,* 8 N.J. Misc. 135, 149 Atl. 33 (1930). Although engineer's certificate did not show on its face that work had been done to his satisfaction, the fact that he gave the certificate to the contractor expressed his satisfaction with the work done.

N.Y.   *Snaith v. Smith,* 7 Misc. 37, 27 N.Y.S. 379 (1894). Where the contract required that the contractor certify in writing that the work had been done to the architect's satisfaction, a certificate stating "there is now due to the contractor the final payment on his contract," specifying the amount, sufficiently complies with the contract.

Grannis & Hurd Lumber Co. v. Deeves, 72 Hun. 171, 25 N.Y.S. 375 (1893), *aff'd,* 147 N.Y. 718, 42 N.E. 723 (1895). Where architect certified that the subcontractor was entitled to a settlement but without prejudice to any claim of the builder, the certificate was proper since it did not judge the claim of each but was intended to permit the subcontractor to enforce its legal rights without prejudicing the builder.

Wyckoff v. Meyers, 44 N.Y. 143 (1870). Where architect certified that the last payment was due the contractor according to the contract, this was the same as certifying that the work was completely finished, as required by the contract.

Va.   *Scotts Ex'r v. Chesterman,* 117 Va. 584, 85 S.E. 502 (1915). Where contractor sent architect a bill for the balance due and the architect endorsed therein the letters "o.k." with his initials and the owner knew of this, the endorsement was a sufficient certification of approval as required by the contract.

Wash.   *Eastham v. Western Constr. Co.,* 36 Wash. 7, 77 Pac. 1051 (1904). Engineer's certificate that he had accepted work was sufficient, although it did not state in the language of the contract that the contract had been fully completed and finished since that necessarily follows when he certifies that he has accepted the work.

U.S.   *Gubbins v. Lautenschlager,* 74 Fed. 160 (1896). Where the contract provided that the work was to be done to the entire satisfaction of the superintendents, a written acceptance was unnecessary, oral acceptance being sufficient.

SOME COURTS HAVE HELD THAT THE CERTIFICATES UNDER CONSIDERATION have not satisfied the contract terms where they have been found to be not final in form or not in strict accordance with contract requirements:

Ill.   *Barney v. Giles,* 120 Ill. 154, 11 N.E. 206 (1887). Where the contract required a certificate that work had been performed and accepted by architect and all damages or allowances deducted, a certificate merely stating that contractors were entitled to a specific payment by the terms of the contract and that the work had been measured was insufficient.

Michaelis v. Wolf, 136 Ill. 68, 26 N.E. 384 (1891). Where the contract required a certificate stating that the work was done in strict accordance with the plans and specifications and that the architect considered payment properly due, a mere order by the architect, requesting the owner to pay the contractor a certain sum "to apply on account," is not a sufficient certificate.

Mass. *Hennebique Constr. Co. v. Boston Cold Storage & Terminal Co.*, 230 Mass. 456, 119 N.E. 948 (1918). Architect's letter which accepts a building on condition that certain items "are satisfactorily attended to at once" is not a final certificate in the form required by the contract.

Congregation Ohab Shalom v. Hathaway, 216 Mass. 539, 104 N.E. 379 (1914). Architect's letter to owner informing him that the contractor had stopped work and had stated that he was not going to do anything about it was not a certificate under the contract that the contractor had failed "to prosecute the work with due diligence."

Mich. *Hanley v. Walker*, 79 Mich. 607, 45 N.W. 57 (1890). Court cited cases holding that if the contract required a certificate to be in writing, there can be no oral approval.

N.Y. *Strauss v. Hanover Realty & Constr. Co.*, 133 App. Div. 743, 118 N.Y.S. 193 (1909). Where architect wrote two letters to contractor, one pointing to defects and the other stating that on his last investigation he found the contractor had done all he had expected except for one question as to damages, they were held not to be the final certificates required by the contract.

Pa. *Zimmerman v. Marymor*, 290 Pa. 299, 138 Atl. 824 (1927). Where contract provided that no payments were to be made by owners until the architect in writing certified a satisfactory completion of the work, a certificate which made no averment of the satisfactory completion of the work was held insufficient.

Tex. *Texas Bldg. Co. v. Collins*, 187 S.W. 404 (1916). Under a contract providing that amount due subcontractor should be fixed by an estimate signed and certified by chief engineer, an unsigned and uncertified instrument was merely a memorandum and not entitled to the legal effect of a final estimate.

PART FIVE

RIGHTS OF ARCHITECTS AND ENGINEERS: COMPENSATION

CHAPTER NINETEEN

Right to compensation

An architect or engineer is entitled to compensation for preparing plans and specifications and supervising construction of a project where he is employed in such capacity and substantially performs his duties under the contract.

The architect or engineer who seeks to recover for his professional services must prove a contract of employment or a promise, either express or implied, to pay for his services. If he fails to make his case certain in this regard, he cannot recover for his work, although it is skillfully performed. Thus, where he volunteers his services in preparing plans in the hope of future employment, and his plans are not accepted, he is not entitled to any compensation.

The contract itself must be valid and binding. The requisites of a valid contract—competent parties, a lawful consideration, a lawful purpose, and mutuality—have been discussed in a previous chapter.

The hazards of entering into a contract with a municipality or other political subdivision have been stressed because the person entering into such a contract is bound at his peril to know the statutory and charter requirements pertaining to its execution. A public contract is valid only if the authority to contract for a given purpose has been conferred and the contract is executed in conformity with the statutory requirements. Unless the contract and method of execution are in accordance with the authority conferred, the great majority of cases hold that the architect or engineer cannot recover for his services, even though on his part the undertaking has been completely performed. Cases so holding are found in the section dealing with the requisites of a valid public contract.

In a few instances, however, some modification has been made of this harsh rule. Although under such a void public contract there can be no recovery pursuant to the terms of the agreement, certain courts have permitted recovery in *quantum meruit,* that is, for the reasonable value of the services, on the theory that honesty and fair dealing require that the municipality pay just compensation for the value of the benefits it has received. This rule does not apply where the contract is contrary to public policy or not within the power of the government to make, but it does afford the architect or engineer protection in those instances where the contract, though properly a function of the municipality or other body, is not made in conformity with charter or statutory provisions.

In addition to the requirement that a valid contract for his services exist, the architect or engineer must properly perform his duties under the contract in order to entitle him to payment for his services. As previously noted, the architect or engineer in performing professional services must exercise the skill and care of those ordinarily skilled in the profession. Negligent performance resulting in defective work may bar the architect's or engineer's recovery for his services or may subject his claim to an offset or counterclaim for damages.

The general rule is that substantial compliance with contract requirements entitles the architect or engineer to the compensation provided for in the contract. Substantial performance is said to be strict performance in all particulars necessary to accomplish the purposes for which the fixture or structure contracted for was designed.

Deviations or omissions in small details are consistent with substantial performance. Where such performance is proved, the owner is obligated to pay the entire contract price subject to deductions for incompleteness or imperfections in matters of detail. Thus, it has been held that where specifications do not exactly comply with the law, a deviation so slight that alterations can easily be made does not prevent the architect from recovering, if he has been given no opportunity to alter the plans.

It has been held that an architect's negligence and delay in furnishing plans will not defeat recovery of his fee although he may be liable in damages. This rule has been applied where the owner has accepted work after performance by the architect.

Recovery by the architect or engineer for services performed pursuant to a contract may also be made to depend upon compliance with specified conditions in the contract. The contract may require that the plans or sketches be accepted by the owner, or that the architect or engineer change and modify the plans to the satisfaction of the owner. If the plans are not approved or the requested alterations executed, the architect has been held not entitled to be paid. Contracts may provide that compensation will be conditioned upon the successful completion of financing arrangements for the intended project. Parties have upon occasion agreed that the architect would be employed to supervise construction of a building for which he has prepared plans and specifications conditioned upon the building being erected. Under such an agreement, if the project is not financed, the building not erected, or a smaller structure erected on different plans, the condition is not met and the architect has no right to require employment.

Where approval by the employer is made a part of the contract, the courts have held that a refusal to accept the work must not be arbitrary or in bad faith. A refusal to accept plans for any extraneous reason not involving the element of performance by the architect, as that building costs are high, constitutes an arbitrary refusal, and does not bar the architect from recovering for plans which have been properly executed.

A provision that plans are to be prepared for a building not to exceed a stipulated cost is enforceable against the designer of the plans; and if he submits plans for a building which would exceed the sum specified if erected in accordance with such plans, he is entitled to recover nothing for his services. This point will be discussed *infra.*

Where plans are entered in competition with other architects the terms of the competition determine the rights of the entrants to payments for their designs. The terms of the competition may reserve the right to reject all designs submitted and return them to the authors without payment. Usual terms provide for award of a prize for the design selected as the best and return of other entries to the competitors without compensation.

The fact that the owner does not proceed with the project and fails to have the proposed building erected does not affect the architect's or engineer's right to be paid if he has submitted proper and acceptable plans. He is in such case entitled to be paid for his plans even if the owner makes no use of them.

The principle that work must be suitable for the purpose for which it is intended, and the principle that recovery cannot be had for services rendered pursuant to an illegal contract, have been used to bar the architect from recovering for his services when he has prepared plans for a structure which cannot lawfully be erected on the site selected by the owner. The architect or engineer must know the building laws applicable to the place where the building will be erected. If he is employed generally to prepare plans for a building of a given style and size, he is entitled to a fee, even if the proposed building cannot be lawfully erected at the place selected by the owner. However, when he is informed of the proposed location, he must know the building restrictions applicable to that place and prepare plans and specifications in conformity with such restrictions. If, according to his plans and specifications, the building cannot be legally constructed, he is not entitled to compensation for services.

This is based on the principle that in any contract of employment there is an implied condition that the work, when completed, will be suitable and proper for the purposes intended. The building ordinance, in effect, becomes a part of the contract between the parties as though it had actually been written into the contract. The courts have also said that the contract is illegal because construction of a building according to plans prepared in violation of a building ordinance would constitute an illegal act. When confronted by contracts which contemplate an illegal purpose, the courts refuse to enforce them and leave the parties where they find them. This rule applies also to ordinances which impose restrictions on particular types of buildings, aside from considerations as to location.

It has been held that the architect cannot recover for plans drawn in violation of building requirements despite the fact that the plans conformed to instructions given him by the owner, since the owner was not aware of such violations. The fact that the owner asked the architect to prepare plans for a building similar to that on an adjacent lot, which also violates the zoning ordinance, barred his right to compensation for such plans. However, where the plans are incomplete or the architect is engaged in making changes to conform them to the statutory requirements at the time his employment is terminated, he can recover the value of his services. This is because the plans are incomplete when work is stopped on them and the owner cannot at that time say that when completed they would have violated the building laws.

The architect is ordinarily required to tender plans to the owner to entitle him to payment for his services in preparing them. Such delivery may be dispensed with, however, if the owner indicates that he will not accept them, as by substituting another architect for the project, or by rejecting the plans as not conforming to the contract requirements.

Recovery by the architect or engineer for superintending construction is likewise conditioned upon a contract of employment and proper performance. If he does not perform his contract or offer to do so, the employer is under no obligation to compensate him. Substantial performance of his services as superintendent entitles him to recover the contract price, less any damages the owner suffers by reason of minor defects. It has been held that damage to the owner to the extent of 25% of the contract price, owing to negligent supervision by the architect, negatived substantial performance and thus entitled the architect to no recovery.

It has been held that where the architect or engineer is employed to prepare plans and specifications and superintend construction for a fixed price, the contract is considered entire and the architect or engineer cannot recover for preparing plans and specifications unless he can offer a sufficient excuse for not having superintended construction. Where the items are provided for separately and the price is apportioned to each, the contract is held divisible or severable, and the architect may recover for one or more items though he cannot recover for the others.

The owner is in all cases responsible for the architect's or engineer's compensation unless there is a different understanding in the contract. Should the architect's plans be transferred to another party who assumes the contract, the original employer is not relieved of liability for the architect's services unless the architect agrees to such substitution.

Where an employer or other person acting for the owner contracts with the architect for his professional services and there is a question of his authority to do so, the architect's right to recover against the owner will depend on the law of agency. The architect cannot recover against the principal if the agent had no actual or apparent authority to enter into a contract on his behalf. Thus, a bank cannot be bound by a contract entered into between its cashier and an architect, where the cashier was given no actual authority to make the contract, and his general authority to bind the bank in financial matters did not extend to the making of contracts for architectural services.

If the architect cannot recover from the owner because the work is defective, he cannot recover from the contractor who is jointly responsible for such defective work.

The death of the owner terminates a contract for architectural services and his personal representatives are not obligated to pay for any work performed after the owner's death. A contract for architectural services made with a firm of architects is terminated by the dissolution of the firm of architects, and the contract is no longer enforceable.

The time of payment for professional services is generally regulated by the contract, but where no time is specified, payment has been held to be due on complete performance.

THE RIGHT OF AN ARCHITECT OR ENGINEER TO BE PAID FOR HIS SERVICES depends upon the existence of a valid contract.

    Ga.   *Southern Land, Timber and Pulp Corp. v. Davis & Floyd Engineers, Inc.*, 135 S.E. 2d 454 (1964). A contract for engineering services held not void for vagueness although the time of performance, the time for payment and the total quantum of payment were not explicitly set out. As to the latter, the court held that the provision by which the owner agreed to pay the engineering firm at specified rates for each hour worked made the contract sufficiently definite.

La.   *Haas v. D'Avanzo*, 45 So. 2d 104 (1950). Where architect's evidence did not establish a definite and certain understanding as to when he was entitled to a fee, he would be allowed a fee only for preliminary plans prepared with the owner's full knowledge and consent.

Taylor v. Panama Ice Co., 16 So. 2d 212 (1944). In engineer's suit to recover balance for professional services, it was held that engineer failed to make his case reasonably certain and so dismissal of the suit was required.

Ghirardi v. Krisler, 161 So. 887 (1935). Where architect made plans and estimates in the hope that he could secure the job as contractor in erecting a proposed building, and where he was not a licensed architect and his plans were not the finished product of an architect, he was not entitled to compensation.

Mich.   *Scott v. Maier*, 56 Mich. 554, 23 N.W. 218 (1885). Architect who volunteers his services in the hope of future employment cannot recover compensation on the basis of his own estimate of the probable cost of the building for preliminary sketches which are not accepted.

N.Y.   *Green v. Messing*, 236 App. Div. 107, 258 N.Y.S. 82 (1932). Architects could not recover where they could not prove a contract of employment by the owner, where the contract pleaded by architects was specifically denied, and the contract pleaded by the owners was entirely different from that asserted by the architects.

Okla.   *Weathers v. Board of Comm'rs of Coal County*, 54 Okla. 723, 154 Pac. 642 (1916). Architect cannot recover on a contract with Board of County Commissioners to erect a courthouse for which no funds have been provided.

Tex.   *Tackett v. Middleton*, 280 S.W. 563 (1926). Contract employing architect, which was separate and distinct from the building contract, was valid where city had sufficient funds on hand to pay the architect, although his claim was to be determined by the total cost of the building for which an appropriation had not yet been made.

Wash.   *Jones v. Brisbin*, 247 P. 2d 891 (1952). Although no explicit oral or written contract exists, where the owner, "with reasonable opportunity to reject offered (architectural) services, takes the benefit of them under cirumstances which would indicate, to a reasonable man, that they were offered with the expectation of compensation, a contract . . . results." The measure of recovery in such cases is the reasonable value of the services offered. In this case, the "benefit" accruing to the owner was not that the plans were used, but that he would have used them had not two sources of financing failed to materialize.

IN A FEW CASES, AN ARCHITECT OR ENGINEER HAS BEEN PERMITTED to recover in *quantum meruit* for services performed and accepted pursuant to a public contract which was held void because it was not executed in conformity with the statutory requirements.

Colo. *Mountjoy & Frewen v. Cheyenne County High School Dist.,* 78 Colo. 162, 240 Pac. 464 (1925). Where, before proper authorization, school board contracted with architects for plans and afterwards used plans, despite invalidity of contract, school district was liable in *quantum meruit* for benefits received.

Tex. *Waller County v. Freelove,* 210 S.W. 2d 602 (1948). Where architect prepared plans for county under contract which was unenforceable because not executed pursuant to requirements, architect could recover on implied contract for reasonable value of his services.

Compare: *Brown v. Mount Vernon Housing Authority,* 279 App. Div. 794, 109 N.Y.S. 2d 392 (1952). Where plaintiff's contract with Housing Authority was specifically conditioned on the approval of the State Division of Housing and such approval was not received, plaintiff could not recover even though said approval was never formally requested by the Authority.

THE RIGHT OF AN ARCHITECT OR ENGINEER TO BE PAID for plans and specifications and supervision of construction depends on the terms of the contract and proper performance of his duties.

D.C. *Cole v. De Bobula,* 38 A. 2d 630 (1944). Architect unjustifiably abandoning contract to furnish plans and specifications for proposed alterations could not recover fee where before abandoning work he had submitted photographs and blueprints of the existing building but no plans or specifications.

Idaho *Nave v. McGrane,* 19 Idaho 111, 113 Pac. 82 (1910). Where plans and specifications are not sufficient for the purposes for which they are intended, as where they are not sufficiently definite, the architect is not entitled to compensation for his services in preparing them.

Ill. *Wehrli v. Rehwoldt,* 107 Ill. 60 (1883). Where architect was employed to superintend erection of a building but did not offer to perform his contract at the proper time, employment of another to supervise the work did not constitute breach of contract, the facts tending to show mutual abandonment of the contract.

Furst v. Board of Education, Highland Park High School Dist., 20 Ill. App. 2d 205, 155 N.E. 2d 654 (1959). "If any work designed or specified by the architect is abandoned or suspended, the architect is to be paid for the services rendered on account of it." This standard contract clause was interpreted to mean that if at any time the contract was abandoned by the Board, the architect could only recover for work done before abandonment. The court also held that "work designated or specified by the architect" referred to his specific plans drawn up for the project at issue and not to the project itself. In this case the Board had decided not to make use of plaintiff-architect's plans and had sought the services of another architect for basically the same facilities as had been originally desired, though of somewhat larger proportions. In rejecting the first architect's claim, the court noted that nowhere did the Board promise to accept plaintiff's plans, and then added ". . . if we were to adopt plaintiff's thinking, the owner would be entirely in the hands of the architect if he or she ever wished to carry out his or her general objective. Such an interpretation could lead to grave inequities which the law will not permit."

Ky.   *Ingram v. State Property and Bldgs. Commission,* 309 S.W. 2d 169 (1957).

La.   *Grosz v. Baton Rouge Realty Co.,* 17 So. 2d 63 (1944). Architect was held entitled to balance due for supervising construction where evidence showed he had diligently performed the contract.

H. A. Bauman, Inc. v. Tilly, 185 So. 504 (1938). One who supervised construction of a building in reliance on a contract for conveyance of such building to him, could recover for services in *quantum meruit* though he could not enforce the contract nor recover damages for its breach.

Maas v. Hernandez, 48 La. Ann. 264, 19 So. 269 (1895). Where contract for fixed amount is entered into between owner and builder, builder may not charge extra for a plan which he prepares and attaches to the specifications as explanatory thereof.

Mo.   *Priestly v. Laederich,* 2 S.W. 2d 631 (1928). In architect's action for services in preparing architectural plans, preparation for starting work under the plans was held to authorize jury's inference that the plans were satisfactory.

Curtis v. Bales, 211 Mo. App. 219, 241 S.W. 83 (1922). Where plans were drawn with provision for connection with heating system, as directed by the owner, though such system did not yet extend to the site of the proposed building, the plans were not on that account worthless and the architect could recover for them.

Pa.   *Hoover v. Paterni,* 13 A. 2d 914 (1940). Architect was held entitled to payment of balance of contract price for drawings where he agreed to make no extra charge if the owner awarded the contract to a named individual and the contract was performed by the architect and the work awarded to said individual.

Thayer v. McCaslin, 314 Pa. 553, 171 Atl. 898 (1934). County controller could be compelled by *mandamus* to approve claim of architects under contract with city commissioners for services properly performed under a valid contract.

R.I.   *Wolf v. Dimond,* 129 Atl. 342 (1925). Owner who accepted plans prepared by an architect six months before he contracted with the architect for supervision, could not object to defects in plans in subsequent suit by architect to recover for supervisory services, especially where he accepted them on the judgment of a contractor.

Tex.   *Scarbrough v. Wheeler,* 172 S.W. 196 (1915). One who furnishes plans for fixtures and furniture for building in compliance with contract, and such plans are accepted by the owners, may recover reasonable value of services rendered though the contract requires that the services shall be to the entire satisfaction of the owner before he is required to pay for them.

U.S.   *Mayer v. Wells,* 222 Fed. 881 (1915). Architect who prepared plans which did not conform to building code and were rejected by owner, and later corrected the plans but never submitted the changes to the owner, could not recover for his services, since he failed to comply with an important provision of the contract.

Kinney v. Manitowoc County, 135 Fed. 491 (1905). Architects could not recover value of their plans and specifications which were not used except to enable board to abandon project, where they did not furnish complete working plans and specifications as provided in the contract and furnished no proof as to the fair value of the use of plans.

THE ARCHITECT OR ENGINEER MAY RECOVER for professional services, notwithstanding the fact that the work is defective or incomplete, when he has substantially performed.

Cal.   *Pieri v. Rasebrook,* 128 Cal. App. 2d 250, 275 P. 2d 67 (1954).

Del.   *Brinckle v. England,* 25 Del. 16, 78 Atl. 638 (1910). If the architect prepares plans and specifications which substantially conform to the owner's directions, he can recover the fair and reasonable value of plans though the owner rejected them.

Ga.   *Block v. Happ,* 144 Ga. 145, 86 S.E. 316 (1915). On acceptance of work after performance by architect, owner is obligated to pay for work, and any damages he suffers for negligent performance of architect may be set off in recoupment.

N.J.   *Klemm v. Hermann,* 86 N.J.L. 869, 92 Atl. 51 (1914). Where architect's specifications deviated from legal requirements so slightly that alteration could easily have been made, and architect was not given an opportunity to make alterations, he was entitled to compensation for his services.

N.M.   *Rapp v. Board of Educ. of Las Vegas,* 34 N.M. 526, 284 Pac. 761 (1927). In order for architect to recover for drawing plans for public or governmental building, it is essential that all statutory requirements regarding such contract be met.

N.Y.   *Nieman-Irving & Co. v. Lazenby,* 263 N.Y. 91, 188 N.E. 265 (1933). If in the performance of a contract, architect exercises skill and diligence but through oversight or lapse causes some damage to the owner, damages may be offset against his recovery. *Gompert v. Healy,* 149 App. Div. 198, 133 N.Y.S. 689 (1912). Where owner was damaged to extent of 25% of contract price by action of architect in permitting installation of a plumbing system which deviated from the plans, architect had not substantially performed the contract and could not recover for his services.

Okla.   *Raitman v. McCune,* 167 Okla. 511, 30 P. 2d 878 (1934). Where an architect admits that but trivial or inconsequential amount of work remained to be done at time owner discharged him, and there was no evidence as to cost of superintending such trivial amount of work, a verdict awarding him full compensation for completion of work will not be set aside on appeal because the contract has not been completed.

Ore.   *White v. Pallay,* 119 Ore. 97, 247 Pac. 316 (1926). Architect, having exercised reasonable care and diligence in examining building site and preparing plans and specifications, can recover compensation and is not liable in damages for defective foundation.

Tex.   *Capitol Hotel Co. v. Rittenberry,* 41 S.W. 2d 697 (1931). Architect's failure to audit accounts does not affect his right to recover fee if owner did not look to him to audit the accounts. His negligence and delay in finishing plans may render him liable in damages although it does not affect his recovery of fee.

Wis.   *Foeller v. Heintz,* 137 Wis. 167, 118 N.W. 543 (1908). Owners must pay architect entire contract price for substantial completion of work, subject to deductions for incompleteness in matters of detail.

U.S.   *Dick v. Jullien,* 51 App. D.C. 355, 279 Fed. 993 (1922). If owner is damaged by incompetent or negligent services rendered by architect, architect may not recover fee, or his claim may be subjected to an offset for damages.

Kinney v. Manitowoc County, 136 Fed. 491 (1905). Where architects were to furnish seven sets of working plans and only furnished four sets, which in twenty particulars failed to give guidance to enable contractors to bid, the contract was not sufficiently performed to permit recovery.

WHERE THE ARCHITECT'S OR ENGINEER'S COMPENSATION is by terms of the contract dependent upon fulfillment of a particular condition, he is entitled to be paid only if such condition is fulfilled or waived.

Cal.   *Harris v. Central High School Dist.,* 45 Cal. App. 669, 188 Pac. 617 (1920). Where architect's plans are accepted "when modified and changed to satisfaction of the board," his contract of employment is complete when plans are accepted by the board and no request for changes made.

Ill.   *Mallinger v. Shapiro,* 329 Ill. 629, 161 N.E. 104 (1928). Evidence that architect contracted to procure loan for building operations as part of agreement to pay him for drawing plans, and did not do so, held to support judgment denying him recovery.

Ind.   *Geddis v. Greene County,* 20 Ind. App. 274, 50 N.E. 581 (1898). Where plans were not to be paid for unless used and plans were orally adopted for purpose of receiving bids and later abandoned for imperfections, architect was not entitled to compensation.

Kan.   *Blair v. Smith County School Dist.,* 94 Kan. 144, 146 Pac. 347 (1915). Where plans and specifications for school building are approved by school board conditioned upon board's letting construction contract for specified sum, and board is unable to do so, architect is not entitled to compensation.

Mass.   *Benton v. Springfield YMCA,* 170 Mass. 534, 49 N.E. 928 (1898). Where plans are offered in competition, the right may be reserved to reject any and all submitted and to return same without compensation to competitors.

Mo.   *Cann v. Church of Redeemer,* 111 Mo. App. 164, 85 S.W. 994 (1905). Where contract required architect to furnish plans for proposed church to satisfaction of vestrymen, their rejection of plans on the ground that they called for too expensive a building, defeated architect's right to recover for work.

Walsh v. St. Louis Exposition & Music Hall Ass'n, 101 Mo. 534, 14 S.W. 722 (1890). Where the architect was to be employed to supervise construction when his amended plans and contract were approved by board, he was not entitled to be employed as architect of building on nonfulfillment of such conditions.

N.Y. *Pierce v. Board of Educ. of Union Free School Dist.,* 125 Misc. 589, 211 N.Y.S. 788 (1925), *aff'd,* 216 App. Div. 787, 214 N.Y.S. 904 (1926). Architect held entitled to recover for preliminary sketches since he rendered services pursuant to contract of employment, but he could not recover for further services because the building, according to his plans, would exceed amount appropriated.

N.D. *Welch Mfg. Co. v. Herbst Dep't Store,* 52 N.D. 113, 204 N.W. 849 (1925). Where contract provides that architect's plans shall be changed until approved by owner, and owner finds them satisfactory and requests further architectural services, owner becomes liable in damages to architect where he arbitrarily prevents architect from completing agreement.

Pa. *Hewitt v. Webb,* 253 Pa. 406, 98 Atl. 609 (1916). Where contract for preparation of plans provided that if work was carried out it should be given to architects, and separate charge was made for preparation of plans, owners were not required to employ architects in constructing smaller building on different plans.

Tex. *Ellerd v. Sodeberg,* 222 S.W. 674 (1920). Persons who employed architect to prepare plans were liable for his services despite nonperformance of his agreements to finance building, which were independent representations. But if the architect fraudulently made agreements without intent to perform them, he could not recover.

Frost v. Grimmer, 142 S.W. 615 (1912). Where architect proved he prepared plans and specifications, owner had burden of proving he was not to pay for work except on the condition that the architect sold certain bonds and building was erected.

Utah *Pack v. Wines,* 44 Utah 427, 141 Pac. 105 (1914). Where plaintiff was to draw plans gratis for a dwelling and his payment was conditioned upon his obtaining a satisfactory bid for its construction, but in case another's bid was accepted plaintiff was to be paid for plans, and plaintiff was unable to obtain a satisfactory bid and no other bid was accepted, he was not entitled to be paid for his plans.

Wash. *Baker v. Central Methodist Church,* 118 Wash. 402, 203 Pac. 977 (1922). Where architects were to be paid upon acceptance of sketches only, failure to accept sketches, if not arbitrary, bars their right to recovery.

Stoddard v. King County, 22 Wash. 2d 868, 158 P. 2d 78 (1945). Where contract employing architect was contingent upon owner obtaining a federal grant which never materialized, architect could not recover for his services rendered.

U.S. *Mayer v. Wells,* 222 Fed. 881 (1915). If architect prepares incorrect specifications and thereafter corrects them but does not submit them for owner's approval, he may not recover therefor. *Audsley v. New York,* 74 Fed. 274 (1896). Where by terms of competition prizes are to be awarded for the six best plans, architect who offers no evidence to show that his plans were among the best six selected by the committee, is not entitled to recover.

FAILURE OF THE EMPLOYER TO USE PLANS AND SPECIFICATIONS prepared by an architect or engineer in accordance with the contract does not affect the right to recover for such services. Delivery of the plans is not necessary where the employer refuses to accept them.

(a) Failure to use plans

Ill. *Hill v. Frost,* 27 Ill. App. 2d 313, 169 N.E. 2d 691 (1960).

Ky. *Davis v. Pendennis Club,* 230 Ky. 465, 19 S.W. 2d 1078 (1929). Architect may recover for services in preparing plans and specifications, although employer did not use the plans.

La. *Leba v. Sills,* 175 A. 2d 599 (1961).
Nolan v. Perloff, 10 La. App. 618, 119 So. 754 (1929). Builder who employs architect to prepare plans and specifications, which he later receives, is liable to pay for them whether or not they are used.

Miss. *Greco v. Lutnick,* 55 So. 2d 139 (1951).

N.J. *Singer v. Parker,* 166 Atl. 325 (1933). Architect who prepares plans and specifications for proposed house may recover therefor, although owners do not build, provided plans and specifications are properly prepared.

Wash. *Jones v. Brisbin,* 247 P. 2d 891 (1952).

Wis. *Hand v. Agen,* 96 Wis. 493, 71 N.W. 899 (1897). Architect employed to prepare plans for and supervise construction of a building for 4% of lowest bid would be entitled to 2½% of such bid for his plans where the building was not constructed, and in preparing plans for and supervising construction of another house he would be entitled to 2½% of the bid if he were discharged with cause, but 4% if he were discharged without cause.

(b) Delivery of plans

Mass. *Schwender v. Schrafft*, 246 Mass. 543, 141 N.E. 511 (1923).
Where owner has in effect refused to accept plans and specifications as not conforming to contract requirements, no delivery is necessary to entitle architect to compensation in absence of a refusal on his part to deliver them.

Mich. *Brandt v. Munz*, 250 Mich. 172, 229 N.W. 463 (1930). Architect, who had been replaced by another after drawing preliminary sketches, could sue for part performance without delivering sketches, which were mere evidence of performance.

N.Y. *Hill v. Sheffield*, 117 N.Y.S. 99 (1909). Where employer, ignorant of the rule that drawings and specifications are property of architect, employed architect to prepare plans for alteration of building, architect could not recover for his services without delivery of drawings.

Wis. *Clas v. State*, 196 Wis. 430, 220 N.W. 185 (1928). State's retention of plans and specifications after bids disclosed that the cost would exceed the amount appropriated was held not to render it liable to the architect, since plans and specifications are of no practical value unless they are employed in the actual construction.

AN ARCHITECT OR ENGINEER MUST KNOW THE BUILDING RESTRICTIONS applicable to the place where the building for which he prepares plans is to be erected, and if, according to his plans and specifications, the building cannot lawfully be erected at such place, he is not entitled to compensation for his services.

Cal. *Davis v. Boscou*, 72 Cal. App. 323, 237 Pac. 401 (1925). Where plans drawn for proposed building violated provisions of state housing act and certain city ordinances, and architect was discharged while engaged in correcting same to conform to legal requirements, architect was held to be entitled to recover the reasonable value of his services.

N.J. *Klemm v. Hermann*, 86 N.J.L. 689, 92 Atl. 51 (1914). Where architect's specifications for building deviated from law so slightly that alteration could easily have been made, and architect was given no opportunity to alter plans, he was held entitled to recover compensation for his services.

N.Y. *Weiser v. Stadium of Canarsie*, 137 Misc. 881, 244 N.Y.S. 61 (1930). Where, after plans had been approved by building department, it appeared that zoning regulations did not permit erection of theatre and owner did nothing thereafter, architect was held entitled to recover for work done since contract was partly performed and services for which architect was engaged were not primarily illegal.

Burger v. Roelsch, 77 Hun. 44, 28 N.Y.S. 460 (1894). Architect was not entitled to recover for breach of building contract by owner where construction of building according to contract would have been in direct violation of city building ordinance.

Pa. *Meneice v. Camp Kadimah Co.,* 157 Pa. Super. 380, 43 A. 2d. 621 (1945). Contractor held entitled to recover for services in constructing swimming pool, though pool could not be used for public purposes as not conforming to requirements of health department, since equipment of pool as public swimming pool is different from mere construction of pool which violates neither statute nor public policy.

Medoff v. Fisher, 257 Pa. 126, 101 Atl. 471 (1917). Architect could not recover for plans for movie picture theater which, if put to the use for which it was contemplated, would have violated law and subjected owner to criminal penalty.

Va. *Bott v. Moser,* 175 Va. 11, 7 S.E. 2d 217 (1940). Architect could not recover from owner for preparing plans and specifications for building to be erected on certain lot where plans did not conform to set-back restrictions in zoning ordinance and architect did not offer to change or redraft them.

Wash. *Bebb v. Jordan,* 111 Wash. 73, 189 Pac. 553 (1920). Where owner of vacant lot requested architect to draw plans for building like the one on an adjoining lot, architect could not recover for services where building would have violated city ordinance, and it was immaterial that building on adjoining lot also violated city ordinance, owner having no knowledge of such violation.

Progress Amusement Co. v. Baker, 106 Wash. 64, 179 Pac. 81 (1919). Where defendant contracted to erect for lease to plaintiff a theater, which should be counterpart of another in another city, and building failed to comply with fire ordinances of city in which erected, plaintiff was not compelled to accept such building, and he could recover deposit he had given.

AN ARCHITECT OR ENGINEER WHO CONTRACTS TO FURNISH PLANS and specifications under an entire contract must fully perform the contract to be entitled to compensation, but where the contract is severable, he may recover for the portion of work he has performed.

D.C. *Sterling v. Marshall,* 54 A. 2d 353 (1947). Where engineering contract provided for fee of 10% of construction cost for preparing plans, obtaining bids, and supervising construction of wall, but owner made complete performance impossible, contract could be considered severable and elements of compensation divisible, recovery being allowed on *quantum meruit.*

Leba v. Sills, 175 A. 2d 599 (1961). "Payment of forty (40) percent of this fee ($2,000) will be due at the time the drawings are ready to be submitted to the District for permit and the specifications are completed; an additional forty (40) percent when approval is obtained and the final twenty (20) percent when the structure is substantially completed." The "whens" were interpreted as "ifs" and the contract was held severable when the permit was refused and the architect sued for the entire fee.

Ga.   *Spalding County v. W. Chamberlin Co.,* 130 Ga. 649, 61 S.E. 533 (1908). Where architect was employed to prepare plans, specifications, and superintend construction for specified percentage of contract price, he could not recover for plans and specifications where no excuse was offered for not superintending construction. *Swanson v. Chase,* 107 Ga. App. 295, 129 S.E. 2d 873 (1963). Where the architect was prevented by the owner from meeting some of his obligations under the contract, he was entitled to recover as if he had fully performed.

La.   *Woodward v. White,* 125 So. 2d 509 (1960).

N.Y. *Spencer v. New York,* 179 App. Div. 69, 166 N.Y.S. 177 (1917). Under contract to pay architects 2½% of estimated contract price for plans and specifications and 2½% of actual construction cost for supervision, they are entitled to 5% on work completed, plus 2½% for plans on buildings never constructed.

Okla. *Board of Comm'rs of Kingfisher County v. Vahlberg,* 198 Okla. 527, 180 P. 2d 144 (1947). A contract for professional services under which architect was to be paid a certain percentage of the total "upon completion of the preliminary studies" and a further percentage "upon the completion of specifications and general working drawings" was a severable contract, and, where the architect had completed specifications and general working drawings, he was entitled to recover the payments specified for such services even though the project was thereafter abandoned.

Wash. *Gauntt v. Chehalis County,* 72 Wash. 106, 129 Pac. 888 (1913). Where architect contracted to prepare plans and specifications for 2½% of cost of building, and to superintend construction for additional 2½%, but in case contract not let, compensation to be $1,000 for plans and specifications, architect held entitled to $1,000, as no contract for construction based on his plans had been let.

U.S. *Audubon Bldg. Co. v. F. M. Andrews Co.*, 187 Fed. 254 (1911). Where contract apportioned price to each item of architect's services, architect could recover for working drawings and specifications furnished, although he could not recover for superintendence because he has acted in derogation of his duties owed to his employer.

AN OWNER WILL NOT BE LIABLE FOR PROFESSIONAL SERVICES rendered pursuant to a contract which is entered into by one who purports to act as his agent, but in fact has no actual or apparent authority to contract in his behalf.

Ariz. *Litchfield v. Green*, 43 Ariz. 509, 33 P. 2d 290 (1934). Where employee of owner commissions architect to prepare plans for owner, and there is a question of his authority to act, architect's recovery will depend on law of agency.

Ark. *Swearingen v. C. W. Bulger & Son*, 117 Ark. 557, 176 S.W. 328 (1915). Even if agent knew he had no authority to contract with architect for professional services, agent is not personally liable if architect knew agent exceeded his authority in making contract.

Colo. *Princess Amusement Co. v. F. E. Edbrooke Architect Co.*, 58 Colo. 207, 144 Pac. 893 (1914). Where architect was employed by amusement company to render professional services and a new corporation was organized, which made payment on account of architect's services, it was held that contract was adopted and acted upon by all parties and measured architect's compensation.

Ind. *Gaddis v. Barton School Tp.*, 89 Ind. App. 369, 164 N.E. 499 (1929). Under statute providing that no township debt may be created except by advisory board in manner prescribed by statute, recovery under contract made with school trustees denied.

Iowa *Driscoll v. Indep. School Dist. of Council Bluffs*, 61 Iowa 426, 16 N.W. 291 (1883). In cases of agency, in employment of architect, principal may be bound for architect's compensation for preparing plans, although agent had no authority to accept plans but only to cause them to be prepared.

Ky. *Bates v. Starkey*, 212 Ky. 347, 279 S.W. 348 (1926). Where owner contracted to pay architect 1% of cost of construction on completion of plans and 2% when contract was awarded, death of owner before acceptance of bid terminated contract and architect was not entitled to anything over 1%.

O'Kain v. Davis, 186 Ky. 184, 216 S.W. 354 (1919). Where architect's plans, drawn for an individual, are transferred in the architect's presence to a hotel company, which assumes architect's contract, the individual is not released from liability for architect's services because mere silence on the part of the architect does not constitute a release of the individual.

Mich. *Harley v. Blodgett Eng. & Tool Co.,* 230 Mich. 510, 202 N.W. 953 (1925). If architect cannot recover for his services from owner, who sets up defective workmanship as defense to payment, he cannot recover from contractor who was joint wrongdoer responsible for such defective work.

Mo. *Eckel v. Gruebel,* 226 S.W. 983 (1920). Where theatrical promoter employs architect to prepare plans, with knowledge of owner who examines plans, architect may recover for his services from promoter or owner.

Tex. *Reuter v. Nixon State Bank,* 206 S.W. 715 (1918). Architect may not recover under contract where he was employed by bank cashier whose authority to bind bank in usual financial affairs did not extend to making contracts for architectural services even though the architect did not know the cashier was acting in an illegal position.

U.S. *Stanley J. Haw & Associates v. Boss,* 222 F. Supp. 936 (1963). The court held that defendant who had signed the contract for architectural services as "agent for a Minnesota Corporation to be formed who will be the obligor" was personally liable for amount due on contract after abandonment of building project for which plans had been drawn.

THE TIME OF PAYMENT FOR PROFESSIONAL SERVICES may be fixed by contract, and where not so fixed payment is due on completion of performance.

Ga. *Southern Land Timber & Pulp Corp. v. Davis & Floyd Engineers, Inc.,* 135 S.E. 2d 454. "As for time of payment, if nothing is specified in the contract, the time is at the completion of the contract."

Ky. *Mock v. First Baptist Church,* 252 Ky. 243, 67 S.W. 2d 9 (1934). A promise to pay for architectural services when owner is financially able to do so means payment is to be made within reasonable time.

La. *Grosz v. Baton Rouge Realty Co.,* 17 So. 2d 63 (1944). Where contract does not stipulate time when architect's compensation is payable, it is due on completion of performance.

Tenn. *Holston Union Nat. Bank v. Knox County,* 179 Tenn. 259, 165 S.W. 2d 382 (1942). County may withhold funds due architect for public improvements until the improvements are completed and accepted in order to indemnify itself against loss or damage due to defective workmanship or failure to complete work, and architect's creditors, therefore, cannot attach such funds before work is completed and accepted.

CHAPTER TWENTY

Amount of compensation

The amount of the architect's or engineer's compensation is measured by the terms of his contract with the owner. Where the contract does not make provision for compensation, the owner is liable for the reasonable value of the services properly rendered by the architect or engineer.

Where compensation is provided in the contract between owner and architect or engineer, the contract measures the amount of such compensation; i.e. fixed fee, percentage of the cost of construction, architect's or engineer's costs and expenses plus a certain sum, any of the standard schedules adopted by the A.I.A., the reasonable value of services rendered. In case of ambiguity on this point, express provisions as to the architect's compensation will be conclusive over implications of a different basis arising from any other provisions.

The rule is well established that on the trial of an action parol (oral) evidence cannot be introduced to vary the terms of a written contract. This rule is applicable to contract terms respecting the amount of compensation the parties have agreed upon. However, where the contract terms are ambiguous, or the written agreement does not contain any specific provision with respect to compensation, oral evidence is admissible to explain the meaning of the ambiguous terms or to show the agreement of the parties when the contract is silent.

If no compensation has been agreed upon either in a written contract or by oral agreement, the architect or engineer may recover the reasonable value of his services, which he has the burden of proving.

A common stipulation in owner-architect contracts provides for a certain percentage of the cost of the work as the architect's fee. Under such stipulation the architect is entitled to the specified percentage on the cost of the completed structure, and the employer cannot, by discharging him before the building is completed, limit his fee.

"Cost of the work" is held to mean the actual cost to the owner. Therefore, the architect suing to recover his fee must show the actual cost, not an estimate. In case of a change of plans he is entitled to a commission only on the actual cost, although that is less than the cost originally contemplated. Furthermore, the architect or engineer has been held not to be entitled to an additional amount paid by the surety to complete construction on the contractor's default since cost to the owner did not embrace cost to the contractor, or any third party.

If the architect's compensation is based on the "estimated cost," it means the amount it is estimated the building will cost if erected according to the plans and specifications.

Under those contracts where the cost of construction has a bearing on the architect's compensation, only that construction for which the architect's plans or specifications provide will be included in determining cost. Any additional work which may be done for which the architect's plans are not used cannot be included with that for which he is to be paid.

If the architect, at the request of the owner, does work in addition to that called for by the contract, he is entitled to be compensated for it. He is in such event entitled to the reasonable value of his services, or at the contract rate for extras. In some instances where the rate for extra work is not specifically mentioned in the contract it has been fixed at the rate specified in the contract for the regular work, but this is not always the case.

Where plans are changed by the order of the owner, the architect has been held entitled to recover for his work in making the changes whether the changes were made after the bids were received or after the contract was let. Under a percentage of cost contract, an architect who made changes in the plans at the order of the owner, which increased the cost of the building, could not recover extra compensation for his services in making such changes, where he was paid a percentage on the increased cost of the building.

If the parties agree that the plans are to be prepared for a building not to exceed a specified cost, and by reason of changes ordered by the owner the cost exceeds the limit set, the architect is nevertheless entitled to compensation for his work; and if, according to the contract, his fee is computed on a percentage of the cost, he is entitled to be paid the specified percentage of the actual cost of the structure as erected.

In one case where an architect contracted to superintend construction for a lump sum, and the owner made changes during the progress of the work requiring a longer time to complete the building than originally planned, the architect was held entitled to be paid for the extra work entailed by reason of the changes.

Where the owner repudiates the contract or by other action on his part makes it impossible for the architect or engineer to complete his work under the agreement, the architect or engineer, in the majority of cases, recovers the reasonable value of the work performed up to the time his services are terminated. The agreed contract price is admissible in evidence as bearing on the value of services rendered and, if a specified basis for measurement of his compensation is agreed upon, that basis may be applied to the portion of work he has performed before the contract is breached by the owner. It has also been held that on the owner's breach, the compensation set forth in the contract between owner and architect or engineer is not controlling in determining the reasonable value of his services. Where the architect is to receive a specified percentage of the cost of constructing the building designed by him, and the owner makes performance impossible by contracting with another person for the work, the architect is not limited to a recovery on the basis of the actual cost of the finished work since it is not constructed according to the design he has been requested to prepare. He is in such event entitled to the reasonable value of the services he has rendered irrespective of the cost of the structure as it is finally erected on the site.

As an alternative to suit for the reasonable value of his services, the architect or engineer may sue for damages for the loss he has sustained by the owner's breach. The measure of damages is the profit the architect could have made if allowed to complete the contract. This is arrived at by allowing the architect the contract price less the reasonable cost he would have incurred in completing the work.

In one case illustrating this alternative recovery, the owner, while secretly intending to use photographic copies of the architect's plans, represented to him that he did not intend to build and was through with the architect's services, and negotiated a settlement with the architect for the work performed on the basis of such representations. His fraudulent conduct in thus inducing the architect to act to his prejudice avoided the settlement (accord and satisfaction) reached by the parties. It was held that since the owner prevented the architect from carrying out his plans, the architect's measure of damages was not merely the value of his services up to the time of the breach, but also the profit he would have derived if permitted to complete the work. The profit was ascertained by deducting the cost of completing the plans and supervising construction from the contract price.

It has been held that where the architect's profits are too remote and speculative to be capable of clear proof, the architect may recover the loss caused by his outlay and expenditure toward the performance of his services.

In a few early cases, the architect was permitted to recover the agreed contract price on the owner's breach without deducting costs and expenses.

The rule that under a contract for personal services the person employed is required, if he can, to minimize his loss resulting from the employer's breach by finding other work, has been held not to apply to the services of an architect.

The parties may, in their contract, provide that in the event the owner abandons the project for which the architect or engineer is employed to render services, the architect or engineer will be compensated for his work up to the time of abandonment. Under an A.I.A. standard form of owner-architect contract the provision reads:

> "If any work designed or specified by the Architect is abandoned or suspended, the Architect is to be paid for the services rendered on account of it."

Some contracts provide that whether the work is executed or whether its execution be suspended or abandoned in part or in whole, payments to the architect are to be made as provided for in the contract.

Both the above clauses and others which are similarly worded have been held to operate in legal effect as a reservation to the owner of the right to abandon the contract though the right to abandon is not specifically asserted. Abandonment under such a stipulation, therefore, did not constitute a breach of the contract by the owner and did not entitle the architect to anything for loss of his opportunity to complete the contract. At the same time, such clauses fixed the measure of the employer's liability on abandonment, and entitled the architect to a fee based upon the work done by him up to that point according to the payments or percentage of payment then due.

It has been held that, where architects were entitled to compensation "based upon the entire cost of the building" and the owner abandoned the project, compensation could not be measured by the bids submitted which were much in excess of the architect's estimates owing to the greatly increased cost of labor and materials due to the First World War. The court held that "the percentages then due" were to be measured by the cost estimated by the architects themselves pior to the advance in labor and materials caused by the war.

In another case where the contract provided that, until a definite estimate of cost was furnished, the charges should be based on proposed cost, and work was abandoned on receipt of the bids, it was held that the lowest bid which was rejected as too high could not be used as a basis for determining proposed cost. The evidence disclosed that the parties had in mind a proposed sum on which the architects based their first charge, and this sum determined the architects' fee.

In some cases of contract termination the courts may be unable to grant recovery to the architect according to the terms of the contract. Thus, where the contract provides for percentage payments based on the "estimated cost" or "actual cost," and no estimate has been furnished by the architect and the project abandoned, the courts cannot enforce the parties' intent. In such case the architect is permitted to recover the reasonable value of his services, and he is permitted to prove such value by producing expert testimony on the trial of the action.

In two Michigan cases where the architects' compensation was to be a certain percentage of the "cost of the work" and no contract for construction was let, the architects were held not entitled to compensation on the basis of the lowest bids submitted for the project. The courts held that the architects were entitled to the specified fee only if contracts for construction of the projects were let. In neither case was any estimated cost mentioned. In one case, the architect received no compensation whatsoever. In the other, he was awarded a percentage of the cost of a building constructed on a much smaller scale than that contemplated by the original plans. Had the architects sued for the reasonable value of their services, instead of relying on the contract, it is probable that they would have recovered in both instances.

Some architect-owner contracts have stipulated that in the event of abandonment of the project by the owner, the architect should receive a specified sum in payment for his services up to that point. Such provisions for "liquidated damages" are permissible and, where the courts find that they are not responsible or unconscionable, they have been enforced.

An architect or engineer who attempts to recover for the reasonable value of his services has the burden of proving such value. Testimony of expert witnesses as to the customary charges of other architects in the locality is admissible upon the question of the value of the architect's services. Such customary charges may be those based on the A.I.A. schedule of recommended charges, and expert witnesses may base their opinion as to value in part on such schedules.

The testimony of an architect or an engineer as to value will be given the same weight as that of any other expert witness. The jury may give it such weight as it wishes, and it may decline to accept it altogether. It may base its verdict as to value upon its own knowledge, experience, and deductions from all the evidence. Wherever expert opinion is not plainly at variance with the facts, the court or jury may follow such opinion. In general, the courts state that the reasonable value of professional services may be shown by any relevant evidence of such value.

WHERE A CONTRACT FOR ARCHITECTURAL OR ENGINEER SERVICES contains an express stipulation as to the amount of compensation, or the method of determining the amount, such stipulation controls.

Cal. *Jones v. Lewis,* 35 Cal. App. 2d 398, 95 P. 2d 698 (1939). Evidence held to sustain finding that owners agreed to pay architect reasonable value of his work in preparing plans and specifications for remodeling of hotel.

Stacy-Judd v. Stone, 124 Cal. App. 165, 12 P. 2d 143 (1932). Where contract for architectural services is ambiguous as respects payments, oral evidence is permitted to explain meaning thereof.

Green v. Connell, 97 Cal. App. 325, 275 Pac. 472 (1929). Evidence held to sustain finding that compensation was to be stipulated percentage of certain amount, and not such percentage of actual cost of building as it was finally constructed.

Colo. *Princess Amusement Co. v. F. E. Edbrooke Architect Co.,* 58 Colo. 207, 144 Pac. 893 (1914). Where contract for architectural services was adopted by successor to original owner and by architect, contract measured architect's compensation.

D.C. *Leba v. Sills,* 175 A. 2d 599 (1961).

Ill. *Llewellyn v. Board of Educ. of Cicero-Stickney High School Tp.,* 324 Ill. 254, 154 N.E. 889 (1926). Architect may recover for services, though no work was let, where his compensation in that event is fixed according to schedule of A.I.A.

Chicago v. Hunt, 227 Ill. 130, 81 N.E. 243 (1907). Where owner employs engineer to superintend installation of pumps for certain percentage of contract price, and contract names a certain sum with proviso for increase under certain conditions, engineer is entitled to compensation based on increased price when conditions are met.

La. *Haase v. Brumfield,* 137 So. 2d 680 (1962). There being no agreement as to architect's fee, plaintiff-architect was held entitled to recover the reasonable value of services. "Reasonable value" interpreted to mean value to the owner, so that architect could only recover for work which was consistent with the cost limitations imposed by the owner.

La. *Fuhrmann v. Catanese,* 44 So. 2d 230 (1950). Evidence held to establish oral contract that A.I.A. standard form of agreement between owner and architect was to be used as guide between parties and architects to be paid 6% of cost of building.

Mass.   *Atwood v. Boston*, 310 Mass. 70, 37 N.E. 2d 131 (1941). Where architect was to be paid percentage of cost of school not to exceed $1,800,000, and he submitted bill on basis of $1,300,000 because he felt building could be constructed for that amount, and the school was not built, he was not entitled to recover on the larger amount.

Perkins v. Hanks, 188 Mass. 120, 74 N.E. 314 (1905). Rule applied that express provision as to amount of compensation must control implication of different rate arising from another provision of contract.

Minn.   *Irwin v. Gould Elevator Co.*, 107 Minn. 233, 119 N.W. 1065 (1909). Where contract provided that architect receive 7% on certain sum and should not be held responsible for delays, however caused, but that, if he failed to have elevator completed on date named, he should receive only 6%, architect held entitled to only 6% on delayed completion of the elevator though he had been diligent in his efforts to have it finished on the proper day.

N.J.   *Frank Grad & Sons v. Newark*, 17 N.J. Misc. 354, 9 A. 2d 676 (1939). Where city agreed that architect's fees on city project should be in accord with A.I.A. schedule of fees, the fact that the schedule did not refer to W.P.A. projects did not preclude recovery of fees in accordance with schedule.

Pa.   *Osterling v. Allegheny County*, 272 Pa. 458, 116 Atl. 385 (1922). In architect's contract for enlargement of building, superintending of removal of old building on land acquired to permit enlargement, and testing of steel used, were held to be part of architect's "work" on which he was entitled to commission.

S.C.   *National Loan & Exchange Bank v. Gustafson*, 157 S.C. 221, 154 S.E. 167 (1930). Where contract provides that architect may recover stipulated sum out of amount retained by owner as liquidated damages for contractor's delay, recovery by architect may be had only to extent owner is allowed damages against contractor.

U.S.   *Calhoun County v. Roberts*, 136 F. 2d 59 (1943). Where statute authorizing county to construct bridge required payment of entire cost from proceeds of bonds, county could not incur general obligation to pay engineering fees except out of proceeds of such funds.

Smithmeyer v. United States, 147 U.S. 342 (1893). Where architects agreed to take annual salaries for services rendered government and thus departed from general rule of architects measuring compensation by customary fees of their profession, their action precluded application of any other contract or usage as to payment.

WHERE THE CONTRACT FOR ARCHITECTURAL OR ENGINEERING SERVICES makes no provision for compensation, the owner is liable for the reasonable value of the services rendered.

Ga. *Douglas v. Rogers,* 10 Ga. App. 486, 73 S.E. 700 (1912). Where employer decides not to erect building because of estimated cost, but retains plans and specifications, in the absence of a guaranty as to cost or an agreement as to compensation, architect is entitled to recover reasonable value of services in preparing plans and specifications.

Ill. *DeLeuw, Cather & Co. v. Joliet,* 327 Ill. App. 453, 64 N.E. 2d 799 (1945). Where engineer was employed by city to do engineering work and no price for services was mentioned, he was entitled to recover reasonable value of services rendered.

Sutton v. Board of Educ. of Casey Tp. High School, 259 Ill. App. 193 (1931). Where evidence in action by architects for services failed to show reasonable value thereof, recovery must be had, if at all, upon the contract.

Meissner v. Reichhold, 177 Ill. App. 21 (1913). Compensation to which architect is entitled for preparing preliminary plans and specifications, which are necessarily incomplete, was fixed at one percent of estimated cost of building, that being held reasonable and customary.

La. *Henry v. Pelican Cold Storage & Warehousing Co.,* 160 So. 843 (1935). Finding that engineer, who gave expert advice on demolition of structure 60 by 192 feet and 28 feet high and devoted some 50 hours to work, was not entitled to recover $350 as reasonable value of services, held supported by evidence.

Nolan v. Perloff, 10 La. App. 618, 119 So. 754 (1929). Fee of 5% for preparing plans and specifications for renovation of old 3-story store building is considered reasonable, when employer admits he offered to pay 5% and there is expert testimony that such charge is reasonable.

Me. *Coombs v. Beede,* 89 Me. 187, 36 Atl. 104 (1896). In the absence of agreement as to architect's compensation he is entitled to be paid reasonable value of his services.

Mich. *Brandt v. Munz,* 250 Mich. 172, 229 N.W. 463 (1930). A sum of $4,000 is not excessive compensation for architect's plans and preliminary drawings for theater costing over $400,000.

N.D.   *Marshall v. Hocking*, 63 N.D. 546, 249 N.W. 111 (1933). Law implies liability for reasonable value of architect's services if parties had not contracted for fixed compensation.

R.I.   *Kent v. Darman*, 137 Atl. 467 (1927). Fact that architect cannot state definitely how much time he spent in preparing plans does not defeat his action for compensation for his services, the element of time being but one of the considerations in determining compensation.

Tex.   *First State Bank of Eastland v. Phelps*, 67 S.W. 2d 900 (1934). Architect's compensation of 5% of total cost of building constructed will be considered reasonable.

Frost v. Grimmer, 142 S.W. 615 (1912). Where architect makes plans and specifications for another, law implies a promise to pay for work done.

Wash.   *Jones v. Brisbin*, 247 P. 2d 891 (1952).

Where compensation is to be determined on a "percentage of cost" and that cost is not ascertained because the project is not constructed, the architect's fee may be jeopardized, depending upon the wording of the architect's contract. Some authorities have held that where a project was not built because bids were in excess of the owner's budget cost, the architect could not recover as his fee a percentage of the estimated cost of construction as reflected in such bids. Other legal authorities have held that if a building is not constructed because the owner does not have the funds and there was no specific budget cost within which the architect was required to furnish plans and specifications, the letting of a contract was not a necessary prerequisite for the architect to recover the contract percentage of an estimated cost.

Where the architectural contract is terminated before the building is constructed because of the death of the architect, the appropriate compensation to be paid under a contract providing for a fee based upon a percentage of construction cost raises a related problem. For example, in *Rowland v. Hudson County*, 13 N.J.S. 166, 80 Atl. 2d 433 (1951), the widow of an architect instituted an action against Hudson County, N.J. for the reasonable value of the latter's services before his death, the court held inadmissible evidence as to the probable cost of the structures to be built had his plans been completed. These plans were as to one building ninety percent and as to another fifty percent complete. The contract provided for payment at the rate of six percent of the cost of the work. Although recognizing that architects are often paid on estimated costs of projects they work on, the court denied the admissibility of such evidence, relying on

1. The fact that building costs had substantially increased since the date of the architect's appointment.
2. The uncertainty as to whether the plans would have been satisfactory to the board and whether the award for construction would have been made thereon, especially in view of the rapid turnover on the board.
3. The substantial possibility that large-scale revision would have been found necessary.
4. The degree of incompleteness of the plans.

"Estimated cost," when used as a basis for compensation, means the estimated reasonable cost of construction according to the plans and specifications.

Cal.   *Havens v. Donohue,* 111 Cal. 297, 43 Pac. 962 (1896). Where compensation of architect, who has fully performed contract, is to be specified percentage of cost, owner cannot limit architect's commission by discharging him before building is completed.

Conn.   *Lambert v. Sanford,* 55 Conn. 437, 12 Atl. 519 (1887). Where architect's fee is based on estimated cost, this means reasonable cost of building erected in accordance with architect's plans and specifications and not necessarily amount of estimate made by builder, or estimate agreed upon by parties, or bid accepted by employer.

Ga.   *Swanson v. Chase,* 107 Ga. App. 295, 129 S.E. 2d 873 (1963).

Ill.   *Cooney v. Belleville,* 311 Ill. App. 553, 37 N.E. 2d 361 (1941). Contract providing payment to engineer of 4% of construction cost, payable 3% as soon as funds available and 1% in monthly installments as work progresses, entitles engineer to 4% of cost of actual construction, not 3% of estimated cost of project.

Ky.   *Foster v. Sellards,* 263 Ky. 752, 93 S.W. 2d 834 (1936). Architect's compensation, which is percentage of cost, is measured by contract price, not by cost to owner occasioned by contractor's failure to pay for materials. Architect is not entitled to compensation on cost of additional story where his plans and specifications were not used in construction of such story.
Saad v. Bates, 208 Ky. 542, 271 S.W. 568 (1925). Where architect was to receive 3% of cost of building for plans and specifications, but owner abandoned such plans and specifications in large measure and constructed building costing much more, architect held entitled to recover on cost of building which he designed, and not on cost of building constructed.

La.   *Burk v. Livingston Parish School Bd.*, 191 La. 364, 185 So. 284
(1938). Where contract provided as architect's fee 10% of cost
of alterations, architect was restricted to 10% of total cost of work
to owner, notwithstanding alleged custom of profession under
which architect would be entitled to 6% of estimated cost and 4%
of actual cost of work.

Nolan & Torre v. Metairie Ridge Nursery Co., 165 La. 312, 115
So. 574 (1928). Under "cost plus" contract architects held not entitled to fee for work not constituting "material changes involving
the services of an architect" and for which they furnished no plans
and specifications.

Churchill v. Thomas, 2 La. App. 153 (1926). Where architect's
compensation was fixed at 5% of lowest bid, but no bids were asked
for, his recovery was based on *quantum meruit*.

Minn.   *Wick v. Murphy*, 54 N.W. 2d 805 (1952). In an action to foreclose a mechanic's lien for architectural services under a contract
which provided that the compensation was to be based upon the
total cost of construction, it was held that the architect's compensation could not be based on a rejected bid substantially in excess
of the limitation placed by the owners on the cost of construction.

N.Y.   *Spencer v. New York*, 179 App. Div. 69, 166 N.Y.S. 177 (1917).
Under a contract to pay architects 2½% of estimated contract price
for the plans and specifications and 2½% of the actual construction
cost for supervision, they are entitled to 5% on work completed
plus 2½% on the buildings never constructed but for which they
furnished plans and specifications.

Lawton v. Roseno, 125 App. Div. 628, 110 N.Y.S. 14 (1908).
Where architect sues for compensation based on cost of building,
he must prove actual cost, and recovery cannot be based on testimony of experts as to what was reasonable cost of finished work.

Israels v. Macdonald, 123 App. Div. 63, 107 N.Y.S. 826 (1907),
app. dismissed, 193 N.Y. 598, 86 N.E. 1125 (1908). Where compensation is based on cost of building, "actual cost" must govern,
that being provable, and not estimate of architect or experts or
amount named in papers filed with building department.

Pa.   *Pellegrini v. Radiant Soc.*, 347 Pa. 21, 31 A. 2d 551 (1943). Under
contract entitling architect to 6% of cost of construction, where low
bid was $77,659, and at owner's request architect revised plans for
building to cost $57,557, but owner abandoned project, architect's
fee was properly calculated on higher figure, where owner admitted that was reasonable estimated cost on architect's plans.

Simsohn v. Wetter, 111 Pa. Super. 523, 170 Atl. 422 (1934). Under contract whereby consulting engineer was to be paid 10% of "total cost of installation" of all work for which engineer prepared plans and specifications, engineer was entitled to compensation only if work was done pursuant to his plans and specifications.

Edwards v. Hall, 293 Pa. 97, 141 Atl. 638 (1928). Architect requested to furnish plans for house to cost $50,000 on commission basis but furnished plans entailing expenditure of $80,000, held entitled to commission on cost first suggested.

Osterling v. Carpenter, 230 Pa. 153, 79 Atl. 405 (1911). Where architect's compensation was fixed at 5% of cost of tomb, architect held entitled to fee on tomb costing $40,000, although parties originally intended a $75,000 tomb, because plans started therefor had been altered at request of employer, without objection by architect, so as to call for $40,000 tomb.

Wis. *Kuenzi v. Radloff,* 253 Wis. 575, 34 N.W. 2d 798 (1948). Where architect was to be paid 3% of estimated value of project, which was never completed, he was entitled to recover compensation on basis of his estimate in absence of showing by owner establishing lower value.

U.S. *Shanley v. Hennigson,* 57 F. Supp. 227 (1944). Where two architects and engineer entered into contract for division of fixed fee pro-rated on basis of construction cost of work performed by each and work terminated before completion, division of fee was to be made according to estimated construction costs.

Pettee v. Nashua, 50 F. 2d 50 (1931). Under percentage of cost contract engineers held not entitled to compensation on additional amount paid by surety to complete construction on default of original contractor, since cost of undertaking meant cost to employer, not cost to contractor or any other third party.

IF THE ARCHITECT OR ENGINEER, AT THE REQUEST OF THE OWNER, performs services in addition to those called for by the contract, he is entitled to extra compensation for such work.

Cal. *Martin v. McMahan,* 95 Cal. App. 75, 271 Pac. 1114 (1928). Where architect's plans are changed by owner to increase cost of building, architect is entitled to compensation, notwithstanding provision limiting compensation if cost exceeds certain amount.

Colo. *Princess Amusement Co. v. F. E. Edbrooke Architect Co.,* 58 Colo. 207, 144 Pac. 893 (1914). Where owner decides to erect new building instead of remodeling old building, architect's compensation will be based on amount provided under remodeling contract, where employment is continued without change.

Ga. *Wallin v. Savannah,* 27 Ga. App. 788, 109 S.E. 920 (1921). Architect is not entitled to extra compensation for making changes in plans necessitated by increased costs to bring cost of building within authorized limit.

Ill. *Alden v. Stromsen,* 347 Ill. App. 439, 106 N.E. 2d 837 (1952). In a suit for engineering fees the defendant relying upon plaintiff's estimate as to the total cost of the engineering services rendered, which was approximately $1,175, the court, in upholding a verdict for $4,746.82, declared it was within the province of the jury to determine whether or not additional services were involved and authorized, and the nature, extent and value thereof.

Ind. *Weatherhogg v. Jasper County,* 158 Ind. 14, 62 N.E. 477 (1901). Where architect, under percentage of cost contract, is to prepare plans for a building not to exceed a certain sum and to make changes without additional expense, and employer orders changes, making building costs exceed specified sum, architect is entitled to recover fee on basis of actual cost.

Ky. *McDonald Bros. v. Whittley County Ct.,* 8 Ky. L. Rep. 874 (1887). Where architects, without limiting time for construction, contracted to superintend construction for specified sum, they could recover only that sum, although building contract provided that if architects made changes for superintending work extending over longer time than contemplated by contract they could recover additional compensation.

Md. *Harrison v. McLaughlin Bros.,* 108 Md. 427, 70 Atl. 424 (1908). Where architect performs extra work, compensation for which is not provided in contract, he must sue on the contract, and agreement as to compensation fixed in contract will control as to payment for extra work.

Mich. *Johnson v. O'Neill,* 181 Mich. 326, 150 N.W. 835 (1915). Where at request of owner plans for building were changed, architect held entitled to recover for labor in making changes, whether made after bids were received on preliminary plans or after contract was let.

Mo. *Baker v. Pulitzer Pub. Co.,* 103 Mo. App. 54, 77 S.W. 585 (1903). Architects who do work in addition to that contracted for may recover reasonable value thereof, if owner promised to pay reasonable value or ordered extra work.

Pa. *Osterling v. Allegheny Trust Co.,* 260 Pa. 64, 103 Atl. 528 (1918). Where architect is employed at specified compensation, and performs other services of same general character without new contract or agreement as to change in compensation, he is entitled to rate of compensation in original contract since presumption is parties intend original rate to continue.

Osterling v. First Nat. Bank, 262 Pa. 448, 105 Atl. 633 (1918). Where architect contracted to perform architectural services for 5% of cost of work, and contract was let upon original plans, but actual cost was increased because of changes made for which he prepared revised drawings, architect held entitled only to specific percentage of final cost, and not to extra compensation for preparing revised drawings.

Tex. *First State Bank of Eastland v. Phelps,* 67 S.W. 2d 900 (1934). Where contractor abandoned project after one-third of building had been completed, and architect furnished extra supervision to complete the remainder of the building, he was entitled to reasonable compensation for such extra services.

Smith v. Bruyere, 152 S.W. 813 (1913). Where architect contracted to superintend construction for lump sum and owner made changes during progress of work requiring longer time to complete building than contemplated, architect was entitled to recover compensation for his extra work.

Wis. *Sterling Eng. & Constr. Co. v. Berg,* 161 Wis. 280, 152 N.W. 851 (1915). Where architect contracted to prepare plans for and superintend construction of a three-story building for 1% of cost thereof, he was entitled to reasonable value of extra services in adding another story and compensation provided in contract did not measure compensation for such extra services.

U.S. *Van Pelt v. United States.* 82 Ct.Cl. 671 (1936). Whether certain work done by architect in changing drawings was extra work held question of law, and, where Secretary of Treasury did not determine amount because he considered such work not extra, court had jurisdiction of claim for compensation.

WHERE A CONTRACT FOR PROFESSIONAL SERVICES ENTERED INTO BY AN OWNER and an architect or engineer is breached by the owner, the architect or engineer may sue for the reasonable value of services already performed, or he may sue to recover damages for the loss sustained by the owner's breach.

Cal. *Bostock v. Hulse,* 54 Cal. App. 2d 334, 128 P. 2d 912 (1942). Evidence that engineer, employed to prepare plans and specifications for and superintend demolition and reconstruction of building, submitted plans and specifications and procured building permit before employer wrongfully terminated employment, sustained finding he was entitled to $300 which represented ¾ of the agreed compensation.

Kimes v. Davidson Inv. Co., 101 Cal. App. 382, 281 Pac. 639 (1929). City planning architect, on city's repudiation of his contract to plan and lay out tract of land, could sue for reasonable value of services performed.

Conn.   *Polak v. Kramer*, 116 Conn. 688, 166 Atl. (1933). Where owner repudiated contract with architects for services in connection with remodeling of building, architects were entitled to recover at least reasonable value of services performed.

Johnson & Burns, Inc. v. Hayden, 98 Conn. 185, 119 Atl. 50 (1922). Where owner, while secretly intending to use photographic copies of plans, told architect he was through with his services and did not intend to build, settlement with architect on basis of work performed was avoided through his fraud, and architect was entitled to recover, not only value of services to time of breach, but also profit he would have derived on completion of work, which is ascertained by deducting cost of such completion and supervision from contract price.

D.C.   *Sterling v. Marshall*, 54 A. 2d 353 (1947). Where owner rendered performance by engineers impossible by contracting for work independently of contract after asking for new plans involving higher cost, engineers were not limited to recovery of percentage of actual cost of final job, as provided by contract, but were entitled to reasonable value of work.

Ga.   *Swanson v. Chase*, 107 App. 295, 129 S.E. 2d 873 (1963). Where owner repudiated the contract, the architect was entitled to recover even for those services unperformed.

Mich.   *Davey v. Sanders*, 253 Mich. 137, 234 N.W. 128 (1931). Evidence held to warrant recovery of $6,000 for owner's breach of contract with architect for preparing plans for and erecting a six-story building for $204,720.

Ky.   *Gaffney v. Switow*, 211 Ky. 232, 277 S.W. 453 (1925). Architects whose contract for work was breached by employer were not required to do other work to minimize loss, and were entitled to recover contract price less reasonable cost they would have incurred in doing work.

N.J.   *Wilkinson v. Orange Mountain Land Co.*, 103 N.J.L. 683, 137 Atl. 591 (1927). Architect could recover contract price for services less deduction for unperformed work, where defendant wrongfully prevented performance.

Klemmt v. Yeskel, 102 N.J.L. 418, 131 Atl. 871 (1926). Where owner abandoned construction project, compensation set forth in agreement between architect and owner held not controlling in determining reasonable value of services rendered by architect prior to abandonment.

N.Y.   *Bintz v. Mid-City Park Corp.,* 223 App. Div. 533, 229 N.Y.S. 390 (1928). Architect's damages on defendant's abandoning contract for architect's services in furnishing plans for and supervising construction of swimming pool and dance hall held to be agreed commission.

Zadek v. Olds, Wortman & King, 166 App. Div. 60, 151 N.Y.S. 634 (1915). Where after architect has partly performed contract for architectural services and employers deprive him of opportunity to complete it, he may elect to recover in *quantum meruit* for value of services actually rendered, or damages for employer's breach.

Hunter v. Vicario, 146 App. Div. 93, 130 N.Y.S. 625 (1911). Where contract provided that architect was to receive, as compensation for his services, one-half of the amount saved on lowest estimate he could obtain and lowest bid owner obtained, and owner abandoned contract before architect could fully perform, architect could recover value of services in *quantum meruit.*

N.D.   *Welch Mfg. Co. v. Herbst Dep't Store,* 52 N.D. 113, 204 N.W. 849 (1925). Where profits are too remote and speculative to be capable of clear proof required by law to permit recovery therefor, architect may recover loss occasioned by his outlay and expenditure toward performance.

Ore.   *Jacob Berger v. School Dist.,* 122 Ore. 124, 256 Pac. 652 (1927). On owner's repudiation of contract for architectural services, architect may elect to sue in *quantum meruit,* or on contract for full contract price at end of time specified for performance, or on contract for loss of the profits incurred.

White v. Pallay, 119 Ore. 97, 247 Pac. 316 (1926). Where owner breached contract providing that he would employ architect in erection of another building in consideration of architect's reducing fee, architect could regard contract as rescinded and rely on *quantum meruit* in action for services.

Pa.   *Knapp v. Teyssier,* 96 Pa. Super. 193 (1930). Architect prevented by owner from fully performing contract may recover fair value of services.

Tex.   *Harlingen Indep. School Dist. v. C. H. Page & Bro.,* 48 S.W. 2d 983 (1932). Measure of damages for breach of contract for

architect's services is profit architect could have made if allowed
to complete contract.

Phelps v. Connellee, 285 S.W. 1047 (1926). Architect wrongfully
discharged was entitled to contract price for services. Fact that
damages could have been mitigated by architect's finding employment was held by court to be a matter of defense and, since it
had not been raised at the trial, the court refused to determine
question as to whether the architect had such duty to mitigate
damages.

Lone Star Creamery Co. v. Carpenter, 285 S.W. 899 (1926). Where
the architect's fee, provided by the contract, was 6% of the cost
of construction, and he was discharged after completing two-
thirds of the plans, his recovery was limited to ⅔ of 4½%, 1½% having
been deducted as customary charge for supervision.

Wash.   *Blackwell v. Ranier Golf & Country Club,* 120 Wash. 384, 208
Pac. 21 (1922). Where architect's employment to render professional services was conditioned on architect taking club membership, and construction work was partially performed, in architect's
action for compensation for work already done he was not entitled
to a refund of his payment for membership.

Gould v. McCormick, 75 Wash. 61, 134 Pac. 676 (1913). Where
owner breached his contract with architect for superintending
construction of building, measure of damages was the difference
between the contract price and cost to architect of completing
work.

W.Va.   *Berry v. Huntington Masonic Temple Ass'n,* 80 W.Va. 342,
93 S.E. 355 (1917). Contractor's liability to engineer for drawings
which he was required to furnish under contract was a proper
item of recovery in action against owner for breach of contract,
even though some of drawings were disapproved by architect.

WHERE A CONTRACT PROVIDES THAT ON ABANDONMENT BY THE OWNER the
architect is to be paid for his services, such stipulation reserves to the
owner the right to terminate the contract and the architect is then entitled to compensation for services rendered prior to its termination.

Cal.   *Stevenson v. San Diego County,* 26 Cal. 2d 842, 161 P. 2d 553
(1945). Where contract with county for architectural services provided for progressive payments and reserved to county right to
abandon work upon payment of compensation due, approval by
county of preliminary plans and estimates fixed the architect's
right to recover initial percentage payments provided for under

contract, notwithstanding subsequent abandonment of the project by the county.

Miller v. San Francisco Church Extension Soc'y, 125 Cal. App. 85, 13 P. 2d 824 (1932). Provision in contract that, whether work be executed or whether its execution be suspended or abandoned, payments are to be made to architect as thereinafter provided is, in legal effect, a reservation to employer of right to abandon contract and fixes employer's liability in the event of abandonment by him.

Russell v. Stillwell, 106 Cal. App. 88, 288 Pac. 785 (1930). Where contract stipulated a certain sum as liquidated damages to architect in case satisfactory bond issue could not be arranged after completion of plans, architect held entitled to such sum on happening of contingency.

D.C.   See *Leba v. Sills,* 175 A. 2d 599 (1961).

Ill.   *Llewellyn v. Board of Educ. of Cicero-Stickney High School Tp.,* 324 Ill. 254, 154 N.E. 889 (1926). Stipulation in contract providing for payment to architect in accordance with A.I.A. schedule in event project was abandoned by the owner was applied.

Lenst v. Board of Education, Highland Park High School Dist., 20 Ill. App. 2d 205, 155 N.E. 2d 654 (1959).

Iowa   *Shockley v. Paul Davis Dry Goods Co.,* 200 Iowa 1034, 205 N.W. 966 (1925). Where architect's compensation was to be 5% of cost of building estimated at $250,000, and if project abandoned $2,500 plus expenses, it was held such amount was not inequitable and should be treated as liquidated damages and not as a penalty.

Ky.   *Dittoe v. Morgan,* 268 S.W. 1065 (1925). Where work was abandoned on receipt of bids, under a contract providing that until a definite estimate of the cost was furnished charges should be based on proposed cost it was held lowest bid rejected as too high could not be treated as cost of construction in determining architect's compensation, since contract contemplated that proposed cost should be used under such circumstances.

O'Kain v. Davis, 186 Ky. 184, 216 S.W. 354 (1919). Where architect was to be paid 3½% of cost of building on awarding of contract and 1½% on completion, but $250 for preliminary services in event building was not erected within certain time, architect was held entitled to only $250 on abandonment of project, though he had completed working drawings and specifications.

Mass.   *Kilham v. O'Connell,* 315 Mass. 721, 54 N.E. 2d 181 (1944). Evidence held sufficient to justify finding that parties entered into percentage of cost contract and that architects completed preliminary sketches, entitling them to first installment payment on the basis of a reasonably estimated cost, before owner abandoned project.

Atwood v. Boston, 310 Mass. 70, 37 N.E. 2d 131 (1941). Where contract with city authorized city to discontinue architect's services at any time, in which case payment was to be made *pro rata,* and city made two payments according to bills presented, after which it terminated the contract, the architect was not entitled to recover any further sum for his services.

Mich. *Loyal Order of Moose v. Faulhaber,* 327 Mich. 244, 41 N.W. 2d 535 (1950). When the contract provided that the architect was to be paid a certain percentage based upon a reasonable cost estimated on completed drawings and specifications, or, if bids were received, then based upon the lowest bonafide bid, and the lowest bid was rejected as too high and the project abandoned, the architect was not entitled to receive compensation on the basis of the lowest bid.

Wetzel v. Roberts, 296 Mich. 114, 295 N.W. 580 (1941). Where fees under contract for architectural services were based upon total amount it would cost to do work, limitation to stipulated cost was a "condition precedent" to the execution of the contract and the architect could not recover under contract for his services since no construction was let because all bids were greatly in excess of the specified limitation.

Minn. *Burner v. Northwestern Bible & Missionary Training School,* 161 Minn. 480, 201 N.W. 939 (1925). Where, by consent of parties, work under contract employing architects was abandoned because of war conditions it was held that architects should be paid reasonable value of services in preparing preliminary studies.

Mo. *Curtis v. Bales,* 211 Mo. App. 219, 241 S.W. 83 (1922). Where architect's fee under contract was 3½% of lowest bid if owner abandoned project, and owner reserved right to abandon project if bids showed cost to be in excess of specified amount, owner could not abandon work and deprive architect of all compensation, especially where lowest bid was within limitation of cost.

Ore. *Bergholtz v. Oregon City,* 116 Ore. 18, 240 Pac. 225 (1925). Where contract provided as architect's fee certain percentage of estimated cost of building in case work was abandoned whether architect's estimate of probable cost of building was reasonably near actual cost was held to be a question for the jury.

Pa. *Orth v. Board of Public Educ.*, 272 Pa. 411, 116 Atl. 366 (1922). Where contract reserves right of owner to terminate contract on payment of percentages then due, and contract is terminated because of increased costs due to war, architect is entitled to percentage due, based on his estimated cost, not on cost shown by bids.

Wash. *Bebb v. Jordan*, 111 Wash. 73, 189 Pac. 553 (1920). Architect could recover reasonable value of services on incomplete plans discarded by employer for new plans which violated building ordinance, contract for plans for original building not becoming merged with contract for second set of plans.

Wis. *Mitterhausen v. South Wisconsin Conference Ass'n*, 245 Wis. 353, 14 N.W. 2d 19 (1944). Where percentage of cost contract provides that, if work designed or specified by architect is abandoned or suspended, he shall be paid for services rendered on account of it, architect held entitled to payment for work he has performed (up to abandonment) on cost, estimated on the basis of the partial bids received.

Shipman v. State, 42 Wis. 377 (1877). Under contract providing certain sum in payment for architect's complete services, architect who did not superintend portion of work could sue for reasonable value of services in preparing plans for that portion, since contract afforded no means to distinguish value of plans from value of superintendence.

THE REASONABLE VALUE OF THE ARCHITECT'S OR ENGINEER'S services may be shown by any relevant evidence of such value. Under this rule, evidence can be admitted as to the customary charges of architects for professional services, such as charges based on the schedule of A.I.A. chapters, and expert opinion as to value of architectural services rendered.

Cal. *Kimes v. Davidson Inv. Co.*, 101 Cal. App. 382, 281 Pac. 639 (1929). Correspondence tending to show contract of employment and price for work held admissible as bearing on value of services in action based upon *quantum meruit*.

Laver v. Hotaling, 115 Cal. 613, 47 Pac. 593 (1897). Customary rates of compensation established by association of architects are merely evidence of value in suit by architect for reasonable value of his services.

La. *Henry v. Pelican Cold Storage & Warehousing Co.*, 160 So. 843 (1935). In determining value of services of engineer employed to give expert advice on demolition of structure, court may follow expert opinion of another engineer if not plainly at variance with facts.

Sully v. Pratt, 106 La. 601, 31 So. 161 (1901). Owner is not bound by schedule of charges obtaining among architects where he is not apprised of such schedules.

Mass.   *Byam v. Carlisle-Ayer Co.,* 272 Mass. 176, 172 N.E. 113 (1930). Where parties had stipulated that, if architect was entitled to recover at all, $1,500 was a reasonable figure, jury, however, was not bound by their agreement, and they could determine that a reasonable charge, based upon all the circumstances and in their judgment, was $750.

Mich.   *Brandt v. Munz,* 250 Mich. 172, 229 N.W. 463 (1930). Evidence of architects' customary fees for similar services held admissible upon issue of damages.

Scott v. Maier, 56 Mich. 554, 23 N.W. 218 (1885). Mere custom among architects will not entitle architect to be paid percentage based on his own estimate, where he volunteers his services in the hope of future employment.

Neb.   *Davis v. South Omaha School Dist.,* 84 Neb. 858, 122 N.W. 38 (1909). Where architect testifies as expert witness as to value of another architect's services, jury may decline to accept his opinion, and may base verdict as to value upon their own knowledge, experience, and judgment of all the evidence.

N.C.   *Green v. Bechtel,* 193 N.C. 94, 136 S.E. 294 (1927). Evidence as to market value of land at date of contract and at time of breach held competent in architect's action for services, where such land was to be conveyed to corporation in which the architect had an interest and to be computed as one half his fees.

Pa.   *Knapp v. Teyssier,* 96 Pa. Super. 193 (1930). In an action by an architect for services, fair value of his services may be shown by any relevant evidence of such value.

R.I.   *Kent v. Darman,* 137 Atl. 467 (1927). Architects testifying as expert witnesses may base opinion as to value of professional services in part on A.I.A. standard charges, since evidence of customary charges by other achitects in vicinity is a proper element in determining such value.

U.S.   *Mason v. United States,* 4 Ct.Cl. 495 (1868). Schedule of prices established by A.I.A. in city of New York is not proper value for services performed by architects in other parts of the country.

CHAPTER TWENTY-ONE

Effect of cost limitation on compensation

*Where an architect or engineer undertakes to prepare plans for a struc-
ture not to cost more than a specified sum, he is not entitled to compensation unless the structure can be erected for the stipulated sum. However,
where there is no agreement as to cost, or where the architect or engineer
merely furnishes an estimate of the cost, his right to compensation is not
affected if the actual cost exceeds the estimate or the amount the owner
expects, or is willing to pay.*

The contract between the owner and architect or engineer may state
a limitation as to the cost of the proposed project, and the architect or
engineer is in such event bound to prepare plans meeting such limitations. The parties may specifically provide that conformity to this requirement should be a condition to the architect's right to compensation. If
the architect's plans require an expenditure in excess of the agreed
limitation, he will not be entitled to any compensation. However, there
need be no distinct agreement that the architect will forfeit his right to
compensation if the cost proves to be more than the limit agreed upon.
If there is a limitation as to cost, with which the architect or engineer
does not comply, the courts have generally said that he is entitled to no
compensation whatsoever because noncompliance with this condition is
a complete failure to carry out the contract.

There may be special circumstances which warrant the modification or
nonapplication of this rule. Thus where there is a provision limiting the
cost, but the architect's plans are changed by the owner to increase the
cost, after being drawn as contemplated by the parties, the architect may
recover the agreed compensation for his services. It has also been held
that if the architect is informed of a limitation as to the cost after he has
begun the work, and his plans when completed call for an expenditure

in excess of the limitation, he can recover for services rendered up to the time he was notified to limit the cost to a particular sum.

In one case where an architect prepared plans for an armory which could not be built for the sum stipulated, he was held entitled to recover for the actual value of his services because the court determined that his work was of value to the employer in the final determination as to the style, character, and cost of the armory. In this case it appeared that the employer had thereafter increased the appropriation for the armory on realizing that the type of building it desired could not be constructed for the sum originally allocated to the project.

Some courts have modified the above rule by denying recovery to the architect or engineer only if the actual cost of construction is "substantially" more than the stipulated amount. Thus where the contract provided for a building to cost "about $100,000" and the architect's plans contemplated an expenditure of $102,000, exclusive of the architect's fees which would bring the total to $107,000, the court held that there had been a substantial compliance with the contract. Again, in another case, preparation of plans calling for a building which would cost $75,000 was held sufficient compliance with a contract to prepare plans for a building estimated to cost $70,000.

Although the written contract itself fixes no maximum cost for the building, parol (oral) evidence is admissible on the trial of the action to show that a maximum cost was agreed upon. Where a written contract exists, it is deemed to state finally the intent of the parties and the terms upon which they agreed and prior negotiations are deemed to have been merged into and settled by the contract as finally stated. For that reason, the courts uniformly hold that evidence of oral agreement is not admissible to vary or contradict the written contract. However, oral understandings are always permitted to explain ambiguous parts of the contract or to show the parties' agreement as to a matter upon which the contract is incomplete or totally silent. It is for this latter reason that evidence of the parties' agreement as to cost, though not in writing, is usually, though not always, permitted to be shown.

Where the amount specified for construction is exceeded, as shown by bids for the work, and the architect's plans are for that reason unsatisfactory, he is not entitled to be given the opportunity to modify his plans to bring the cost within the limit imposed. The owner may reject the plans and terminate the architect's employment without paying him for his services. On the other hand, the owner may waive the limitation as to cost, as by accepting the plans and specifications and accepting bids for the work, and if he does so, he must pay the architect for the plans and specifications and for any other services.

An architect or engineer contracting with a public or governmental body to render professional services is charged with the knowledge of any limitation imposed on such body as to the amount of money it may expend for a given project. He may therefore not recover compensation if he prepares plans and specifications calling for an amount in excess of the limit.

The amount of money made available for construction purposes may depend upon the size of the appropriation for the project, the amount specified by resolution of the appropriate body, or the amount realized from the sale of a bond issue.

A somewhat different situation is presented when the sum named in the contract is only by way of estimate, or the architect is requested to furnish an estimate. The estimate in such case is a statement of the probable cost and does not amount to an undertaking that the building will cost no more than the sum specified. It is merely an expression of the architect's professional opinion as to the cost of the building when erected. Should it be incorrect the architect is not deprived of his right to payment for his services, unless it is attributable to a want of skill or negligence resulting in damage to the owner.

In those cases where the cost of construction is not fixed in the agreement but the architect is employed to prepare plans according to instructions given him by the owner as to the size, style, and details of construction, he is entitled to compensation notwithstanding the fact that the plans, when completed, call for a building which will cost more than the owner had in mind.

The question as to whether the architect is under a duty to ascertain the sum which the owner proposes to spend does not often arise when the owner either has in mind a definite figure which he conveys to the architect, or seeks the advice of the architect as to the cost of the particular kind and style of building he desires. But when the owner specifies in detail the size and type of building he is interested in and, without referring to cost, requests the architect to prepare plans accordingly, the architect is generally under no duty to inquire as to the cost of the structure. This is particularly the case if the owner is a person of business experience and financial ability, able to pay for a structure of the kind and style he selected. The fact that the building when completed will cost more than the owner expected to pay does not defeat the architect's right to compensation.

AN ARCHITECT WHO IS EMPLOYED TO PREPARE PLANS for a building to cost not more than a specified sum is generally not entitled to compensation if his plans call for an expenditure in excess of such sum. Some courts permit recovery if the actual cost is not "substantially" more than the stipulated sum. Where the owner orders substantial changes in plans or construction, he may be deemed to have waived his rights under the cost limitation agreement.

Ark.   *Almand v. Alexander,* 180 Ark. 947, 23 S.W. 2d 611 (1930). Where contract fixed no maximum cost upon which architect's compensation was to be computed, oral evidence was properly received to show maximum cost agreed upon, and architect could not recover balance of compensation on cost exceeding agreed limit.

Cal.   *Rowell v. Crow,* 93 Cal. App. 2d 500, 209 P. 2d 149 (1949). Where architect entered into oral contract to draw plans for a hotel, cost not to exceed $250,000, but hotel was constructed according to plans which would cost more than twice that much and architect's plans were never used, he was held entitled to no compensation.

   Martin v. McMahan, 95 Cal. App. 75, 271 Pac. 1114 (1928). When architect's plans are drawn for a building not to exceed a certain sum, but are later changed by owners so as to increase the cost of the building, architect held entitled to compensation on final cost within cost limitation after certain items were eliminated.

   Pieri v. Rosebrook, 128 Cal. App. 2d 250, 275 P. 2d 67 (1954). Where owner ordered substantial changes in plans and construction, he was deemed to have authorized the increased costs.

Del.   *Brinckle v. England,* 2 Boyce (Del.) 16, 78 Atl. 638 (1910). If an employer places a limitation on the cost of proposed alterations, and architect's plans provide for alterations exceeding such limit, architect can recover only for such services as were rendered before receiving notice setting forth the limitation on cost.

D.C.   *Eberhard v. Mehlman,* 60 A. 2d 540 (1948). Architect could not recover for plans for remodeling store where he violated cost limitation for work set by owner.

Ga.   *Feltham v. Sharp,* 99 Ga. 260, 25 S.E. 619 (1896). Where architect's plans call for a building exceeding the stipulated sum of $4,000 by over $3,000, architect held not entitled to compensation.

Ill.   *Ada Street M.E. Church v. Garnsey,* 66 Ill. 132 (1872). Where number of architects submitted plans for church, one of which was accepted upon condition construction cost would not exceed certain sum, the architect held not entitled to compensation by reason of acceptance where the plans were rejected when it was ascertained that the church could not be built for such sum.

Kan.   *Blair v. Smith County School Dist.,* 94 Kan. 144, 146 Pac. 347 (1915). Where plans and specifications approved by school board were conditioned upon the letting of a construction contract not exceeding a specified sum, and board was unable to let contract for sum within limit, architect preparing such plans was not entitled to compensation for his services.

Ky. *Minary v. Hammon,* 294 Ky. 51, 170 S.W. 2d 873 (1943). In architect's suit to recover for plans and specifications, jury was instructed to grant recovery if architect had merely agreed to draw plans and had done so, but to deny recovery if architect promised to prepare plans with limitation as to cost, and exceeded such limitation.

La. *Andry & Feitel v. Ewing,* 15 La. App. 272, 130 So. 570 (1930). Architect failing to furnish plans for building within cost limit held not entitled to fees.

Rosenthal v. Gauthice, 69 So. 2d 367 (1953).

Bruno v. Gauthice, 70 So. 2d 693 (1954). The court indicated that where no timely objection is made to plans whose cost is in excess of agreed amount and where plans are found satisfactory by the owner, cost limitation condition may be waived.

Tsoi v. Ebenezer Baptist Church, 153 So. 2d 592 (1963).

MacDonnell v. Dreyfous, 144 La. 891, 81 So. 383 (1919). Where architect agreed to prepare plans for building to cost about $50,000 and plans called for building costing $69,000, architect was not entitled to be paid for plans.

Me. *Cf. Coombs v. Bede,* 89 Me. 187, 36 Atl. 104 (1896). Instruction to jury that, if architect prepared plans for building exceeding cost limitation set by owners, he could not recover for services was held erroneous, since it would punish architect for what might be merely honest mistake or miscalculation.

Md. *Williar v. Nagle,* 109 Md. 75, 71 Atl. 427 (1908). Architect cannot recover compensation for plans where building cannot be erected, except at cost materially in excess of amount specified. *Harrison v. McLaughlin Bros.,* 108 Md. 427, 70 Atl. 424 (1908). Where percentage of cost contract recited that the cost would not exceed $12,000, architect was held entitled to recover a fee on the total cost exceeding $12,000 where the increased cost was the result of changes made by the owner.

Mass. *Blackall v. Duthie-Strachan,* 258 Mass. 551, 155 N.E. 604 (1927). Architects agreeing to compute commission on estimated cost or price at fixed figure are bound by limitation, though alterations increasing cost were made without modification of the agreement for commission.

Mich. *George Wagschall Associates, Inc. v. West,* 362 Mich. 676, 107 N.W. 2d 874 (1961). General rule that cost limitation must be respected applied to engineer who was responsible only for the construction of certain electrical and mechanical facilities of a large project. Interestingly, in this case, the cost limitation was for the entire project and the court derived a limitation for the above-mentioned facilities by applying to the total cost limitation that percentage representing the standard costs of such operations divided by the standard total construction costs for such projects.

Zannoth v. Booth Radio Stations, 333 Mich. 233, 52 N.W. 2d 678 (1952). Architect may recover for work performed before cost limitation is set.

Minn. *Wick v. Murphy,* 54 N.W. 2d 805 (1952).

Mo. *Hellmuth v. Benoist,* 144 Mo. App. 695, 129 S.W. 257 (1910). Where employment of architect was dependent on plans being furnished for house that would not cost more than $10,000, he could not recover in absence of compliance with limitation.

Kurfiss v. Martin, 130 Mo. App. 469, 110 S.W. 32 (1908). Though architect cannot recover for plans calling for a building which cannot be erected for specified sum, if, at employer's request, he furnishes plans for another building to be erected at less cost, he is entitled to reasonable compensation for additional plans unless they are furnished on condition employer accept them, and he does not.

Campbell v. Evens & Howard Sewer Pipe Co., 286 S.W. 2d 399 (1956).

N.C. *Hite v. Aydlett,* 192 N.C. 166, 134 S.E. 419 (1926). Architect who prepared plans for building, the cost of which exceeded the sum stipulated, held not to have performed contract so as to entitle him to compensation.

Tex. *Baylor University v. Carlander,* 316 S.W. 2d 277 (1958). Parole evidence as to cost limitation was not admissible in this case where written agreement was found to be a complete integration of all agreements. The court also subscribed to the rule that "where the cost of construction is not fixed in the agreement employing an architect, nor estimated by him, but the plans are prepared according to details dictated by the owner, . . . the fact that the plans when completed call for a building which will cost more to erect than the owner expected or was willing to pay, will not preclude the architect from recovering compensation for his services in making the plans."

Vaky v. Phelps, 194 S.W. 601 (1919). Contention that plans for building which would cost $75,000 was not compliance with contract to prepare plans for building to cost $70,000 was untenable. *Smith v. Dickey,* 74 Tex. 61, 11 S.W. 1049 (1889). Where building was to cost "about $100,000" and architect's plans when completed would require expenditure of $102,000 exclusive of architect's and building superintendent's fees, bringing total cost to $107,000, court found sufficient compliance with contract.

Utah *Parrish v. Tahtaras,* 318 P. 2d 642 (1957). Where plaintiff-architect was ready, able and willing to modify plans drawn up so as to reduce the cost of their use in construction to below the cost limitation, and was authorized by the owner to do so, he was entitled to recover when defendant-owner decided to abandon the project.

Wash. *Bissell v. McCormack,* 162 Wash. 482, 298 Pac. 697 (1931). Under contract denying architect compensation if his plans call for an expenditure in excess of the agreed limit, owner may waive limitation by accepting bids on plans and specifications and by having contracts prepared and delivered to successful bidders, and in such event he must pay architect reasonable value of his services.

Svarz v. Dunlap, 149 Wash. 663, 271 Pac. 893 (1928). Architect agreeing not to charge for plans and specifications if cost exceeds estimated cost, may recover if owner causes increased cost by ordering changes in plans and specifications.

Graham v. Bell-Irving, 46 Wash. 607, 91 Pac. 8 (1907). Where architect agreed to prepare plans for structure not to exceed $25,000 and lowest bid for construction was $35,000, held plans were not in accordance with contract and architect could not recover for them where owner offered to return them.

Warburton v. Tacoma School District No. 10, 55 Wash. 2d 746, 350 P. 2d 161 (1961).

AN ARCHITECT OR ENGINEER WHO IS EMPLOYED BY A STATE or political subdivision thereof may generally not recover compensation for plans calling for an expenditure in excess of the appropriation or other limit permitted by law.

Architect held not entitled to recover in the following cases.

Conn. *Cooper v. Derby,* 83 Conn. 40, 75 Atl. 140 (1910). No recovery by architect where plans called for building to cost more than the limit imposed on legislative committee which hired architect, he being charged with knowledge of such limitation.

Me. *Lane v. Town of Harmony,* 112 Me. 25, 90 Atl. 546 (1914). Where architect knew limit of cost of building desired by town and falsely misrepresented what building would cost during negotiations leading up to contract, his fraud permitted town to avoid contract.

Mass.   *Vinal v. Nahant*, 232 Mass. 412, 122 N.E. 295 (1919). Architect could not recover for plans where bids exceeded fixed amount specified in contract and architect was held not entitled to modify plans to bring cost within limit.

Mich.   *Stratton v. Detroit*, 246 Mich. 139, 224 N.W. 649 (1929). Where city was unauthorized to contract for sanatorium costing over $700,000 no implied liability arose for architect's commission on larger amount.

N.M.   *Rapp v. Board of Educ. of Las Vegas*, 34 N.M. 526, 284 Pac. 761 (1927). Where bids on architect's original plans exceeded authorized cost of construction, he could not recover for modified plans upon which bids were within limit, where auditorium and gymnasium were omitted in said plans without written consent of Board.

N.Y.   *Pierce v. Board of Educ. of Union Free School Dist.*, 125 Misc. 589, 21 N.Y.S. 788 (1925), *aff'd*, 216 App. Div. 787, 214 N.Y.S. 904 (1926). Where, in reliance on architect's estimate, school district voted appropriation but rejected plans when bids exceeded appropriation, architects were bound to know compensation was conditioned upon the cost and therefore they could not recover. *Lord v. New York*, 171 App. Div. 140, 157 N.Y.S. 127 (1916), *aff'd*, 221 N.Y. 663, 117 N.E. 1075 (1917). No recovery was allowed to architect where contract stipulated cost of construction according to plans should be "within the total appropriation." *Bernstein v. New York*, 143 App. Div. 543, 127 N.Y.S. 987 (1911). No recovery by architect where cost, according to his plans, exceeded authorized amount, even though final plans, at direction of city commissioner, embraced many features not appearing in original plans. *Horgan & Slattery v. New York City*, 114 App. Div. 555, 100 N.Y.S. 68 (1906). Where architect's plans contemplated cost in excess of limit fixed by resolution of Armory Board and Board later increased sum and obtained plans from other architects, architect held entitled to recover for reasonable value services as his work was of value on final determination as to style, character of armory, and cost, though Board was under no duty to request any further plans from the original architect.

Pa.   *Ritter v. School Dist. of Harrisburg*, 291 Pa. 439, 140 Atl. 126 (1928). Architect held not entitled to recover compensation where plans for school building contemplated unlawful increase in indebtedness of school district and the costs were beyond the limitation imposed in the contract.

Cf. Altman v. School Dist. of Uniontown, 334 Pa. 336, 5 A. 2d 896 (1939). Fact that school district's constitutional debt limit would have been exceeded if building was constructed according to architect's design was immaterial with respect to validity of architect's separate contract to furnish plans.

S.C. *Beacham v. Greenville County,* 62 S.E. 2d 92 (1950). Where architect contracted to provide plans for remodeling county courthouse at estimated cost of $400,000 and the contract was silent as to cost, but set the architect's fee at 6% of the cost, and subsequently the general assembly ratified the contract and appropriated $400,000 for the purpose of remodeling, but the lowest bid submitted was $863,000 and the project was abandoned, the architect was not entitled to a fee based on 6% of such bid.

Wash. *State v. Pratt,* 31 Wash. 2d 725, 198 P. 2d 814 (1948). Architect could not recover fees for services where estimated cost of construction for which he drew plans exceeded the constitutional limit of indebtedness that the county was permitted.

Wis. *Clas v. State,* 196 Wis. 430, 220 N.W. 185 (1928). Architect dealing with Department of Agriculture is bound by limitation on Commissioner's authority to expend public moneys, whether or not contract involved so provides, and he must furnish plans for a building which can be constructed within the amount appropriated before being entitled to any compensation.

U.S. *Davis v. Hamilton County,* 48 F. 2d 718 (1931). Where engineer was told by public body that cost of bridge was not to exceed certain sum and both parties in dealings with each other construed contract as limiting cost, engineer held not entitled to recover compensation where plans called for excessive cost though written contract did not expressly limit cost.

WHERE NO COST IS FIXED, or where the architect or engineer merely estimates the cost, he may recover compensation though his plans contemplate an expenditure in excess of his estimate or in excess of the cost the owner expected, or is willing to pay.

Cal. *Spaulding v. Pardridge,* 28 Cal. App. 2d 658, 83 P. 2d 80 (1938). Architect could recover for services, though owner abandoned project because he considered cost excessive, where there was no oral agreement limiting cost and written memo was to effect that architect would endeavor to prepare budget within appropriation of owner, and the increased cost of the proposed building was due to changes made and approved by the owner.

Ga. *Douglas v. Rogers*, 10 Ga. App. 486, 73 S.E. 700 (1912). Where owner decides not to build because estimated cost is too high but retains the plans, and there is no guaranty of cost or agreement as to compensation, the architect is entitled to the reasonable value of his services in preparing plans and specifications.

La. *Nolan v. Great Southern Wirebound Box Co.*, 12 La. App. 688, 127 So. 98 (1930). Where owner abandoned project because bids were much in excess of amount he was willing or able to pay, but evidence did not establish his contract with architect set limit on cost, architect was entitled to recover specified percentage of lowest bid, as provided for in contract.

Mercier v. Munich, 9 La. App. 373, 120 So. 522 (1928). Where an architect and builder entered into a contract for alterations to a building for a certain percentage of the total cost, the owner could not refuse to pay the commission by showing that the work cost considerably more than anticipated where the additional cost was due to changes required by the owner.

Mass. *Schwender v. Schrafft*, 246 Mass. 543, 141 N.E. 511 (1923). Architect could recover for plans, though cost exceeded that which owner said he was ready to spend, where owner desired many special features, the cost of which could not be determined until bids were received.

Mo. *Cf. Cann v. Church of Redeemer*, 11 Mo. App. 164, 85 S.W. 994 (1905). Where architect was employed to prepare plans for church building "under the direction and to the satisfaction of" owners, though there was no cost limit, owners acting in good faith might reject plan as unsatisfactory if cost of construction contemplated by plans proved too great.

Tex. *Bueche v. Eickenroht*, 220 S.W. 2d 911 (1949). Where architect prepared plans for building which would cost more than estimated sum desired by owner, but owner did not place said sum as the absolute limit on cost of building, architect could recover for his services.

Texas Delta Upsilon Foundation v. Fehr, 307 S.W. 2d 124 (1957). "Unless the architect is given clear instructions with regard to maximum cost, it is not the architect's province to keep himself informed as to the financial ability of his client."

Utah *Headlund v. Daniels*, 50 Utah 381, 167 Pac. 1170 (1917). Where actual expenditure doubled cost estimated by architect but excessive cost was not due to his negligence or incompetence, and owner received benefits of his services until the building was completed, the owner was estopped from refusing payment to the architect on the ground that the services were unsatisfactory.

Wash. *Bissell v. McCormack,* 162 Wash. 482, 298 Pac. 697 (1931). Where property owners waived limitations on cost of construction by accepting plans and specifications, receiving bids, and having contracts prepared and delivered to two successful bidders, they became bound by an implied contract to pay architect reasonable value of services.

Wis. *Clark v. Smith,* 234 Wis. 138, 290 N.W. 592 (1940). Architects who prepared plans in conformity with owner's instructions were entitled to recover percentage of lowest bid, in accordance with contract terms, though bids were for larger sum than client wished to pay, where he did not set any cost limit and plans and specifications could not be so modified as to keep cost of house within owner's limit.

CHAPTER TWENTY-TWO

Right to mechanics' lien

Architects or engineers, who prepare plans for and supervise the construction of buildings and other structures, are generally entitled to a mechanics' lien under statutes which give a lien in general terms for material and labor furnished in the erection of a building.

The mechanics' lien is purely statutory and is given to those who perform labor or furnish material in the improvement of real property. There has been much litigation as to whether an architect or engineer is entitled to protection under these acts. The courts have reached different conclusions, depending on the interpretation of a given statute, and the court's views as to the architect's or engineer's duties and the character of his work.

In the majority of states, an architect or engineer who furnishes plans and specifications for and supervises the construction of a building is entitled to a mechanics' lien under statutes which give a lien in general terms for work and labor furnished in the construction, improvement, or repair of a building. The courts which adopt this rule point out that the statute makes no distinction between skilled and unskilled labor and should therefore be construed liberally in order to insure to both classes of workmen remuneration for whatever they may do in increasing the value of the owner's real estate.

In holding that an architect or engineer should be protected in his contribution to the construction, the courts reject the contention that the word "labor" means only manual labor or unskilled labor. The preparation of suitable plans and specifications and supervision of construction according to such plans is as essential to the proper construction of a building as is the purely manual part; and the fact that it is of a higher order and requires some architectural or engineering skill is deemed not to impair the right to a lien. In thus including architects and engineers within the meaning of the mechanics' lien laws, the courts have effectuated what they believe to be the general policy of the legislatures to give to any person who has contributed by his labor or by furnishing materials to a structure, a claim upon the property for the improvements. Surveyors, however, have generally been held not entitled to the lien, because of the more distant relationship between their work product and the completed project. See *Wilkinson v. Rome*, 98 So. 2d 435 (1957).

The minority view, which denies the right to a lien for professional services rendered by an architect or engineer, construes this general type of statute more strictly. According to this view, the architect or engineer must be excluded because he is not specifically mentioned in the statute and because he does no work on the building. According to the ordinary and well understood meaning of the terms he is not a "mechanic" or "laborer." Further, it is said that his services in drawing plans and specifications and superintendence cannot properly be called "work or labor upon the building." If he is not specifically mentioned in this type of statute, then, the minority view holds, he is not entitled to its benefits.

In certain states, a distinction is drawn between the preparation of plans and specifications and supervision of construction, a lien being denied where there is no supervision by the architect. In a few cases, the work of supervision only has entitled the architect to a lien, although he also prepared the plans and specifications used in the construction. In other cases, the architect has not been permitted to claim a lien for his plans and specifications used in the erection of the building if he has not also supervised construction. Under this rule, it is held that the mere drawing of plans and specifications is not labor performed upon the building. The supervision of construction, on the other hand, is akin to the performance of the duties of a foreman, skilled mechanic, or superintendent, and comes more nearly within the definition of work performed in the actual construction of the building. Thus, it is the role that the architect plays during the construction that draws his services within the lien law. This appears to have been the more restricted view which prevailed in the nineteenth century. The growing trend toward giving the mechanics' lien laws broader interpretation, and the specific inclusion of architects within the protection of lien laws by the legislatures have placed the architect and engineer in a more favorable position for securing compensation.

Some decisions permit the architect to claim a lien when his plans and specifications are used in the construction of a building even if he does not supervise its erection. Services of the architect in preparing plans and specifications, when they are later used in the construction of the building, are said to be services rendered in its construction under this liberal interpretation.

When the plans and specifications are not later used in the construction of the proposed building, some of the cases hold that no lien is permissible. Since the law contemplates that the lien is to attach to the property which the plans and specifications have enhanced by contributing to the value of the improvement, where there is no such benefit, these cases hold that there is no specific property to which the lien can attach. Other decisions have permitted an architect to claim a lien against property where the proposed improvement was not made and his plans and specifications not used. In one case architects were held entitled to a lien on the ground that they "constructively" contributed to an improvement of the owner's land.

Other cases have interpreted an Illinois statute which provides in part "that any person who shall furnish materials for the purpose of, or in building any house, or perform services as an architect for any such purpose, shall have a lien." Some courts have interpreted this statute as giving the architect a lien not only in building any house, but for the purpose of building any house, and an architect who draws plans for a building, even if he does not superintend its construction, performs services for the purpose of building it. Other cases in the same state have denied the architect's right to a lien under similar circumstances.

Although the right to a mechanic's lien is established by statute, it has been held that the right can be waived. Generally, however, consideration or its various substitutes must be shown to establish a waiver [*Colvin Lumber & Coal Co. v. J.A.G. Corp.*, 260 Minn. 46, 109 N.W. 2d 425 (1961); *Brimwood Homes, Inc. v. Knudsen Builders Supply Co.*, 385 P. 2d 982 (Utah, 1963)].

It is important to note that the architect is generally entitled to a mechanic's lien only for the value of the services which he actually renders. This is not of course to say that he cannot recover in full for damages sustained by other legal means.

While the cases which follow are grouped in certain categories, to illustrate the various ways in which the laws operate, it is important to bear in mind that the question in each state is one of interpretation of the local statute. Furthermore, it is inadvisable to rely exclusively on past decisions of the courts, since the mechanics' lien laws are purely statutory and have been subject to numerous changes by the legislatures.

THE GENERAL RULE IS THAT AN ARCHITECT OR ENGINEER, who prepares plans and specifications for and superintends the erection of a building, is entitled to a mechanics' lien under statutes which give a lien in general terms for work and labor furnished in the erection of a building.

The rule in a minority of jurisdictions is that an architect or engineer is not entitled to a mechanics' lien under such statutes. In the following cases the majority and minority views are listed separately.

(a) Majority view—architect or engineer entitled to a lien.

Ala. *Hughes v. Torgerson*, 96 Ala. 346, 11 So. 209 (1892).

Cal. *Pacific Mut. Life Ins. Co. v. Fisher*, 109 Cal. 566, 42 Pac. 154 (1895).

Colo. See *Trustee Co. v. Bresnahan*, 119 Colo. 311, 203 P. 2d 499 (1949); *Rara Avis Gold & Silver Min. Co. v. Bouscher*, 9 Colo. 385, 12 Pac. 433 (1886). Services of superintendent of mine held similar to those of an architect, who is entitled to a lien.

Conn. *Marchetti v. Sleeper*, 100 Conn. 339, 123 Atl. 845 (1924).

Del. *May v. Howell*, 2 Harr. 221, 121 Atl. 650 (1922).

Fla. *Robert L. Weed, Architect, Inc. v. Horning*, 159 Fla. 847, 33 So. 2d 648 (1947).

Ill. *Taylor v. Gilsdorff*, 74 Ill. 354 (1874). Lien conferred for services as "architects and superintendents."
Cf. Adler v. World's Pastime Exposition Co., 126 Ill. 373, 18 N.E. 809 (1888). Lien of architect specifically conferred by statute does not embrace services in keeping books, auditing accounts, material settlements with contractors, nor services as supervising architects in the improvement of grounds and accessories, the latter being work of a landscape gardener.

Ind. *Beeson v. Overpeck*, 112 Ind. App. 195, 44 N.E. 2d 195 (1942). *Marcisz v. Osborne*, 118 N.E. 2d 378 (1954). Contractor entitled to lien for supervisory labor performed.

La. *National Homestead Ass'n v. Graham*, 176 La. 1062, 147 So. 348 (1933). Architect employed as supervising engineer was held entitled to a lien.
Mercier v. Munich, 9 La. App. 373, 120 So. 522 (1928). Firm acting as architect and contractor held entitled to a lien.

Mich. *Chesnow v. Gorelick*, 246 Mich. 571, 225 N.W. 4 (1929). Architect held entitled to a lien for drawing plans and specifications and for supervision where contract for services was indivisible.

Minn. *Lamoreaux v. Andersch*, 128 Minn. 261, 150 N.W. 908 (1915); *Wentworth v. Tubbs*, 53 Minn. 388, 55 N.W. 543 (1893); *Gardner v. Leck*, 52 Minn. 522, 54 N.W. 746 (1893); *Knight v. Norris*, 13 Minn. 473 (1868).
See *Minneapolis Builders' Supply Co. v. Calhoun Beach Club Holding Co.*, 186 Minn. 635, 244 N.W. 53 (1932). Where architect executed a satisfaction of his mechanics' lien to float a first

mortgage upon the property under construction, his lien was re-
linquished and it was found, therefore, to be subordinate to the
lien of other claimants involved in the transaction.

Mo.   *Fagan v. Brock Motor Car Co.,* 282 S.W. 135 (1926).

Mont.   *Caird Eng. Works v. Seven-Up Gold Mining Co.,* 111 Mont.
471, 111 P. 2d 267 (1940).

Neb.   *Von Dorn v. Mengedoht,* 41 Neb. 525, 59 N.W. 800 (1894). See
also *Fiske v. School Dist. of Lincoln,* 58 Neb. 163, 78 N.W. 392
(1899).

Nev.   *Paterson v. Condos,* 55 Nev. 134, 28 P. 2d 499, *rehearing den.,*
55 Nev. 60, 30 P. 2d 283 (1934).

N.J.   *Furlong v. Housing Auth. of Newark,* 132 N.J. Eq. 341, 28 A. 2d
424 (1942); *Truck v. Allard,* 87 N.J.L. 721, 94 Atl. 583 (1915).

N.M.   *Johnson v. McClure,* 10 N.M. 506, 62 Pac. 983 (1900).

N.Y.   Application of Bralus Corp., 282 App. Div. 959, 125 N.Y.S. 2d
786, *aff'd.* 307 N.Y. 626 (1954); *Otto L. Spannhake, Inc. v. Mountain Constr. Co.,* 159 App. Div. 727, 144 N.Y.S. 968 (1913); *Swasey
v. Granite Spring Water Co.,* 158 App. Div. 549, 143 N.Y.S. 838
(1913); *Rinn v. Electric Power Co.,* 3 App. Div. 305, 38 N.Y.S.
345 (1896). See also *Stryker v. Cassidy,* 76 N.Y. 50, 32 Am. Rep.
262 (1879). Architect held entitled to a lien for superintending
construction.

N.D.   *Friedlander v. Taintor,* 14 N.D. 393, 104 N.W. 527 (1905).
See also *Buckingham v. Flummerfelt,* 15 N.D. 112, 106 N.W. 403
(1906).

Ohio   See *Phoenix Furniture Co. v. Put-in-Bay Hotel Co.,* 66 Fed. 683
(1895), *infra.*

Pa.   *Silfies v. Austin,* 104 Pa. Super. 344, 158 Atl. 661 (1932). Mechanics' lien may be filed for architect's services in preparing plans
and specifications if coupled with "inspection" and issuance of
certificates during construction.
See *Hoekstra v. Hopkins,* 87 Pa. Super. 15 (1926); *Dyer v. Wallace,*
264 Pa. 169, 107 Atl. 754 (1919); *Bank of Pennsylvania v. Gries,*
35 Pa. 423 (1860); *St. Clair Coal Co. v. Martz,* 75 Pa. 384 (1874).

R.I.   *Field & Slocomb v. Consolidated Mineral Water Co.,* 25 R.I.
319, 55 Atl. 757 (1903).

S.C.   *Williamson v. Hotel Melrose,* 110 S.C. 1, 96 S.E. 407 (1918).

Tex.   *Sanguinett & Staats v. Colorado Salt Co.,* 150 S.W. 490 (1912).

Va.   *Cain v. Rea,* 159 Va. 446, 166 S.E. 478 (1932).

Wash.   *Gould v. McCormick,* 75 Wash. 61, 134 Pac. 676 (1913).
See also *Spalding v. Burke,* 33 Wash. 679, 74 Pac. 829 (1903);

Nason v. Northwestern Milling & Power Co., 17 Wash. 142, 49 Pac. 235 (1897).

Seattle Lighting Fixture Co. v. Broadway Central Market, 156 Wash. 189, 286 Pac. 43 (1930). Where architect made plans for building to be erected by a lessee under a lease, but the lease had not been made at the time he did the work, it was held that the lessee was not the agent of the owner and the architect could not have a lien on the property, and where he failed to show what part of claim due was for supervising construction, for which he could have a lien and what part was for the plans, his claim was dismissed.

W.Va.   See *Wetzel & T. Ry. Co. v. Tennis Bros. Co.*, 145 Fed. 458 (1906), *infra*.

Wis.   *Neumann v. Strandt*, 195 Wis. 610, 219 N.W. 348 (1928).

U.S.   *Phoenix Furniture Co. v. Put-in-Bay Hotel Co.*, 66 Fed. 683 (1895). See also *Wetzel & T. Ry. Co. v. Tennis Bros. Co.*, 145 Fed. 458 (1906). Corporation held entitled to a lien for services of its officers and servants.

(b) Minority view—Architect or engineer held not entitled to a lien.

Mo.   *Raeder v. Bensberg*, 6 Mo. App. 445 (1879).

N.C.   *Stephens v. Hicks*, 156 N.C. 239, 72 S.E. 313 (1911). Architect who furnishes plans and specifications is not entitled to a lien.

Ohio   *Pierson Lumber Co. v. Roehm*, 43 Ohio App. 151, 183 N.E. 795 (1932).

Tenn.   *Howe v. Kaucher-Hodges & Co.*, 13 Tenn. App. 367 (1930); *Thompson v. Baxter*, 92 Tenn. 305, 21 S.W. 668 (1893).

A FEW DECISIONS HAVE PERMITTED AN ARCHITECT who has drawn plans and specifications and supervised construction of a building to have a lien for superintendence only.

Fla.   *Palm Beach Bank & Trust Co. v. Lainhart*, 84 Fla. 662, 95 So. 122 (1922).

Mass.   *Mitchell v. Packard*, 168 Mass. 467, 47 N.E. 113 (1897); cf. *Libbey v. Tidden*, 192 Mass. 175, 78 N.E. 313 (1906). Where contract for preparing plans and specifications and supervising construction is entire, and there is no lien for preparing plans, there can be no lien for supervision. See also *Look v. Springfield*, 292 Mass. 515, 198 N.E. 661 (1935).

IN A NUMBER OF JURISDICTIONS AN ARCHITECT OR ENGINEER IS ENTITLED to a lien in the absence of his superintendence for preparing plans and

specifications used in the construction of a building. In other jurisdictions
an architect is not entitled to a lien in such event.

(a) Architect or engineer entitled to a lien.

Cal.   *Hornlein v. Bohlig,* 37 Cal. App. 646, 174 Pac. 697 (1918).

Colo.   *Park Lane Properties v. Fisher,* 89 Colo. 591, 5 P. 2d 577 (1931).
        Where the fundamental principles of architect's plans were used
        in constructing a building, the architect was entitled to a lien.
        The fact that identical plans were not used did not deprive him of
        his lien.

Conn.   *Marchetti v. Sleeper,* 100 Conn. 339, 123 Atl. 845 (1924).

Del.   *Girdler Corp. v. Delaware Compressed Gas Co.,* 7 Harr. 344,
        183 Atl. 480 (1936). Claimant held not entitled to a mechanic's
        lien for furnishing engineering information enabling subcontractor
        to design and build plant in absence of showing that plant became
        part of building on which lien claimed.

Ill.   *Nimmons v. Lyon & Healy,* 197 Ill. App. 376 (1916). *Cf. Ohren-
        stein v. Howell,* 227 Ill. App. 215 (1922).

Neb.   *Henry & Coatsworth Co. v. Halter,* 58 Neb. 685, 79 N.W. 616
        (1899).

N.M.   *Gaastra, Gladding & Johnson v. Bishop's Lodge Co.,* 35 N.M.
        396, 299 Pac. 347 (1931).

N.Y.   *Application of Bralus Corp.,* 282 App. Div. 959, 125 N.Y.S. 2d
        786, *aff'd* 307 N.Y. 626 (1954).

N.D.   *Buckingham v. Flummerfelt,* 15 N.D. 112, 106 N.W. 403 (1906).
        Architect held not entitled to a mechanic's lien for services in pre-
        paring plans and specifications where the building was actually
        constructed pursuant to a different plan.

Wis.   *Fitzgerald v. Walsh,* 107 Wis. 92, 82 N.W. 717 (1900).

(b) Architect or engineer not entitled to a lien.

Fla.   *Palm Beach Bank & Trust Co. v. Lainhart,* 84 Fla. 662, 95 So.
        122 (1922).

Mass.   *Libbey v. Tidden,* 192 Mass. 175, 78 N.E. 313 (1906); *Mitchell
        v. Packard,* 168 Mass. 467, 47 N.E. 113 (1897).

Mo.   See *Raeder v. Bensberg,* 6 Mo. App. 445 (1879).

N.Y.   (Prior to 1916 when lien law was amended).
        Otto L. Spannhake, Inc. v. Mountain Constr. Co., 159 App. Div.
        727, 144 N.Y.S. 968 (1913); *Swasey v. Granite Spring Water Co.,*
        158 App. Div. 549, 143 N.Y.S. 838 (1913); *Thompson-Starrett Co.
        v. Brooklyn Heights Realty Co.,* 111 App. Div. 358, 98 N.Y.S. 128
        (1906); *Rinn v. Electric Power Co.,* 3 App. Div. 305, 38 N.Y.S.
        345 (1896).

N.C.   *Stephens v. Hicks,* 156 N.C. 239, 72 S.E. 313 (1911).

Ohio   *Stark v. McConnell,* 8 Ohio Supp. 23 (1940); *Robert V. Clapp Co. v. Fox,* 124 Ohio St. 331, 178 N.E. 586 (1931).

Pa.   See *Hoekstra v. Hopkins,* 87 Pa. Super. 15 (1926); *Bennett v. Frederick R. Gerry Co.,* 273 Pa. 585, 117 Atl. 345 (1922); *Prouse v. Stocker,* 74 Pa. Super. 55 (1920); *Dyer v. Wallace,* 264 Pa. 169, 107 Atl. 754 (1919); *Rush v. Able,* 90 Pa. 153 (1879); *Price v. Kirk,* 90 Pa. 47 (1879).

THERE IS A DIVERGENCE IN VIEWS AS TO WHETHER AN ARCHITECT or engineer is entitled to a lien for drawing plans and specifications never used in the construction of a proposed building.

(a) Architect or engineer not entitled to a lien.

Iowa   *Foster v. Tierney,* 91 Iowa 253, 59 N.W. 56 (1894).

Neb.   See *Fiske v. School Dist. of Lincoln,* 58 Neb. 163, 78 N.W. 392 (1899).

N.D.   See *Buckingham v. Flummerfelt,* 15 N.D. 112, 106 N.W. 403 (1906).

Wash.   *Lipscomb v. Exchange National Bank,* 80 Wash. 296, 141 Pac. 686 (1914).

Wis.   *Clark v. Smith,* 234 Wis. 138, 290 N.W. 592 (1940).

(b) Architect or engineer entitled to a lien.

Ill.   *Crowen v. Meyer,* 324 Ill. 46, 174 N.E. 55 (1931); *Cf. Mallinger v. Shapiro,* 244 Ill. App. 228 (1927), *aff'd,* 329 Ill. 629, 161 N.E. 104 (1928); *cf. Ohrenstein v. Howell,* 227 Ill. App. 215 (1922); *Freeman v. Rinaker,* 185 Ill. 172, 56 N.E. 1055 (1900).

It has been held in New York that an architect is entitled to a lien not only where the project was never constructed, but where the services only consisted of the preparation of preliminary plans [Application of Bralus Corp., 307 N.Y. 626 (1954)]. In construing the applicable statutory language, the Court stated that nothing contained in the law "disallows architect's plans which are preliminary in nature, provided they have progressed to a point where they can be characterized as 'plans' within the meaning of that term as it is used in the building trades." The Court further pointed out that more than rough sketches would be required to render lienable an architect's charges. However, drawings which are sufficiently formal to be called plans, and which have been prepared to assist the owner in determining whether he wants the project constructed according to such design, qualify for the filing of a lien under the law even though such drawings leave some ultimate details to be selected and to be subsequently added.

PART SIX

LIABILITY OF THE ARCHITECT
OR ENGINEER

CHAPTER TWENTY-THREE

Liability for negligence or fraud

An architect or engineer is liable to the owner for damages resulting from his negligence in performing architectural or engineering services. He is also liable for any fraud practiced on the owner. An architect may be held liable to third parties with whom he has no contractual relationship.

An architect or engineer implies by every contract that he possesses sufficient knowledge, skill, and ability to render professional services with reasonable competence and without negligence. He will therefore be held to the duty of exercising reasonable skill and care ordinarily expected of members of the architectural and engineering profession. If he exercises his functions in a negligent and improper manner, he will be liable in damages to the owner for injuries resulting directly from his defective performance.

The owner may bring action against the architect or engineer for the damages he has sustained as a result of improper performance. More frequently, however, the question of the architect's or engineer's liability arises in suits commenced by him against the owner for payment for his services. On the owner's refusal to pay for his work, the architect's only recourse is to resort to the courts if he wishes to be paid. He may then be met with the defense by the owner that he has not properly performed the contract; and the owner himself may claim a set-off or counterclaim for the amount of damage he has sustained.

The architect may be held liable for furnishing improper plans and specifications, which, when followed, result in the construction of a defective building. He may also be liable for damages for a defective building which results from improper supervision of construction by him.

In line with the principle that the architect or engineer will be held to the duty of exercising reasonable care, is the corollary rule that he is not responsible for all defects or omissions unless he has given a specific warranty as to the end product. It is a question of fact to be decided by the jury or the trial court whether the architect has exercised reasonable care. If it is found that he has, a number of cases have held that he is entitled to the contract price even though the building is defective in some particulars. In other cases, the owner has been entitled to offset the expense incurred in correcting the defects against the contract price. In an undertaking of broad scope involving many details it is not improbable that some mistakes will be made, but if the architect has substantially performed the contract, he will be deemed to have fulfilled the duty imposed on him. However, where defects and omissions run through the entire system of his plans, so that they are useless to the owner or contractor, he will receive no payment.

An action against an architect for damages resulting from construction according to defective plans furnished by the architect cannot succeed where it is not proven that the plans were followed in all important particulars. An architect has, therefore, not been held liable for collapse of a portion of a structure or the death of a person caused by such collapse where it was not shown that that portion of the building was erected according to his plans. An immaterial variance or a departure by the contractor from the plans in a separate and independent part of the building does not relieve the architect of responsibility unless such departure applies to the defective portion or to a part which is structurally related to the defective member.

An architect may also be liable for delay in furnishing plans and specifications if, by his delay, he prevents the continuity of the work by the contractors. The owner may recover from him any added expense he incurs which is directly attributable to the architect's delay.

The architect also subjects himself to liability for negligent supervision of the work even though he has furnished adequate plans. In supervising construction he is charged with the task of seeing that the plans are not deviated from in any important particular and that the work of the contractors and subcontractors is properly performed. It is also the architect's responsibility to see that proper materials are used and his duty includes not only inspection but also condemnation of improper materials. Proper supervision further includes compliance with the requirements of the applicable building laws.

A person who acts as both architect and builder is responsible for proper plans and proper construction. If he is sued for damages for defective construction, he cannot claim that the work was done according to the plans and specifications when he has also drawn the plans and specifications.

Where the owner deals with the contractor independently of the architect, and the architect can do no more than warn the owner of defective workmanship and materials, the architect is not responsible for any resulting defective construction.

An architect may also be liable for negligently issuing certificates of performance which result in injury to the owner. However, some courts have held that the architect could not be sued because of the immunity implicitly conferred upon him as arbitrator under the basic contract.

An architect or engineer implies by the nature of his employment that he will perform the required services with reasonable skill, ability, and judgment and without negligence. He is bound to furnish a reasonable degree of skill and care to produce a building of the kind called for without marked defects in character, strength, or appearance.

In the absence of a specific agreement to that effect, the architect does not imply that his plans will be perfect; and where he possesses ordinary knowledge and experience, and uses his best judgment, he is not liable for faults in construction resulting from defects in the plans. He may expressly contract, however, that his plans will be satisfactory, or he may make such representation of architectural skill as will amount to a warranty. The exact nature of his duty may be defined by the particular agreement that he has made with the interested parties.

If he is employed to superintend construction of a building, he will not be liable for every defect in construction. He is responsible only for those defects which result from his failure to exercise reasonable care and skill. The mere fact that some of the material may be defective or that some construction work is not done in a workmanlike manner is not sufficient to establish as a matter of law that he has not fully performed the contract.

An architect or engineer may be held liable to third parties with whom he has no contractual relationship for injury or death arising from plans which are negligently prepared, or resulting from some act or failure to act during his supervision of the project. The area of such liability is dependent upon the state in which the litigation is resolved, as there are material differences in the rule of liability to third persons in the various jurisdictions.

AN ARCHITECT OR ENGINEER WHO CONTRACTS to furnish professional services, is under a duty to perform such services with reasonable skill, care, and diligence.

Fla. *Bayshore Development Co. v. Bonfoey,* 75 Fla. 455, 78 So. 507 (1918). Architect owes to employer duty to exercise skill, ability, judgment, and taste, reasonably and without neglect.

Me. *Lane v. Town of Harmony*, 112 Me. 25, 90 Atl. 546 (1914). Persons with whom architect contracts to furnish plans for building have right to believe it will not cost substantially more than he represents.

Coombs v. Beede, 89 Me. 187, 36 Atl. 104 (1896). Responsibility of architect is essentially same as that which rests upon lawyer to his client or upon physician to his patient. The architect implies he possesses skill and ability, including taste, sufficient to enable him to perform services ordinarily and reasonably well. But his undertaking does not imply or warrant satisfactory result and error of judgment is not necessarily evidence of want of skill or care.

Md. *Hammaker v. Schleigh*, 157 Md. 652, 147 Atl. 790 (1929). Contractor is entitled to rely on architect's judgment in performing work according to plans and specifications.

Mich. *Chapel v. Clark*, 117 Mich. 638, 76 N.W. 62 (1898). Law does not imply warranty or guaranty of perfection of plans, but requires only exercise of ordinary skill and care in light of present knowledge.

Mo. *Beattie Mfg. Co. v. Heinz*, 120 Mo. App. 465, 97 S.W. 188 (1906). Contractor is entitled to rely on plans and specifications showing level floor.

N.Y. *Major v. Leary*, 241 App. Div. 606, 268 N.Y.S. 413 (1934). The law does not expect or require absolute perfection but tests efficiency of architect by rule of ordinary and reasonable skill usually exercised by one of that profession.

Dunne v. Robinson, 53 Misc. 545, 103 N.Y.S. 878 (1907). Architect must exercise his skill and ability reasonably and without neglect.

Hubert v. Aitken, 15 Daly 237, 2 N.Y.S. 711 (1888). When new conveniences are introduced into homes and become the customary means of securing the comfort of the average citizen, the architect is expected to possess technical learning respecting them.

Pa. *Edwards v. Hall*, 293 Pa. 97, 141 Atl. 638 (1928). Architect who fails to deliver plans in time for successful continuation of work is accountable for damages.

Osterling v. Frick, 284 Pa. 397, 131 Atl. 250 (1925). Architect has duty to supply plans and specifications without undue delay.

Reilly v. Rodef Sholem Congregation, 243 Pa. 528, 90 Atl. 345 (1914). Architect may not delay in furnishing necessary detailed drawings to prejudice of contractor.

William Miller & Sons Co. v. Homeopathic Medical & Surgical Hospital, 243 Pa. 502, 90 Atl. 394 (1914). Under contract investing architect with complete supervision over construction project, especially mentioning soil tests, held architect's duty to make proper soil tests.

Follansbee Bros. Co. v. Garrett-Cromwell Eng. Co., 48 Pa. Super. 183 (1907). Duty of architect depends on particular agreement.

Tex. *Pierson v. Tyndall*, 28 S.W. 232 (1894). Architect is bound to exercise such skill and diligence as is ordinarily required of architects, and fact that owner pays for work he knows is defective does not stop him from claiming damages.

Wash. *School Dist. of Kings County v. Josenhans*, 88 Wash. 624, 153 Pac. 326 (1915). Owner may, as against architect, rely upon sufficiency of construction when architect certifies it has been completed in accordance with plans and specifications although he may have detected what seems to be a faulty construction.

THE ARCHITECT DOES NOT GUARANTEE AGAINST DEFECTS in his plans, except as he contracts or represents to that effect. His duty is only to exercise ordinary care and skill.

Ky. *Kortz v. Kimberlin*, 158 Ky. 566, 165 S.W. 654 (1914). While an architect represents that he possesses the skill and ability necessary to practice his profession, he does not guarantee that his plans will be perfect and is liable only for failure to exercise reasonable skill in the preparation of plans.

Mich. *Bayne v. Everham*, 197 Mich. 181, 163 N.W. 1002 (1917). Architect is not warrantor of his plans and where he possesses requisite skill and knowledge and uses best judgment, he is not liable for defective plans and specifications.

Chapel v. Clark, 117 Mich. 638, 76 N.W. 62 (1898). Where an architect possesses the knowledge and experience of those ordinarily skilled in the profession, and uses his best judgment, he is not liable for faults in construction resulting from defects in his plans.

Okla. *Smith v. Goff*, 325 P. 2d 1061 (1958).

Pa. *Bloomsburg Mills, Inc. v. Sordoni Construction Co.*, 401 Pa. 358, 164 A. 2d 201 (1960). "While an architect is not an absolute insurer of perfect plans, he is called upon to prepare plans and specifications which will give the structure so designed reasonable fitness for its intended purpose, and he impliedly warrants their sufficiency for that purpose."

Tex. *American Surety Co. v. San Antonio Loan & Trust Co.*, 44 Civ. App. 367, 98 S.W. 387 (1906). If architect exercises skill and care of those ordinarily engaged in business and uses his best judgment, he is not liable for faults in construction caused by defects in his plans.

Va. *Surf Realty Corp. v. Stending*, 195 Va. 431, 78 S.E. 2d 901 (1953).

Wash. *Niver v. Nash*, 7 Wash. 558, 35 Pac. 380 (1893). Where architect sold plans for a building, knowing the purposes for which they were to be used, and represented that he was a competent and skillful architect and that the building would be well lighted and first class in every respect, such representations amounted to a warranty that the plans were as he represented them to be.

AN ARCHITECT EMPLOYED TO SUPERVISE CONSTRUCTION is liable to the owner only for those defects in construction which result from his failure to exercise reasonable skill and care.

Cal. *Pancoast v. Russell*, 307 P. 2d 719 (1957). Where contract between owner and architect provides for general supervision, architect ruled liable to owner for breach of contract for superficial supervision in connection with the approval of the contractor's work, it being the architect's duty to secure workmanlike adherence to the building contract.

Monson v. Fischer, 118 Cal. App. 503, 5 P. 2d 628 (1931). Contract provision that architect should exercise reasonable diligence to discover defects in materials must be construed in light of usual twenty-eight day test for determining strength of concrete.

Iowa *Schreiner v. Miller*, 67 Iowa 91, 24 N.W. 738 (1885). Court determined that a house is not constructed with reasonable care where foundation is so defective as to cause walls to crack and architect was held liable in damages for negligent supervision.

Ky. *Kortz v. Kimberlin*, 158 Ky. 566, 165 S.W. 654 (1914). A supervising architect is not liable for every defect in construction if he uses reasonable care and diligence in seeing that the work is properly done.

N.M. *Gaastra v. Holmes*, 36 N.M. 175, 10 P. 2d 589 (1932). Where the owner deals with the building contractor independently of the architect who furnished the plans and specifications, the architect does not warrant sound construction of the building.

N.Y. *Lindeberg v. Hodgens*, 89 Misc. 454, 152 N.Y.S. 229 (1915). Architect who assumes duty of supervision must exercise due care in its performance.

Straus v. Buchman, 96 App. Div. 270, 89 N.Y.S. 226 (1904), *aff'd,* 184 N.Y. 545, 76 N.E. 1109 (1906). Duty of supervising architect was to see not only that beams were properly placed but that placing conformed to requirements of statute.

R.I. *Chiaverini v. Vail,* 61 R.I. 117, 200 Atl. 462 (1938). Where architect visited construction work about every day, either before day's work began or after completion, but never during its progress, held he did not supervise work with meaning of contract.

S.C. *Avent v. Proffitt,* 109 S.C. 48, 95 S.E. 134 (1918). Where work was to be done under the direction of an architect, it was his duty not merely to inspect but to see that proper materials were used and to condemn defective construction.

Wis. *Foeller v. Heintz,* 137 Wis. 169, 118 N.W. 543 (1908). If builder by inexcusable fault of supervising architect departs from plans agreed upon, damages may be charged to architect.

AN ARCHITECT OR ENGINEER IS LIABLE IN DAMAGES to the owner for his negligence in preparing plans and specifications, in supervising construction, and for delay in furnishing plans and specifications to the owner.

Cal. *Benenato v. McDougall,* 166 Cal. 405, 137 Pac. 8 (1913). Where the cost of a building exceeded the limitation specified by the owner, he could not recover damages against the architect, where the architect stated he could not estimate the cost accurately and the contractors refused to do the work for a fixed price but were engaged on a percentage of the cost basis.

Fla. *Bayshore Development Co. v. Bonfoey,* 75 Fla. 455, 78 So. 507 (1918). Architect held liable for negligence and lack of skill in preparing plans and specifications.

Iowa *Schreiner v. Miller,* 67 Iowa 91, 24 N.W. 738 (1885). Architect held liable for negligence in preparing plans and specifications and supervising construction of house.

Ky. *Kortz v. Kimberlin,* 158 Ky. 566, 165 S.W. 654 (1914). A supervising architect is not liable for every defect in construction if he uses reasonable care to insure proper construction, and the mere fact that some material and work is defective does not conclusively establish that he has not fully performed the contract.

Mich. *Chapel v. Clark,* 117 Mich. 638, 76 N.W. 62 (1898). Where an architect possesses the knowledge and experience of those ordinarily skilled in the profession and uses his best judgment, he is not liable for faults in construction resulting from defective plans.

N.J. But see *State v. Ireland,* 126 N.J.L. 444, 20 A. 2d 69, *app. dismissed,* 127 N.J.L. 558, 23 A. 2d 560 (1942). An architect who, through neglect or violation of a building code, prepares defective plans for a building and the building in turn collapses because of the architect's faulty plans, killing an occupant, is subject to indictment for manslaughter.

N.M.   *Gaastra v. Holmes,* 36 N.M. 175, 10 P. 2d 589 (1932). Where the owner deals with the contractor independently of the architect, who furnished the plans and specifications, the architect is not responsible for defective workmanship or materials.

N.Y.   *Straus v. Buchman,* 96 App. Div. 270, 89 N.Y.S. 226 (1904), *aff'd,* 184 N.Y. 545, 76 N.E. 1109 (1906). Where the supervising architect permitted beams to be improperly placed and in violation of the city building law, he was held liable for the damage to the owner resulting from defective construction.

Hubert v. Aitken, 15 Daly 237, 2 N.Y.S. 711 (1888), *re-argued,* 5 N.Y.S. 839 (1889), *aff'd,* 123 N.Y. 655, 25 N.E. 954 (1890). Where he relied on specifications furnished him by contractor, architect was held liable for inadequacy of chimneys designed by him for steam heating purposes.

Slutzky v. Hinderstein, 97 N.Y.S. 2d 255 (1950). In a contractor's suit to foreclose mechanic's lien the owner counterclaimed for poor workmanship and materials, and the contractors alleged the architect's approval of work.

Ore.   *White v. Pallay,* 119 Ore. 97, 247 Pac. 316 (1926). Architect was held not liable for the settling of a building foundation where the court found that he had used reasonable care in examining the site and preparing plans and specifications.

Pa.   *Edwards v. Hall,* 293 Pa. 97, 141 Atl. 638 (1928). Architect was held liable for the damages resulting to the owner or contractor for his failure to deliver plans and specifications in time for the successful continuation and completion of the work.

Osterling v. Frick, 284 Pa. 397, 131 Atl. 250 (1925). Architect was held liable for damages sustained by the owner due to his unreasonable delay in furnishing the plans and specifications.

R.I.   *Chiaverini v. Vail,* 61 R.I. 117, 200 Atl. 462 (1938). Architect could not escape liability for extra expense caused by error in his plans on the ground that such expense was caused by the contractor's failure to check the plans.

S.C.   *Avent v. Proffitt,* 109 S.C. 48, 95 S.E. 134 (1918). Architect was held liable for failure properly to inspect and condemn defective material and construction.

Tex.   *Capitol Hotel Co. v. Rittenberry,* 41 S.W. 2d 697 (1931). An architect is liable to the owners for loss sustained if, through want of skill or through fraud, he has misled the owners by his estimates and caused them to spend more than they contemplated. *Presnall v. Adams,* 214 S.W. 357 (1919). Where the same person is the architect and the superintendent of construction, he is liable in both capacities for lack of skill and care in the construction of a building.

Wash. *Niver v. Nash,* 7 Wash. 558, 35 Pac. 380 (1893). In an action by an architect for the value of his plans and services as superintendent of construction, the owner may counterclaim for damages sustained from defects in the architect's plans.

WHERE THE SAME PERSON IS BOTH THE ARCHITECT AND THE BUILDER, he is responsible for both the plans and construction.

Cal. *Goldberg v. Underhill,* 95 Cal. App. 2d 700, 213 P. 2d 516 (1950). Owner was held entitled to recover damages from an architect, also acting as contractor, resulting from the defective plans prepared by the architect and for defective construction work under his supervision.

La. *Louisiana Molasses Co. v. Le Sassier,* 52 La. Ann. 2070, 28 So. 217 (1900). A surety company for an architect who, as builder, contracted to carry out his own plans, cannot escape liability for defective work by taking the position that the defect was in the plans, not in the work.

Neb. *Lincoln Stone & Supply Co. v. Ludwig,* 94 Neb. 722, 144 N.W. 782 (1913). Where a person contracts to erect a building and furnishes plans and specifications therefor, a claim that the work was done according to the plans and specifications is not a good defense to a counterclaim for damages for defective construction.

AN ARCHITECT MAY BE LIABLE for negligently issuing certificates of performance which result in injury to the owner.

Ariz. *Carviolini v. Scholler & Fuller Associated Architects,* 89 Ariz. 24, 357 P. 2d 611 (1960). In an action by building contractors against the architect, the court held that the charge of wilful and malicious conduct causing damage to the plaintiff stated a cause of action. The court pointed out that on the face of the complaint there was no controversy between the owner and the contractor which would support the claim that the architects were acting in a judicial capacity and hence were clothed with immunity.

N.C. *City of Durham v. Reidsville Engineering Co.,* 255 N.C. 98, 120 S.E. 2d 504 (1961). The court in this case was receptive to the argument of immunity probably because of the somewhat limited role of the engineer in the execution of the contract.

THE OWNER DOES NOT WAIVE HIS CLAIM AGAINST THE ARCHITECT or engineer for damages resulting from negligent performance by accepting work with latent defects, by accepting delayed performance, or by settling with contractors who may also have been guilty of negligent performance.

Cal.　*Pancoast v. Russell*, 307 P. 2d 719 (1957). The court held that the plaintiff-owner did not waive his rights against the defendant-architect when the latter paid the contractor with knowledge of certain defects. The court explained that the payment was made with the understanding that the defects would be corrected and that the payment was not voluntary, but followed certification by the architect.

Mich.　*Bailey v. Jones*, 243 Mich. 159, 219 N.W. 629 (1928). Execution by the owner of renewal notes to the architect for services rendered, after discovery of defects in materials and workmanship, showed intent not to claim damages for defects.

N.Y.　*Schwartz v. Kuhn*, 71 Misc. 149, 126 N.Y.S. 568 (1911). Fact that owner settled with builders, who were equally at fault with the architects, for defective construction does not affect his right to recover against the architects.

Dunne v. Robinson, 53 Misc. 545, 103 N.Y.S. 878 (1907). Payment to an architect on account, made without knowledge of the defective character of the plans, does not constitute acceptance or waiver of the defects.

Pa.　*Edwards v. Hall*, 293 Pa. 97, 141 Atl. 638 (1928). Owner's acceptance of delayed plans does not deprive him of a claim against the resultant damage, though he fails to complain of delay and later uses the plans, where, under the circumstances, the owner had no choice in the matter.

Osterling v. Frick, 284 Pa. 397, 131 Atl. 250 (1925). Owner is not estopped from claiming damages against an architect for negligence and delays because he permitted the architect to remain in charge and settled with the contractors, especially where he made frequent protests to the architect and a change without the architect's consent would have been difficult.

Tenn.　*J. R. Hale & Sons v. R. C. Stone Engineering Co.*, 14 Tenn. App. 461 (1932). Where work is accepted with the knowledge that it has not been completed according to the contract, or under such circumstances that such knowledge may be imputed, acceptance will be deemed a waiver of defective performance, but this rule does not apply to latent defects not discoverable by competent inspection performed at the time the building was completed.

Tex. *Pierson v. Tyndall*, 28 S.W. 232 (1894). Payment to the contractors, upon a certificate of the architect, for work which the owner knew was not in accordance with the specifications, does not prevent the owner from recovering against the architect for defective plans and specifications and negligent supervision.

AN ARCHITECT OR ENGINEER IS NOT LIABLE FOR DAMAGES resulting from defective construction where it is not shown that his plans were followed as to that portion of the construction found defective.

La. *Day v. National U.S. Radiator Corp.*, 241 La. 288, 128 So. 2d 660 (1961). The approval of a shop plan authorizing the fabrication of the items in the plan did not create liability in the architect for a defective boiler, because the evidence was clear that the plan was not followed by the subcontractor who installed the boiler.

Mich. *Bayne v. Everham*, 197 Mich. 181, 163 N.W. 1002 (1917). In an action against an architect for the death of a workman by collapse of a portion of a garage where the evidence showed that the architect's plans and specifications were deviated from in necessary and vital aspects, there could be no recovery against the architect.

N.Y. *Lake v. McElfatrick*, 139 N.Y. 349, 34 N.E. 922 (1893). Owner cannot recover damages against an architect for alleged defective plans resulting in the collapse of an arch where departure from the plans may have been the direct cause of the collapse of the arch.

Wash. *McGuire v. United Brotherhood of Carpenters*, 50 Wash. 699, 314 P. 2d 439 (1957). In a suit by architects to recover the contract price for plans prepared, the owner cross-complained that the completed building was unsatisfactory due to defects in such plans. The court dismissed the cross-complaint on the grounds that the defective parts of the building were not constructed according to the plans.

The relationship between principal and agent is one of trust. Thus, an architect's or engineer's duty toward his client must meet a high standard. A fraudulent act by an architect or engineer will not only subject him to liability for damages, but will jeopardize his right to practice. Where such fraud is practiced or is attempted to be practiced by a combination of two or more persons, the participants may be made criminally responsible for a conspiracy to defraud. An architect and contractor who act in collusion to change drawings and specifications for the purpose of using less materials and materials of inferior quality in order to defraud the public body with whom they have contracted will be guilty of a conspiracy to defraud such body.

AN ARCHITECT OR ENGINEER WHO INDUCES AN OWNER TO ENTER into a contract with him through intentional misrepresentations or who seeks to defraud the owner during the performance of the contract, is liable to the owner for damages resulting from his misrepresentations or fraud.

Cal.   *Palmer v. Brown,* 127 Cal. App. 44, 273 P. 2d 306 (1954). In an action by architects to recover a portion of the contract price for architectural services rendered, the owner cross-claimed on several counts, one of which was that the architects had fraudulently issued certificates to the contractors before the work was completed and before the materialmen had been paid. The court held on the cross-claim it presented a jury question because there was evidence that at the same time the architect had accepted another job from the same contractor and had received payments therefor.

Goldberg v. Underhill, 95 Cal. App. 2d 700, 213 P. 2d 516 (1950). Evidence supported recovery of damages by the owners against an architect for fraud and misrepresentations with respect to the cost of the building proposed by the architect.

Edward Barron Estate Co. v. Woodruff Co., 163 Cal. 561, 126 Pac. 351 (1912). Owner who employed an architect on his fraudulent representations that he had great knowledge and skill as an architect and that the maximum cost of the building would not exceed a certain sum, could, on discovering the fraud, when the building was partially completed, repudiate the contract, complete the building itself, and sue for fraud.

Hall v. County of Los Angeles, 74 Cal. 502, 16 Pac. 313 (1888). Architect was held entitled to recover for his services in drawing plans where the county did not establish its contention that the architect practiced fraud by procuring the adoption of his plans through the advocacy of an agent who pretended to be an unbiased expert.

Me.   *Lane v. Harmony,* 112 Me. 25, 90 Atl. 546 (1914). Where the architect knows the limitation of cost of the building desired by his client, his intentional concealment of the truth, or his materially false statements as to what the building will cost, will avoid his contract.

Mass. *Corey v. Eastman,* 166 Mass. 279, 44 N.E. 217 (1896). A fraudulent combination between an architect and builder pursuant to which the architect gives false certificates as to the amount of work and materials furnished, inducing the owner to pay the builder, gives the owner a good cause of action against the architect for his damages.

N.Y. *Unity Sheet Metal Works, Inc. v. Farrell Lines, Inc.,* 101 N.Y.S. 2d 1000 (1950). Where subcontractor brought action for wrongful refusal of engineers to certify that the general contractor was entitled to be paid for work done by the subcontractor, thus inducing a breach of contract between the owner and general contractor, the alleged acts constituted the commission of a willful wrong warranting recovery in tort even if the acts could not be classified as an inducement of breach of contract.

A COMBINATION OF AN ARCHITECT OR ENGINEER and one or more other persons to cheat and defraud the party with whom a contract for professional services has been entered into makes such persons civilly and criminally liable.

Kan. *School Dist. v. Ferrier,* 122 Kan. 15, 251 Pac. 425 (1926). Evidence held to sustain jury's finding that architect and builder had not conspired to defraud school district by preparing new set of drawings calling for the use of fewer materials and materials of inferior quality in the construction of a schoolhouse.

N.Y. *People v. Connolly,* 253 N.Y. 330, 171 N.E. 393 (1930). Engineer was convicted of conspiracy to defraud city by so drafting specifications for a sewer project that bidders were compelled to use a special kind of pipe sold by a certain dealer, thereby enabling him to charge exorbitant prices for such pipe, and forcing the city to let contracts for the sewer at prices far in excess of reasonable cost.

The liability of architects or engineers to third persons for injury sustained because of a defective design or improper supervision during construction appears to be expanding. The traditional rule was that any liability arising from design which created a hazardous condition, terminated upon the completion and acceptance of the building by the owner. Insofar as supervision is concerned, it has been generally held that an architect or engineer will not be charged with liability for nonfeasance. However, more recently some courts have indicated that acceptance of a project by the owner will not bar liability as against the architect by third parties for latent defects, and that an architect can be charged with liability for failing to stop a contractor's work if the contractor's methods or procedures are creating a hazardous or dangerous condition at the site.

AN ARCHITECT OR ENGINEER MAY BE LIABLE TO THIRD PERSONS who are injured by his negligence, but the courts differ as to the extent of such liability.

Ark. *Erhart v. Hummonds*, 232 Ark. 133, 334 S.W. 2d 869 (1960). Employees of a contractor were injured as the result of a slide during excavation work. The court said that it was a question for the jury as to whether the architect was negligent in failing to stop all work until shoring was furnished which would make the site safe for workmen.

Cal. *Paxton v. Alameda County*, 119 Cal. App. 2d 393, 259 P. 2d 934 (1953). After stating the test of negligence as whether the architect "uses the care ordinarily exercised in the cases by respectable members of his profession practicing in the same locality," the court went on to say that a departure from that practice is not in itself conclusive of negligence so that proof is required of any alleged unsafe conditions.

Montijo v. Swift, 33 Cal. Rptr. 133 (1963). The plaintiff brought an action against the architect for injuries sustained as a result of a fall in a bus depot. She charged that the defendant had been negligent in not extending the stairway handrail to the base of the stairway. The court found sufficient evidence to support a verdict for her. It specifically rejected the rule, in an action for personal injuries, that the acceptance of the work terminates the architect's liability.

Ill. *Miller v. DeWitt*, 59 Ill. App. 2d 38, 208 N.E. 2d 249, aff'd in part Supreme Court of Illinois, Docket No. 39428 (1966). Contractor's employees were injured from collapse of roof due to inadequate shoring. It was held that the architect had the duty to stop the contractor's work if he knew or should have known that the contractor's method of shoring was unsafe and hazardous.

Iowa *Trunk & Gordon v. Clark*, 163 Iowa 620, 145 N.W. 277 (1914). Architect is bound to prepare plans and specifications with reasonable degree of skill and such as will produce building of kind called for without marked defects in character, strength, or appearance.

Schreiner v. Miller, 67 Iowa 91, 24 N.W. 738 (1885). Architect is bound to furnish proper plans and to see that house is at least reasonably well constructed.

La. *Day v. National U.S. Radiator Corp.*, 241 La. 288, 128 So. 2d 660 (1961). The claim against the architect was that he had negligently approved plans for a boiler and had negligently supervised its installation. As to the former, the court concluded that the items in the plan were not approved as a shop plan for fabrication. As to the latter, the court held that the architect under the contract was charged with the obligation of ensuring that the completed work was satisfactory. He was not charged with inspecting the methods of the contractor or subcontractor.

Mo. *Lottman v. Barnett*, 62 Mo. 159 (1896). Supervising architect was held liable for the death of a workman injured by a falling wall resulting from the collapse of an appliance on which it rested where the architect had approved the method adopted for raising the wall.

N.Y. *Ramos v. Shumavan*, 21 A.D. 2d. 4, 247 N.Y.S. 2d 699 (1964). Supervising engineer was sued for injuries to contractor's employees resulting from the collapse of forms. The complaint was dismissed on the ground that the engineer's function was to see to it that the owner obtained a project which complied to the plans and specifications. The engineer had no contractual duty regarding the safety of workmen.

Persichilli v. Triborough Bridge and Tunnel Authority, 21 App. Div. 2d 819, 251 N.Y.S. 2d 733 (1964), *modified*, 16 N.Y. 2d 136, 262 N.Y.S. 2d 476 (1965). Action against engineer supervising construction of a new roadway for the death of a contractor's employee, who was asphyxiated on the job. Specifically, the engineer was charged with the failure to provide safety equipment. The Appellate Division stated the long-standing rule that the defendant could not be liable to a third party for non-feasance (omissions as opposed to positive acts) in a negligent supervision case where he is not in control of the work, but held that there was sufficient evidence for the jury to have found the requisite control.

Olsen v. Chase Manhattan Bank, 10 App. Div. 2d 539, 205 N.Y.S. 2d 60, 9 N.Y.S. 2d 829, 215 N.Y.S. 2d 773 (1960). An employee of a contractor was injured when struck by a pneumatic drill which fell from a temporary platform above him. The court held the accident occurred because of the manner in which the contractor's work was being performed, for which the architect is not responsible, and that a charge of non-feasance will not support liability by third persons against an architect.

Inman v. Binghamton Housing Authority, 3 N.Y. 2d 137, 143 N.E. 2d 895 (1957). The architects were charged with negligently designing a stoop from which the infant plaintiff fell. The court held that although the owner had accepted the project the architect could be sued by a third party for latent defects. The absence of a protective railing, however, did not constitute a latent defect. *Clinton, et al. v. Boehm, et al.*, 139 App. Div. 73, 124 N.Y.S. 789 (1910). An architect could not be charged with liability for the death of a contractor's employee who was injured on the project. The architect's duty is to see to it that the plans and specifications are followed. However, an architect is not called upon to inspect or review the means and methods utilized by contractors in fulfilling their contract.

Potter v. Gilbert, 130 App. Div. 632, 115 N.Y.S. 425 (1909). An employee of a contractor was killed by the collapse of a wall. The architect was charged with failing to exercise due diligence in supervising construction. The action was dismissed as the complaint charged merely an omission of duty, which constitutes nonfeasance for which an architect may not be held liable by third parties.

U.S.   *Geare v. Sturgis*, 56 App. D.C. 364, 14 F. 2d 256 (1926). An architect who designed a building is not liable to a third person injured by its collapse after the building has been completed and accepted by the owner.

AN ARCHITECT OR ENGINEER MAY BE HELD LIABLE TO A BONDING COMPANY for issuing certificates of payment which were not justified by the percentage of completion of the contractor's work.

Miss.   *National Surety Corp. v. Malvaney*, 221 Miss. 190, 72 So. 2d 424 (1954). An architect was deemed liable to the owner's surety for the unjustified release of retainage funds to a contractor, leaving unpaid many of the debts incurred in the construction of the project.

U.S.   *Peerless Insurance Company v. Cerny & Associates, Inc.*, 199 F. Supp. 951 (1961). Architect liable in negligence to owner's surety on ground that certification by architect to owner of certain payments to contractor were unjustified. Architect deemed to owe a duty to owner's surety even though there was no privity of contract between them.

CHAPTER TWENTY-FOUR

Bases for computing damages

The measure of damages which the owner may recover from the architect or engineer for defective work may be computed on two bases: (1) the difference between the value of the building as actually designed and constructed and the value as it would have been if the building had been properly constructed, or (2) the cost of remedying the defects, if that can be done without unreasonable or disproportionate expense.

As has been pointed out, the responsibility of the architect for damages to the owner often arises in actions by the architect to recover the contract price for alleged complete services. Negligence on the part of the architect does not defeat his entire claim for compensation if he has substantially performed the contract. To constitute substantial performance of a contract to supervise and direct the construction of a building, the structure as completed must accomplish the owner's purpose. Incompleteness in detail which has been said to be consistent with substantial performance is the kind which can be remedied structurally, practicably, and reasonably—that is, without excessive expenditure or destruction of any material part of the building.

The rules permitting a builder to recover upon an entire building contract only substantially performed, less damage for incompleteness of detail, apply to a contract for supervision of the execution by an architect. Where the damage is slight, the architect may recover the contract price less the cost of supplying the defects. Such defects are generally considered as a matter for offset or counterclaim, and not as a complete defense to the architect's claim for payment. Further, when repairs are necessary to correct improper construction, they must be made as economically as possible consistent with proper workmanship and proper construction.

The architect will be liable only for the damages naturally resulting

279

from delay or defective construction, not for the remote consequences of his acts. The owner who claims damages must also prove the extent to which he has been damaged. Where there is no testimony or showing of any special items of expense incurred on account of improper plans or defective work done by the architect, the owner cannot deduct any amount by way of offset from the balance which the architect proves to be due. However, where the owner's counterclaim for negligence and unskillful performance by the architect is in excess of the amount claimed by the architect, and the owner's damage is proven, then he is entitled to a judgment for the difference.

DAMAGES WHICH THE OWNER MAY RECOVER against the architect or engineer for defective construction may be measured by the cost of remedying the defects, where that is practicable, or by the difference between the value of the building as erected and the value of the building as it would have been if properly constructed according to the agreement of the parties.

Fla.   *Bayshore Development Co. v. Bonfoey,* 75 Fla. 455, 78 So. 507 (1918). Measure of damages for architect's negligence in designing and supervising construction of building is amount equal to the difference between the value of the building as actually designed and constructed, and value as it would have been had the building been properly constructed. Loss of rentals due to delays in occupying the premises is too remote and speculative an item of damage to be considered.

Iowa   *Trunk & Gordon v. Clark,* 163 Iowa 620, 145 N.W. 277 (1914). The measure of damages for an architect's negligence in planning and supervising construction is to be determined as follows: Where defects can be corrected without unreasonable or disproportionate expense, such expense measures the damage sustained; where the defects cannot be remedied at a reasonable expense, the value of the building as erected and the value as it would have been if properly constructed, measures the damages. *Schreiner v. Miller,* 67 Iowa 91, 24 N.W. 738 (1885). Where a house, through repairs and alterations costing about the sum claimed by the architect for his services, could be made to be of the value it would have been if properly constructed, the owner was held entitled to recover such sum upon his counterclaim.

Neb.   *Lincoln Stone & Supply Co. v. Ludwig,* 94 Neb. 722, 144 N.W. 782 (1913). The owner's measure of damages against the architect for improper construction is the difference between the value of the building as constructed and what its value would have been if it had been constructed according to the contract.

N.Y. *Lindeberg v. Hodgens,* 89 Misc. 454, 152 N.Y.S. 229 (1915). The negligence of an architect in supervising construction gives his employer who has accepted his services a cause of action for damages for correcting the defects but will not defeat the architect's action to recover fees for his services.

Schwartz v. Kuhn, 71 Misc. 149, 126 N.Y.S. 568 (1911). Where defective construction is due to both defective plans and negligent supervision, the owner may show the cost of putting the buildings into the condition in which they would have been if properly constructed, and may recover a sum leaving him as well off as he would have been had the architect fully performed the contract in accordance with proper plans and specifications.

Lord v. Comstock, 20 Jones & S. 548 (1885). The owner's measure of damages for defective work is either the difference in value between the product of the architect's work and the house as it should have been, or the cost of remedying the defects and, if time was of the essence, the loss of rental value during the time required to make the necessary alterations. Architect was held not responsible for the loss of a year's rent upon a lease, such damage not being within the legal contemplation of the parties.

Pa. *Osterling v. Frick,* 284 Pa. 397, 131 Atl. 250 (1925). Where the owner's damages due to the architect's negligence cannot be shown with entire accuracy because like injuries have been inflicted by other persons, he will not be denied recovery if the damages can be fairly estimated from the evidence.

R.I. *Holland v. De Nunzio,* 165 Atl. 374 (1933). In the absence of a showing by the owner of special items of expense incurred on account of the engineer's defective work, the court cannot deduct any amount by way of recoupment from the balance the engineer proves to be due for his services rendered.

Tex. *Capitol Hotel Co. v. Rittenberry,* 41 S.W. 2d 697 (1931). Owner's measure of damages for architect's overestimation of the cost of a hotel was not the excess cost of the building but a sum compensating him for the loss sustained, taking into account the contemplation of the parties that the owner receive a reasonable return on his investment. The architect's negligence in delaying completion made him liable only for the damages naturally resulting from the delay, and not for interest on the amount of money borrowed by the owner.

Larrimore v. Comanche County, 32 S.W. 367 (1895). Evidence describing the defects in a building, with opinions of witnesses as to the manner and cost of remedying such defects, furnished the jury with sufficient data to enable it to estimate the damages to the building caused by the defect.

Wash.   *School Dist. v. Josenhans,* 88 Wash. 624, 153 Pac. 326 (1915). The measure of damages recovered by a school district for the collapse of a roof under the weight of snow was the cost of constructing the damaged second story, erecting a temporary roof, and repairing the damage to the lower story.

Wis.   *Foeller v. Heintz,* 137 Wis. 169, 118 N.W. 543 (1908). The owner's measure of damages, where the architect has substantially performed the contract, is the reasonable cost of remedying the defects which can be practicably remedied so as to make the structure conform as closely as possible to the agreement, and the difference between the value of the structure so completed and the building agreed upon by the parties.

PART SEVEN

PROPERTY RIGHT OF ARCHITECT OR ENGINEER IN HIS PLANS

CHAPTER TWENTY-FIVE

Common law copyright and contract

An architect or engineer has a common law copyright in plans and designs he has drawn, whereby he is entitled to the exclusive possession and use of his work until he publishes it. In the absence of a contract provision to the contrary, a client is entitled to plans and specifications which he has accepted and paid for. Registration of a plan or design by an architect or engineer in accordance with the terms of the Copyright Act protects him against infringement of his work even after it has been published. The copying of some substantial or material portion of an "original" plan or design which has been copyrighted may constitute infringement.

The extent to which an architect or engineer has an exclusive right in the use of plans he has drawn, in the reproduction of these plans, or in the reproduction of a building according to plans designed by him may be determined by the common law, statute, or contract.

As between owner and architect, the rights to ownership and use of plans are now generally the subject of contract between them. A standard form of contract adopted by the A.I.A. contains the following provision on this point:

> "Drawings and specifications, as instruments of service, are the property of the architect whether the work for which they are made be erected or not."

Under this stipulation the plans and specifications remain the property of the architect even after the building for which they are drawn is constructed and the architect paid for his services. The owner cannot resist the architect's demand for payment for his services on the ground that the architect has not delivered the plans to him. Even where the owner decides not to build, he must pay for the plans which the architect has prepared, and is entitled to keep.

In the absence of such an agreement between the client and architect, a somewhat different rule applies. An architect is ordinarily no longer the owner of the plans and specifications which he designs and which are furnished to and accepted and paid for by the owner. In such case, on acceptance of and payment for the plans, the owner is entitled to them. They become his property, and the architect cannot subsequently prevent the owner from using them in constructing another building. Nor does he have a right to receive additional compensation when they are used again, since he has already been paid for them under the original contract.

The fact that there may be a custom among architects that an architect is entitled to retain the plans which he prepares for a client, is not necessarily conclusive on others outside the profession. A client is not bound by this practice if at the time he entered into a contract with an architect he did not know of this custom and the contract did not include a provision covering it. Thus it has been held that where a client refused to pay for architectural services unless the plans were delivered to him, it was held that in the absence of knowledge on his part of a custom that drawings and specifications remain the property of the architect, he was not liable for the services claimed until the drawings were delivered to him.

Apart from the question of ownership of plans on completion of his services, the architect is the owner of his plans before they have been accepted and paid for. As the product of his skill and ability, they are property for which he is entitled to be remunerated. The client cannot, therefore, by fraud or deception deprive the architect of the right to complete the contract while retaining the benefits of his work.

The architect's right to be safeguarded against appropriation of his plans by other persons is protected by the common law copyright. This is distinct from copyright secured under the Copyright Act and operates independently of any statute. A common law copyright protects the architect's right in the design of plan which he has created only so long as he retains control of the work and until it is "published" (a term of art meaning some act which renders the work common property). As a creator of a unique intellectual production the architect has a property right in any architectural plan he has designed and no copyright statute is required to protect him against use of the plan by anyone without his permission. As long as copies of the plans remain in his office, in the hands of his client, or others similarly situated, they are personal property, and no other person may, without authorization, take them or use them without becoming liable for their use.

If the plans or copies are stolen, the architect may maintain an action to recover them. If they are lost, the court may grant him relief by barring the finder from using the plans without his consent. Should the plans fall into the hands of another architect who represents that they are his own and uses them in the construction of a building, there is little question that the architect who designed them has a legal remedy for such unauthorized use. However, where a client employs an architect to prepare plans for a building and the architect without his knowledge or consent copies the plans of another architect, it has been stated that the employer is not responsible. As to the preparation of plans, the architect is said to be acting for himself as an independent contractor and not as an agent for whose wrongful act the owner would be liable.

Once the architect's or engineer's work has been published he no longer has an exclusive right either in the design or in its reproduction. What amounts to unrestricted publication has from time to time been considered by the courts. In an early case it was held that an architect had a common law right of property in his design of a novel and artistic porch only before its publication by its application to a building which he erected.

Until recently, the few jurisdictions that had the matter before them had ruled that the filing of plans with a Building Department amounts to a publication so as to terminate the architect's common law copyright [*Wright v. Eisle,* 86 App. Div. 356, 83 N.Y.S. 887 (1903); *Tumey v. Little,* 18 Misc. 2d 462, 186 N.Y.S. 2d 94 (1959); *DeSilva Constr. Corp v. Herrald,* 213 F. Supp. 184 (M.D., Fla. 1962)].

In *Wright v. Eisle, supra,* an architect had prepared plans and specifications for a residence and filed the plans with the building department to procure a building permit. A house was erected under his supervision according to his plans and he received compensation from his client for these services. The defendant, a person who was not connected with either of the parties, desired to have a similar house built. On finding the figure named by the architect for a duplicate of his plans and specifications too high he procured the services of another architect. The second architect prepared plans for a building which, when constructed, conformed substantially to that designed by the original architect who then sued the owner of the second building.

The court dismissed his complaint, stating that he had lost his common law copyright by filing the plans with the building department. It emphasized that he had superintended the construction of a house under these plans and had been paid for the work. This, the court said, is as far as common law right of copyright extends since the law protects him only in the first publication of his work.

Within the last seven years the highest courts of two states have rejected the rule that the filing of plans with a public agency constitutes a publication terminating common law copyright privileges. These decisions were justified on the theory that it was unrealistic to attribute to the architect an intention to abandon his property rights when all he had done was to comply with a governmental ordinance whose purpose was no broader than to protect the public by ensuring that all buildings erected were sound in design [*Smith v. Paul,* 174 Cal. App. 2d 744, 345 P. 2d 546 (1959); *Edgar H. Wood Associates, Inc. v. Skene,* 347 Mass. 351, 197 N.E. 2d 886 (1964)].

Unrestricted exhibition of a project or its exposure to public view has also been held to constitute a general publication of the work [*Gendell v. Orr,* 13 Phila. 191 (Pa. Common Pleas 1879); *Kurfuss v. Cowherd,* 233 Mo. App. 397, 121 S.W. 2d 282 (1938), cf. *Smith v. Paul,* 174 Cal. App. 2d 744, 345 P. 2d 546 (1959)]. However, the Supreme Judicial Court of Massachusetts in *Edgar H. Woods Associates, Inc. v. Skene,* 347 Mass. 351, 197 N.E. 2d 886 (1964), came to the opposite conclusion, holding that the fact that a building is built from plans and is open to the gaze of the public may be a publication of the general design or idea of the building but cannot constitute a publication of the exact plans which would permit a duplication of such plans by anyone without compensation to the architect.

A contractor who has been employed by the owner to construct a building according to plans prepared by an architect has a right to the possession of the architect's plans while he is engaged in the construction. He is entitled to use the plans as long as they are necessary to the execution of the work. It has been held that while he is engaged on the project any unwarranted taking of the plans by the architect so as to deprive the contractor of their use constitutes a trespass for which the architect will be held liable even though he remains the owner of the plans. Following completion of the work, however, the contractor has no further interest either in the possession or the use of the plans and, depending upon the contract between owner and architect, they become the property of the owner or remain that of the architect.

IN THE ABSENCE OF A CONTRACT PROVISION TO THE CONTRARY, plans, once accepted and paid for by the client, become his property; the fact that there may be a custom among architects that the property in plans belongs to them is not conclusive upon a client who enters into the contract in ignorance of it.

Ind.   *Hutton v. School City of Hammond,* 194 Ind. 212, 142 N.E. 427 (1924). Where an architect, pursuant to contract, had furnished plans and specifications for a house and supervised its construction, and the owner, who had lost the plans, five years later demanded of the architect books and papers containing the data from which they had been drawn, the owner's right to such data was not so clear as to justify issuance of an injunction to compel their surrender.

Minn. *McCoy v. Grant,* 144 Minn. 92, 174 N.W. 728 (1919). Court found that architect and owner had contracted that architect should remain owner of the plans used in the construction of the owner's house, that the owner should not use them again without paying for them, and that the owner had procured the same plans for the construction of a second building under a valid contract to pay for them.

Neb. *Berlinghof v. Lincoln County,* 128 Neb. 28, 257 N.W. 373 (1934). Where an architect furnished plans and specifications for and supervised the construction of a courthouse for an agreed commission on the cost of the completed structure, the county was held not liable to the architect for a further commission because some years later it expended more funds to change the building and its newly appointed achitect used the first architect's original plans and specifications.

N.Y. *Hill v. Sheffield,* 117 N.Y.S. 99 (1909). Where an owner, ignorant of the A.I.A. rule that "drawings and specifications as instruments of service are the property of the architect," employed architects to prepare plans and specifications for alteration of a building, the drawings belonged to him, and the architects could not recover for their services without delivering the drawings.

Tumey v. Little, 186 N.Y.S. 2d (1959).

AN ARCHITECT OR ENGINEER HAS A COMMON LAW COPYRIGHT IN HIS PLANS and specifications while they are in his possession and before their publication, and they may not be appropriated or used without his consent.

Ala. *Lunsford v. Deitrich,* 86 Ala. 250, 5 So. 461 (1889). Architect, when prosecuted for larceny of plans from builder, could show, in action for malicious prosecution, universal custom that drawings remain property of architect, builder only being entitled to use them until the building is completed. Court held that taking the plans without the builder's consent while he was entitled to use them would constitute trespass, but whether it amounted to larceny would depend on whether it was done secretly and fraudulently with the intent to deprive the builder of his special property in them, or openly, under a claim of right.

Iowa *Driscoll v. Independent School Dist. of Council Bluffs,* 61 Iowa 426, 16 N.W. 291 (1883). Where plaintiffs alleged that school boards employed another architect to copy plans prepared by plaintiff, which board used to erect a building, but there was no evidence to show the other architect copied the plans, or was employed to copy plans, or that the plans were in his possession except for the short time when he and other architects were before the board, there was insufficient evidence to present to the jury on this question.

Minn. *McCoy v. Grant,* 144 Minn. 92, 174 N.W. 728 (1919). Though plans may have been filed with building inspector, it is not necessary to consider what effect this has on the architect's property in them as against the owner, where the parties contract that as between themselves, the plans and specifications shall remain the property of the architect and the owner shall not use them again without paying for them.

Mo. *Kurfiss v. Cowherd,* 233 Mo. App. 397, 121 S.W. 2d 282 (1938). An architect is protected against appropriation of his plans by common law copyright until they are released for unrestricted publication. Where a house, built in accordance with an architect's plans and with the architect's consent, is thereafter open to public inspection, this amounts to unrestricted publication, and his exclusive property right in the plans is thereby extinguished.

N.Y. *Wright v. Eisle,* 86 App. Div. 356, 83 N.Y.S. 887 (1903). An architect who files plans and specifications for a house with the building department thereby publishes his work to the world and has no exclusive right in the design or in its reproduction, especially where he later superintends construction of the building for which he is paid, and the building is exposed to the public view.

Pa. *Mackay v. Benjamin Franklin Realty & Holding Co.,* 288 Pa. 207, 135 Atl. 613 (1927). Where architect acted as an independent contractor and used the ideas of another architect by allegedly copying his plans, without the knowledge of his client, the client could not be held responsible for his action.

Glendell v. Orr, 13 Phila. 191 (1879). An architect has a common law right of property in his design of a novel and artistic porch before its publication by application to a building which he has erected.

U.S. *Smithmeyer v. United States*, 25 Ct.Cl. 481, 500 (1890), *aff'd*, 147 U.S. 342 (1893). "... there was no intrinsic property in the architect's design. It was not covered by copyright. If an architect's plans are lost or stolen, it may be that a court of equity will enjoin a person not entitled to them from using them; but if he voluntarily makes an unrestricted surrender of them he loses all right or property in them; and when they are tendered to a party for inspection, then, by a usage so universal and self-apparent that it can not be questioned, it is mutually understood to be a tender of the services which produced the plans and are embodied in them."

CHAPTER TWENTY-SIX

The copyright act

While the architect's or engineer's common law copyright in his design ends once he has published his work, his protection may be extended if he registers his work under the Copyright Act. The Act then supersedes the common law and permits the owner to release copies of his design provided he has stamped them with his brand. The law permits the owner of copyrighted matter to print, reprint, publish, copy, and sell the copyrighted work. The owner also has the corollary right to execute and complete the copyrighted work if it is a model or a design for a work of art.

Architectural plans may fall within either of two categories of work classified as copyrightable. One category (Sec. 5 (g) includes "works of art, models or designs for works of art." This section is limited to inchoate works of art and would include models or designs of architects. Another category (Sec. 5 (i) includes "drawings or plastic works of a scientific or technical character." Under Copyright Office rules, architectural plans and designs for engineering works are included in this classification.

The limitations on the copyright protection available to the architect should be clearly noted. The copyright prohibitions clearly extend to the reproduction of the plans themselves. Whether they extend as well to the use of plans in the construction of a building, where there is no reproduction of such plans, is a matter that has yet to be resolved. In any case, the copyright prohibitions clearly do not extend to the duplication of a structure where no reference is made to the copyrighted plans.

In order to be protected by copyright a work must be "original." The degree of originality may be slight. It should not be confused with artistic merit, which is not required, nor must it necessarily be novel. What is required is independent thought and not a mere repetition or copying of the work of others. All the essential elements of the design may be in common use. It is the arrangement or combination of the elements which makes for originality. In one case where a design for a memorial had been copyrighted, it was contended by the person alleged to have infringed upon it that all essential elements were in common use prior to the copyright. The court regarded this as immaterial and stated that the combination of elements in the design and their plan or arrangement made the work original. Since the defendants had not shown any work similar to the design or proved that anyone had produced a similar combination of elements, the argument that the work was not copyrightable failed.

The copyright law protects also reproductions of existing works in different adaptations, arrangements, or media of expression. The protection extends to the old and new matter in combination on the theory that the original work plus the new matter constitutes new work. In one instance, a design or a miniature shrine was copyrighted, the principal elements of the design being taken from a shrine established by the Roman Catholic Church. While the various elements embodied in the design were symbols of worship and therefore deemed common property, the arrangement of these elements in an original fashion satisfied the criteria of originality and independent labor so as to permit copyright of the design.

The copyright law does not protect ideas, but only the media or forms in which they are expressed. An idea may be expressed in totally different manners, and it is the manner in which it is expressed that is the subject of copyright. In one case, which illustrates the difference between the idea, which cannot be protected, and the manner of expressing it, which can, an engineer had procured a copyright of a drawing showing a novel bridge approach designed to unsnarl traffic congestion. He had presented his plans before a municipal body, which subsequently constructed a bridge approach similar to the engineer's idea. The engineer then sued for infringement of his copyrighted drawing.

The court decided that the design had been conceived from other sources, namely a bridge already constructed in another locality. It went on to say that, even if his idea had been copied, he could not recover for infringement. His drawing showing a bridge approach would not prevent anyone from using and applying the system of traffic separation set forth in his design. The engineer's system of traffic separation embodied an idea and this idea anyone could utilize. Before an exclusive right can be obtained in an invention or discovery, the court stated, it must be subject to the examination of the patent office. The court compared the design with a book containing a system of shorthand. There is no copyrightable material in the system itself but the explanation as to the use of the system is copyrightable.

Whether a copyright has been infringed by the reproduction of another work without the copyright owner's consent is a question of fact for a court or jury to determine. It must determine whether the similarities in the two works are mere coincidence or the result of plagiarism, for it may happen that a person has by independent thought and creative ability produced a work of art that bears substantial resemblance to a work which has been registered. The test of infringement, then, is whether an original independent production has been made, or whether the work is merely a copy of the original registered work. A "copy" has been described as that which comes so near the original as to give every person seeing it the idea created by the original.

The general rule is that copying of some substantial or material portion of the copyrighted work will constitute infringement. It is not necessary that the whole work be copied but it is sufficient if so much is taken that the value of the original work is noticeably diminished or the labors of the authors are substantially appropriated by another. It has been stated that a criterion for determining whether infringement exists is whether an ordinary reasonable person would fail to differentiate between the two works or would consider them dissimilar by reasonable observation.

Whether an architect is protected against copying of uncopyrighted plans when they are published in a magazine or other periodical which is itself copyrighted has not been decided. However, the inference may be drawn from other cases on similar points that the architect is not protected unless his individual contribution is copyrighted and is so labelled in the magazine. A copyright notice in a periodical is said to cover everything in the work provided that copyright in all of the contents belongs to the one whose name appears on the notice of copyright. If the publication does not have exclusive right to the article or design as owner, then it would appear that separate notice is required in the part belonging to the contributor.

If the architect submits a plan to a magazine and the plan is accepted and paid for, the plan may become the property of the magazine, and reproduction of it by third persons would constitute infringement for which the magazine, not the author of the design, would have a remedy. If the architect remains the owner he can best be protected against copying of his work by registering it as a copyright and placing a notice of copyright on the design appearing in the periodical. The purpose of the notice is to warn the public against infringement, and if it does not appear on each copy of the work reaching the public, the protection afforded by the copyright is lost.

AN ARCHITECT OR ENGINEER WHO COPYRIGHTS A PLAN OR DESIGN will be protected against infringement of his work. However, there can be no copyright of an idea or system.

U.S. *Allegrini v. DeAngelis,* 59 F. Supp. 248 (1944). Where the principal elements of plaintiff's copyrighted miniature shrine and of defendant's miniature shrine, alleged to be an infringement, were taken as a common source from a shrine established by the Roman Catholic Church, mere resemblance would not justify a finding of infringement.

Muller v. Triborough Bridge Authority, 43 F. Supp. 298 (1942). A copyright of a drawing showing a novel bridge approach designed to unsnarl traffic congestion is not infringed if such drawing is copied, since the system of traffic separation shown therein embodied an idea, which cannot be copyrighted.

It may be that certain structures can acquire the status of "works of art" and thus provide the additional copyright protection of prohibiting the reproduction of such structures or the use of the plans thereof. One authority on copyright law offers the Eiffel Tower and the Statue of Liberty as examples of structures falling within that class. That the standard may occasionally be lowered for "works of art" is evidenced by the following case: *Jones Bros. Co. v. Underkoffler,* 16 F. Supp. 729 (1936). Copyrighted design for a memorial, which was an independent work of the artist, was infringed by a monument which the evidence showed was copied, though with several changes and in another medium.

APPENDIX

FORMS

The following clauses, which are for the most part alternative provisions (although in some instances supplementary in nature), deal primarily with the construction contract. Although the owner or his attorney should assume the ultimate responsibility for the provisions contained in a construction contract, the architect or engineer is generally expected, at least initially, to provide the framework for that agreement.

The General Conditions of the Construction Contract issued by the American Institute of Architects provide the basis for a majority of construction contracts prevalently in use. This document serves a significant and important function, and may be obtained at the offices of the Institute at 1735 New York Avenue, N.W., Washington, D.C. The form provisions contained in this appendix are merely suggested as possible alternative or supplementary provisions to some of those contained in the A.I.A. document, dependent upon the nature of the project, the circumstances of the parties, and the objectives to be achieved. Some of the provisions offered have a different premise from those contained in the A.I.A. document. The authors make no recommendation as to their use.

Forms should not be used by rote. The study or analysis of alternative provisions in respect to any subject normally included in a construction contract will often pinpoint problems that should be dealt with, which otherwise might be overlooked through the unquestioned use of a form. In considering alternatives, the architect or engineer will be in a position to draft a more meaningful and comprehensive contract for consideration by owner and contractor.

Alternative or additional clauses dealing with the following subject matters have been included in this appendix:

Architect's or Engineer's Authority and Status
Audit of Contractor's Books and Records
Changes in the Work
Construction Schedule
Contractor's Obligations in Performing the Work
Contractor's Right to Stop Work or Terminate Contract
Correction of Work
Delays and Extensions of Time
Guarantees
Indemnification of Owner and Architect or Engineer

Insurance
Interpretation and Execution of Plans and Specifications
Liens and Claims
Liquidated Damages
Occupancy by Owner
Patents
Payments to Contractor
Protection of Work and Property
Representations of Contractor
Rights of the Owner to Terminate Contract
Separate Contracts and Mutual Responsibility of Contractors
Shop Drawings
Specifications by Manufacturer, Brand, Trade Name, or Catalogue Number
Subcontractors
Substitution of Equal or Comparable Materials
Subsurface Conditions
Use of Premises
Withholding of Payments to Contractor

ARCHITECT'S OR ENGINEER'S AUTHORITY
AND STATUS

1.

The Architect shall give all orders and directions contemplated under this contract and specifications relative to the execution of the work. The Architect shall determine the amount, quality, acceptability, and fitness of the several kinds of work and materials which are to be paid for under this contract and shall decide all questions which may arise in relation to said work and the construction thereof. The Architect's estimates and decisions shall be final and conclusive, except as herein otherwise expressly provided. In case any question shall arise between the parties hereto relative to said contract or specifications, the determination or decision of the Architect shall be a condition precedent to the right of the Contractor to receive any money or payment for work under this contract affected in any manner or to any extent by such question.

The Architect shall decide the meaning and intent of any portion of the specifications and of any plans or drawings where the same may be found obscure or be in dispute.

Any differences or conflicts in regard to their work which may arise between the Contractor under this contract and other contractors performing work for the Owner shall be adjusted and determined by the Architect.

Nothing herein contained shall be construed to prevent any court proceedings in case of alleged arbitrary or capricious decisions on the part of the Architect.

2.

All claims of the Owner or Contractor and all questions or disputes relating to the execution and progress of the work and the Contractor's performance (including the amount, quality, acceptability and fitness of the work and materials which are to be or have been provided under this contract), and all claims, questions or disputes involving the interpretation of the Contract Documents shall be determined or decided by the Architect.

All determinations, decisions, interpretations, and certifications of the Architect shall be final, binding, and conclusive.

As the Architect is the interpreter of the conditions of the contract and the judge of its performance, he shall side neither with the Owner nor with the Contractor, but shall use his powers under the contract to enforce its faithful performance by both.

In the case of the termination of the employment of the Architect, the Owner shall appoint a capable and reputable Architect against whom the Contractor makes no reasonable objection, whose status under the contract shall be that of the former Architect.

3.

The Architect shall be the Owner's representative during the construction period. The Architect will make periodic visits to the site to familiarize himself generally with the progress and quality of the work and to determine in general if the work is proceeding in accordance with the Contract Documents.

The Architect will not be required to make exhaustive or continuous on-site inspections to check the quantity or quality of the work and he will not be responsible for the Contractor's failure to carry out the construction work in accordance with the Contract Documents.

The Architect may condemn the work as failing to conform to the Contract Documents and he shall have the authority to stop the work whenever such stoppage shall be necessary in his opinion to insure the proper execution of the Contract.

In the case of the termination of the employment of the Architect, the Owner shall appoint a capable and reputable Architect against whom the Contractor makes no reasonable objection, whose status under the Contract shall be that of the former Architect.

4.

To prevent all disputes and litigation, it is further agreed by and between the parties to this contract, that said engineer shall in all cases determine the amount or the quantity of the several kinds of work which are paid for under this contract, and he shall determine all questions in relation to said work, and the construction thereof, and he shall in all cases decide every question which may arise relative to the execution of this contract on the part of the said Contractor, and his estimate and decision shall be final and conclusive; and such estimate and decision, in case any question shall arise, shall be a condition precedent to the right of the party of the second part to receive any money or compensation for anything done or furnished under this agreement.

AUDIT OF CONTRACTOR'S BOOKS AND RECORDS

5.

If the Contractor's compensation, or any part thereof, is based upon cost, the Contractor agrees that its books and records which relate to such cost and to the Contractor's performance hereunder shall at all reasonable times be subject to audit by the Owner or Architect, or their authorized representatives. The Contractor further agrees that his plant shall be subject to inspection at all reasonable times by the Owner or Architect, or by their authorized representatives. Compliance with this Article shall constitute a condition precedent to the issuance of a certificate of payment by the Architect.

6.

The Contractor shall check all material and labor entering into the work and shall keep such full detailed accounts as may be necessary for the proper financial management under this Contract, and the system shall be such as is satisfactory to the Owner. The Contractor shall preserve all such records for a period of at least two (2) years after the final payment is made by the Owner to the Contractor under this Contract. The Contractor shall require all of its subcontractors to keep similar records of those parts of the work which have been let to them by the Contractor on a cost-plus or any type of escalation basis, and to preserve all such records for at least such same period. The Owner and its representatives shall be afforded access to, and have the right to audit, all of the Contractor's books, papers, correspondence, instructions, receipts, vouchers, memoranda and other records relating in any way to the services or work performed or furnished by the Contractor or by any of its subcontractors under, because of or as a result of this Contract, within such period, and the Contractor shall require each such subcontractor to afford access to the Owner to all his records relating or pertaining in any way to any such work let to him on a cost-plus or any type of escalation basis and to give the Owner the right to audit such records during such period. If the Owner shall require a certification of independent certified public accountants, not employees of the Contractor, the reasonable expenses of making the necessary audit and obtaining such certification shall be reimbursable costs if paid by the Contractor.

CHANGES IN THE WORK

7.

Without invalidating the contract, the Owner may order extra work or make changes by altering, adding to, or deducting from the work, the contract sum being adjusted accordingly, and the consent of the Surety being first obtained where necessary or desirable. All the work of the kind bid upon shall be paid for at the price stipulated in the proposal, and no claims for any extra work or materials shall be allowed unless the work is ordered in writing by the Owner or its Architect, acting officially for the Owner, and the price is stated in such order.

No changes in the work covered by the approved contract documents shall be made without having prior written approval of the Owner. Charges or credits for the work covered by the approved change shall be determined by one or more, or a combination, of the following methods:

(a) Unit bid price previously approved.
(b) An agreed lump sum.
(c) The actual cost of:
   1. Labor, including foremen.
   2. Materials entering permanently into the work.
   3. The ownership or rental cost of construction plant and equipment during the time of use on the extra work.
   4. Power and consumable supplies for the operation of power equipment.
   5. Insurance.
   6. To the above cost there shall be added a fixed fee to be agreed upon but not to exceed fifteen percent (15%) of the estimated cost of the work. The fee shall be compensation to cover the cost of supervision, overhead, bond, profit and any other general expenses.

No claim for extra work or cost shall be allowed unless the same was done in pursuance of a written order of the Architect, as aforesaid, and the claim presented with the first estimate after the changed or extra work is done. When work is performed under the terms of subsection of these General Conditions, the Contractor shall furnish satisfactory bills, payrolls and vouchers covering all items of cost, and when requested by the Owner, give the Owner access to accounts relating thereto.

8.

The Owner, without invalidating the Contract, may order extra work or make changes by altering, adding to, or deducting from the work, the Contract sum being adjusted accordingly. All such work shall be executed under the conditions of the original Contract, except that any claim for extension of time caused thereby shall be determined by the Architect at the time of ordering such change.

The Contractor shall not be entitled to any extra compensation for claimed extra work unless he has performed such work in pursuance of a written order signed by the Owner or the Architect. The Contractor, when so ordered, shall proceed promptly in accordance with said order.

The value of any such extra work shall be determined as follows:

1. By unit prices named in the Contract, if applicable. Such unit prices shall be deemed to cover completed work in place and shall include all labor, material, equipment, supervision, taxes, insurance, overhead, fee, etc. The Contractor shall, within ten (10) working days from the date of receipt of Architect's letter of instruction, furnish to the Architect for his approval a comprehensive detailed breakdown of all materials and labor with unit prices arranged in a form as approved by the Architect. The quantities against which said unit prices are to apply are to be measured by actual quantities, irrespective of trade customs to the contrary, and it is understood that unit prices stated in the Contract are so based. Any question or dispute concerning quantities shall be determined by the Architect.

2. If no applicable unit price is stated in the Contract, by agreement for a lump sum price between Owner and Contractor. To this end the Contractor shall furnish to the Architect, for consideration by the Owner, a proposal, in writing, within ten (10) working days of receipt of Architect's letter of instruction, containing a detailed breakdown of the material and labor to be furnished in connection with such extra work, together with a detailed estimate of the cost of such material and labor to the Contractor. The proposal shall also contain the lump sum fee for which the Contractor will undertake to perform the extra work. All backup material and breakdown submitted by the Contractor shall be typewritten, and all items shall be fully described and explicit. Upon request by the Architect, all backup material shall be supported by letters from manufacturers, fabricators, producers, etc.

3. If the Owner and Contractor cannot agree, by the actual cost of labor and material to the Contractor, plus 10% of said costs for overhead and profit, but not to exceed the lowest sum for which the Contractor offered to perform the extra work in negotiating for a lump sum agreement under subparagraph "2" above. If the work is to be performed by a subcontractor, the actual cost of labor and materials to the contractor shall be measured by the actual cost of labor and material to the subcontractor, plus 10% to cover the subcontractor's overhead and profit, plus 5% to cover the Contractor's overhead and profit. However, the total sum payable hereunder shall not exceed the lowest sum which the Contractor offered to perform the extra work in negotiating for a lump sum agreement under subparagraph "2" above.

4. In the event that the Contractor fails to submit a breakdown as provided in subparagraph "1" above, or a proposal as provided in subparagraph "2" above, whichever is applicable, within the time period provided in said subparagraphs,

then it shall be understood and agreed that the work to be performed is not deemed by the Contractor to entitle him to extra compensation, and the Contractor shall perform said work without any extra compensation.

The Contractor shall keep and present in such form as the Architect may direct, a correct account of the costs, together with vouchers, and the Contractor agrees that his books and records and the books and records of any subcontractor who performs the work, may be audited by the Owner's accountant if deemed advisable by the Owner. Costs may include all items of labor and materials, rental of equipment, power, premiums on public liability, property damage and workmen's compensation insurance, social security and unemployment insurance. It shall not include drafting time, such time being deemed included in overhead. Any question concerning the propriety of the costs claimed by the Contractor shall be determined by the Architect.

In the event that the change directed by the Owner constitutes a reduction in the work for which the Owner is entitled to a deduction from the contract sum, the value of such deduction to be credited to the Owner shall be determined as follows:

(a) By unit prices named in the contract, if applicable.

(b) If no applicable unit prices, by agreement between Owner and Contractor.

(c) If Owner and Contractor cannot agree, by the determination of the Architect, who, in making such a determination, shall estimate the cost of labor and materials saved to the Contractor, plus a reasonable sum to be deducted as an allowance covering overhead and profit.

If the Contractor claims that any instructions, by drawings or otherwise, constitute a change in the work entitling him to extra compensation under this contract, he shall give the Architect written notice thereof within ten (10) working days after the receipt of such instructions, and in any event before proceeding to execute the work. No such claim shall be valid unless so made. The Architect shall determine whether such instruction constitutes a change in the work entitling the Contractor to extra compensation and if he so determines, the work must be authorized as provided under this Article above. If the Architect determines that such instruction does not constitute a change in the work entitling the Contractor to extra compensation, the Contractor shall forthwith comply with such instruction at his own cost and expense. Contractor and Architect shall negotiate deduction in contract time when any deduction in contract amount is made. Architect shall have power of final decision in such negotiations.

9.

If the Contractor claims that any instructions, by drawings or otherwise, constitute a change in the work entitling him to extra compensation under this contract, he shall give the Architect written notice thereof within a reasonable time after the receipt of such instructions, and in any event before proceeding to execute the work. No such claim shall be valid unless so made. The Architect shall determine whether such instruction constitutes a change in the work entitling the Contractor to extra compensation and if he so determines, the work must be authorized as provided under paragraph above. If the Architect determines that such instruction does not constitute a change in the work entitling the Contractor to extra compensation, the Contractor shall forthwith comply with such instruction at his own cost and expense.

CONSTRUCTION SCHEDULE

10.

Immediately after execution and delivery of the contract, and before the first period payment is made, the Contractor shall deliver to the Owner an estimated construction progress schedule in form satisfactory to the Owner, showing the proposed dates of commencement and completion of each of the various subdivisions of work required under the contract documents and the anticipated amount of each monthly payment that will become due the Contractor in accordance with the progress schedule. The Contractor shall also furnish, on forms to be supplied by the Owner, (a) a detailed estimate giving a complete breakdown of the contract price and (b) periodical itemized estimates of the work done for the purpose of making partial payments thereon. The costs employed in making up any of these schedules will be used only for determining the basis of partial payments and will not be considered as fixing a basis for additions to or deductions from the contract price.

11.

The Contractor, prior to commencing the work and subject to the approval of the Architect, shall establish a schedule of progress for the work as a whole, and for the various parts, in such form as the Architect shall direct; and the Contractor shall comply with and adhere to such schedule. The parts of the work performed by each subcontractor, and the time schedule applicable to each part, shall be acknowledged and accepted by each such subcontractor in the subcontract. The Contractor shall also furnish a materials delivery schedule and shall inform the Architect immediately of any delay, or potential delay, or deviation from such schedule. The Contractor shall keep the Architect and his subcontractors and other contractors informed monthly as to actual progress made. The construction schedule shall be revised monthly; it shall show latest percentage of each item of work completed together with last percentage of work completed.

It shall be the responsibility of the Contractor to distribute copies of the approved operation schedule to all interested parties and to prepare and distribute any revisions of said schedule at his cost and expense.

Each Contractor and subcontractor shall be furnished a copy of the "Schedule of Progress" and each shall so prosecute his work that he not only maintains his progress in accordance with such Schedule but also shall cause no delays to other contractors and subcontractors engaged on the work.

Should the Contractor, either in person or through a subcontractor fail to maintain progress according to the approved operations schedule or cause delay to another contractor or subcontractor, he shall furnish such additional labor and/or services or work such overtime as may be necessary to bring his operations up to schedule. Failure to maintain schedule or to take the above steps to regain the agreed operations schedule shall constitute a default on the part of the Contractor.

12.

Before award of the Contract, the Contractor for General Construction Work will be required to submit evidence satisfactory to the Architect that his organization is qualified in the techniques and requirements of the Critical Path Method of Scheduling, as hereinafter specified.

As an alternate, or in the event that the evidence of qualification submitted by the Contractor is not satisfactory, the Contractor shall be required to employ the services of a recognized consultant qualified in the Critical Path Method for planning, scheduling, reporting and evaluating the work under this Contract and of modifying the program as required.

The progress schedule shall be prepared by the General Contractor in the Critical Path Method with the arrow diagram and computer printout indicating work to sufficient detail that complete control of the project is possible. Include items such as: placing orders for materials, submissions of shop drawings and samples, delivery of material, and all work activities. Each activity shall be assigned a time estimate by the Contractor. With the exception of material deliveries, the time duration for an activity shall not exceed fifteen days. One day shall be the smallest time unit used. The schedule shall provide for approximately 150 to 200 activities. Form and content of Critical Path Method Schedule shall be as approved by the Architect.

If any portion of the work is let separately by the Owner, such separate Contractor shall cooperate by promptly supplying the General Contractor with work schedule to be incorporated in CPM Schedule.

After completion and approval of the CPM Schedule, the General Contractor shall submit a print of the CPM Schedule and the schedule in computer form showing job identification, job duration, job description, calendar dates for early start, early finish, late start and late finish for each job, total float and the activities critical to completion of the project on schedule. Copies of the Critical Path Method Schedule in final form shall be distributed by the General Contractor to all of the prime contractors and to all of the General Contractor's material suppliers and subcontractors. The CPM Schedule will be reviewed weekly at job meetings and corrections to the work schedule shall be made as required.

At intervals throughout the life of the Contract not greater than once every six weeks or more often as directed by the Architect, a review and new computer printout schedule shall be submitted. This review shall incorporate changes as required from weekly job meetings, information on all activities scheduled to be completed in the previous work period, started in the previous work period and those activities scheduled to be started for the next work period, issued change orders and all other conditions affecting the progress of the work.

The General Contractor shall submit within one week of award of Contract a bar graph type progress schedule to be followed within two weeks by the complete Critical Path Method arrow diagram as specified. It shall be the Contractor's responsibility to maintain the progress of the work in accordance with the approved CPM Schedule and to submit for approval such changes in the Schedule as may be deemed necessary throughout the project life.

The Contractor and each subcontractor shall so prosecute his work that he maintains his progress in accordance with the Critical Path Method schedule, and so that no delays are caused to other contractors and subcontractors engaged on the work. Should the Contractor, either in person or through his subcontractor, fail to maintain progress according to the above schedule, or cause delay to another contractor or subcontractor, he shall furnish or have furnished such additional labor, services or overtime work as may be necessary to bring his operations up to schedule, without any additional cost or expense to the Owner. Failure to maintain schedule or to take the above steps to regain the agreed schedule shall constitute a default under the Contract.

13.

OPERATIONS SCHEDULE.

The Contractor shall establish a schedule of progress for the work as a whole, and for the various parts, in such form as the Architect shall direct; and the Contractor shall comply with and adhere to such schedule. The parts of the work performed by each subcontractor, and the time schedule applicable to each part, shall be acknowledged and accepted by each subcontractor at the time of entering into the subcontract. The Contractor shall also furnish a materials delivery schedule and shall inform the Architect immediately of any delay or deviation from such schedule. The Contractor shall keep his subcontractors and other contractors informed monthly as to actual progress made. Subcontractors shall be notified in writing not less than six weeks in advance of the commencement of their work and shall confirm, in writing, to the Contractor, the expected schedule. No adjustment or extension of the schedule or the time in which the contract is to be performed will be made or granted, except as provided in Article   below. It shall be the responsibility of the Contractor to distribute copies of the approved operations schedule to all interested parties and to prepare and distribute any revisions of said schedule at his cost and expense.

Where there is more than one Prime Contractor, the schedules of each such Contractor, as required above, must be coordinated with the schedules of the other contractors for the purpose of establishing a master schedule for the approval of the Architect. It shall be the responsibility of the General Contractor to prepare the master schedule, to secure agreement from the other Prime Contractors, and, after approval by the Architect, to distribute copies of the approved schedule to all interested parties at his cost and expense.

Contractor and each subcontractor shall so prosecute his work that he not only maintains his progress in accordance with the "Operations Schedule," but also shall cause no delays to other contractors and subcontractors engaged on the work.

Should the Contractor, either in person or through a subcontractor, fail to maintain progress according to the approved operations schedule or cause delay to another contractor or subcontractor, he shall furnish such additional labor and/or services or work such overtime as may be necessary to bring his operations up to schedule. Failure to maintain schedule or to take the above steps to regain the agreed operations schedule, if so determined by the Architect, shall constitute default hereunder.

CONTRACTOR'S OBLIGATIONS
IN PERFORMING THE WORK

14.

The Contractor shall and will, in good workmanlike manner, do and perform all work and furnish all supplies and materials, machinery, equipment, facilities and means, except as herein otherwise expressly specified, necessary or proper to perform and complete all the work required by this contract, within the time herein specified, in accordance with the provisions of this contract and said specifications and in accordance with the plans and drawings of the work covered by this contract and any and all supplemental plans and drawings, and in accordance with the directions of the Architect as given from time to time during the progress of the work. He shall furnish, erect, maintain, and remove such construction plant and such temporary works as may be required. He alone shall be responsible for the safety, efficiency, and adequacy of his plant, appliances, and methods, and for any damage which may result from their failure or their improper construction, maintenance, or operation. The Contractor shall observe, comply with, and be subject to all terms, conditions, requirements, and limitations of the contract and specifications, and shall do, carry on, and complete the entire work to the satisfaction of the Architect and the Owner.

15.

All articles, materials, equipment specified and/or shown on the Drawings shall be new, and they shall be applied, installed, connected, erected, used, cleaned, and conditioned for proper performing, as per manufacturer's directions, and as approved by Architect. The Contractor shall, if required, furnish satisfactory evidence as to the kind and quality of materials.

Each Contractor shall carefully lay out his own work on the job site, verify all field measurements, and make required provisions for the work of other Contractors. Offsets shall be made subject to the Architect's approval wherever it is necessary to clear finished rooms, structural members, or other obstructions.

All workmanship shall be provided to the full satisfaction of the Architect, in the best and most modern available methods, and workmanlike manner.

16.

All work performed by the Contractor shall be in the best workmanlike manner by mechanics skilled and experienced in their respective trades. The workmanship to be furnished by the Contractor shall conform to the best trade practices and the standard of work required throughout shall be of such grade as will bring results of the highest quality only. The Contractor shall at all times enforce strict discipline and good order among his employees and shall not employ on the work any unfit or incompetent person, or anyone not skilled in the work assigned to him. The Architect may require the Contractor to relieve any such person of any further duties on the project.

The Contractor and each subcontractor shall cooperate with and assist other contractors and subcontractors on the job to avoid trade and jurisdictional disputes. If any part of the work to be performed by the Contractor is under the jurisdiction of another trade, he will be required to employ members of that trade to execute the work if necessary to avoid jurisdictional disputes.

All Contractors and subcontractors employed upon the work shall conform to the requirements of the Labor Laws of the State in which the work is performed, and the various Acts amendatory and supplementary thereto, and to all other State and Town Laws, Federal regulations, ordinances, and legal requirements applicable to the performance of the Contract work.

17.

The Contractor shall keep on his work, during its progress a competent superintendent and any necessary assistants, all satisfactory to the Architect. The superintendent shall not be changed except with the consent of the Architect, unless the superintendent proves to be unsatisfactory to the Contractor and ceases to be in his employ. The superintendent shall represent the Contractor in his absence and all directions given to him shall be as binding as if given to the Contractor. Important directions shall be confirmed in writing to the Contractor. Other directions shall be so confirmed on written request in each case. The Architect shall not be responsible for the acts or omissions of the superintendent or his assistants.

The Contractor shall give efficient supervision to the work, using his best skill and attention. He shall carefully study and compare all Drawings, Specifications and other instructions and shall at once report to the Architect any error, inconsistency or omission which he may discover.

In the event that the Owner has entered into more than one prime contract for the construction of the project, then the Contractor for General Construction shall be responsible for the coordination, scheduling and expediting of the work of these separate contractors.

The Contractor shall be solely responsible for Contract execution and completion at the time fixed in the Agreement. It is not incumbent upon the Architect to notify the Contractor when to begin, when to cease or to resume work, nor in any way to superintend in such manner as to relieve the Contractor of responsibility or from consequence of lack of proficiency, neglect or carelessness by him or his employees.

Job meetings shall be attended by each Contractor or his field representative once a week or when called by the Architect.

The Contractor will furnish all plant, labor, materials, supplies, equipment and other facilities and things necessary or proper for or incidental to the work contemplated by this Contract as required by and in strict accordance with the applicable Plans, Specifications and Addenda (hereinafter enumerated) prepared by the Architect, and/or required by and in strict accordance with such changes as are ordered and approved pursuant to this Contract, and will perform all other obligations imposed on him by this Contract.

CONTRACTOR'S RIGHT TO STOP WORK
OR TERMINATE CONTRACT

18.

If the work shall be stopped by order of the court or any other public authority, for a period of three (3) months without act or fault of the Contractor or of any of his agents, servants, employees or subcontractors, the contractor may, upon ten (10) days' notice to the Owner, discontinue his performance of the work and/or terminate the contract, in which event the Owner may take possession of the work and complete the work by contract or otherwise, as the Owner may deem expedient. In such case the Contractor shall not be entitled to receive any further payment until the work is finished. If the unpaid balance of the compensation to be paid to the Contractor hereunder shall exceed the expense of so completing the work (including compensation for additional managerial administrative and inspection services), such excess shall be paid to the Contractor. If such expense shall exceed such unpaid balance, the Contractor shall not be obligated to pay to the Owner any excess of the expense of completing the work over the unpaid balance of the compensation to be paid the Contractor hereunder, nor shall the Owner be obligated to pay any additional sum to the Contractor.

19.

If the work should be stopped under an order of any court, or other public authority, for a period of 30 days, through no act or fault of the Contractor or of anyone employed by him, then the Contractor may, upon seven (7) days' written notice to the Owner and the Architect, terminate this Contract and recover from the Owner payment for all work executed.

If, after issuance of certificate of payment by the Architect, the Owner should fail to pay the Contractor when payment becomes due, then the Contractor may, upon seven (7) days' written notice to the Owner and the Architect, stop the work unless such payment is made before the expiration of said seven (7) days' notice.

CORRECTION OF WORK

20.

All work, all materials, whether incorporated in the work or not, all processes of manufacture, and all methods of construction shall be at all times and places subject to the inspection of the Architect, who shall be the final judge of the quality and suitability of the work, materials, processes of manufacture, and methods of construction for the purposes for which they are used. Should they fail to meet his approval they shall be forthwith reconstructed, made good, replaced and/or corrected, as the case may be, by the Contractor at his own expense. Rejected material shall immediately be removed from the site. Acceptance of material and workmanship by the Owner's inspectors shall not relieve the Contractor from his obligation to supply other material and workmanship when so ordered by the Architect.

If, in the opinion of the Architect, it is undesirable to replace any defective or damaged materials or to reconstruct or correct any portion of the work injured or not performed in accordance with the contract documents, the compensation to be paid to the Contractor hereunder shall be reduced by such amount as in the judgment of the Architect shall be equitable.

The Contractor expressly warrants that his work shall be free from any defects in materials or workmanship and agrees to correct any such defects which may appear within the respective guarantee periods. Neither the acceptance of the completed work nor payment therefore shall operate to release the Contractor or his sureties from any obligations under or upon this contract or the Performance Bond.

21.

The Contractor shall be fully and solely responsible for the removal, replacement, and rectification of all damaged, or defective materials and workmanship in connection with the Contract Work. He shall replace or repair as directed by the Architect, all such damages or defective materials and workmanship before making application for final payment.

The Contractor shall promptly remove from the premises all work condemned by the Architect as failing to conform to the Contract, whether incorporated or not, and the Contractor shall promptly replace and re-execute his own work in accordance with the Contract and without expense to the Owner and shall bear the expense of making good all work of other contractors destroyed or damaged by such removal or replacement.

If the Contractor does not remove such condemned work within a reasonable time, fixed by written notice, the Owner may remove it and may store the material at the expense of the Contractor. If the Contractor does not pay the expenses of such removal within ten (10) days' time thereafter, the Owner may, upon ten (10) days' written notice, sell such materials at auction or at private sale and shall account for the net proceeds thereof, after deducting all the costs and expenses that should have been borne by the Contractor.

If the Owner and Architect deem it inexpedient to require the Contractor to replace and re-execute the defective work or work not performed in conformity with the Contract Documents, then the Contract price shall be reduced in an equitable amount as determined by the Architect.

The Contractor shall remedy all defects with utmost care and expediency. All questions arising under this Article shall be decided by the Architect, notwithstanding final payment.

22.

Any materials or work found to be defective, or not in strict conformity with the requirements of the drawings and specifications, shall be removed immediately from the premises and satisfactory materials or work substituted therefore without delay. This shall include the making good of all work of other Contractors destroyed or damaged by such removal or replacement. The cost of the above replacements shall be at the expense of the Contractor responsible for the defective work or material.

No previous inspection or certificates of payment shall be held as an acceptance of defective work or materials or to relieve the Contractor from the obligation to furnish sound materials and to perform satisfactory work in accordance with the contract requirements. The final payment shall not relieve the Contractor of the responsibility for faulty materials or workmanship and he shall remedy all such defects, paying the cost of any damage to other work resulting therefrom, which shall appear within a period of one year from the date of final certificate.

DELAYS AND
EXTENSIONS OF TIME

23.

If the Contractor shall be delayed in the completion of his work by reason of unforeseeable causes beyond his control and without his fault or negligence, including, but not restricted to, acts of God or of the public enemy, acts or neglect of the Owner, acts or neglect of any other Contractor, fires, floods, epidemics, quarantine, restrictions, strikes, riots, civil commotions, freight embargoes or priority regulations, the period hereinabove specified for completion of his work shall be extended by such time as shall be fixed by the Owner.

No such extension of time shall be deemed a waiver by the Owner of his right to terminate the Contract for abandonment or delay by the Contractor as herein provided or relieve the Contractor from full responsibility for performance of his obligations hereunder.

24.

If the contractor be delayed at any time in the progress of the work by any cause beyond his control and which, in the opinion of the Architect shall entitle the Contractor to an extension of time, such as unavoidable casualties, substantial changes ordered in the work, or other similar occurrences (not including, however, the failure of any subcontractor, material supplier, or any person or persons employed by the Contractor to perform his or their work in the proper manner or in accordance with approved progress schedules), the time to perform or the date of completion shall be extended for such reasonable period as the Architect shall determine. No such extension shall be made for delay the cause of which occurred more than seven (7) days before claim therefor is made in writing to the Architect. In the case of a continued cause of delay, only one claim is necessary.

If no schedule or agreement stating the dates upon which drawings shall be furnished is made, then no claim for delay shall be allowed on account of failure to furnish drawings until two weeks after demand for such drawings, and not then unless such claim be reasonable.

When the Contractor is requested to state in his Form of Proposal the number of calendar days to complete the project, he shall include an estimated average number of days that work may not be performed because of inclement weather. No extensions of contract performance time because of inclement weather will be allowed except for an unusually great number of days of inclement weather above the average as determined from official records.

Contractor shall have no claim against Architect and/or Owner for damages, loss or other expenses which may be attributed to delays as described hereinbefore.

25.

If the Contractor be delayed at any time in the progress of the work by any cause beyond his control (not including, however, the failure of any subcontractor, material supplier, or any person or persons employed by the Contractor to perform his or their work in the proper manner or in accordance with approved progress schedules and which in the opinion of the Architect should entitle the Contractor to an extension of time, the time for the Contractor to perform, or the date of completion, shall be extended for such reasonable period as the Architect shall conclusively determine. Adverse weather conditions, however, shall not constitute a ground for an extension of time, unless in the opinion of the Architect, they are catastrophic in nature, or unless the number of days of inclement weather is substantially and unusually greater than the average for the period involved.

The Contractor shall be entitled to no extension of time for delay the cause of which occurred more than seven (7) days before claim therefor is made in writing to the Architect. In the case of a continuing cause of delay only one claim is necessary.

No claim for delay shall be allowed on account of alleged failure by the Architect to furnish drawings to the Contractor until two (2) weeks after request for such drawings, and not then unless such claim, in the opinion of the Architect, is reasonable.

26.

If the Contractor be delayed at any time in the progress of the work by any cause beyond his control and which, in the opinion of the Architect, should entitle the contractor to an extension of time, such as unavoidable casualties, substantial changes ordered in the work, or other similar occurrences, the time to perform or the date of completion shall be extended for such reasonable period as the Architect shall determine. Adverse weather conditions, however, shall not constitute a ground for an extension of time unless in the opinion of the Architect they are catastrophic in nature.

The Contractor shall be entitled to no extension of time for a delay the cause of which occurred more than seven (7) days before claim therefor is made in writing to the Architect. In the case of a continuing cause of delay, only one claim is necessary.

GUARANTEES

Neither the final certificate of payment nor any provision in the contract documents, nor partial or entire occupancy of the premises by the Owner, shall constitute an acceptance of work not done in accordance with the contract documents or relieve the Contractor of liability in respect to any express warranties or responsibility for faulty materials or workmanship. The Contractor shall remedy any defects in the work and pay for any damage to other work resulting therefrom, which shall appear within a period of one year from the date of final acceptance of the work or date of Owner's occupancy, whichever is earlier, unless a longer period is specified. The Owner will give notice of observed defects with reasonable promptness.

27.

The Contractor shall guarantee all work performed and materials furnished by him to be free from inherent defects. For the duration of the stipulated guarantee period the Contractor shall, at his own expense, repair and/or replace any defective materials and workmanship upon notice of an Owner's representative.

The duration of the guarantee period, and acceptance date following final acceptance of the work, shall be as defined in the "Form of Contract."

In addition to the guarantees set forth herein Contractor will be responsible for the performance of all equipment in connection with and relating to this contract whether installed and/or connected by the Contractor or another subcontractor. This applies to such equipment as motor disconnect devices supplied and installed by the electrical contractor. The Contractor will supervise the installation and testing of any of the aforesaid work by other subcontractors and will be responsible for the functioning thereof.

The Contractor further guarantees that all equipment installed in connection with this contract will meet the design conditions and performance requirements set forth by the Architect. In the event the Contractor believes any equipment he is to install will not be adequate to meet these requirements he will so notify the Architect. If any equipment is found after installation and upon testing as called for in "Testing and Adjusting" hereof to be inadequate to meet the design conditions or performance requirements, the Contractor will replace such equipment with proper equipment at no cost to the Owner, and will pay for all damages to work of other trades caused by said replacements.

The Contractor will be responsible for all leaks in all pipes for a period of one (1) year from the date of acceptance of work under this contract. He shall repair at no cost to the Owner all such leaks which occur after completion of this contract upon twenty-four (24) hours notice thereof by the Owner. Leaks which occur prior to the date of acceptance shall be repaired at once. He is responsible for any damage caused by such leaks and the repair thereof and will reimburse the Owner for all expenses incurred thereby.

28.

The Contractor shall guarantee all materials and workmanship against defects which may appear within a period of one (1) year from the date of issuance of a final certificate, unless a longer period is provided in any special guarantee. Neither the issuance of a final certificate, nor final payment to the Contractor, nor any provision in the Contract Documents, shall relieve the Contractor of responsibility for faulty materials or workmanship, and he shall remedy, at his own cost and expense, any defects due thereto, and pay for any damage to other work resulting therefrom, which shall appear within a period of one (1) year from the date of final certificate, or within the period of any longer guarantee required under the Contract Documents. Neither the foregoing nor any provision in the Contract Documents, nor any special guaranteed time limit shall be held to limit the Contractor's liability for defects to less than the legal limit of liability in accordance with the law of the place of building. All questions arising under this Article shall be determined by the Architect.

29.

In addition to any specific guarantees required by the Specifications for the work, the Contractor shall furnish to the Owner with his application for final payment a written guarantee of all the work against defects in material or workmanship for a period of one (1) year from the date of acceptance.

Should the manufacturer or supplier of any equipment or material extend to the Contractor a guarantee in excess of one (1) year, the Contractor shall extend his guarantee to the Owner for such equipment or material for an equivalent period of time.

Within a reasonable time after receipt of written notice thereof, the Contractor shall make good any defects in material or workmanship which may develop during the one (1) year period (or such other period as provided herein) from the date of acceptance of the completed work by the Owner and any damage to other work caused by such defects or the repairing of such defects, at his own expense and without cost to the Owner.

The above guarantees shall not be construed to modify or limit, in any way, any rights or actions which the Owner might otherwise have against the Contractor under common law or any applicable statute.

INDEMNIFICATION OF OWNER AND ARCHITECT OR ENGINEER

30.

If any legal proceedings shall be brought against the Owner and the Architect on account of any injury to person or to property described herein, the Owner shall give notice thereof to the Contractor who shall, at his own expense, defend such proceedings, pay to satisfy any judgment that may be entered against the Owner and the Architect in any such proceedings and pay all costs or expenses whatever incurred by the Owner and the Architect in any such case in which judgment is rendered against him.

31.

The Contractor agrees to indemnify and otherwise hold harmless the Owner and Architect, their agents, servants and employees, from and against all loss, damage or expense which the Owner or Architect shall sustain, incur, or become liable for on account of claims or suits asserted or instituted against the Owner or Architect arising out of the work performed by the Contractor or his subcontractors, or sub-subcontractors, or arising out of, or failure to perform any work under the contract. This indemnity shall include, but shall not be limited to, any liability or loss or damages arising from injuries or death to persons, or damage to property, occasioned by any work performed by, or any act or omission of, the Contractor, his subcontractors, their agents, servants and employees.

32.

The Contractor shall take out all necessary insurance, free of extra charge, and shall agree to indemnify and save harmless the Owner against loss or expense, by reason of the liability imposed by law upon the Owner for damages because of bodily injuries, including death at any time resulting therefrom, accidentally sustained by any person or persons or on account of damage to property arising out of or in consequence of the performance of this Contract, whether such injuries to persons or damage to property are due or claimed to be due to any negligence of the Contractor, the Owner, his or their employees or agents, or any other person.

33.

The Contractor shall save and hold the Owner harmless from all loss arising out of, or in connection with, suits or claims for injury (including death) to any person or damage to any property that may occur or that may be alleged to have occurred, in the course of the performance of this Contract, whether such claim shall be made by an employee of the Contractor, or by a third person and whether or not it shall be claimed that the alleged damage or injury (including death) was caused through a negligent act or omission of the Contractor, his agents or employees, or otherwise; and, at his own expense, the Contractor shall defend any and all such actions and pay all charges of attorneys and all cost and other expenses arising therefrom.

INSURANCE

34.

The Contractor shall not commence work under this contract until he has obtained all the insurance required under this paragraph and such insurance has been approved by the Owner, nor shall the Contractor allow any subcontractor to commence work on his subcontract until the insurance required of the subcontractor has been so obtained and approved.

(a) *Compensation Insurance:* The Contractor shall procure and shall maintain during the life of this contract Workmen's Compensation Insurance for all of his employees to be engaged in work on the project under this contract and, in case of any such work sublet, the Contractor shall require the subcontractor similarly to provide Workmen's Compensation Insurance for all of the latter's employees to be engaged in such work unless such employees are covered by the protection afforded by the Contractor's Workmen's Compensation Insurance. In case any class of employees engaged in hazardous work on the project under this contract is not protected under the Workmen's Compensation Statute, the Contractor shall provide and shall cause each subcontractor to provide adequate employer's general liability insurance for the protection of such of his employees as are not otherwise protected.

(b) *Contractor's Public Liability and Property Damage Insurance:* The Contractor shall procure and shall maintain during the life of this contract Contractor's Public Liability Insurance in an amount not less than $100,000 for injuries, including accidental death, to any one person, and subject to the same limit for each person, in an amount not less than $300,000, on account of one accident, and Contractor's Property Damage Insurance in an amount not less than $100,000.

(c) *Subcontractors' Public Liability and Property Damage Insurance:* The Contractor shall require each of his subcontractors to procure and to maintain during the life of his subcontract subcontractors' Public Liability and Property Damage Insurance of the type specified in subparagraph (b) hereof in the amounts herein below specified:

Public Liability—Each Person	*$100,000*
Public Liability—Each Accident	*$300,000*
Property Damage	*$100,000*

(d) *Scope of Insurance and Special Hazards:* The insurance required under subparagraphs (b) and (c) hereof shall provide adequate protection for the Contractor and his subcontractors, respectively, against damage claims which may arise from operations under this contract, whether such operations be by the insured or by anyone directly or indirectly employed by him and, also, against any of the following special hazards which may be encountered in the performance of this contract: _____

(if applicable, insert the word "None")

_____

_____

(e) *Proof of Carriage of Insurance:* The Contractor shall furnish the Owner with satisfactory proof of carriage of the insurance required. Insurance certificates must have the ten (10) day notice of cancellation clause noted thereon.

35.

During the life of this contract the Owner shall secure and maintain fire insurance with standard extended coverage and vandalism and malicious mischief endorsement on the building in course of construction in the sum of one hundred percent (100%) of the insurable value thereof, including all materials and equipment therefor incorporated in or stored on the site of the building. This insurance shall be written under the Builder's Risk Completed Value form and shall include the interests of the Contractor and all subcontractors as well as the Owner. The loss, if any, is to be made adjustable with and payable to the Owner as trustee for the insured and contractors and subcontractors as their interests may appear, except in such cases as may require payment of all or a portion of said insurance to a mortgagee as his interest may appear. The trustee shall have the power to adjust and settle any loss with the insurers.

The Contractor shall review in detail all provisions of the Owner's fire and extended coverage insurance described above as it pertains to the interests of the Contractor and subcontractors. If the Contractor determines that the coverage is not adequate for his needs or his subcontractors' needs, or if he desires insurance on materials, tools, forms, scaffolds, sheds, equipment, and structures, he shall request the Owner to effect such additional insurance coverage by appropriate riders or endorsements to the Owner's policies and shall pay the Owner any additional premiums resulting from these additions, or, if he prefers, the Contractor shall secure and pay for such additional coverage.

The Owner, the Contractor, and all subcontractors shall waive all rights as against the others for damages caused by fire or other perils covered by the fire insurance provided by the above paragraphs.

The contractor shall secure and maintain insurance of such types and in such amounts as are necessary to cover his responsibility and liability on a project of the character contemplated under this contract. The Contractor shall not commence work under this contract until he has obtained all insurance required under this Article and such insurance has been approved by the Owner. The Contractor shall maintain all insurance required under this contract during the life of the contract and for not less than one (1) year after the completion of this contract.

Prior to commencing work under this contract, the Contractor shall submit to the Owner through the Architect two (2) copies of each certificate of insurance evidencing insurance coverage as required of him by this Article. Each certificate shall contain a clause stating that the policy will not be cancelled without ten (10) days' prior written notice first having been furnished to the Owner, the Contractor, and the Architect. If required by the Owner, the Contractor shall furnish copies of the insurance policies to the Owner for his review and approval.

The Contractor's insurance under this Article as a minimum shall include the following coverage:

1. Insurance as will protect him from claims under workmen's compensation acts and other employee benefit acts, including disability benefit insurance, in the minimum amount required by statute as provided by the state or other political subdivision in which this work is performed.

2. Comprehensive general liability insurance written in amounts of not less than $200,000 for bodily injury, including death resulting therefrom, for any one person injured or killed, and $500,000 for any one accident or occurrence where more than one person is injured or killed; and in not less than the sum of $100,000 for property damage as the result of any one accident or occurrence, and not less than $200,000 aggregate for each year of the policy period. Said insurance shall cover bodily injury to, or death of, persons, or damage to, or destruction of, property, resulting from the execution of work provided for under this contract, or due to or arising in any manner from any omission or any act of negligence of the Contractor and/or any subcontractor and/or any independent contractor performing on behalf of the Contractor in respect to this project, and their respective employees or agents, including damage to adjacent property. Such insurance shall also cover bodily injury, death, or property damage caused by the condition or state of repair of the premises or other property of the Owner or Architect upon, about, or in connection with which any work incidental to the execution of this contract is performed.

3. Comprehensive general contingent liability insurance covering the contingent liability of the Owner, written in the amount of not less than $100,000 for each accident, and $200,000 aggregate for each year of the policy period.

4. Comprehensive automobile liability insurance written in amounts of not less than $200,000 for bodily injury or death for each person in any one accident, and $500,000 for bodily injury or death sustained by two or more persons in

any one accident. Said insurance shall be in the minimum amount of $50,000 for each accident to cover property damage liability. The insurance shall cover owned, non-owned, or rented vehicles, and include loading and unloading thereof.

36.

CONTRACTOR'S INSURANCE.

(A) Each Contractor shall secure and maintain insurance of such types and in such amounts as are necessary to cover his responsibility and liability on a project of the character contemplated under this contract, and shall require all of the subcontractors to carry similar insurance. No Contractor shall commence work under this contract until he has obtained all insurance required under this Article and such insurance has been approved by the Owner, nor shall any Contractor allow any subcontractor to commence work on his subcontract until appropriate insurance has been obtained by the subcontractor. The Contractor shall maintain all insurance required under this contract during the life of the contract and for not less than one (1) year after the completion of this contract.

Prior to commencing work under this contract, the Contractor shall submit to the Owner, through the Architect, two copies of each certificate of insurance evidencing insurance coverage as required by this Article. Each certificate shall contain a clause stating that the policy will not be cancelled without ten (10) days' prior written notice having first been furnished to the Owner, the Contractor, and the Architect. If required by the Owner, the Contractor shall furnish copies of the insurance policies to the Owner for his review and approval.

(B) The Contractor shall secure insurance under this Article as a minimum, which shall include the following coverage:

1. *Statutory Liability Insurance.* The Contractor shall secure and maintain such insurance as will protect him from claims under Workmen's Compensation Acts and other employee benefit acts in the minimum amount required by statute as provided by the State or other political subdivision in which this work is performed, and the Contractor shall secure employer's liability insurance with limits of not less than $100,000 for all damage or bodily injury from one or more claims arising from each accident or occupational disease.

2. *Comprehensive General Liability Insurance.* The contractor shall secure and maintain liability insurance which shall cover liability on account of:

   (a) Bodily injury to, or death of, persons, or damage to or destruction of property, resulting from the execution of work provided for under this contract, or due to or arising in any manner from any omission or any act of negligence of the Contractor and/or any subcontractor and/or any independent contractor performing on behalf of the Contractor in respect to this project, and their respective employees or agents, including damage to adjacent property.

   (b) Bodily injury to or death of Contractor or any subcontractor or any of their respective employees or agents, due to the condition or state of repair of the premises or other property of the Owner or Architect upon, about, or in connection with which any work incidental to the execution of this contract is performed.

(c) Loss, damage, or expense because of bodily injury to or death of persons, or because of damage to or destruction of property resulting from operation of an elevator or a material hoist if either or both are operated on or in connection with work under this contract.

(d) Defects in materials, products, or equipment installed under this contract which may become evident within one (1) year of acceptance of the building, including damage to the building or its contents.

(e) Contractual obligations, with specific reference to the obligation of the Contractor to hold the Owner harmless as provided in these specifications.

(f) Policies for comprehensive general liability insurance shall be written in amounts of not less than $200,000 for bodily injury, including death, resulting therefrom, for any one person injured or killed, and $500,000 for any one accident or occurrence where more than one person is injured or killed; and in not less than the sum of $50,000 for property damage as the result of any one accident or occurrence, subject to an aggregate limit of not less than $100,000.

3. *Comprehensive Automobile Liability Insurance.* The Contractor shall secure and maintain, and shall require each subcontractor to secure and maintain, comprehensive automobile liability insurance covering owned, non-owned, or rented vehicles, and including loading and unloading thereof, with limits of $200,000/$500,000 for each accident, and general property damage liability insurance with limits of not less than $50,000 for each accident.

4. Bodily injury coverage under both comprehensive general and comprehensive automobile liability insurance shall include "occurrence" basis wording, which means an event or continuous or repeated exposure to conditions which unexpectedly cause injury during the policy period.

5. No insurance required under this Article shall be carried by an insurer not authorized to do business within the State in which this contract is performed.

INTERPRETATION AND EXECUTION OF PLANS AND SPECIFICATIONS

37.

The Contractor shall keep at the site of the work one copy of the Plans and Specifications signed and identified by the Architect, and shall at all times give the Architect and representatives of the Owner access thereto. Anything shown on the Plans and not mentioned in the Specifications, or mentioned in the Specifications and not shown on the Plans, shall have the same effect as if shown or mentioned, respectively in both. In case of any conflict or inconsistency between the Plans and Specifications, the Architect's decision shall govern. Any discrepancy between the figures and drawings shall be submitted by the Contractor to the Architect, whose decision thereon shall be conclusive.

38.

The work required of the Contractor shall consist of all work indicated or described on the drawings and specifications, or either of them, and work reasonably inferable therefrom, except those items specifically noted as provided under another contract, provided by the Owner, or not in contract.

The Contract Documents are complementary and what is called for by any one shall be binding as if called for by all. The intention of the Documents is to include all labor and materials, equipment and transportation, necessary for the proper and complete execution of the work. All materials and services necessary to construct a complete project shall be provided, whether or not called for or shown.

It is the intent of these Specifications and Drawings to call for finished work, tested, complete, and ready for operation.

Computed dimensions shall have precedence over scale dimensions, and large scale Drawings over small scale Drawings.

These Plans and Specifications are presented to the Contractor with the understanding that he is expert and competent in the preparation of contract bid prices on the basis of information such as is contained in these documents, which do not include assurance as to their complete accuracy and validity in all details, and which may depend upon interpretation by Owner's representatives and other authorities for proper execution during the course of construction.

For the above reason, the Contractor shall understand that his submission of an unqualified bid commits him to perform all work expressed and implied in the Drawings and Specifications. Such submission commits him, without extra compensation, and within the scope of the Contract to the following:

1. To provide, with the sole exception of the Architect's written pre-bid date clarification described hereinafter, the items or arrangements of greater quantity, better quality or higher cost in the event that a conflict or disagreement, or omission with regard to such items or arrangements occurs between the Drawings and Specifications or within either one. The Architect shall be final judge of the greater quantity and/or better quality of items and arrangements in the event of said conflict, disagreement or omission. If Contractor, before bidding, obtains a written decision by the Architect as to which item or arrangement, in conflict, disagreement or omission is required, that decison shall govern.

2. To abide by the rules and regulations of all authorities (utility companies, code enforcement bureaus, etc.) having jurisdiction over the work.

3. To subcontract, or otherwise arrange to have any work, called for in the Drawings and Specifications, which does not come within the jurisdiction of the local trade unions, done by such persons whose performance of the work will not create jurisdictional or other disputes which might delay the completion of the project.

4. Any apparatus, appliances, material not shown on Drawings but which is mentioned in the Specifications, or vice-versa, or anything which may be necessary to make the work complete and perfect in all respects and ready for operation, even if not particularly specified, shall be furnished, delivered and installed by this Contractor the same as though specifically shown on the Drawings or mentioned in the Specifications, without any additional expense to the Owner.

5. To coordinate his work or adjust same to that of other trades involved at the project, so that conflicts in space do not occur.

39.

(a) The work required of the Contractor shall consist of all work indicated or described on the Drawings and Specifications, or either of them, and work reasonably inferable therefrom, except those items specifically noted as provided under another contract, provided by the Owner, or not in contract. The intention of the documents is to include all labor and materials, equipment, tools, water, power, light, transportation, and other facilities necessary for the proper and complete execution of the work. The Contract Documents are complementary and what is called for by any one of these shall be as binding as if called for by all.

Additional instructions or drawings to clarify the Drawings and Specifications may be furnished by the Architect as the work progresses. The work shall be executed in accordance with such instructions or drawings.

(b) Where typical or representative detail is shown on the Drawings, this detail shall constitute the standard in workmanship and materials throughout corresponding parts of the building, and where necessary, the Contractor is required to adapt such details for use in said corresponding parts of the building, said adaption, however, shall be subject to the approval of the Architect.

(c) References to known standards by number, symbol or title shall comply with the latest revision thereof. The referred standards shall have the full force and effect as though written out in full in the Specifications. Referred standards may be secured from the appropriate sources as required. The Architect will furnish upon request information as to how copies of standards may be obtained.

Reference to technical society, organization or body is made in the Specifications in accordance with the following abbreviations:

ACI	American Concrete Institute
AIA	American Institute of Architects
AISC	American Institute of Steel Construction
ASA	American Standards Association
ASHRAE	American Society of Heating, Refrigerating and Air-Conditioning Engineers
ASME	American Society of Mechanical Engineers
ASTM	American Society for Testing and Materials
AWS	American Welding Society
FS	Federal Specifications
NBFU	National Board of Fire Underwriters
NEC	National Electric Code
UL	Underwriters' Laboratories, Inc.

(d) The Specifications are generally divided into trade sections for the purpose of ready reference, but such sections are arbitrary, and the Contractor will be permitted to allot the work of subcontractors at his own discretion regardless of the grouping of the Specifications. It shall be his responsibility to settle definitely with each subcontractor the portions of the work which each will be required to do and the Owner assumes no responsibility whatever for any jurisdiction claimed by any of the trades involved in the work.

(e) Each Contractor shall examine all drawings relating to the work of all Contractors and shall become fully informed as to the entire scope, extent, and character of the project and the relation of his work with other Contractor's work.

(f) If the Drawings and Specifications are not in agreement, the one requiring the greater quantity or superior quality shall prevail as determined by the Architect.

LIENS AND CLAIMS

40.

The Contract agrees that he will indemnify and save the Owner harmless from all claims growing out of the demands of subcontractors, laborers, workmen, mechanics, materialmen, and furnishers of supplies and equipment. The Contractor shall furnish satisfactory evidence that all obligations of the nature hereinabove described have been paid, discharged, or waived. If the Contractor fails so to do, then the Owner may, after having served written notice on the said Contractor, either pay unpaid bills of which the Owner has written notice, deduct or withhold from the Contractor's unpaid compensation a sum of money deemed reasonably sufficient to pay any and all such lawful claims, until satisfactory evidence is furnished that all liabilities have been fully discharged, whereupon payments to the Contractor shall be resumed in accordance with the terms of this Contract, but in no event shall the provisions of this Contract be construed to impose any obligations upon the Owner to the Contractor, his surety, or to any subcontractors, materialmen, or to any person to whom the Contractor is obligated. In paying any unpaid bills of the Contractor, the Owner shall be deemed the agent of the Contractor and any payments so made by the Owner shall be considered as payment made under the Contract by the Owner to the Contractor, and the Owner shall not be liable to the Contractor for any such payment made in good faith.

In no event shall the final payment to the Contractor, nor any part of the retained percentage, be due and payable until the Contractor shall deliver to the Owner a complete release and discharge of all liens arising out of this Contract, receipts in full showing payment of all subcontractors and materialmen and an affiidavit that so far as he has knowledge or information, the release and receipts include all the labor and material for which a lien could be filed; but the Contractor may, if any subcontractor refuses to furnish a release or receipt in full, furnish a bond satisfactory to the Owner to indemnify him against any lien, and to discharge any lien that has been filed. If any lien remains unsatisfied after all payments are made, the Contractor shall refund to the Owner all monies that the latter may be compelled to pay in discharging such a lien, including all costs and a reasonable attorney's fee.

41.

The Contractor shall execute a Waiver of Lien simultaneously with the signing of the Contract, agreeing that the said Contract shall be performed, constructed, finished and delivered to the Owner, free from all claims, liens, or charges in favor of the Contractor of any party, firm or corporation entitled to such lien. Said waiver to be recorded in the County in which the work is to be done.

LIQUIDATED DAMAGES

42.

It is hereby understood and mutually agreed, by and between the Contractor and the Owner, that the date of beginning, rate of progress, and the time for completion of the work to be done hereunder are *essential conditions* of this contract; and it is further mutually understood and agreed that the work embraced in this contract shall be commenced on a date to be specified in the work order.

The Contractor agrees that said work shall be prosecuted regularly, diligently, and uninterruptedly at such rate of progress as will insure full completion thereof within the time specified. It is expressly understood and agreed, by and between the Contractor and the Owner, that the time for the completion of the work described herein is a reasonable time for the completion of the same, taking into consideration the average climatic range and usual industrial conditions prevailing in this locality.

If the said Contractor shall neglect, fail or refuse to complete the work within the time herein specified, then the Contractor does hereby agree, as a part consideration for the awarding of this contract, to pay to the Owner the amount specified in the contract, not as a penalty but as liquidated damages for such breach of contract as hereinafter set forth, for each and every calendar day that the Contractor shall be in default after the time stipulated in the contract for completing the work.

The said amount is fixed and agreed upon by and between the Contractor and the Owner because of the impracticability and extreme difficulty of fixing and ascertaining the actual damages the Owner would in such event sustain, and said amount is agreed to be the amount of damages which the Owner would sustain and said amounts shall be retained from time to time by the Owner from current periodical estimates.

It is further agreed that time is of the essence of each and every portion of this contract and of the specifications wherein a definite and certain length of time is fixed for the performance of any act whatsoever; and where under the contract an additional time is allowed for the completion of any work, the new time limit fixed by such extension shall be of the essence of this contract: *Provided,* that the Contractor shall not be charged with liquidated damages or any excess cost when the delay in completion of the work is due:

(a) To any preference, priority or allocation order duly issued by the Government;

(b) To unforeseeable cause beyond the control and without the fault or negligence of the Contractor, including, but not restricted to, acts of God or of the public enemy, acts of the Owner, acts of another contractor in the performance of a contract with the Owner, fires, floods, epidemics, quarantine restrictions, strikes, freight embargoes, and unusually severe weather; and

(c) To any delays of subcontractors or suppliers occasioned by any of the causes specified in subsections (a) and (b) of this article.

Provided, further, that the Contractor shall, within seven (7) days from the beginning of such delay, notify the Owner, in writing, of the causes of the delay, who shall ascertain the facts and extent of the delay and notify the Contractor within a reasonable time of its decision in the matter.

43.

Time shall be especially considered as the essence of this contract on the part of the Contractor[s], and in case the Contractor[s] shall fail in the due performance of the works to be executed under this contract by and at the time or times herein mentioned or referred to, or at other than the day or days to which the period of completion may have been extended ... may be liable to pay to the board, as and for liquidated damages, and not as penalty, the sum of $... for each and every ... which may elapse between the appointed and actual time of completion and delivery hereinbefore mentioned or provided for, which sum is hereby agreed upon, fixed, and determined as the damage which will be suffered by such failure to complete within the time named; and the Owner or city may deduct the same from any moneys in their hands due or to become due to the Contractor[s]; and such payments or deduction shall not in any degree release the Contractor[s] from the further obligations and penalties in respect of the fulfilment of the entire contract, nor any right which the board might have to claim, sue for, and recover compensation and damages for non-performance of this contract at the time hereby stipulated.

OCCUPANCY BY OWNER

44.

The Contractor shall allow the Owner to take possession of and use any completed or partially completed portion of the structure or work, or to place and install as much furniture and equipment during the progress of the work as is possible without interference before its entire completion; such possession and use of structure or work of such placing and installation of equipment, or both, shall not in any way evidence completion of the work or any part of it.

45.

The Contractor shall arrange for partial or complete occupancy, or the operation of the apparatus previous to final acceptance when directed by the Architect. The Owner shall have the right to occupy the buildings and to operate the apparatus. The occupation or use of apparatus will not constitute acceptance of such work.

46.

The Owner has the right to occupy or use any completed or partially completed portion of the work when such occupancy and use are in its best interest, notwithstanding the time of completion for all of the work. If such occupancy or use increases the cost of the work or delays its completion, the Contractor shall be entitled to extra compensation or extension of time or both. Such claims for extra compensation or extension of time, to be valid, shall be made in writing within seven (7) days of the Owner's notification to the Contractor of its intent so to occupy or use.

PATENTS

47.

The Contractor shall hold and save the Owner and its officers, agents, servants, and employees harmless from liability of any nature or kind, including cost and expenses, for, or on account of, any patented or unpatented invention, process, article, or appliance manufactured or used in the performance of the contract, including its use by the Owner, unless otherwise specifically stipulated in the contract documents.

If the Contractor uses any design, device or materials covered by letters, patent or copyright, he shall provide for such use by suitable agreement with the Owner of such patented or copyrighted design, device or material. It is mutually agreed and understood that, without exception, the contract prices shall include all royalties or costs arising from the use of such design, device or materials in any way involved in the work. The Contractor and/or his sureties shall indemnify and save harmless the Owner of the project from any and all claims for infringement by reason of the use of such patented or copyrighted design, device or materials or any trademark or copyright in connection with work agreed to be performed under this contract, and shall indemnify the Owner for any cost, expense or damage which it may be obliged to pay by reason of such infringement at any time during the prosecution of the work or after completion of the work.

48.

The Contractor shall indemnify the Owner against liability, including costs, for infringement of any United States letters patent arising out of the manufacture or delivery of supplies or out of construction, alteration, modification, or repair of real property (hereinafter referred to as "construction work") under this contract, or out of the use or disposal by or for the account of the Owner of such supplies or construction work. The foregoing indemnity shall not apply unless the Contractor shall have been informed as soon as practicable by the Owner of the suit or action alleging such infringement, and shall have been given such opportunity as is afforded by applicable laws, rules, or regulations to participate in the defense thereof; and further, such indemnity shall not apply if: (i) the infringement results from compliance with specific written instructions of the Architect directing a change in the supplies to be delivered or in the materials or equipment to be used, or directing a manner of performance of the contract not normally used by the Contractor; or (ii) the infringement results from the addition to, or change in, the supplies furnished or construction work performed, which addition or change was made subsequent to delivery or performance by the Contractor; or (iii) the claimed infringement is settled without the consent of the Contractor, unless required by final decree of a court of competent jurisdiction.

49.

The Contractor shall pay all royalties and license fees. He shall defend all suits or claims for infringement of any patent rights and shall save the Owner harmless from loss on account thereof, except that the Owner shall be responsible for all such loss when a particular process or product is specified by it unless the Contractor shall have information that a particular process or product specified infringes on a patent, in which event he shall be responsible for loss on account thereof unless he promptly gives such information to the Architect and the Owner.

PAYMENTS TO CONTRACTOR

50.

Not later than the fifteenth (15th) day of each calendar month the Owner will make a partial payment to the Contractor on the basis of a duly certified and approved estimate of the work performed during the preceding calendar month under this contract, but to insure the proper performance of this contract, the Owner shall retain ten percent (10%) of the amount of each estimate until final completion and acceptance of all work covered by this contract: *Provided:* That the Owner, at any time after fifty percent (50%) of the work has been completed, if it finds that satisfactory progress is being made, may make any of the remaining partial payments in full: *Provided, further,* that on completion and acceptance of each separate building, public work, or other division of the contract, on which the price is stated separately in the contract, payment may be made in full, including retained percentages thereon, less authorized deductions.

In preparing estimates the material delivered on the site and preparatory work done may be taken into consideration.

All material and work covered by partial payments made shall thereupon become the sole property of the Owner, but this provision shall not be construed as relieving the Contractor from the sole responsibility for the care and protection of materials and work upon which payments have been made or the restoration of any damaged work, or as a waiver of the right of the Owner to require the fulfillment of all of the terms of the contract.

51.

After receipt of the Contractor's requisition, the Architect will review it and will issue a certificate of payment for the amount, if any, he determines should be paid by the Owner to the Contractor.

No certificate issued nor payment made to the Contractor, nor partial or entire use or occupancy of the work by the Owner, shall be an acceptance of any work or materials not in accordance with this Contract. The Contractor by his acceptance if the final payment under the Contract, warrants that he has received payment in full for his performance of the Contract and waives all claims against the Owner in connection with the work.

In order to secure the proper performance of this Contract, the Owner shall retain ten percent (10%) of the payments to be made, in accordance with the valuation of the work done, which retainage shall be paid with the final payment after the issuance of the final certificate.

A final certificate will be issued by the Architect when all work is completed and accepted, provided, however, the Contractor shall be obligated prior to the issuance of the final certificate to furnish a maintenance bond in the amount of twenty-five percent (25%) of the contract, in a form and with sureties satisfactory to the Owner and Architect, covering the obligations of the Contractor to correct, repair and make good any and all defects or damages that may occur because of faulty workmanship or materials for a period of one (1) year from the date of the issuance of the final certificate of payment.

PROTECTION OF WORK AND PROPERTY

52.

The Contractor shall at all times safely guard the Owner's property from injury or loss in connection with this Contract. He shall at all times safely guard and protect his own work, and that of adjacent property, from damage. The Contractor shall replace or make good any such damage, loss or injury unless such be caused directly by errors contained in the Contract or by the Owner, or his duly authorized representatives. All passageways, guard fences, lights, and other facilities required for protection by local authorities or local conditions must be provided and maintained.

53.

The Contractor shall take over and assume all responsibility for the entire premises assigned to him, maintain all existing protections and provide and maintain all additional protections as required by the Architect and governing laws, regulations and ordinances. He shall carefully protect any existing curbs, walks, and paving; existing sewers, water mains, gas mains, and other public utilities; and trees and shrubs liable to be damaged during construction. All protections shall be removed from the premises when directed.

The Contractor shall be responsible for any damage caused by him or his workmen to the property of the Owner, or to the work or materials of the subcontractors and shall make good, at his own expense, any loss, damage, or injury without cost to the Owner.

Any work damaged by failure to provide proper protection shall be removed and replaced by new work at the expense of the Contractor responsible for such damage.

The Contractor shall protect adjacent property from injury, arising in connection with this contract, as well as the Owner's property.

54.

The Contractor shall assume all responsibility for the entire premises assigned to him, maintain all existing protections and provide and maintain all additional protections as required by the Architect and governing laws, regulations and ordinances. He shall carefully protect any existing curbs, walks, and paving; existing sewers, water mains, gas mains, and other public utilities; trees and shrubs liable to be damaged during construction.

Protect all existing trees, shrubbery and foliage in such a manner as not to injure roots, trunk or branches. Only trees that interfere with construction shall be removed. However, no trees shall be removed without consent of the Architect.

No trees, foliage, or shrubs should be cut or damaged in any way by any Contractor in order to permit passage for delivery of any equipment, materials, etc., to buildings without the approval of the Architect and Owner in writing.

The Contractor shall be fully responsible for any damages caused to any existing trees or shrubs, replace same as approved by Architect, and at no additional costs.

Any existing landscaping areas which become damaged in any way by any operations of any Contractor shall be replaced with equal quantities and like quality as approved by Architect, and at no additional cost to Owner.

All protections shall be removed from the premises when directed by the Architect.

The Contractor shall be responsible for any damage caused by him or his workmen to the property of the Owner, or to the work or materials of the subcontractors and shall make good, at his own expense, any loss, damage, or injury without cost to the Owner.

Any work damaged by failure to provide proper protection shall be removed and replaced by new work at the expense of the Contractor responsible for such damage.

The Contractor shall protect adjacent property from injury, arising in connection with this Contract, as well as the Owner's property.

If any legal proceedings shall be brought against the Owner and the Architect on account of any injury to person or to property described herein, the Owner shall give notice thereof to the Contractor who shall, at his own expense, defend usch proceedings, pay to satisfy any judgment that may be entered against the Owner and the Architect in any such proceedings, and pay all costs or expenses whatever incurred by the Owner and the Architect in any such case in which judgment is rendered against him.

Any existing structures or portions of existing structures that are affected or damaged in any way due to any operations under this Contract shall be repaired, and/or replaced as required and/or directed by the Architect or the Owner, to the Architect's full satisfaction at no additional costs.

55.

The Contractor shall continuously provide and maintain adequate protection of all his work from damage and shall protect the Owner's property and all adjacent property from injury or loss arising in connection with this Contract. The Contractor shall perform his work in such manner as to insure against injury or damage to the Owner's property or to adjacent property. He shall make good any damage, injury, or loss which results or which is contributed to by his failure to comply with these requirements.

The Contractor shall take all necessary precautions for the safety of employees on the work, and shall comply with all applicable provisions of Federal, State, and Municipal safety laws and building codes to prevent accidents or injury to persons on, about or adjacent to the premises where the work is being performed. He shall erect and properly maintain at all times, as required by the conditions and progress of the work, all necessary safeguards for the protection of workmen and the public and shall post danger signs warning against the hazards created by such features of construction as protruding nails, hoists, hatchways, scaffolding, window openings, stairways and falling materials; and he shall designate a responsible member of his organization on the work, whose duty shall be the prevention of accidents. Neither the Owner nor the Architect shall have any responsibility for safety of employees on the work or safety of working conditions.

All pertinent precautions for accident prevention recommended by the Building Trades Employers Association, or by State or local laws and regulations, shall be considered to form a part of the Contractor's obligation under this Contract.

Whenever serious or fatal accident occurs at the site during construction, the Contractor shall immediately notify the Owner and the Architect. The Contractor shall investigate the accident to determine the cause thereof.

In an emergency affecting the safety of life or of the work or of adjoining property, the Contractor, without special instruction or authorization from the Architect or Owner, is hereby permitted to act, at his discretion, to prevent such threatened loss or injury, and he shall so act, without appeal, if so authorized or instructed. Any compensation, claimed by the Contractor on account of emergency work, shall be determined by agreement or by the Architect.

The General Contractor shall provide approved temporary enclosures for all exterior openings, as soon as the building is closed and otherwise made weathertight, or whenever necessary in order to provide suitable working conditions within the building. For this purpose, the permanent window enclosures may be utilized, except that at least one quarter (¼) of the window area in each space shall be provided with temporary cloth screens to permit the exit of water vapor from the building at all times, or shall be otherwise equipped to effect the same result. The permanent door enclosures shall not be used as temporary enclosures, but temporary batten doors with proper hardware to make them self-closing shall be provided.

All finished surfaces shall be protected by the General Contractor generally but not limited to the following: All door and window sills; the jambs and soffits of all openings used as passageways, or through which material is handled, shall be cased and protected adequately against possible damage resulting from the conduct of the work of all contractors; stairs shall be provided with temporary planking on treads.

All surfaces shall be clean and not marred upon delivery of the building to the Owner. The Contractor shall, without extra compensation, refinish all surfaces in such spaces where these surfaces prove to have been inadequately protected, and are damaged.

Tight wood sheathing shall be laid under any materials that may stain, damage or discolor concrete and stored on finished cement surfaces; planking shall be laid before moving any materials over finished areas. Wheelbarrows used over such areas shall have rubber tired wheels.

The General Contractor shall provide the necessary safeguards to prevent accidents, to avoid all unnecessary hazards and protect the public, the work and the property at all times, including Sundays, holidays and other times when no work is being done. The General Contractor shall be in charge of the building until its acceptance by the Owner. He shall be responsible for all damage done to the building construction and finishes and shall make good all damages caused by lack of proper precautions.

If watchman services are furnished by the General Contractor, this shall not be construed as guaranteeing other contractors against loss or damage. If other Contractors deem additional protection necessary for their own interests, they shall provide such protection. Each Contractor shall be responsible for any of his property, fixtures, fittings, tools, equipment, etc., that may be injured or stolen, either before or after the installation in the building, and shall make good such damage or loss at his own sole expense.

The General Contractor shall provide and maintain an adequate number of hand fire extinguishers located at the approximate location of permanent fire extinguishers indicated to be provided on the drawings, or at locations approved by the Architect, and take other precautions necessary to prevent fires.

The General Contractor shall from commencement to completion of building operation, keep all parts of site and building free from accumulation of water, no matter what the source or cause of water and to this end, he shall supply, maintain, and operate all pumping and bailing equipment such as pumps, containers, hose, piping, strainers, fuel, power, etc., at no additional cost to the Owner. He shall direct any such accumulation of water so that no damage is done to the building or other property on or adjoining the premises and he shall repair and make good damages, including any erosion caused by his operations.

The Contractor shall take special precautions against damage to materials and work installed in freezing weather, by providing adequate special heat and coverings. The ground surfaces under footings and pipe lines, and all masonry shall be protected against freezing or ice formation.

The General Contractor shall maintain the building and all approaches clear of snow and ice. Each Contractor shall remove such other snow and ice as may be required for proper protection and prosecution of his work.

REPRESENTATIONS OF CONTRACTORS

56.

The Contractor represents and warrants:

(a) That he is financially solvent and that he is experienced in and competent to perform the type of work or to furnish the plant, materials, supplies or equipment, to be so performed or furnished by him; and

(b) That he is familiar with all Federal, state, municipal and department laws, ordinances, orders and regulations, which may in any way affect the work of those employed therein, including, but not limited to, any special acts relating to the work or the project of which it is a part; and

(c) That such temporary and permanent work required by the contract as is to be done by him can be satisfactorily constructed and used for the purpose for which it is intended, and that such construction will not injure any person or damage any property; and

(d) That he has carefully examined the Plans and Specifications, and addenda, if any, and site of the work and that, from his own investigations he has satisfied himself as to the nature and location of the work, the character, quality and quantity of surface and sub-surface materials likely to be encountered, the character of equipment and other facilities needed for the performance of the work, the general and local conditions, and all other materials which may in any way affect the work or its performance.

57.

The Contractor shall be required, prior to the execution of the Contract Documents, to review the same, including the Plans and Specifications, to verify that they are complete and contain no ambiguity, errors or omissions. In the event the Contractor finds any error, omission, ambiguity or incompleteness in the Contract Documents, or otherwise is of the opinion that the work is shown on the drawings or specified in such a manner as will make it impossible to produce a first-class piece of work, he shall so notify the Architect. The lack of such notification shall exclude the entertainment of any excuse for failure by the Contractor to carry out the work in a satisfactory manner, and as complete acceptability by him of all Contract Documents, and as a waiver of rights to future claims arising from omissions, discrepancies, ambiguities, incompleteness or errors, and the Contractor shall bear any cost or expense for the supplying of materials and labor to correct any damage or defect in the work caused by any such omission, error, conflict, or inadequacy in said Contract Documents. Nothing contained herein, however, shall require the Contractor to review the Contract Documents for the purpose of determining the completeness or desirability of aesthetic effects.

58.

The Contractor represents and warrants that he has studied and thoroughly familiarized himself with the Contract in its entirety, the site, and all current equipment labor and material market conditions, such that he accepts responsibility for and is prepared to execute and shall fulfill completely by his construction work the design intent of the Contract without exception and without reservation. The Contractor further represents and warrants that he has carefully examined the Contract in detail and that he accepts all of the documents as adequate in all respects to meet the requirements specified.

The Contractor represents and warrants that he has good title to all materials and supplies used by him in the work, free from all liens, claims, or encumbrances. No materials or supplies for the work shall be purchased by the Contractor or by any subcontractor subject to any chattel mortgage or under a conditional sale contract or other security agreement by which an interest is retained by the seller.

RIGHTS OF THE OWNER
TO TERMINATE CONTRACT

59.

In the event that any of the provisions of this contract are violated by the Contractor or by any of his subcontractors, the Owner may serve written notice upon the Contractor and the Surety of its intention to terminate the contract, such notices to contain the reasons for such intention to terminate the contract, and, unless within ten (10) days after the serving of such notice upon the Contractor such violation or delay shall cease and satisfactory arrangement of correction be made, the contract shall, upon the expiration of said ten (10) days, cease and terminate. In the event of any such termination, the Owner shall immediately serve notice thereof upon the Surety and the Contractor, and the Surety shall have the right to take over and perform the contract, provided, however, that if the Surety does not commence performance thereof within five (5) days from the date of the mailing to such Surety of notice of termination, the Owner may take over the work and prosecute the same to completion by contract or by force account for the account and at the expense of the Contractor, and the Contractor and his Surety shall be liable to the Owner for any excess cost occasioned the Owner thereby, and in such event the Owner may take possession of and utilize in completing the work such materials, appliances, and plant as may be on the site of the work and necessary therefor.

60.

(a) The Owner, subject to conditions set forth below, may terminate the Contract for any of the following causes:

1. The Contractor's bankruptcy, whether by filing a petition in bankruptcy, or for arrangement or for reorganization under the Bankruptcy Act of the United States, or by being adjudged a bankrupt.
2. A general assignment made by the Contractor for the benefit of his creditors.
3. The appointment of a receiver on account of the Contractor's insolvency.
4. Refusal or failure of the Contractor to supply enough properly skilled workmen or proper materials.
5. Failure of the Contractor to make prompt payment to subcontractors, or for material or labor.
6. Disregard by the Contractor of laws, ordinances, or the instructions of the Architect.
7. Failure of the Contractor to commence work when notified to do so by the Owner.

8. Abandonment of the work by the Contractor.
9. An unreasonable or willful delay of the Contractor's performance or the awarding of necessary subcontracts or the placing of necessary material or equipment orders.
10. The inability of the Contractor to complete in the time required by the Contract Documents.
11. Other substantial violation of any provision of the Contract.

(b) Termination of the Contract by the Owner shall be without prejudice to any other right or remedy, and shall be subject to the following conditions:

1. The Architect's decision that sufficient cause exists to justify such action.
2. Seven (7) days' written notice given by the Owner to the Contractor and his surety, if any.

(c) Termination of the Contract as set forth above shall entitle the Owner to take possession of the premises and of all materials, tools, and appliances thereon, and finish the work by whatever method he may deem expedient.

(d) Payments after termination of Contract:

1. Termination of the Contract shall deprive the Contractor of any right to further payment until the work is finished.
2. Should the unpaid balance of the balance of the Contract price exceed the expense of finishing the work, including compensation for additional architectural, managerial, and administrative services, such excess shall be paid to the Contractor.
3. Should such expense exceed such unpaid balance, the Contractor shall pay the difference to the Owner.
4. The expense incurred by the Owner as herein provided, and the damage incurred through the Contractor's default, shall be certified by the Architect.

61.

(a) The Owner may terminate this contract by notice in writing from the Owner to the Contractor. Any such termination shall be effective upon the receipt by the Contractor of such notice of termination except to the extent that the Contractor shall have such time as the Contractor acting reasonably and prudently after receiving such notice of termination shall require to stop all such work and to cancel all subcontracts, orders and contracts for materials, supplies and facilities which the Contractor is notified to cancel in such termination notice, which in no event shall be more than seven (7) days from the receipt of such notice of termination; and the Contractor shall for a reasonable time thereafter, if requested by the Owner, do such work as may be necessary to preserve and protect any work already in progress and any materials, tools and equipment at the site or in transit.

(b) In the event of such termination, full and complete settlement of the following claims shall be made:

1. The Owner shall assume and become liable for all obligations, commitments and claims that the Contractor may have in good faith undertaken or incurred in accordance with this Contract in connection with the work so terminated prior to the receipt by the Contractor of notice of such termination; and the Contractor shall execute and deliver all such papers and

take all such steps, including, but not limited to, the legal assignment of its contractual rights as the Owner may require for the purpose of fully vesting in the Owner the rights and benefits of the Contractor under such obligations and commitments.

2. The Owner shall reimburse the Contractor for any expenses incurred by the Contractor for the protection of the work and property, as provided in section (a) of this Article.

3. The Owner shall reimburse the Contractor for all expenditures made and expenses incurred prior to the effective date of such termination and not previously reimbursed.

4. There shall be an equitable adjustment of the Fee on the basis of the value and extent of the services performed by the Contractor in accordance with this Contract in relation to the total services the Contractor would have performed had the Contractor fully completed all of the work, pursuant to this Contract. The Owner shall pay the Contractor the amount determined as provided in this subsection (4) less any payments theretofore made by the Owner on account of the Fee.

5. The Owner shall reimburse the Contractor for all reasonable legal fees and expenses of counsel approved by the Owner, paid by the Contractor in connection with such termination.

(c) In the event that the Owner and the Contractor cannot agree as to what the adjustment shall be under the foregoing subsection (b) of this Article then the Architect shall make such determination.

(d) Notwithstanding anything herein contained, in the event that such termination is due to the fact that the Contractor has failed to prosecute the work diligently or properly, or to supply a sufficient number of properly skilled workmen, or to supply a sufficient amount of proper materials, or to make prompt payment to subcontractors or for material or labor, or has persistently disregarded laws, ordinances or any rules or regulations by governmental or local agencies, or has otherwise been guilty of a substantial violation of any provision of this Contract, or was adjudged a bankrupt, or the Contractor has made a general assignment for the benefit of creditors, or a receiver has been appointed on account of the Contractor's insolvency, or there has been a change of any officers of the Contractor, then, the Contractor shall not be entitled to receive any payment on account of the Contractor's Fixed Fee until and unless the work is finished; and any fees for services similar to those to be performed by the Contractor paid by the Owner for finishing the work shall be deducted from the fee otherwise due the Contractor under this Contract. In the event of termination of this Contract, for any reason mentioned in this section (d) then the Owner may, at its option, take possession of any tools and equipment belonging to the Contractor used in connection with any of the work performed by the Contractor pursuant to this Contract. In such case, if any of the Contractor's tools and equipment are retained by the Owner, the Owner shall pay the Contractor a reasonable rental therefor.

62.

(a) If the Contractor refuses or fails to prosecute the work, or any separable part thereof, with such diligence as will insure its completion within the time specified in this contract, or any extension thereof, or fails to complete said work within such time, the Government may, by written notice to the Contractor, terminate his right to proceed with the work or such part of the work as to which there has been delay. In such event the Government may take over the work and prosecute the same to completion, by contract or otherwise, and the Contractor and his sureties shall be liable to the Government for any excess cost occasioned the Government thereby, and for liquidated damages for delay, as fixed in the specifications or accompanying papers, until such reasonable time as may be required for the final completion of the work, or if liquidated damages are not so fixed, any actual damages occasioned by such delay. If the Contractor's right to proceed is so terminated, the Government may take possession of and utilize in completing the work such materials, appliances, and plant as may be on the site of the work and necessary therefor.

(b) If the Government does not terminate the right of the Contractor to proceed, as provided in paragraph (a) hereof, the Contractor shall continue the work, in which event he and his sureties shall be liable to the Government, in the amount set forth in the specifications or accompanying papers, for fixed, agreed, and liquidated damages for each calendar day of delay until the work is completed or accepted, or if liquidated damages are not so fixed, any actual damages occasioned by such delay.

(c) The right of the Contractor to proceed shall not be terminated, as provided in paragraph (a) hereof, nor the Contractor charged with liquidated or actual damages, as provided in paragraph (b) hereof because of any delays in the completion of the work due to unforeseeable causes beyond the control and without the fault or negligence of the Contractor, including, but not restricted to, acts of God, or of the public enemy, acts of the Government, in either its sovereign or contractual capacity, acts of another contractor in the performance of a contract with the Government, fires, floods, epidemics, quarantine restrictions, strikes, freight embargoes, and unusually severe weather, or delays of subcontractors or suppliers due to such causes: *Provided,* That the Contractor shall within ten (10) days from the beginning of any such delay, unless the Contracting Officer shall grant a further period of time prior to the date of final settlement of the contract, notify the Contracting Officer in writing of the causes of delay. The Contracting Officer shall ascertain the facts and the extent of the delay and extend the time for completing the work when in his judgment the findings of fact justify such an extension, and his findings of fact thereon shall be final and conclusive on the parties hereto, subject only to appeal as provided in Clause   hereof.

SEPARATE CONTRACTS AND
MUTUAL RESPONSIBILITY OF CONTRACTORS

63.

The Contractor shall cooperate and work in harmony with all other contractors engaged to the building, and shall allow them and their employees the usual access through such portions of the building as are under his control. He shall arrange and carry on all work in such manner as not to unnecessarily hinder or delay any other contractor in the progress of his work.

64.

Should the Contractor be caused to sustain damages, whether through delay in performance or any other cause, by any other separate contractor on the work, the Contractor agrees that no claim or action shall lie or be maintained against the Owner or Architect, but must be asserted solely against the contractor causing said damages. If the Contractor should cause damage to any separate contractor on the work by reason of the Contractor's failure to properly perform under this contract, he will assume the responsibility and liability for such damage, and such separate contractor may assert his claim against the Contractor as a third party beneficiary hereunder. If such separate contractor makes a claim against the owner or sues the Owner on account of any damage alleged to have been so sustained, the Contractor agrees that he will hold the Owner harmless against any such claim or suit, and that he will reimburse the Owner the cost of defending such suit, including a reasonable attorney's fee, and if any judgment against the Owner arises therefrom, the Contractor shall pay or satisfy it and shall pay all costs incurred by the Owner.

65.

The Owner reserves the right to let other contracts in connection with this work under similar General Conditions. The Contractor shall afford other contractors reasonable opportunity for the introduction and storage of their materials and the execution of their work, and shall properly connect and coordinate his work with theirs.

If any part of the Contractor's work depends for proper execution or results upon the work of any other contractor, the Contractor shall inspect and promptly report to the Architect any defects in such proper execution and results. His failure so to inspect and report shall constitute an acceptance of the other contractor's work as fit and proper for the reception of his work, except as to defects which may develop in the other contractor's work after the execution of his work.

To insure the proper execution of his subsequent work the Contractor shall measure work already in place and shall at once report to the Architect any discrepancy between the executed work and the Drawings.

Contractors shall provide all other interested parties with adequate setting plans for their materials, and shall provide and install or have installed anchorages and building materials, all of which shall be done in a manner to avoid delay in the work of others. Except as may be mutually agreed, to avoid delay in the work, each Contractor shall provide and set or have set all anchors, ties, inserts, sleeves, nailings, duct boxes, etc., required for his work, and shall build into his work the chases, materials and work of others. The Contractor shall cooperate with other contractors in the installation of sleeves, chases, openings, inserts, hangers, and other devices or provisions necessary for the later installation of work that is not installed concurrently with work in progress, and in providing temporary openings of adequate size for passage of large or bulky items or equipment without damage to finished work. The expense of cutting or patching (or of the replacement of damaged materials) resulting from the failure to satisfy these requirements, shall be borne by the Contractor so at fault. Each Contractor shall furnish and install all specialized equipment required for the installation of his work, except as may otherwise be mutually agreed with the General Contractor.

66.

The Owner plans to execute this project by awarding a single General Contract, the work of all trades of which shall proceed simultaneously. The Owner may elect to execute portions of the project construction responsibility by means of award of separate contracts.

(a) The Contractor shall coordinate his operations with those of all subcontractors, and any separate contractors.

(b) Cooperation will be required of all subcontractors, and contractors, in the arrangements for the storage of materials and in the detailed execution of the work.

(c) The Contractor, including his subcontractors, shall keep informed of the progress and the details of work of all subcontractors and contractors, and shall notify the Architect immediately of lack of progress or defective workmanship on the part of subcontractors and contractors.

(d) Failure of the Contractor to keep informed of the work progressing on the site and failure to give notice of lack of progress or defective workmanship by others shall be construed as acceptance by him of the status of the work as being satisfactory for proper coordination with his own work and the project schedule.

(e) It is agreed that the Contractor shall not be entitled to any damage or extra compensation from the Owner on account of any work performed by the Owner or other contractors, that in any way affects the work under this Contract.

(f) In case the Contractor, by his own acts or the acts of any person or persons in his employ, shall unnecessarily delay, in the opinion of the Architect, the work of the Owner or other contractors, by not properly cooperating with them or by not affording them sufficient opportunity or facility to perform work as may be specified, the Contractor shall, in that case, pay all costs and expenses incurred by such parties due to any such delays and he hereby authorizes the Owner to deduct the amount of such costs and expenses from any monies due or to become due the Contractor under this Contract, based on the investigations and recommendations of the Architect. Nothing contained in this paragraph shall, however, relieve said Contractor from any liability or damage resulting to the Owner on account of such delay or delays.

SHOP DRAWINGS

67.

Submit for approval, with such promptness as to cause no delay in work, scale and full size transparencies accompanied by white prints of shop drawings as required. Architects will retain white prints and return transparency marked as follows:

1. *Approved.* Do not resubmit shop drawings.
2. *Disapproved.* Resubmit shop drawings promptly for approval in same manner described above.
3. *Approved as Noted.* Proceed with work but resubmit shop drawings.

Upon receiving Architect's approval of shop drawings, promptly distribute copies to affected trades.

Where it is difficult to prepare shop drawing transparencies such as for "cuts," "booklets," "photographs," submit four (4) copies for architectural trades, five (5) copies for mechanical and structural trades. Distribute copies in same manner as shop drawings.

Shop drawing transparency shall be ozalid, litho, C.B., or original shop drawing tracing; sharp, clear, distinct for reproduction. Transparency shall have blank space on right hand side, inside or outside border, not less than eighty (80) square inches, for imprinting of receipt and approval stamps.

Shop drawings shall be complete in every detail, including provisions required of various trades and separate Contracts, connections with other work, cutting, fitting, drilling required and any and all other necessary information as per usual trade practice as required for any specific purpose. When such drawings are required to be submitted to Building Authorities, submit them to and secure approval of authorities.

Wherever shop drawings state or imply "by others," or "not-in-contract," the General Contractor shall, before submitting drawings to the Architect, mark same, identifying such others and/or Contract.

Submit shop drawings at sufficiently early date, allowing enough time for checking, fabrication. Architect may withhold approval on any shop drawing until shop drawings indicating all items related to each other have been submitted. Submit (and resubmit) shop drawings for such related items at approximately the same date to permit coordinated checking. Contractor shall be responsible for delays resulting from failure to cause subcontractors to submit drawings at required dates.

Check shop drawings of various trades for measurements, size of members, materials and details to make sure that they conform to intent of Drawings and Specifications and for contract requirements. Correct drawings found to be inaccurate or otherwise in error. Shop drawings, at time of submission, shall bear stamp of approval of Contractor as evidence that such drawings and/or details have been checked by Contractor. Drawings submitted without such stamp of approval will be returned to Contractor for resubmission and will not be considered; in such event it will be deemed that Contractor has not complied with requirements of this Article and shall bear risks of delays as if no drawings or details had been submitted.

Where specified or required, shop drawings for work of one trade shall have been checked by subcontractors of related trades, and shall have received their stamp of approval before being submitted to Architects.

Shop drawings which involve change in or variance with Contract Drawings shall be so noted by Contractor and Architects duly advised in writing of recommended change and reasons therefor.

Architect will check and approve shop drawings as aid to Contractor. Approval of drawings by Architects will be general and shall not relieve Contractor from responsibility for deviations from Drawings and Specifications or for proper performance of work covered by Contract. Correct errors in and omissions from work without extra cost to Owner, whether or not work was installed in accordance with approved shop drawing.

Accompany each submission of shop drawings with transmittal letter listing drawings submitted by number and title.

Do no work until drawings are approved.

Drawings and Specifications on the work: Contractor shall keep one copy of all Drawings and Specifications on the work, in good order, available to the Architect, Field Engineer and their representatives.

68

Shop drawings shall be complete in every detail, including provisions required of various trades, connections with other work; cutting, fitting and drilling required and other necessary information as per usual trade practice and as required for any special purpose.

1. Shop drawings shall indicate relationship with work of other trades in respective assembled positions. The Contractor shall be responsible for shop drawing detailing to the extent of coordination with other trades and contractors, in addition to all other requirements specified herein.

2. If shop drawing details indicate conditions not properly accommodating the work of other trades or Contractors, or if the details as submitted reveal conditions that in the opinion of the Architect are not compatible with the appearance of the building, the Architect shall have the right to adjust details as necessary. Subsequent re-submissions of shop drawings to reflect amended conditions shall be without additional cost to the Owner.

Each Contractor shall check the shop drawings of his subcontractors for quantities, measurements, size of members, materials and details to ascertain that they conform to the intent of the Drawings and Specifications and to the Contract requirements and shall correct drawings found to be inaccurate or otherwise in error before submitting them to the Architect. Shop drawings at the time of submission shall bear a stamp of approval of the prime Contractor as evidence that such drawings and/or details have been checked by the Contractor. Any drawings submitted without such stamp of approval or which appear to be inadequately checked by the Contractor shall be returned to the Contractor and shall not be considered as an official submission.

If the drawing, as submitted, indicates departure from Contract requirements which the Architect finds to be in the interest of the Owner and to be so minor as not to involve change in Contract price or time of performance, he may approve the drawing. The Contractor shall call to the attention of the Architect in writing any deviation from the Drawings and Specifications in any shop drawing, and the submission of such drawing shall mean that the Contractor warrants that such drawing is in complete accord with the Contract Documents unless stated to the contrary.

If submitted shop drawings deviate considerably from the requirements of the Contract Documents, the Contractor shall pay the Architect for such additional work required to coordinate such shop drawings to the project requirements. Payment to the Architect shall be made on demand and will be established at two and one half times the cost of technical personnel performing such services plus reimbursement for any additional expense.

Approval of shop drawings will be general, is only for conformance with the design concept of the project and compliance with the information given in the Contract Documents, and is subject to coordination by the Contractor with other trades; it is not an approval of quantities, or dimensions, nor an authorization for extra work. Where work "by other contractors" is approved it shall not be construed as eliminating this work from the Contract Documents. The Architect's approval of such drawings, schedules, or cuts shall not relieve the Contractor from responsibility for deviations from Drawings or Specifications, unless he has in writing called the Architect's attention to such deviations at the time of submission, and has received from the Architect, in writing, permission for such deviations, nor shall it relieve him from responsibility for errors of any sort in shop drawings or schedules. The Contractor shall correct errors in and omissions from work without additional cost to the Owner, whether or not work was installed as per approved shop drawings.

All shop drawings, schedules and cuts shall contain the following information:

1. Job title and shop drawing number.
2. Date and dates of revisions.
3. Prime Contractor's name and certification that shop drawing has been checked and approved by him.
4. Specification page and paragraph number.
5. Details of fabrication, assembly and erection.
6. Materials used.
7. All required dimensions.
8. Details of relation to and connection with contiguous work. Work noted to be "by others" shall be identified by the Contractor on the shop drawings by name of trade or separate Contractor responsible for such work.
9. Information on all items of equipment, e.g., electrical characteristics, hp rating, etc.
10. All protective coatings and factory finishes.

Shop drawing submissions which fail to comply with the above requirements will be returned to the Contractor and shall not be considered as an official submission. In such event, it will be deemed that the Contractor has not complied with requirements of this Article, herein specified, and he shall bear the risks of delays as if no drawings or details at all had been submitted.

The Architect shall not be required to review shop drawings within any stated period of time, it being understood that the minimum time in which the Architect shall review shop drawings shall be ten (10) working days from the date of receipt of an initial submission, and not less than twenty (20) working days for drawings to be reviewed by a consultant of the Architect, and not less than five (5) and ten (10) working days respectively from the date of receipt of subsequent submissions.

Shop drawings shall be stamped by the Architect with the following classifications:

1. *Approved:* No corrections, no marks. Contractor shall submit copies for distribution.
2. *Approved as Noted:* A few minor corrections. All items may be fabricated as marked up without further resubmission. Submit copies for distribution.
3. *Approved as Noted—Resubmit:* Minor corrections. Items not noted to be corrected may be fabricated at the Contractor's option. Contractor shall resubmit drawings with corrections noted.
4. *Disapproved:* Major corrections or not in accordance with the Contract Documents. No items shall be fabricated. Contractor shall correct and resubmit drawings.

The Contractor shall make no changes in excess of those noted by the Architect unless these additional changes are brought to the attention of the Architect in writing. The Contractor shall be responsible for information that pertains solely to the fabrication processes or to techniques of construction.

All Shop Drawings shall be resubmitted until they are returned "approved as noted" or "approved."

Initial shop drawings shall be submitted as follows:

1. All drawings, schedules, etc., shall be submitted originally in single copy to the Architect as an ozalid transvellum print suitable for reproduction. Blue prints, black and white prints, or any other opaque print will not be acceptable.

2. Corrections and classification (approval or disapproval) will be marked on this ozalid print by the Architect or his consultant.
3. The Architect will make one print each for himself and his consultant, if any, of all initial and subsequent shop drawings. These prints will be made at a regular blue printing concern at established rates. These costs shall be payable upon the Architect's billing, and shall be included in the Contract Price.
4. The Ozalid will be returned to the Contractor.
5. If the ozalid submission is returned "approved" or "approved as noted" the Contractor shall then supply a minimum of six (6) blueprints, printed from the ozalid, for distribution.
6. If the ozalid submission is returned "approved as noted—resubmit" or "disapproved," the original drawing shall be corrected and a new ozalid transparency submitted for final approval. After final approval, the Contractor shall then supply a minimum of six (6) blueprints, printed from the approved ozalid, for distribution.
7. Any submissions which are not reproducible as ozalids such as cuts, catalog sheets, etc., shall be submitted in seven (7) copies to the Architect.

69.

The Architect will review shop drawings for conformity with design concept only and his approval shall not in any way relieve the Contractor from his obligation to conform to plans and specifications, nor shall such approval be deemed an authorization to deviate from the plans and specifications. The Contractor is responsible for dimensions to be confirmed and correlated at the job site, for information that pertains solely to the fabrication processes or to techniques of construction, and for coordination of the work of all trades. The Contractor shall make any corrections required by the Architect, file with him six (6) corrected copies, and furnish such other copies as may be needed.

The above clause is not intended to prevent a Contractor or subcontractor from recommending changes which will improve or simplify the work or permit him to utilize new or special techniques, but to point out the necessity for notice and approval of such changes, since they may affect other parts of the work.

SPECIFICATION BY MANUFACTURER, BRAND, TRADE NAME, OR CATALOGUE NUMBER

70.

The naming of manufacturers in the specifications does not necessarily indicate that such manufacturers' stock or catalogue products are acceptable or meet the requirements of the drawings and specifications. It shall be the obligation of the Contractor to ascertain if the stock or catalogue products of the named manufacturers meet all of the requirements of the drawings and specifications, and if they do not the Contractor shall not be entitled to select such stock or catalogue products.

The naming of brand, trade name, or catalogue number in the specifications shall be for the convenience of the Contractor only and does not necessarily indicate that such brand, trade name, or catalogue number is acceptable or satisfies the requirements of the plans and specifications. The only acceptable criteria for approval of items to be used in construction shall be the elaborated and detailed standards of the Architect as enumerated in the specifications and drawings, and it shall be the obligation of the Contractor to ascertain if the designated brand, trade name, or catalogue number satisfies such criteria.

Where an item is designated by manufacturer, brand, trade name or catalogue number, and is not otherwise described or specified, and if the manufacturer producing such item is no longer in business or no longer manufactures such item, the Contractor shall consider the item as standard to be matched with equal products of other fabricators. Such substitution shall be proposed in writing within fifteen (15) working days of award of contract and shall be subject to the approval of the Architect and at no extra cost to the Owner of any kind, and without extension of contract time.

If the Architect is satisfied that no equal exists, he may allow use of other items, more or less costly, with corresponding extra charges or credits.

71.

Whenever a material or article required is specified or shown on the plans by using the name of the proprietary product or of a particular manufacturer or vendor, any material or article which will perform adequately the duties imposed by the general design will be considered equal and satisfactory, providing the material or article so proposed is of equal substance and function and meets with the approval of the Architect.

"At the Architect's request, the Contractor shall gather and submit such evidence as is required to satisfy the Architect. The cost of any test, mock-up, transportation and other expenses shall be borne by the Contractor making the submission."

SUBCONTRACTORS

72.

As soon as the Contractor has been notified by the Architect that the contract has been awarded to him, and before the Contract Documents have been executed, he shall promptly submit for approval, names and addresses of subcontractors (in addition to those listed in his proposal) and the work that is contemplated to be sublet to them. The execution of Contract Documents is subject to above approval.

Each subcontract shall contain the following clause:

"The subcontractor agrees to be bound to the Contractor by all the terms of the General Conditions, Conditions, drawings and specifications (which are made a part of the contract between the Owner and the Contractor, dated _____ as to said work and other work), and to assume toward the Contractor all of the obligations and responsibilities as to the subcontractor's work that the Contractor by such documents has assumed toward the Owner. The subcontractor agrees that the Contractor shall at all times have the right, with the written consent of the Owner to assign this subcontract to the Owner and in the event of such assignment the Owner shall have the right to terminate this subcontract in the event of delays caused by 'strikes' upon the same terms and conditions as are contained in the said contract between the Owner and Contractor."

73.

The Contractor may utilize the services of specialty subcontractors on those parts of the work which under normal contracting practices are performed by specialty subcontractors.

The contractor shall not award any work to any subcontractor without prior written approval by the Architect, which approval will not be given until the Contractor submits to the Owner a written statement concerning the proposed award to the subcontractor, which statements must contain a description of the work and materials which the proposed subcontractors are to perform and furnish any other information tending to prove that the proposed subcontractors have the necessary facilities, skill, integrity, past experience and financial resources to perform the work in conformity with the contract documents, and such other information as the Architect may require.

The Contractor shall not employ any subcontractor to whom the Architect may have objection. If after the approval of any subcontractor by the Architect, the Architect requires a change in such subcontractor, the contract price shall be increased or decreased by the difference in cost occasioned by such change as determined by the Architect, provided however the Contractor shall not be required to employ any subcontractor against whom he has a reasonable objection.

As soon as the Contractor has been advised that the contract has been awarded to him, he shall promptly submit for approval the statements covering the following subcontractors:

Subcontractors (Electro-Mechanical)

Subcontractors (General Construction)

The Contractor agrees that he is as fully responsible to the Owner for the acts and omissions of his subcontractors and of persons either directly or indirectly employed by them, as he is for the acts and omissions of persons directly employed by him, and the Contractor shall be fully responsible for the correlation of the work to be done by each of his subcontractors and he shall require each subcontractor to perform his work at the times required by the progress schedule and as required by the conditions of the project.

Nothing contained in the Contract Documents shall create any contractual relation between any subcontractor and the Owner, and nothing in the Contract Documents shall create any obligation on the part of the Owner to pay or to see to the payment of any sums to any subcontractor.

The Contractor agrees to bind every subcontractor, and every subcontractor agrees to be bound by the terms of all Contract Documents, as far as applicable to his work. The Contractor shall provide in his contract with each subcontractor that before beginning his work, each subcontractor shall carefully examine the condition of the building and of the work done by others which might affect his work, and shall report to the Contractor immediately any condition that would adversely affect the quality of his work. Failure to make such a report before beginning his work shall constitute acceptance by him of the conditions then existing as suitable to receive or accommodate his installation. The following provisions shall also be included in the subcontract:

THE SUBCONTRACTOR AGREES:

To be bound to the Contractor by the terms of the Contract Documents and to assume toward the Contractor all the obligations and responsibilities that the Contractor, by those documents, assumes toward the Owner.

To submit to the Contractor applications for payment in such reasonable time as to enable the Contractor to apply for payment under the "Application for Payment" paragraph of these General Conditions.

THE CONTRACTOR AGREES:

To pay the Subcontractor, upon the payment of certificates, if issued under the schedule of values described in the "Application for Payment" paragraph of these General Conditions, the amount allowed to the Contractor on account of the Subcontractor's work to the extent of the Subcontractor's interest therein.

To pay the Subcontractor, upon the payment of certificates, if issued otherwise than as in the above subparagraph, so that at all times his total payments shall be as large in proportion to the value of the work done by him as the total amount certified to the Contractor is to the value of the work done by him.

To pay the Subcontractor to such extent as may be provided by the Contract Documents or the Subcontract, if either of these provides for earlier or larger payments than the above.

To pay the Subcontractor on demand for his work or materials as far as executed and fixed in place, less the retained percentage, at the time the Certificate for payment should issue, even though the Architect fails to issue it for any cause not the fault of the Subcontractor.

To pay the Subcontractor a just share of any fire insurance money received by him, the Contractor, under the "Fire Insurance with Extended Coverage" paragraph of these General Conditions.

To make no demand for liquidated damages or penalty for delay in any sum in excess of such amount as may be specifically named in the Subcontract.

That no claim for services rendered or materials furnished by the Contractor to the Subcontractor shall be valid unless written notice thereof is given by the Contractor to the Subcontractor during the first ten (10) days of the calendar month following that in which the claim originated.

To give the Subcontractor an opportunity to be present and to submit evidence in any proceeding involving his rights.

74.

Before awarding any subcontracts, the Contractor shall notify the Architect in writing of the names of the subcontractors proposed for the principal parts of the work, and for such other parts as the Architect may direct, and shall not employ any to whom the Architect may have objection. The names of subcontractors shall be furnished and approved and secured prior to the issuance by the Architect of any certificate of payment.

If, after the approval of any subcontractor by the Architect, the Owner requires a change in such subcontractor, the Contract price shall be increased or decreased by the difference in cost occasioned by such change as determined by the Architect.

The Contractor shall not be required to employ any subcontractor against whom he has a reasonable objection.

The Contractor agrees that he is as fully responsible to the Owner for the acts and omissions of his subcontractors and of persons either directly or indirectly employed by them, as he is for the acts and omissions of persons directly employed by him.

Nothing contained in the Contract Documents shall create any contractual relation between any subcontractor and the Owner.

The Contractor shall provide in his contract with each subcontractor that before beginning his work, each subcontractor shall carefully examine the condition of the building and of the work done by others which might affect his work and shall report to the Contractor immediately any condition that would adversely affect the quality of his work. Failure to make such a report before beginning his work shall constitute acceptance by him of the conditions then existing, as suitable to receive or accommodate his installation.

The Contractor shall be solely responsible for the correlation of the work to be done by each of his subcontractors, including the performance of such parts of the work described in each Section of the Specifications as he may delegate specifically to any subcontractor.

All phases of work shall be coordinated to eliminate interferences from the installations of all trades. Interfering installations shall be relocated to provide clearances and headroom. If directed by the Architect, additional shop drawings shall be submitted showing the means suggested for correcting conflicts or difficulties.

Each subcontractor shall perform his work at time required by the Critical Path Method Schedule and as required by the conditions of the project.

SUBSTITUTION OF EQUAL
OR COMPARABLE MATERIALS

75.

Materials or products specified by the elaborated and detailed standards of Architect as enumerated in the Specifications and on Drawings shall be the basis of the bid and shall be furnished under the Contract unless otherwise authorized in writing by the Architect in accordance with the procedures outlined below.

(A) *Before Bid Acceptance:*

1. Requests for approval of items other than those specified will be considered if submitted by bidders in writing at least ten (10) days prior to bid date with full and complete documentation as specified hereinafter under B-2, and indicating what approximate difference, if any, will be made in base bid price, including changes in cost of all work affected thereby.

   All bidders will be notified, in writing, of any such approval.

2. If Contractor bases his bid on any other item or items not specified or approved as outlined above, he does so entirely at his own risk.

(B) *After Bid Acceptance:* Contractor may submit comparable materials and manufacturers to Architect for approval only under the following conditions, which will be rigidly adhered to:

1. Submission shall be made early enough in course of job and with allowance of sufficient time for Architect decision, so that job progress is not delayed. Any delay caused by any proposed substitution will be the responsibility of the Contractor.

2. Submission shall be made with full and complete documentation to include: manufacturer's literature, printed Specifications, samples, test reports, names of local jobs on which employed with names of jobs' Owners and Architects, and information on cost differential between specified and proposed items. Incomplete or inadequate documentation will result in rejection of submission.

3. Architect's decision shall be final and conclusive, and he reserves the right to disapprove any submission.

(C) *Differences Regarding Submissions Before or After Bid Acceptance:*

1. Greater consideration will be given to submissions received before bid acceptance.

2. Submissions after bid acceptance will be judged with the entire burden of proof in regard to comparable qualities, and cost differential (or lack of cost differential) involved, as full responsibility of Contractor making such submission.

(D) *Tests and Analysis of Proposed Substitutes:* Architect reserves the right to submit proposed substitutes to tests and analysis. The type of test and/or analysis and the testing laboratory or facility by which the test and/or analysis will be made shall be chosen by the Architect. Quantities of the item in question required for these tests and/or analysis shall be determined by the Architect, and furnished by the submitting Contractor directly to the testing laboratory. All costs of tests and/or analysis shall be paid by the Contractor.

76.

If materials, items or methods are specified by trade name or name of manufacturer, no substitution will be permitted, whether equal or not, unless "or equal" is expressly specified, or substitutions of equals are permitted to the Contractor by requirement of law. Where substitution is permitted, the specifying of a material, item or method by trade name or name of manufacturer shall be deemed for the purpose of establishing the standard of quality. Where substitution is permitted, the Architect shall be the sole and conclusive judge as to the quality of substitute. To receive consideration, requests for substitution shall be submitted to the Architect within thirty (30) days after signing of Contract.

Any request by the Contractor for approval of a material, item or method as equal to that specified, shall be accompanied by written proof adequate to establish such equality and by a citation of several situations wherein the substitute material has been successfully used. Any approvals of a substitute by governmental or other agencies, obtaining of certificates, etc., which are a requirement of law or the Contract Documents or deemed desirable by the Architect shall be the responsibility of the Contractor and shall be secured at his expense. If required by the Architect, the Contractor, at the Contractor's expense, shall run or secure tests of the requested substitute in order to establish its equality.

If any substitution requested by the Contractor requires additional services on the part of the Architect to make such substitution acceptable to him, the Contractor shall pay the Architect for such services at a rate equal to two and one half times the cost of technical personnel performing such services plus reimbursement of any additional expense.

When, in the various Sections of the Specifications, additional requirements as to responsibility in case of substitution of materials are set forth, such additional requirements shall govern for the particular Contract in which they occur. It is the intent of these Specifications that the changes requested by the Contractor in makes or brands of materials or requirements specified or indicated on the Drawings, shall place the burden of coordination with other Contractors on him, and should these changes require revision of his work or work of others, cost of such changes shall be borne by the Contractor requesting the substitution.

77.

Where substitution of materials is permitted, the Architect shall be the sole and conclusive judge as to the quality of such substitute. Any request by the Contractor for approval of a material, item, or method as equal to that specified, shall be accompanied by written proof adequate to establish such equality, and by a citation of several situations wherein the substitute material has been successfully used. If required by the Architect, the Contractor, at his expense shall run or secure tests of the requested substitute in order to establish its equality. Any items submitted as a substitute shall comply in all respects with the specifications and/or catalog descriptions of the material, item, or method specified by name or catalog number. If requested, the Contractor shall furnish special guarantees warranting qualities of substituted items.

The Contractor shall give the Architect promptly in writing the names of the manufacturers of all materials and fabricated items he intends to provide, none of which shall be ordered until the manufacturer is approved. The Architect will not issue any certificate for payment until all names are approved.

All materials are subject to approval by the Architect both before and after incorporation in the building.

Price differences for substitutions shall include not only costs of labor and materials, but also costs to all other trades affected by the substitutions.

SUBSURFACE CONDITIONS

78.

Should the Contractor encounter subsurface and/or latent conditions at the site materially differing from those shown on the Plans or indicated in the Specifications, he shall immediately give notice to the Architect of such conditions before they are disturbed. The Architect shall thereupon promptly investigate the conditions, and if he finds that they materially differ from those shown on the Plans or indicated in the Specifications, he shall at once make such changes in the Plans and/or Specifications as he may find necessary, any increase or decrease of cost resulting from such changes to be adjusted in the manner provided herein for adjustments as to extra work and/or additional work and changes.

79.

Bidders shall visit the site and shall be responsible for having ascertained pertinent local conditions such as location, accessibility and general character of the site or building, the character and extent of existing work within or adjacent to the site, existing conditions under which he will be obligated to operate in performing his part of the work, or which will in any manner affect the work under this Contract, and any other work being performed thereon at the time of the submission of his bid. No claims for extra compensation based on ignorance of existing conditions will be considered.

It shall be the obligation of the Contractor to satisfy himself as to the sub-surface conditions of the site prior to bidding upon the Contract or executing the Contract, and the Contractor shall not be entitled to any extra compensation if the actual sub-surface conditions differ from those contemplated unless the Contractor could not by appropriate investigation and/or tests ascertain a reasonable approximation of such conditions. Any sub-surface information secured or furnished by the Owner or Architect shall not be deemed as part of the Contract Documents and is not guaranteed by either of them in any respect, it being the responsibility of the Contractor to determine for himself all sub-surface conditions.

If in the performance of the Contract, sub-surface or latent conditions at the site are found to be materially different from those contemplated, or unknown conditions of unusual nature are disclosed, differing materially from the conditions usually inherent in the work of the character shown and specified, the attention of the Architect shall be called immediately to such conditions before they are disturbed. Upon such notice the Architect shall issue such instructions to the Contractor as he finds necessary for the proper performance of the work, and the Contractor shall comply with such instructions.

Should the Contractor encounter, or the Owner discover, during the progress of the work sub-surface and/or latent physical conditions at the site materially differing from those shown on the drawings or indicated in the specifications, or unknown physical conditions of an unusual nature differing materially from those ordinarily encountered and generally recognized as inhering in work of the character provided for in the drawings and specifications, the Architect shall be notified promptly in writing of such conditions before they are disturbed. The Architect shall thereupon promptly investigate the conditions, and if he finds that they do so materially differ the contract shall be modified to provide for any increase or decrease of cost and/or difference in time resulting from such conditions.

80.

Test boring data is offered in good faith solely for the purpose of placing the Contractor in receipt of all the information available to the Owner, and in no event is to be considered a part of the Contract Documents. The Contractor must interpret such data according to his own judgment and acknowledges that he is not relying upon the same as accurately describing the sub-surface conditions which may be found to exist. The Contractor further acknowledges that he assumes all risks contingent upon the nature of the sub-surface conditions to be actually encountered by him in performing the work covered by the Contract, even though such actual conditions may result in the Contractor performing more, or less work than he originally anticipated.

USE OF PREMISES

81.

The Contractor expressly undertakes at his own expense:

(a) To take every precaution against injuries to persons or damage to property;

(b) To store his apparatus, materials, supplies and equipment in such orderly fashion at the site of the work as will not unduly interfere with the progress of his work or the work of any other contractor;

(c) To place upon the work or any part thereof only such loads as are consistent with the safety of that portion of the work;

(d) To *frequently* clean up all refuse, rubbish, scrap materials, and debris caused by his operations, to the end that at all times the site of the work shall present a neat, orderly and workmanlike appearance;

(e) Before final payment to remove all surplus materials, temporary structures, including foundations thereof, plant of any description and debris of every nature resulting from his operations, and to put the site in a neat, orderly condition;

(f) To effect all cutting, fitting or patching of his work required to make the same to conform to the plans and specifications and, except with the consent of the Architect, not to cut or otherwise alter the work of any other contractor.

82.

The Contractor shall confine his apparatus, storage of materials and construction operations to the limits indicated by ordinances or permits or as may be directed by the Architect. He shall not unreasonably encumber the premises with his materials.

The Contractor shall not load or permit any part of any structure to be loaded to such an extent as to endanger its safety.

The Contractor shall enforce any instructions of the Architect or the Owner regarding signs, advertising, fires, danger signals, barricades and smoking.

The introduction of materials and access and egress of workmen shall be restricted to such places and in such manner as approved by the Architect.

In the utilization of ground area, the necessary protection of pavement, curbs, walks, structures, and other permanent improvements shall be installed and maintained.

In storing materials within any structure, or when used as a shop, etc., the Contractor shall consult with the Architect and shall restrict his storage to spaces designated for such purposes. The Contractor will be held responsible for any repairs, patching or cleaning arising from such use.

Ground storage shall be similarly restricted.

The Contractor shall not trespass or enter upon areas that are noted as being restricted.

Plumbing fixtures shall not be used for emptying water from any buckets, pails or other containers.

All temporary structures shall be of substantial construction, neat appearance, and shall be painted a uniform grey unless otherwise directed.

83.

The Contractor shall at all times keep the premises free from accumulation of waste materials or rubbish caused by his employees or work, and at the completion of the work he shall remove all his rubbish from and about the building and all his tools, scaffolding and surplus materials and shall leave his work "broom-clean" or its equivalent, unless more exactly specified. In case the Contractor shall fail to perform his obligations hereunder, the Owner may remove the rubbish and charge the cost to the Contractor in an amount to be determined by the Architect.

All materials shall be stored in a neat and orderly manner, and those subject to weather damage shall be protected against the weather by floored weatherproof temporary storage sheds.

Storage piles and sheds shall be located within the Contract limits, as specifically approved by the Architect, and shall be moved if so necessary because of interference with the work of any Contractor.

Materials stored within the building shall be distributed in such a manner as to avoid overloading of the structural frame, and never shall be concentrated in such a manner as to exceed the equivalent of fifty (50) pounds per square foot uniformly distributed loading. Stored materials shall be moved if they interfere with the progress of the work.

Materials shall not be stored or located where they will interfere with the use or occupancy of existing facilities.

84.

Owner reserves the right to require the Contractor to so organize his work that portions of the building or buildings or equipment therein will be complete and ready for occupancy before the entire completion of the project, and to take possession and occupy any portion of the premises prior to the completion of the entire Contract without in any way waiving any of the provisions or requirements of the Contract, particularly in regard to time of completion, acceptance of the work, protection and responsibility, and insurance. The occupancy of the building or any portion thereof does not constitute an acceptance of any work nor does it waive the Owner's right to liquidated damages. Prior to such occupancy, however, the Architect, a representative of the Owner, and Contractor shall fully inspect the portions of the building to be occupied, preparing a complete list of omissions of materials, faulty workmanship, or any items to be repaired, torn out or replaced. Owner will assume responsibility for maintenance and operating costs of premises so occupied and for repair of damage not itemized on this list.

WITHHOLDING OF
PAYMENTS TO CONTRACTOR

85.

The Owner may withhold from the Contractor so much of any approved payments due him as may in the judgment of the Owner be necessary:

(a) To assure the payment of just claims due and unpaid to any persons supplying labor or materials for the work;

(b) To protect the Owner from loss due to defective work not remedied; or

(c) To protect the Owner from loss due to injury to persons or damage to the work or property of other contractors, subcontractors or others caused by the act or neglect of the Contractor or any of his subcontractors. The Owner shall have the right as agent for the Contractor to apply any such amounts so withheld in such manner as the Owner may deem proper to satisfy such claims or to secure such protection. Such application of such money shall be deemed payments for the account of the Contractor.

86.

Partial payments by the Owner to the Contractor shall become due on a date in each month as agreed upon by the parties at the time of signing the Contract, upon the issuance by the Architect of a certificate of payment.

The Architect may withhold or, on account of subsequently discovered evidence, nullify the whole or part of any certificate to such extent as may be necessary in his opinion to protect the Owner from loss on account of:

1. Failure of the Contractor to perform properly under the Contract Documents.
2. Defective work not remedied.
3. Claims filed or reasonable evidence indicating probable filing of claims.
4. Failure of the Contractor to make payments properly to subcontractors or to pay for material or labor.
5. A reasonable doubt that the Contract can be completed for the balance then unpaid.
6. Damage to another Contractor.
7. Damages to the Owner arising from delay or other default of the Contractor.

Index of cases

Andry & Feitel v. Ewing, 245
Bruno v. Gauthice, 245
Burk v. Livingston Parish School Bd., 230
C. G. Kershaw Contracting Co. v. Crowley, 4, 116
Charbonnet v. Board of Architectural Examiners, 39
Churchill v. Thomas, 230
Day v. National U.S. Radiator Corp., 273, 277
Fritz Jahncke, Inc. v. Fidelity & Deposit Co., 116, 138
Fuhrmann v. Catanese, 225
Garrett v. Verlander, 129
Ghirardi v. Krisler, 206
Grosz v. Baton Rouge Realty Co., 208, 218
Haas v. D'Avanzo, 206
Haase v. Brumfield, 225
H. A. Bauman, Inc. v. Tilly, 208
Harnischfeger Sales Corp. v. Sternberg Co., Inc., 45
Hatchitoches Motor Co. v. Campbell, 101
Henry v. Pelican Cold Storage & Warehousing Co., 227, 239
Leba v. Sills, 213
Louisiana v. McIllhenny, 86
Louisiana Molasses Co. v. Le Sassier, 271
Maas v. Hernandez, 208
MacDonnell v. Dreyfous, 245
Mahoney v. St. Paul's Church, 190
Mercier v. Munich, 255
National Homestead Ass'n v. Graham, 255
New Orleans v. Bayley, 8
New Orleans v. Lagman, 8
New Orleans v. Leibe, 9
New Orleans v. O'Neil, 9
New Orleans v. Pohlmann, 9
Nolan v. Great Southern Wirebound Box Co., 250
Nolan v. Perloff, 213, 227
Nolan & Torre v. Metairie Ridge Nursery Co., 230
Rabinowitz v. Hurwitz-Mintz Furniture Co., 4, 6, 30
Rosenthal v. Gauthice, 245
Sully v. Pratt, 240
Taylor v. Panama Ice Co., 206
Theobalds v. Connor, 9
Tsoi v. Ebenezer Baptist Church, 245
Woodward v. White, 216

Maine

Bunker v. City of Old Town, 82
Coombs v. Beede, 227, 245, 266

Jacques v. Otto Nelson Co., 133
Kerr v. State, 116
Lane v. Town of Harmony, 108, 247, 266, 274
Seretto v. Rockland, S. T. & O. H. Ry., 121, 156
State v. Beck, 5

Maryland

Aetna Indem. Co. v. Waters, 168
Baltimore & O. R.R. Co. v. Brydon, 119
Baltimore Cemetery Co. v. Coburn, 103
Hammaker v. Schleigh, 266
Harrison v. McLaughlin Bros., 232, 245
Hughes v. Model Stoker Co., 139
Lynn v. Baltimore & O. R.R. Co., 119
McNulty v. Keyser Office Bldg. Co., 103
Seventh Baptist Church v. Andrew & Thomas, 116
Stark v. Christie, 39
Williar v. Nagle, 245

Massachusetts

Atwood v. Boston, 226, 238
Benjamin Foster Co. v. Commonwealth, 152
Benton v. Springfield Y.M.C.A., 80, 86, 211
Blackall v. Duthie-Strachan, 245
Burns v. Thorndike, 103
Byam v. Carlisle-Ayer Co., 240
Congregation Ohab Shalom v. Hathaway, 197
Corey v. Eastman, 275
Crane Constr. Co. v. Commonwealth, 103
C. W. Hunt Co. v. Boston Elev. Ry. Co., 116
Dahlstrom Metallic Door Co. v. Evatt Constr. Co., 98
Derby Desk Co. v. Connors Bros. Constr. Co., 168
Edgar H. Woods Associates, Inc. v. Skene, 288
Edge Moor Bridge Works v. Bristol County, 87
Evans v. Middlesex County, 119
Feldman v. Desantis, 180
Gaffey v. United Shoe Machinery Co., 101
Gillis v. Cobe, 181
Handy v. Bliss, 122
Hathaway v. Stone, 116
Hebert v. Dewey, 121
Hennebique Constr. Co. v. Boston Cold Storage & Terminal Co., 175, 197
James Elgar Inc. v. Newhall, 185

Subject index

371